Textiles and Clothing
of Việt Nam

ALSO BY MICHAEL C. HOWARD

*Transnationalism in Ancient and Medieval Societies:
The Role of Cross-Border Trade and Travel*
(McFarland, 2012)

*Transnationalism and Society:
An Introduction* (McFarland, 2011)

Textiles and Clothing of Việt Nam
A History

MICHAEL C. HOWARD

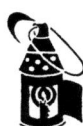

McFarland & Company, Inc., Publishers
Jefferson, North Carolina

LIBRARY OF CONGRESS CATALOGUING-IN-PUBLICATION DATA

Names: Howard, Michael C., author.
Title: Textiles and clothing of Việt Nam : a history / Michael C. Howard.
Description: Jefferson, North Carolina : McFarland & Company, Inc., Publishers, 2016. | Includes bibliographical references and index.
Identifiers: LCCN 2016034297 | ISBN 9781476663326 (softcover : acid free paper) ∞
Subjects: LCSH: Textile fabrics—Vietnam—History. | Textile design—Vietnam—History. | Ethnic costume—Vietnam—History.
Classification: LCC NK8878.6.V5 H675 2016 | DDC 746.09597—dc23
LC record available at https://lccn.loc.gov/2016034297

BRITISH LIBRARY CATALOGUING DATA ARE AVAILABLE

ISBN (print) 978-1-4766-6332-6
ISBN (ebook) 978-1-4766-2440-2

© 2016 Michael C. Howard. All rights reserved

No part of this book may be reproduced or transmitted in any form or by any means, electronic or mechanical, including photocopying or recording, or by any information storage and retrieval system, without permission in writing from the publisher.

Front cover photograph © 2016 YunYulia/iStock

Printed in the United States of America

McFarland & Company, Inc., Publishers
Box 611, Jefferson, North Carolina 28640
www.mcfarlandpub.com

Table of Contents

Preface   1
A Note on Spelling   4
A Note on Translation   5
Adminstrative Map of Việt Nam   6
Introduction   9
    Technology and Materials   9
        Looms 9; *Fibers* 11; *Dyes* 18
    Change, Status and Identity   19

1. Ancient Clothing   23
    Bark-cloth   23
    Ancient Bronze Age Northern Việt Nam   26
    Ancient Bronze Age Yúnnán   32
    Ancient Bronze Age Guìzhōu   40
    Nán Yuè and Chinese Ruled Việt Nam   46
    Chămpa   54

2. Feudal   66
    Đại Việt   66
    Chămpa   75
    Mekong Delta Khmer and Chăm   76

3. Modern Việt Nam   82
    Nguyễn Dynasty   82
    French Colonial Period   88
    Independent Việt Nam   96

    Between pages 100 and 101 are 8 color plates containing 18 photographs

4. Ethnic Minorities in Northern Việt Nam   101
    Kadai Groups   103
        Cờ Lao 103; *La Chí* 103; *La Ha* 104; *Pu Péo* 104

Tai Groups   104
   Tày 105; *Nùng* 107; *Thái* 108; *Lào* 116; *Lự* 118; *Bố Y and Giáy* 119;
   Cao Lan 121
Mon-Khmer Groups   121
   Thổ 121; *Mường* 121; *Khơ Mú* 122; *Xinh Mun* 123; *Kháng* 123;
   Mảng 123; *Ơ Đu* 123
Hmong-Mien Groups   123
   Hmông 123; *Pà Thẻn* 128; *Dao* 129
Tibeto-Burman Groups   139
   Hà Nhì 139; *Lô Lô* 140; *La Hủ* 142; *Phù Lá* 142; *Si La* 144; *Cống* 145

5. Ethnic Minorities in Southern Việt Nam   146
   Khmer   148
   Chăm   149
   Central Highlands Malayo-Polynesian Groups   151
      Gia Rai 152; *Ê Đê* 154; *Ra Glai* 155; *Chu Ru* 156
   Central Highlands Mon-Khmer Groups   156
      Tà Ôi and Cơ Tu 156; *Bru* 159; *Ba Na and Rơngao* 160; *Giẻ Triêng*
      162; *Xơ Đăng* 163; *Hrê* 165; *Rơ Măm* 167; *Brâu* 167; *Mnông* 167; *Xtiêng*
      173; *Mạ* 175; *Cơ Ho* 177; *Chơ Ro* 178

Chapter Notes   181
References   197
Index   205

Preface

Clothing and Textiles in Việt Nam is a survey of the clothing styles and types of textiles produced in Việt Nam since antiquity. This is the first time that such a study has been published in English on this important topic. The work is an outgrowth of my earlier research during the late 1990s and early 2000s on the textiles and dress of Việt Nam's ethnic minorities that resulted, among other things, in the publication of three books on the topic in 2002. That research included both ethnographic fieldwork and exploration of the early prehistory and history of the region. In regard to the latter I was especially interested in the early history of Tai-speaking peoples in northern Việt Nam and of the kingdom of Chămpa in the south. My research on ethnic textiles and dress in Việt Nam also led in 2007 to my involvement in a project by the Meadows Museum of Art at Centenary College in Shreveport, Louisiana, on French artist Jean Despujols and his visit to Indochina in the late 1930s. My work in relation to the project included study of the textiles and dress of the people of Việt Nam during the French colonial period.

Since the early 2000s I have been especially interested in the survival of cultural traditions related to dress and textiles and efforts at reviving and modernizing such traditions in Việt Nam. Cultural revival among ethnic groups was the theme of a project by the Việt Nam Ethnic Minorities Arts and Literature Association that I participated in between 1999 and 2003 and has informed much of my work in recent years with the ASEAN Traditional Textiles Arts Community (ASEANTTAC). ASEANTTAC held a symposium in 2013 in Thái Nguyên, Việt Nam, on the theme of "Heritage, Tradition & Connection in Textiles among ASEAN Weaving Communities" in collaboration with the Museum of the Cultures of Vietnam's Ethnic Groups and another in 2015 in Chiang Mai, Thailand, on the theme of "Connecting Centuries of Tradition" in collaboration with Payap University. These symposia highlight the contemporary importance of textile traditions in Việt Nam and other Southeast Asian countries.

The present study begins with a look at weaving technology, fibers, and dyes. While most clothing in Việt Nam today is made of industrially woven cloth, industrial weaving is a relatively recent development in the country and many of the country's ethnic minorities still weave cloth by hand on a variety of types of loom. As for fibers, the Bronze Age cultures of northern Việt Nam are associated with some of the earliest production of silk and silk has a long and important history in Việt Nam. In contrast, cotton has a shorter history in Việt Nam and in modern times most cotton thread has been imported. Other fibers, such as kapok and hemp, were widely used prior to the advent of cotton and such fibers are still used by some minority groups. As elsewhere, most cloth in Việt Nam today is colored using commercial dyes, but the country has a rich tradition of employing natural dyes and many of these are still used by highland minority groups.

Our history of clothing and textiles begins with a look at the use of bark-cloth in Việt Nam. Bark-cloth appears to have its origins in southeastern China, in an area adjacent to Việt Nam. Bark-cloth was widely made throughout ancient Việt Nam and it has survived in a few remote areas up to the present. We then look at the Bronze Age cultures of northern Việt Nam and neighboring Yúnnán and Guìzhōu that are of relevance to the history of clothing and textiles in Việt Nam. What we know of clothing and textiles from this period comes largely from human figures depicted in bronze from which we can learn about the shape of clothing, but little about the colors and fibers used. Over the next thousand or so years the history of Việt Nam is essentially that of a Chinese-ruled north and the independent kingdom of Chămpa in the south that was influenced by Indian culture. In both instances, clothing styles developed that included local and imported elements with the clothing of elites being especially prone to external influences. During this period the style of dress of elites in the north in particular tended to mirror Chinese fashions. These patterns of dress persisted during the feudal period after the end of Chinese rule in the north in the independent kingdom of Đại Việt and in Chămpa. Among the topics discussed in relation to this period are the numerous edicts relating to dress issued by the various rulers of Đại Việt.

The early 19th century witnessed the creation of a unified Việt Nam and an end of the independent kingdom of Chămpa in the lowlands (thus, reducing the Chăm to a small minority with its feudal elite gone), but much of the highlands remained autonomous. This meant that, while the style of clothing worn by people in the lowlands became increasingly uniform, there was still considerable variation in the northern and southern highlands where people continued to wear their local styles of clothing. Also important was the fact that while modernity had begun to manifest itself in some ways in Nguyễn-ruled Việt Nam, the clothing styles of lowlands common people and elites remained firmly rooted in the past. Modernity became much more evident under French colonial rule and gradually the French brought the highlands more tightly under central authority. Nevertheless, ethnic divisions within colonial society meant that many forms of traditional clothing were retained, especially away from urban areas. Of particular importance was modification of the traditional female tunic during the 1920s in accordance with contemporary tastes to create the modern *áo dài*, which today is recognized worldwide as a Vietnamese national symbol. The history of this garment along with other fashion trends are discussed in sections covering the French colonial period and the post-colonial period when Việt Nam for a time was divided into two countries with governments that exerted very different influences on the types of clothing people wore.

Preface

While a large majority of the Vietnamese population belongs to the Kinh ethnic group, Việt Nam remains an ethnically diverse country. Many of its ethnic minorities have distinctive clothing and textile traditions and these are discussed in the final two chapters of the book. These ethnic minorities include groups such as the Thái that have lived in Việt Nam since antiquity as well as groups such as the Hmông that migrated to the country in modern times, bringing with them their traditions of dress and weaving. The first of these chapters covers the highland minority groups of northern Việt Nam. The majority of the people belonging to these groups speak Tai languages. Among the northern highland groups the Thái are of particular importance since it is from their homeland that many of the Tai speaking groups in neighboring Laos and Thailand migrated and the origins of the clothing and textile traditions of Tai speaking groups in these countries can be traced back to the Thái of Việt Nam. The second of these chapters covers ethnic minorities in southern Việt Nam. These include the Chăm in the lowlands that are among the most important producers of hand-woven textiles in present-day Việt Nam and a variety of groups in the Central Highlands. Recent social and economic changes in the Central Highlands have served to diminish wearing traditional clothing and making hand-woven textiles. Nevertheless, weaving by hand continues among many of these groups and traditional clothing is still worn, although increasingly only for special occasions.

A Note on Spelling

I have used *Hànyǔ pīnyīn* with its system of diacritics to transcribe Chinese words such as those for dynasties, people, places, and ethnic groups in China. I have used the Vietnamese alphabet (*chữ Quốc ngữ*) with its system of diacritics for Vietnamese words such as those for types of dress, dynasties, people, places, and ethnic groups in Việt Nam. In the case of ethnic groups, for example, I have used the spellings found in SIL International's *Ethnologue* for the language, the *Hànyǔ pīnyīn* spelling for the name of the groups in China, and the *chữ Quốc ngữ* spelling for the names of groups in Việt Nam.

A Note on Translation

It is not always easy to translate Vietnamese words (or the words used in the languages of various minority groups in Việt Nam) for objects of clothing precisely into English, especially since the types of clothing the peoples in Việt Nam (and China) have worn historically differ markedly from those in the West. This is particularly an issue when it comes to finding the best English terms to use for the various types of long garments worn by men and women in Việt Nam (and China). English writers have described these garments using a variety of words, including robes, tunics, and gowns. In the present work I will use the term gown for looser fitting, flowing long garments and tunic for long garments that fit the body more tightly, such as the modern *áo dài*.

Next two pages: **Việt Nam Provinces [1 Bắc Ninh, 2 Vĩnh Phúc, 3 Hà Nam, 4 Hưng Yên, 5 Hải Dương, 6 Ninh Bình]. Map by NgaViet.**

Administrative Map of Việt Nam

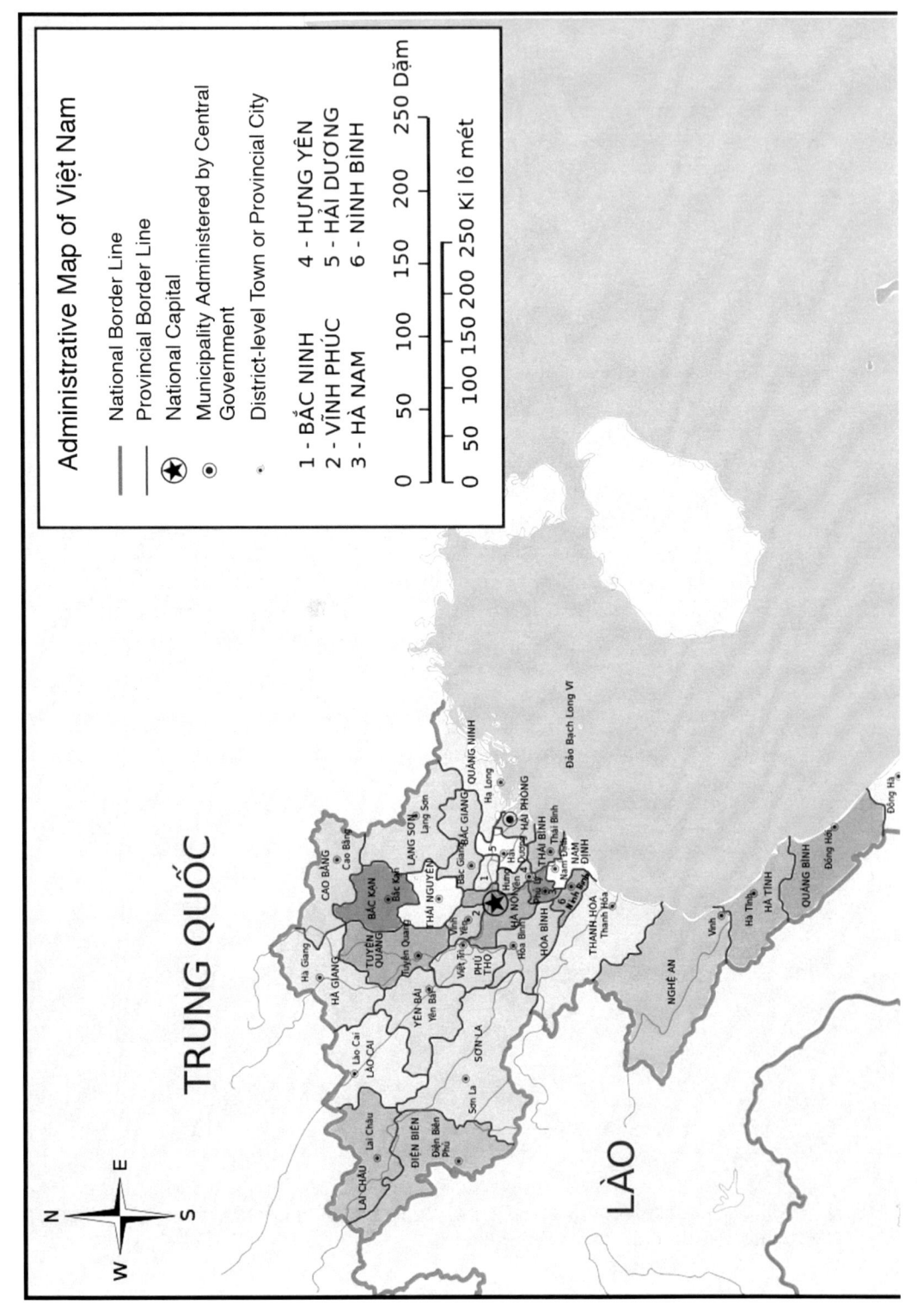

Administrative Map of Việt Nam

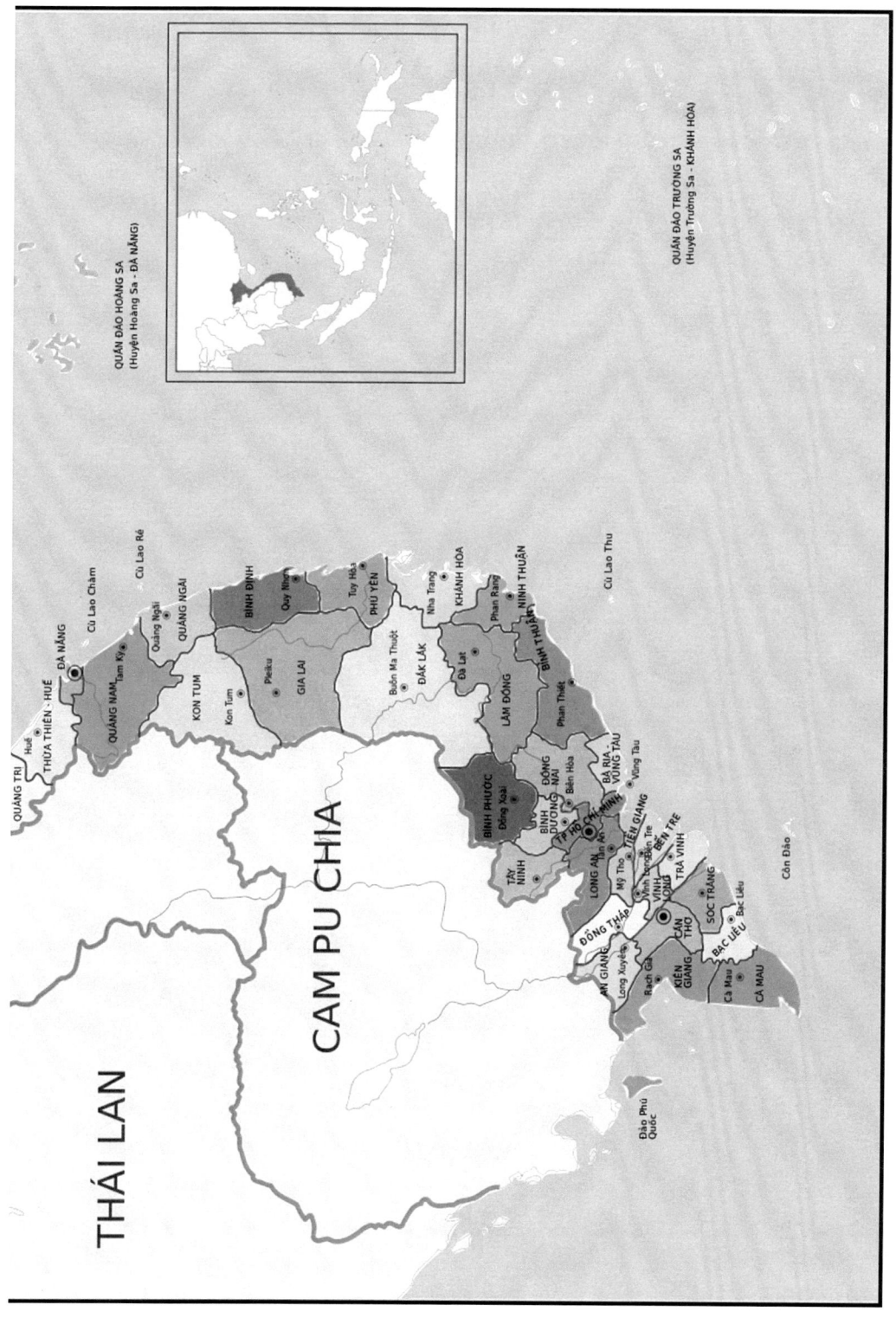

Introduction

The *áo dài*, a long tight-fitting tunic worn with trousers, is popularly associated with Vietnamese dress worldwide. In fact, few other countries can boast an item of clothing that has become so widely recognized as a national symbol. Women in Việt Nam as well as ethnic Vietnamese women in other countries commonly wear *áo dài* on any occasion when they wish to emphasize their national or ethnic identity. It is important to recognize, however, that the *áo dài* is a relatively recent creation in the long history of dress in Vietnam and only the most prominent part of Việt Nam's varied history of clothing styles.

The history of textiles and clothing in Việt Nam reflects ancient Bronze Age traditions associated with a variety of peoples living in Việt Nam, a long period of Chinese rule and cultural influence, and a much shorter period of French colonial rule. Dynamic responses to Chinese and other forms of outside influence has been an important feature of the history of Vietnamese dress for over two thousand years that has created distinctive styles of Vietnamese clothing of which the *áo dài* is only one of many examples over the centuries.

Technology and Materials

Looms. Loom weaving in Việt Nam dates back into antiquity and is associated with the arrival of early Austro-Tai speaking migrants from the north 2,500 to 3,000 years ago. Traditional hand operated looms include various types of back-strap looms, combination back-strap and frame looms, and frame looms. The earliest type is a foot-braced back-strap loom. Ancient bronze images of women weaving on this type of loom have been found in Yúnnán as well as on the Indonesian island of Flores (probably having been made in northern Việt Nam or an adjacent area and brought to Flores as a trade item).[1] Foot-braced back-strap looms ceased to be used by most people speaking Austro-Tai languages long ago, the Lí of Hǎinán Island in China being an exception.[2] Weaving technology using this type of loom diffused from Austro-Tai peoples to some Mon-Khmer and Malayo-Polynesian peoples and they are still used by many Mon-Khmer peoples in the Central Highlands of Việt Nam.[3]

Foot-braced back-strap looms restrict the size of the cloth woven to about twice

Introduction

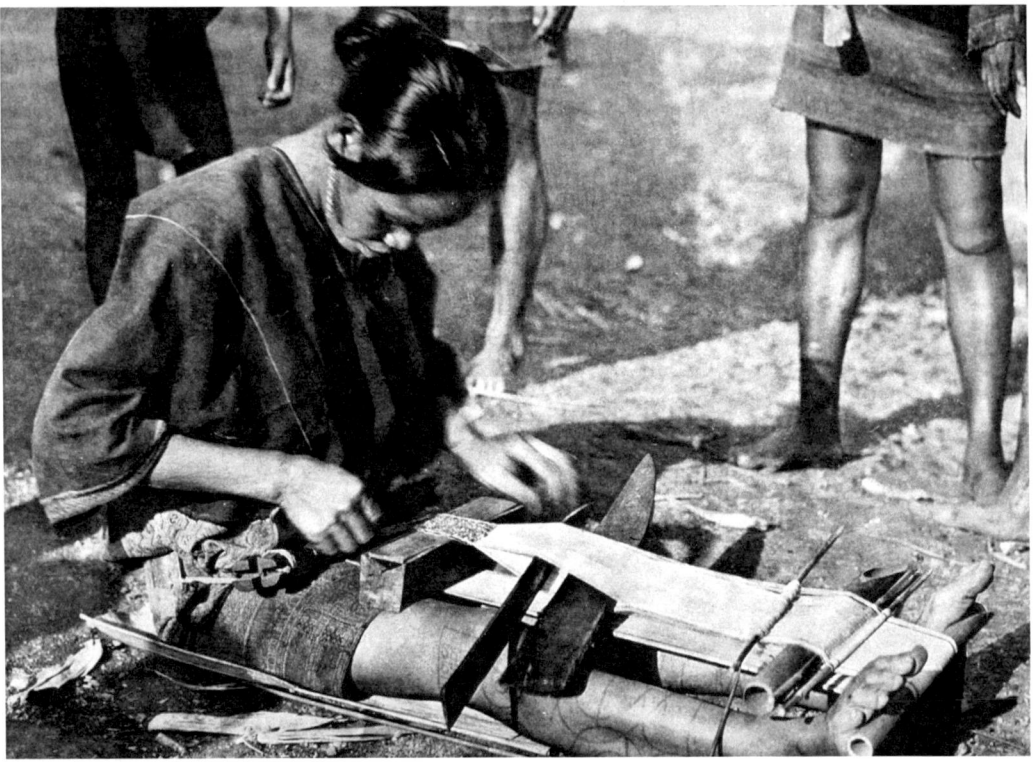

Lí woman weaving on a foot-braced backstrap loom, Hăinán Island (from Stübel, *Die Li-Stämme der Insel Hainan*, fig. 42).

the length of the weaver's legs and a width that is not much greater than that of the weaver's body. Individual woven pieces can be stitched together to produce larger pieces of cloth. Malayo-Polynesian peoples overcame the length issue by attaching the warp beam to an independent object such as posts secured in the ground, a tree trunk, or part of a house. Anthropologists in Việt Nam commonly refer to this type of back-strap loom as an "Indonesian" loom, reflecting its place of origin. Malayo-Polynesian peoples in Việt Nam such as the Chăm, Gia Rai (aka Jarai), and Ê Đê (aka Rhadé) use this type of loom. In the north some weavers overcame the length issue by attaching the back-strap to a frame and placing the warp threads on a roller. This type of loom, which can be referred to as a combination back-strap and frame loom, is used by some groups speaking Tai languages such as the Nùng and some Tày subgroups, as well as by the Hmông and Pà Thẻn.[4]

Replacing the back-strap altogether with a breast-beam that is also attached to a frame allows weavers to produce wider pieces of cloth (in addition to reducing back strain) and various types of such frame looms gradually came into widespread use in Việt Nam. The arrival of the French led to the introduction of modern power looms to Việt Nam in the late 19th century and resulted in the disappearance of hand weaving

Technology and Materials

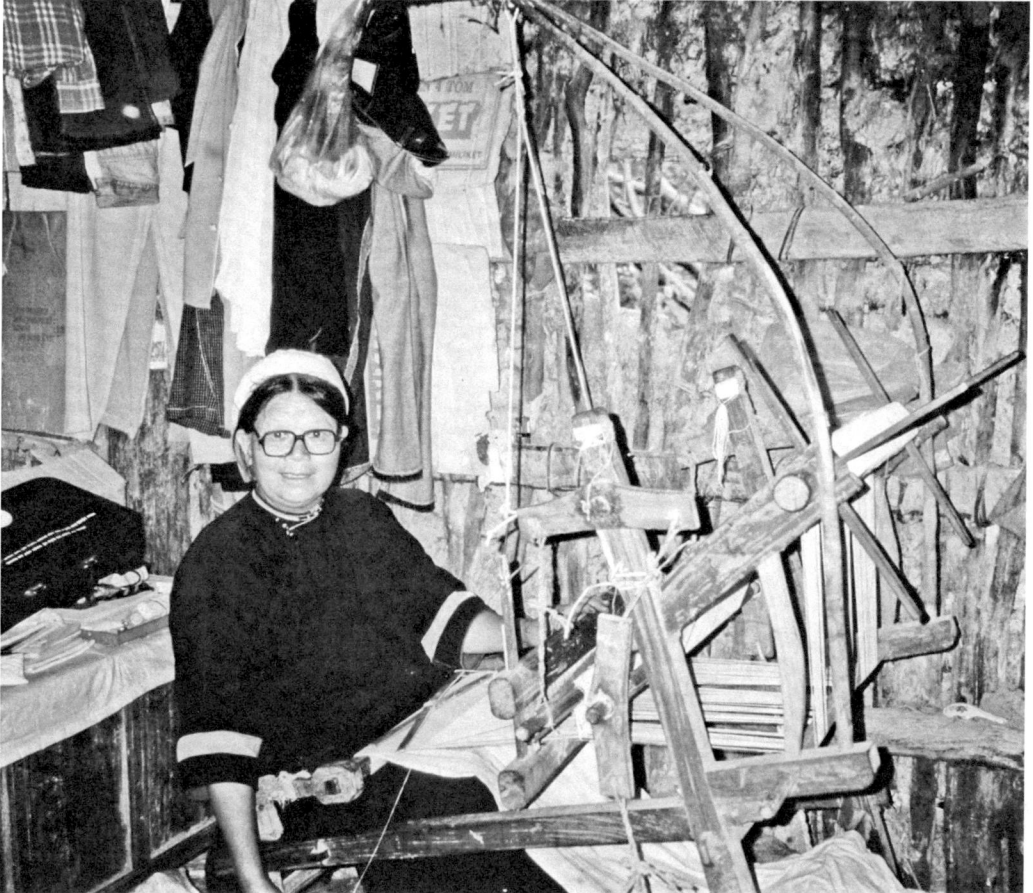

Nùng An woman weaving on a combination backstrap and frame loom, Quảng Uyên District, Cao Bằng Province.

in most of the country over the next couple of decades. Today, hand weaving using pre-industrial looms is found only among Việt Nam's minority groups.

Fibers. The oldest type of cloth produced in Việt Nam was made from beaten tree bark. Trees belonging to the Moraceae family are the source of material for most of this bark-cloth. These include *Artocarpus altilis* (breadfruit), *Antiaris toxicaria* (*sui* in Vietnamese, *upas* in Malaysia, a popular source of whitish bark-cloth and well known for the poisonous quality of its latex, which is used arrow tips), *Broussonetia papyrifera* (paper mulberry), and *Ficus* (fig) trees. Most ethnic groups in Việt Nam have traditions of making bark-cloth, but today it is encountered only on rare occasions among a few minority groups in the Central Highlands. Paper mulberry pulp is also used for making paper, something that probably has its origins in bark-cloth production.

The silk cotton tree (*Bombax ceiba* Linn., *Bombax malabaricum* DC., *cây gạo*

Introduction

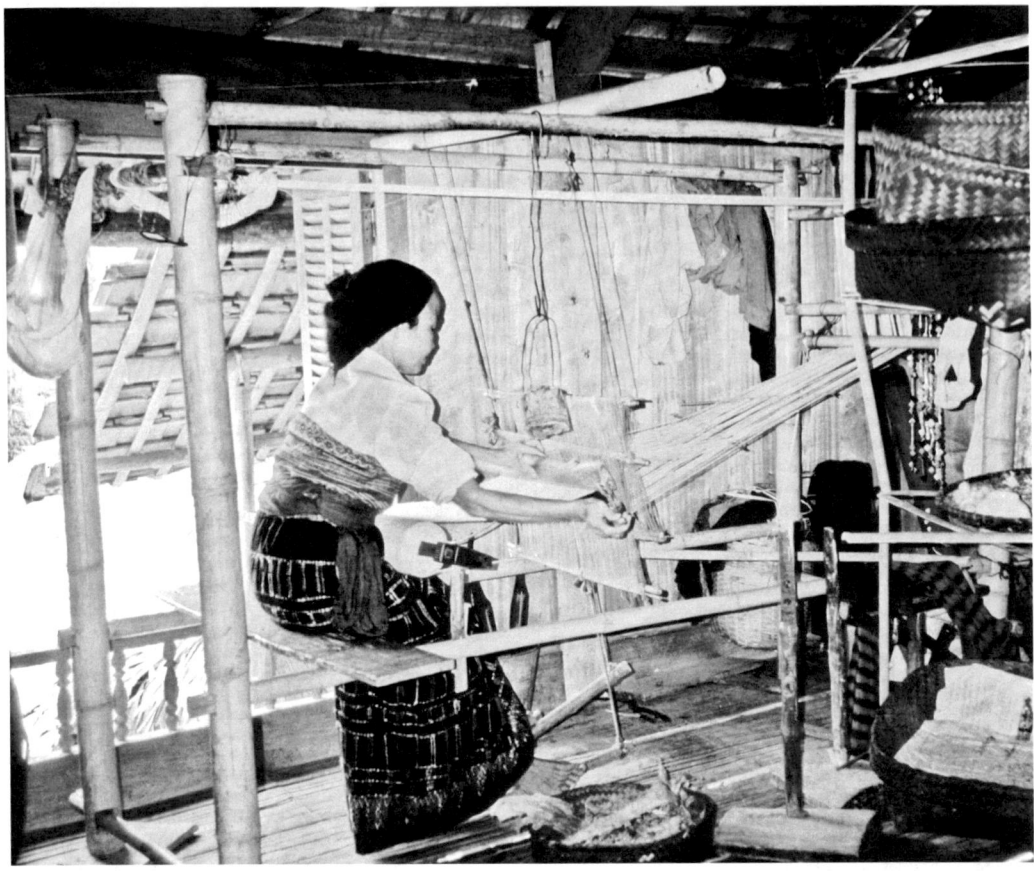

Thái (Tái Dăm sub-group) woman weaving on a frame loom, Quan Sơn District, Thanh Hoa Province.

in Vietnamese), which is sometimes referred to as a kapok tree, and silk are the two best documented sources of fibers used to weave cloth in ancient Việt Nam. The early Tai inhabitants of northern Việt Nam produced silk (*lụa* in Vietnamese) and some highland Tai villages still produce their own silk thread and cloth. Quasi-mythical legend links the origin of silk to Princess Hoàng Phủ Thiếu Hoa, the daughter of Hùng Định Vương, one of the Tai kings of Văn Lang. According to the legend, silk weaving in Việt Nam first took place in Cổ Dó village (in modern Ba Vì District, Hà Tây Province). This legend can be interpreted as linking the origin of silk production in Việt Nam to the arrival of the Tai people known as Lò Yuè (aka Lạc Việt) in northern Việt Nam probably in the 600s BC (to be discussed further in the next chapter). Production of raw silk and weaving silk cloth became increasingly widespread in northern Việt Nam after the time of the Hùng kings. In feudal Đại Việt both were almost universal household activities in the Red River Delta (*Đồng bằng sông Hồng* or *Châu thổ sông Hồng* in Vietnamese) as well as among highland Tai peoples. There were, however, important distinctions between the common silk cloth produced by households for domestic consumption and the higher quality silk cloth produced for elites and later for export. Weaving of this higher quality silk cloth took place primarily in a few centers clustered in and around the capital of Thăng Long, including locales not only in Hà Tây Province, but also in Sơn Tây, Bắc Ninh and Hải Dương provinces.[5] There were over a dozen types of silk produced during the feudal period with the finest types domestically being reserved for the nobility. In addition to plain weave silk, weavers also produced silk with supplementary weft (aka brocade) patterns called *gấm*.

As will be discussed later, after increasing in the 16th and early 17th centuries, silk production in Việt Nam went into decline in the late 17th century for a variety of political, environmental, and economic reasons. It declined even further in the 19th century in the face of competition from imported silk cloth from China, Japan, and France. In response, French colonial authorities made an effort to promote sericulture and silk weaving starting in the late 1890s.[6] The French promoted sericulture in Hải Dương Province in Tonkin and in Thanh Hóa, Quảng Nam, and Bình Định provinces in Annam. The main silk filatures and weaving industries were located in Nam Định and Phú Phong (Bình Định Province), with smaller operations found in Tân Châu (An Giang Province) and Hà Tây Province (especially the village of Vạn Phúc). Tân Châu was famous for its black silk (*lụa lãnh mỹ a*) that is made using a dye from *Diospyros mollis* fruit (*mặc nưa*). These efforts met with limited success, but on the whole silk production in Việt Nam remained relatively small until recently, when efforts again were made to revive the industry. This included promotion of the area around Bảo Lộc (Lâm Đồng Province) as a center of sericulture and silk production, employing migrants from the Red River Delta, with a large factory in Bảo Lộc town. Despite some ups and downs, on the whole these efforts have been successful and at present Việt Nam is the world's 7th leading producer of silk.

Austro-Tai speaking peoples have an ancient tradition of using the silk cotton tree (*Bombax ceiba* Linn., *Bombax malabaricum* DC.) to produce cotton-like kapok thread by non-Chinese peoples in much of southern China, especially in the southeast. Schafer mentions Táng Dynasty Chinese sources referring to such thread from Guǎngxī using such terms as "mountain wool" and "tree floss."[7] Kapok thread (like that made from hemp) is made by the more labor-intensive process of hand splicing rather than being spun on a spinning wheel like cotton. In large part because of this difference, by the time of the Táng Dynasty throughout most of China as cotton had become more readily available kapok was used only as stuffing. It is perhaps the way kapok was used in China during the Táng Dynasty that led Khun and Needham mistakenly to state since "the fibre cannot be spun" that "it can only be used for such purposes as stuffing sleeping bags."[8] Schafer also wrongly claims, "kapok cannot be woven" in a discussion of cotton and kapok in ancient Việt Nam, perhaps for the same reason.[9]

Deng says the "Lao-ai tribe" (probably referring to Ai Lào in Yúnnán) was growing

Introduction

the *Gossypium arboreum* variety of cotton from the Indus Valley by the AD 200s.[10] Citing the 5th century *Hou Han Shu* (Book of the Later Han), he argues generally that "the South Asian species (*Gossypium arboreum* and *Gossypium barbadense*) [arrived in China] through a southern route overseas from India to Burma, Vietnam and to China's Hainan Island, Yunnan, Guangxi and Guangdong."[11] The earliest mention of South Asian cotton by the Chinese refers to it being used by Southwestern Barbarians and it is several centuries before there are references to its use in the southeast. It is likely that it's early appearance in southern Yúnnán relates to Ai Lào having a well-established trade link with India via Myanmar, with textiles being the main trade items (discussed in the next chapter).

Although the highland environment of southern Yúnnán and northeastern Myanmar is far less suitable for growing cotton than the lowlands of South Asia, the Tai and a number of Tibeto-Burman peoples from this region appear to have a fairly long history of growing cotton and of exporting it to the north. Many of the Karen groups in Myanmar in particular have a history of growing and exporting cotton to China.[12] The Tai-speaking Shan in Myanmar also have a long history of growing cotton and their mythical account of its introduction that appears to link it with South Asia: "the Shans tell how eight Brahmans, four male and four female, came down long since from above and eating of the earth became human: denied a return to heaven, they took up their dwelling in Burma, and multiplying there introduced among its people the cultivation of cotton and the arts of spinning and weaving."[13] In historical times cotton was more widely used than silk among the Tai in Shan State and southern Yúnnán, with silk clothing being worn mainly by members of the nobility. Silk was more widely produced among Tai peoples further to the east in Laos and Việt Nam.

Nán Yuè (i.e., southeastern China and northern Việt Nam) was tied to Indian through overland and maritime trade links. Traders from Shǔ (i.e., Sìchuān) mainly conducted the overland trade and, in the case of northern Việt Nam, the routes passed along the Lô and Red rivers from Yúnnán. Malays and later people from the Middle East mainly carried out the maritime trade with ships stopping at the ports of Fù Nán, Chēnlà, and Chămpa to the south of northern Việt Nam and at Guǎngzhōu immediately to the north. Cotton cloth was a trade item along both routes and cotton growing could have been introduced to northern Việt Nam by either one. In any event, South Asian cotton had arrived in the Guǎngzhōu area by the latter part of the Táng Dynasty era. Schafer says the earliest mention of cotton from this region is in a poem written in the late 700s by Wáng Jiàn (l. 767–ca. 830) that refers to family-based cotton weaving in Guǎngzhōu being as "commonplace as the cultivation of red banana."[14] There are many more references to cotton in the Guǎngzhōu and beyond in the 800s and over the next couple of centuries. Further south in Chămpa, Schafer cites the *Jiù Táng Shū* (Old Book of Tang, presented in 945) and the *Xīn Táng Shū* (New Book of Tang, presented in 1060) referring to the king wearing clothing made of *kārpasa*, a fairly unambiguous Sanskrit reference to a *Gossypium* variety of cotton and not kapok.[15]

Cotton was also produced in Việt Nam at least by the time of the Táng Dynasty and probably earlier, but it is not clear just how extensively it was being grown south of Guǎngzhōu during and in the centuries immediately before and after the Táng Dynasty. In general, however, there was a shift from the use of kapok to cotton in northern Việt Nam during the period of Chinese rule, especially in the lowlands. Kapok continued to be used by some highland ethnic groups in Việt Nam until modern times. At present some Tai-speaking groups still use kapok as stuffing for blankets and pillows. In the case of Chămpa references to cotton cloth usually are to the clothing of the king. In ancient times the Chăm wove with kapok and Chămpa continued to export kapok well into the 1600s, though presumably to be used as stuffing by that time.[16] Both the northern and central regions of independent Đại Việt produced cotton for domestic use and for export. John Crawfurd describes clothing made of cotton cloth being widely worn in central and southern Việt Nam in the early 1800s and lists cotton among the exports from Tonkin and Faifo (Hội An) in the 1600s and early 1800s.[17] He adds that while "They manufacture no fine cotton fabric, nor any thing indeed approaching to it.... Cotton is raised by them in considerable abundance, and of good quality; and from this material there is fabricated particularly in Tonquin [Tonkin], a coarse durable cloth, at so low a price, that it would not be easy to supplant it by the introduction of European manufactures under the most favourable circumstances."[18]

Among the problems with the history of kapok versus cotton based on early accounts is assessing the validity of observations since cotton and kapok cloth are not that different to the casual observer. There are also linguistic problems. Thus, Khun and Needham note in their study of early Chinese technology, "Mien-hua is true cotton. Mu-mien can mean cotton, but also kapok, the cotton-like floss from a tree."[19]

Although cotton eventually became the main material used to make clothing for common people throughout Việt Nam, the country's climate is not ideal for growing it. While it was possible to grow sufficient quantities of cotton to meet demand in areas where the population and the demand for clothing was relatively small, such as in the Central Highlands, this has not been the case with the densely populated Mekong River and Red River delta regions for many centuries. Therefore, most cotton thread and cloth was imported during the French colonial period and this remains the case today. The French established three cotton-spinning mills in northern Việt Nam using raw imported cotton. The largest of these was at Nam Định (southeast of Hà Nội), which was established in 1889, and where silk thread was also produced. Nam Định remains an important center of textile production. In the south, Gò Công in Tiền Giang Province was a center of cotton weaving in the French period.

In discussing silk and cotton it is important to distinguish between thread and woven cloth. This is because hand-made silk and cotton thread has been largely replaced in Việt Nam by industrially manufactured thread. Only women from a few minority groups still make their own silk and cotton thread. Even among those

Introduction

employing handlooms such as the Chăm it is common now to use industrial thread (as well as aniline dyes). Moreover, in addition to industrial thread produced locally, it should be noted that local weavers and weaving factories have been using imported cotton and silk thread from China, Japan, and other countries since the early days of the French colonial period. Thus, Tày weavers in the highlands of northern Việt Nam had access to imported French silk thread even in the early 20th century.

There are a variety of other materials from trees, lianas, and grasses that have been used to make bast fibers for weaving in Việt Nam, although the history of the use of many of these is not well documented. Ramie fiber [*Boehmeria Nivea* (L.) Gaudich] was used to weave cloth extensively in ancient China.[20] The Táng Dynasty *Yüan-Ho Chun Hsien Thu Chih* ("Topography of the Prefectures and Districts of China in the Reign Period Yuan-ho"; i.e., during the reign of Emperor Xiànzōng, r. 805–20) mentions fine ramie cloth being woven in Líen and Kuei counties in northern Lǐng Nán (the border region of modern Guǎngxī, Guǎngdōng, and Húnán).[21] As Kuhn and Needham note, the ramie used in the south is different from that used in the north of China: white or yellow *Boehmeria nivea* (var. *chinensis* Gaudich) was used in the north and green *Boehmeria nivea* (var. *tenassima* Gaudich) was used in the south.[22] Ramie thread is made by hand splicing and in the south cloth was woven on a foot-braced back-strap loom in ancient times. It is not clear how extensively it was used further south of Líen and Kuei counties, but ramie seems mainly to have been a bast fiber used in the north and not widely used in Việt Nam. There are only rare instances of ramie cloth in modern Việt Nam. For example, some Ê Đê Kpă grew ramie in the recent past and made cloth from it.[23]

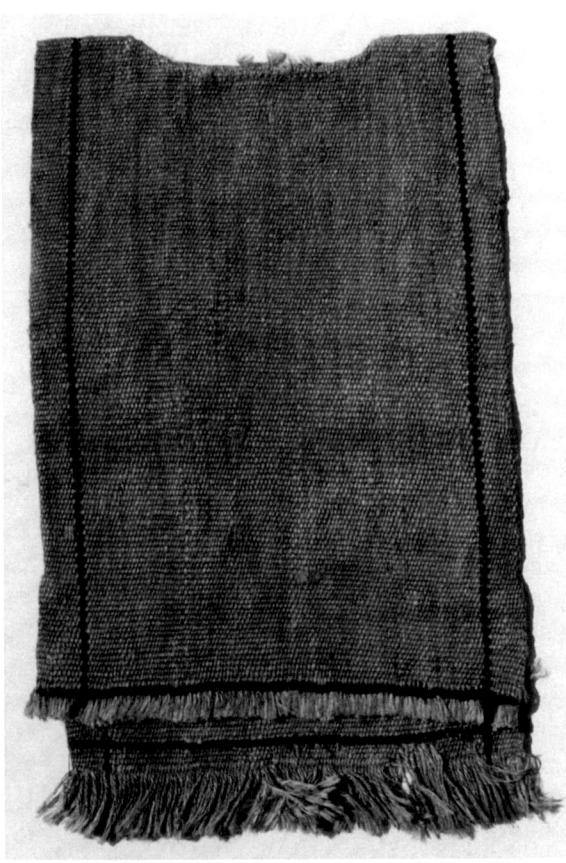

Ê Đê (Kpă sub-group) pullover blouse made from ramie, Krông Bông District, Đắk Lắk Province.

The Southern Barbarians wove hemp (*Cannabis sativa*) cloth much more widely than ramie cloth.[24] Hemp cloth is sometimes mistakenly referred to as linen in published sources. Hemp textiles have

Technology and Materials

a long history in southern China and may have been used by some of the ancestors of people currently living in Việt Nam, but in ancient times people living to the northwest of Việt Nam were the ones primarily making hemp cloth. These include the ancestors of the Hmông and Bố Y. Members of both groups settled in the highlands of northern Việt Nam in the late 1700s and 1800s. A few peoples in the Central Highlands of Việt Nam have been reported to use hemp to make cloth in modern times. These include most sub-groups of Xơ Đăng, the Hrê, and possibly the Gia Rai.

Banana fiber cloth appears to have been widely produced in Nán Yuè and is mentioned as a product of northern Việt Nam in Chinese accounts dating back to the Hàn Dynasty. Kuhn and Needham cite the *Kuang Chih* ("Extensive Records of Remarkable Things") by Kuo I–Kung (l. 420–502) describing banana fiber cloth from Ān Nán (northern Việt Nam), Guǎngxī, and Guǎngdōng being "of fragile but good quality, yellowish-white in colour."[25] During the Táng Dynasty they cite the *Thung Tien* ("Comprehensive Statutes") by Tu Yu (l. 735–812) referring to the economic importance of banana fiber cloth in Fújiàn, Hǎinán, and Ān Nán and to it being sent as tribute to the emperor and the *Yüan-Ho Chun Hsien Thu Chih*

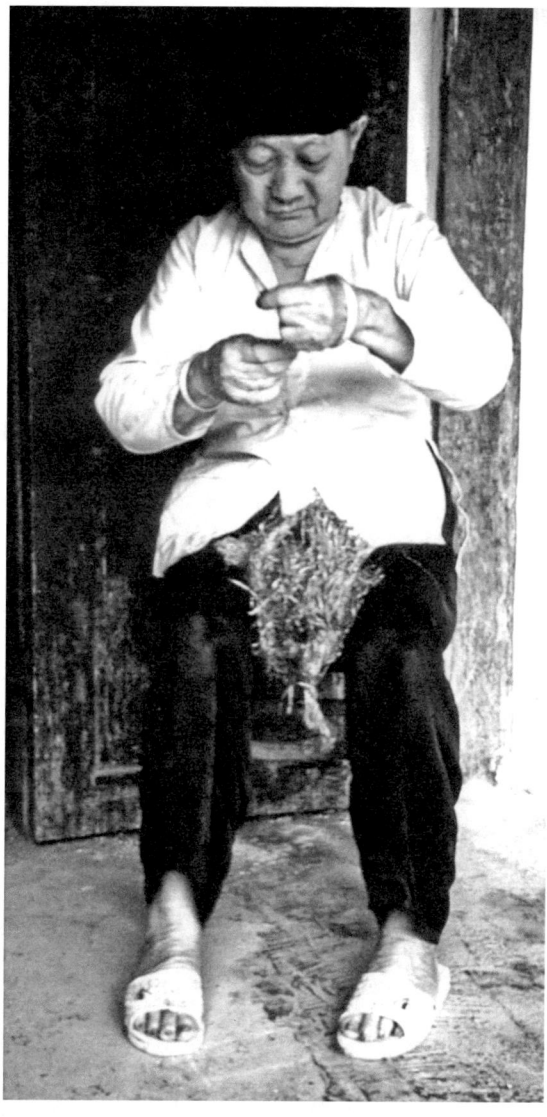

White Hmông woman making hemp tread by hand-splicing, Quản Bạ District, Hà Giang Province.

mentioning banana fiber cloth being made in Guǎngxī and Guǎngdōng.[26] As with other fibers occasionally there are problems with terms used to describe banana fiber cloth. In particular it is sometimes, like hemp, referred to as linen.[27] Two types of banana cloth, called *hi* and *khích*, were produced in Chinese-ruled Giao Chỉ (aka Jiāozhǐ), and banana fiber cloth continued to be produced and remained popular in Việt Nam until the 1700s.

Introduction

There are also a variety of other materials that have been used to make cloth in Việt Nam, but documentation of their use is relatively poor.[28] Asbestos cloth is one particularly interesting type of fabric mentioned by Schafer: "Nonflammable textiles made from mineral asbestos were listed by Yüan Chen [aka Yuán Zhěn, l. 779–831], along with kapok and sago, among the wonderful ware of Nam-Viet."[29]

Dyes. What about dyes?[30] By and large, common people in Việt Nam have tended historically to wear clothing made of cloth that was left undyed or dyed a single color, whereas elites had a preference for more colorful clothing. As for specific dyes, we have already mentioned the black dye from *Diospyros mollis* fruit (*mặc nưa*). Historically blue has been the most common color of clothing. The shade of blue has tended to be dark, often called indigo blue, and sometimes dark enough to look almost black. Lighter shades of blue generally were associated with elite silk clothing. The Vietnamese language uses the same word, *xanh*, for blue and green, but often adds something to indicate a particular shade of blue or green. Thus, *chàm* or *màu chàm* means indigo (as in the dye) and *xanh chàm* or *xanh chàm* can be used to indicate dark blue. In the case of green something is often added to *xanh* to indicate green or a particular shade of green. Thus, *xanh lá cây* refers to tree leaf green. When dyeing a cloth blue, dyers among a particular group or in a particular area in Việt Nam often use a single source for the dye and obtain different shades based on the length of time and number of times the cloth is dyed. In the West it is common to associate what we call indigo blue with *Indigofera tinctoria* L. or common indigo, but in Việt Nam blue dyes traditionally have come from other sources. In Việt Nam the word *chàm* is usually associated with blue obtained with dye from the *Strobilanthes cusia* (Nees) Imlay. However, in ancient times in particular there were also other common sources of *chàm* dye in Việt Nam. Dyer's knotweed, *Persicaria tinctoria* (Aiton) Apach, is a particularly ancient source of blue dye that was once widely used in northern Việt Nam.[31] The liana *Marsdenua tinctoria* R. Brown is another ancient source of *chàm* dye in the region. Cardon provides a photograph of a Sòng Dynasty hemp or kapok skirt from an archaeological site in Guìzhōu with blue batik patterning made using dye from this plant.[32] *Wrightia laevis* J.D. Hooker is another source of blue dye, one that was widely used by the Tày and Nùng in the past.

Red dye (red is *đỏ* in Vietnamese) came from a number of sources in Việt Nam in the past. Lac insect colonies (*Kerria chinensis*, *cánh kiến* in Vietnamese) have a long history of use as a source of red dye in Việt Nam.[33] Various trees can be used as a host for the colonies, such as the *Ficus altissima* Blume, *Combretam quadrangulare* Kurz., and *Albizzia chinensis* (Obs.) Merr. The sappan tree (*Caesalpinia sappan* L. Leguminosae, *vang* or *tô mộc* in Vietnamese) was another popular source of red dye in the lowlands of central and southern Việt Nam. Sappan bark is used for yellow dye and the wood for red dye. Schafer reports that sappan wood dye was exported from Ái-châu (southern Ăn Nán) during the Táng Dynasty.[34] Other less common sources of red dye include *Morinda umbellata* L. root (*nhàu tan* in Vietnamese, also a source of yellow dye), mulberry fruit (*Morus nigra* L.), and rose apple fruit (*Syzygium jambos*).

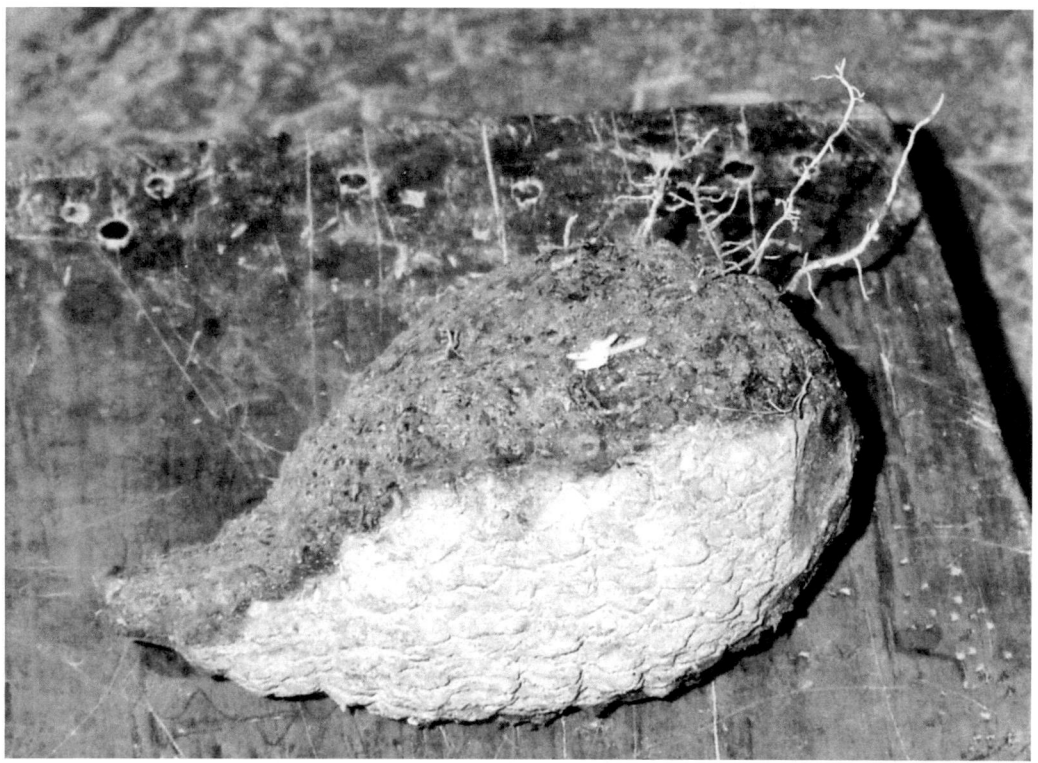

Dye yam (*củ nâu*) used for brown dye.

Yellow (*màu vàng* in Vietnamese) clothing in Việt Nam, as in China, commonly has been associated with royalty. The climbing shrub *Fibraurea tinctoria* Lour. (*dây vàng* in Vietnamese, *huang teng* in Chinese) has been used as a source of yellow dye in southern China and northern Việt Nam.[35] Jackfruit wood (*Artocarpus heterophyllus* Lam., *mít* in Vietnamese) is another source of yellow dye in Việt Nam. Turmeric (*Curcuma longa* L.) is a popular source of yellow dye throughout much of the Asia-Pacific region. It originated in India and spread very early to eastern Asia and the Pacific, being used in China in the AD 600s. Traditionally, however, it was not a major source of dye in Việt Nam.

Brown clothing with the color being produced by the dye yam (*Dioscorea cirrhosa* Lour., *củ nâu* in Vietnamese) has been widely worn by lowland Kinh people in Việt Nam for centuries and the dye is also used by some highland ethnic groups in Việt Nam.[36]

Change, Status and Identity

Styles of dress in Việt Nam prior to the 20th century were relatively conservative. This in part reflects technical factors, such as the fact that the clothing worn by most

Introduction

people was produced within their own household or community using pre-industrial technology, and that most people's knowledge of and exposure to the larger world was quite limited. Most people wore pretty much the same style of clothing that their parents wore as befitted their status within society. As for the last point, what someone wore often reflected ethnicity as well as one's position in society. Thus, many ethnic groups in Việt Nam have distinctive styles of dress. In feudal Kinh (the majority population) society relative status was clearly indicated by the clothing that a person wore. Dress not merely broadly differentiated between the elites and commoners, but also indicated more subtle differences in relative status within these broad categories.

The above does not mean that styles of dress were completely static, otherwise people would still be adorning themselves in leafs and feathers. Changes in dress styles in Việt Nam prior to the 20th century tended to come about for a few reasons and such changes usually were initiated by elites. Conquest and migration have played an important role in changing styles of dress in Việt Nam. Conquests were associated with the introduction of new cultural elements and by the arrival of new peoples that resulted in changes to the cultures of peoples already living in the region conquered. Those arriving included both the conquerors themselves as well as others that arrived following the initial period of conquest. While there are instances where the conquerors decreed a change of dress for the conquered, especially on the part of surviving elites, by and large changes in the wake of conquest have tended to come about as a result of wishing to emulate the dress of those now in power. This process starts with elites and then percolates downward and outward to those of lower status. Such emulation, of course, does not only come about as a result of conquest and the dress of local elites and others often are influenced by fashions emanating from other places, especially from places that are perceived to be centers of civilization possessing superior cultures. Essentially there have been four main periods of conquest and migration that have influenced textiles and styles of dress in Việt Nam.

The first of these periods is what is commonly known as the Đông Sơn era that is liked to the arrival of Tai nobles in northern Việt Nam some 2,500 years ago, which started a process of complete or partial assimilation of many local Mon-Khmer and Kadai peoples that can be referred to as Tai-ization or Tai-ification.[37] This process included the adoption of Tai styles of dress or of dress styles that were influenced by the Tai. The Tái Mười of Nghệ An Province provide an example of complete assimilation in regards to dress and most of the surviving Mon-Khmer minority groups in the highlands of north Việt Nam—such as the Mường, Xinh Mun, and Kháng—wear clothing that is strongly influenced by neighboring Thái.[38] While it is uncertain how many Tai speaking people actually migrated to northern Việt Nam, for present purposes it is their cultural impact and the introduction of particular types of textiles and styles of dress that is important.

The second period is associated with the Chinese conquest of northern Việt Nam over 2,000 years ago and the subsequent centuries of Chinese rule lasting into the AD 900s. Chinese conquest and rule brought about a similar process that of acculturation that can be referred to as Sinification, Sinicization, or Hànification. This was a gradual process that took place over centuries, starting with the Nán Yuè Kingdom period in which the Chinese physical presence was limited and a hybrid Tai-Chinese culture developed and the influence of Chinese dress was primarily among local elites. Once the region was formally incorporated into the Chinese imperial system elites followed Chinese fashions more closely, but migration of Chinese and others to northern Việt Nam was still relatively limited until well after the fall of the Hàn Dynasty when large numbers of Chinese migrants arrived and greatly changed the demographic make-up of Ăn Nán ("Pacified South," aka Annam). Táng-ruled Ăn Nán also attracted non-Chinese migrants from neighboring areas, including people speaking Vietic Mon-Khmer languages from the southwest. A blending of the cultures of various Mon-Khmer, Tai-Kadai, and Chinese peoples in the lowlands of northern Việt Nam during the period of Chinese rule produced the Kinh (aka Việt) people that became the national majority of subsequent Vietnamese states.

After northern Việt Nam became independent from China there began a long history of Vietnamese elites sometimes closely following Chinese fashion and at other times seeking to create local styles that, although still clearly strongly influenced by Chinese dress, had distinctive characteristics. Chinese styles of dress also gradually spread among common people in Kinh society, although in forms that were distinct from the clothing worn by elites, as well as among peoples living in regions surrounding territory formally under Vietnamese rule. In the case of male attire among Kinh commoners and many ethnic minority groups loincloths and other older forms of dress almost universally gave way to Chinese style trousers and shirts. Over the centuries it tended to be female dress that served as a marker of ethnic identity among non-Kinh peoples.

As the Kinh-ruled kingdom of Đại Việt conquered lowland territories to its south that had been part of the kingdom of Chămpa and the Khmer Empire of Kampuchea (*Srok Khmer*) it assimilated a majority of the Chăm and Khmer Krôm (aka Khơ Me Crộm) living in these territories, while leaving minorities of both groups in some locales. The process of Kinhification or Kinhization associated with the conquest of central and southern Việt Nam resulted in the development of regional Kinh cultures with some distinctive features, including styles of dress. Assimilated Chăm and Khmer Krôm adopted such styles of dress. However, while the local styles of Kinh dress influenced the dress of the remaining Chăm and Khmer Krôm these people retained some distinct elements of dress. The Kinh also exerted political control to varying degrees of highland peoples in the north and Kinh culture influenced many aspects of life in the northern highlands, including styles of dress, especially among local elites.

In modern times French rule began a period of modernization and Westernization in Việt Nam that saw the erosion and finally the disappearance of most elements of the older feudal society. There were also important demographic changes under French rule. While the number of French and other Europeans living in Việt Nam was relatively small and often transient they did provide and important cultural presence in the country. In addition, colonial policies encouraged the migration of people from China, with large numbers of them settling in the south in particular. Under the French, Vietnamese began to adopt Western dress. French colonial rule also served to undermine the old distinctions that had been made between the dress of elites and commoners. During the French colonial period this process was largely an urban affair that was closely linked to the rise of a new Vietnamese middle class that valued what it perceived to be modernity. It was a process that accelerated after the end of French colonial rule in both the communist north and non-communist south and later in unified Việt Nam as traditional distinctive Kinh clothing increasingly came to be worn only on special occasions, if at all. As can be seen from the current popularity of the *áo dài,* however, links with the past clearly have persisted and even been revived to form the basis for new fashions.

1

Ancient Clothing

There are essentially five ancient clothing traditions that have contributed to the history of textiles and clothing in Việt Nam. The first and oldest of these is associated with the early use of bark-cloth for clothing that appears to be linked to the arrival of peoples speaking Mon-Khmer (aka Austro-Asiatic) and Kadai languages. The next two are from northern Việt Nam and are associated with the early cultures of what Hirth refers to as the "bronze drum nations," located along and to the south of the Yangtze River and populated by non–Hàn people.[1] This is a vast region that included a number of tribes, confederacies, and kingdoms along and to the south of the Yangtze River (aka Cháng Jiāng). The second clothing tradition is that of the Nán Yuè region of coastal southeastern China and northern Việt Nam and especially its Tai-speaking inhabitants that are associated with Đông Sơn culture in Việt Nam. The third clothing tradition comes from western Guìzhōu and Yúnnán in China, a region that included the ancient kingdom of Diǎn (aka Tien) in Yúnnán and the Yèláng confederacy in Guìzhōu. The fourth clothing tradition is from central and southern Việt Nam and is associated with the kingdom of Chămpa and the Chăm people that speak a Malayo-Polynesian language. The fifth one is associated with the Chinese that ruled lowland northern Việt Nam.

There were peoples occupying Việt Nam prior to the arrival of the Austro-Asiatic and Austro-Tai peoples from the north. These peoples are associated with Hoabinhian (20,000–7,000 BP) and other Neolithic cultures.[2] There are no material remains of the clothing of these peoples, but it is likely that they wore some sort of minimal leaf and twine clothing of the types that were found throughout Southeast Asia prior to the spread of bark-cloth and weaving technology and access to woven cloth through trade for non-weavers. In historical times this style of clothing has been found in some remote areas such as the Andaman Islands and parts of New Guinea.[3] Such clothing vanished long ago in Việt Nam, but there are figures on Đông Sơn bronzes that may depict people wearing leaf skirts.

Bark-cloth

Based on archaeological evidence in the form of stone bark-cloth beaters from southeastern China, bark-cloth was being produced in Guangxi as early as around

1. Ancient Clothing

6,000 BC and in the Guǎngdōng's Pearl River Delta area by 4,600 BC.[4] Beyond China stone bark-cloth beaters have been found in Việt Nam, Laos, Cambodia, Thailand, Peninsular Malaysia, Taiwan, the Philippines, Borneo, Sulawesi, Madagascar, and along the west coast of Latin America. Cameron divides stone bark-cloth beaters into 8 types and, while the earliest types come from the Pearl River region of China, "the widest range of bark-cloth beaters," five types, have been found in Việt Nam.[5] A number of stone bark-cloth beaters have been found in Late Neolithic sites not only in northern Việt Nam (including Hà Giang, Mai Pha, and Hạ Long sites), but also in central and southern Việt Nam.[6]

The distribution of these beaters appears to be linked to the diffusion of bark-cloth making technology form southeast China and this in turn is related to the migration patterns of particular peoples. Southeast China was home to the ancestors of a variety of peoples that subsequently migrated to Việt Nam and elsewhere in Southeast Asia.[7] These include the ancestors of peoples speaking Mon-Khmer, Kadai, Austronesian, and Hmong-Mien languages. In modern times peoples speaking all but Hmong-Mien languages are known to have made bark-cloth. As for Hmong-Mien speaking groups, the Chē people (aka Shē Mín) of ancient Guǎngdōng were the ancestors of the Yáo (Dao in Việt Nam). Some of them moved into the highlands around the time of the arrival of the Tai from the north and retained a distinctive identity, while those that remained in the lowlands were assimilated into Tai and then Chinese populations. It is quite possible that the Chē made bark-cloth, but by the time that Mienic groups began to settle in northern Việt Nam they no longer did. This region of southeast China is widely recognized as the ancestral home of the Austronesian peoples and the Austronesians that left southeast China and spread across Island Southeast Asia and beyond carried the knowledge of bark-cloth making with them. The Austronesian peoples speaking Malayo-Polynesian languages that later settled in central

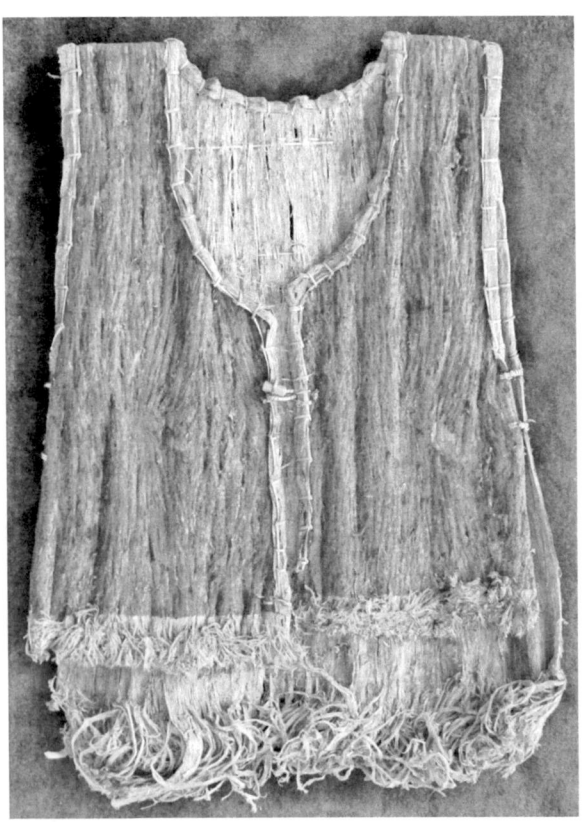

Xơ Đăng, man's vest made of bark-cloth, Kon Tum Province.

and southern Việt Nam from Borneo over 3,000 years ago seem to have made bark-cloth prior to adopting weaving. Among modern Malayo-Polynesian groups in Việt Nam, the Ra Glai who live in the highlands of eastern Ninh Thuận and Khánh Hòa provinces are interesting in this regard since they have no tradition of weaving and only one of making bark-cloth (trading for woven cloth).[8] In addition, while the Ê Đê weave, some of them also have made bark-cloth in recent times. Even the Chăm, who are well known for their weaving, have a tradition of making bark-cloth and it was still made by some Chăm in the early 20th century.[9]

The diffusion of bark-cloth across ancient Mainland Southeast Asia is closely linked to the migration of Mon-Khmer peoples.[10] Early peoples speaking Mon-Khmer languages arrived in Việt Nam during the Late Neolithic Period over 4,000 years ago. This period is represented by sites associated with Hà Giang, Mai Pha, and Hạ Long cultures in northern Việt Nam, the Bàu Tró (Quảng Bình Province) and Lung Leng (Kon Tum Province) sites in central Việt Nam, and several sites in the Đồng Nai region in southern Việt Nam. Stone bark-cloth beaters have been found in many of these Late Neolithic sites. There are still several groups speaking Northern Mon-Khmer languages living in northern Việt Nam, but none of them have made bark-cloth in recent times. Rather they either trade with neighboring Tai peoples for cloth or have learned to weave themselves from the Tai. There are numerous groups speaking Mon-Khmer languages living in the Central Highlands and not only do these peoples have traditions of making bark-cloth, but many continued to make bark-cloth into recent times. Those known to have made bark-cloth in modern times include both peoples that did not learn to weave such as the Chứt of Quảng Bình Province (a group that includes the Rục, May, Arem, Mã Liêng, and Sách) as well as others that did learn to weave such as the Ba Na and Bru.[11]

It is unclear when the ancestors of the groups speaking Kadai (aka Kra-Dai) languages first settled in northern Việt Nam, but they arrived earlier than the Tai (with whom they are closely related genetically).[12] Most Kadai in southeastern China and northern Việt Nam were assimilated by the Tai, but small groups of them on Hainan Island and scattered across the highlands of the Việt Nam-China border region have retained a distinct identity. In Việt Nam they include the La Ha, La Chí, Cờ Lao, and Pu Péo.[13] For the most part these small groups of Kadai adopted the weaving techniques and styles of dress of later migrants, and ceased making bark-cloth. Only the Lí of Hăinán Island have continued to make bark-cloth in modern times (Lí weaving will be discussed in the next section). Lí bark-cloth is interesting for our purposes since it is mentioned in early Chinese sources and because modern examples exist. The Sòng Dynasty author Yue Shi (l. 930–1007), reported that the Lí "make clothes with bark-cloth and blankets with silk cotton."[14] Qīng Dynasty authors such as Gu Yanwu (l. 1613–82) also mention Lí silk cotton tree (i.e., kapok) cloth as well as bark-cloth.[15]

Bark-cloth ceased to be worn in northern Việt Nam long ago (although bark-cloth blankets were still made on occasion in the highlands into the mid–20th century), but an idea of the nature of ancient bark-cloth is possible by looking at modern examples from the Lí and various peoples in the Central Highlands of Việt Nam (aka Tây Nguyên). As noted in the previous chapter, bark-cloth is made primarily from trees belonging to the Moraceae family such as *Artocarpus altilis* (breadfruit), *Antiaris toxicaria* (*sui, upas*), *Broussonetia papyrifera* (paper mulberry), and *Ficus* (fig) trees. These are sources for Lí and Central Highlands bark-cloth and probably were used in ancient times throughout the region as well. As for the style of clothing, some care must be taken since older styles of bark-cloth clothing may have ceased to be worn and clothing made of woven cloth occasionally influences bark-cloth clothing styles. Bark-cloth clothing worn by the Li and in the Central Highlands includes loincloths worn by males and wrap-around skirts worn by females. There are also sleeveless blouses or shirts that open down the front or are fashioned as pullovers or ponchos and blankets. The wrap-around skirts are often secured with a piece of rattan. The Bru made a bark-cloth tubeskirt in the past, but this probably reflects the influence of neighboring Tai people and may not be an ancient style. Tailored garments were assembled using bamboo needles and string made from rattan, vines, and various tree fibers. Unlike some other places in the Asia-Pacific region, examples of bark-cloth produced in Việt Nam are not decorated.

Ancient Bronze Age Northern Việt Nam

Most of ancient northern Việt Nam was part of what early Chinese writings referred to as the Bai Yuè or the Hundred Yuè region stretching along the coast from Fújiàn in the north to northern Việt Nam in the south. Bai Yuè was often further subdivided, including a northern region associated with the Mǐn Yuè (River Yuè) in Fújiàn and a southeastern region associated with the Nán Yuè (Southern Yuè) in the eastern parts of Guǎngxī and Guǎngdōng and northern Việt Nam. Political boundaries in this area varied over time and much of it, especially highland regions, was not under any form of direct political control. It was an area that was occupied by a variety of peoples—the so-called Bai Yuè—primarily speaking Mon-Khmer (aka Austro-Asiatic) and Austro-Tai languages (i.e., Kam-Sui, Kadai, and Tai languages).[16]

People speaking Tai languages were politically and culturally dominant in Bai Yuè for centuries prior to the Chinese conquest and exerted considerable influence on the material culture of the region, including textiles and styles of dress. The ancestry of the Tai people can be traced back to Liángzhǔ Culture (*c.* 3300–2100 BC) in the vicinity of Tài Hú Lake (aka Lake Tai) in northeast Zhèjiāng.[17] While Liángzhǔ Culture is best known for its jade artifacts and being an early site of rice domestication, it also produced some of the oldest pieces of silk known: a herringbone patterned braided silk belt, pieces of silk thread, and a small scrap of woven fabric found in bamboo utensils at Qiangshanyang in Zhèjiāng and dated about 2,750 BC.[18]

Liángzhǔ Culture comes to an abrupt end around 2200–2100 BC, possibly as a result of environmental changes, and its people seem to have migrated south to Fújiàn. Historically the Tai emerge as a distinct entity in Fújiàn around 900–800 BC when the Yuè in this region broke away from the multi-ethnic kingdom of Chŭ (f. 1030 BC). The Chinese at the time sometimes referred to the Tai and others in this area as Man Yi that has been translated as "fringe Yi peoples" or "southern barbarians," but over time the term Yuè was the most common one employed by the Chinese in reference to these people.[19] In the case of the Tai, members of the Lò (aka Luò) clan ruled over the early Tai peoples in Fújiàn and so the Chinese referred to this particular group of Tai people as Lò Yuè (aka Luò Yuè, Lạc Việt).[20]

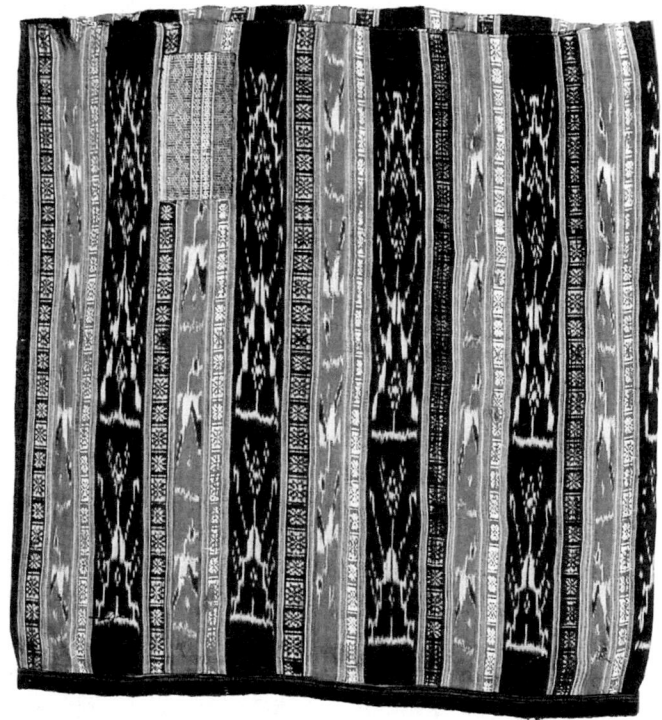

Thái (Tái Dăm sub-group) silk tubeskirt for funeral wear with grey heron and funeral hut motifs woven using weft ikat technique, Thanh Hóa Province.

The Lò Yuè gradually expanded southward into Guăngxī and northern Việt Nam, arriving in the Red River delta region by the 600s or 500s BC.[21] In Việt Nam they founded the kingdom of Văn Lang (aka Xích Quỷ) in what is now Phú Thọ Province northern Việt Nam. A date of 696 BC is usually given for the founding of this kingdom, but the actual date of the founding may be later. The Tai rulers of Văn Lang are commonly referred to as the Hùng kings. Ancient Chŭ's influence can be seen in that early Chinese writings refer to these rulers using the character designating the Mĭ clan, the founding clan of Chŭ, and Văn Lang initially at least may have been a vassal state of Chŭ.[22] Văn Lang can be translated as "country of the tattooed," a form of body decoration widely used by Bai Yuè people. Additional members of the Lò clan fled Fújiàn and settled in northern Việt Nam after the Chinese conquered northern Bai Yuè in 334 BC. The Lò Yuè (Lạc Việt) settled as far south as Nghê An Province in the lowlands and also moved up the Red River and then spread across southern Yúnnán (where they established the *mường* of Ai Lào, aka Muang Ai) and Shan State in Myanmar.[23] All of these Tai speak Southwestern Tai languages and some of the Tai living in southern Yúnnán later moved into the highlands of northwestern Việt Nam to the

1. Ancient Clothing

west of the Red River, where their descendants include Thái, Lào, and Lự. The Lò Yuè that remained in the lowlands of northern Việt Nam gradually assimilated and became part of Kinh society.

Văn Lang's first capital is sometimes referred to as Bạch Hạc, which is often translated as white crane, but is more accurately translated as referring to the grey heron.[24] The grey heron (*Ardea cinera*) was the totem of the Lò clan.[25] To members of the Lò clan and other clans sharing their culture, the grey heron was given the task of transporting male spirits to the spirit world upon death and thus its image figured prominently in objects related to funerals. In addition to Đông Sơn era bronzes, the grey heron motif was employed on tubeskirts worn by Thái noblewomen, especially those worn at funerals. Recently, of course, the grey heron motif has come to be widely used in Việt Nam and identified with that country.

While the Lò Yuè migrated southward generally sticking to the lowlands until they later migrated up the Red River, other Tai migrated into the adjacent highland valleys of western Guǎngdōng, Guǎngxī, Guìzhōu, and southeast Yúnnán provinces in China and Lạng Sơn and Cao Bằng provinces in Việt Nam. The Chinese referred to these people as the Ōu Yuè (East Valley Yuè) and they were later also known as Tây Âu (Xī'ou), Âu Việt, and Huàng. They speak Central Tai languages and today are known as Zhuàng in China and Tày and Nùng in Việt Nam. Most of the Zhuàng in China today live in Guǎngxī Province, but there are also Zhuàng in southwest Guìzhōu and southeast Yúnnán provinces. In Việt Nam they are found living mainly in the highlands east of the Red River from Lào Cai Province (where a few Zhuàng live west of the Red River) in the west to Quảng Ninh Province in the east. There are a couple of early kingdoms associated with these early Ōu Yuè. A noble from Shǔ founded a kingdom named Nam Cường in the highlands of northeastern Việt Nam around 300 BC, with its capital at Nam Bình in Cao Bằng Province. The Gouding kingdom was founded further to the west in Wénshān Zhuàng and Miao Autonomous Prefecture in southeastern Yúnnán. One of Nam Cường's rulers named Thục Phán conquered Văn Lang in 258 BC and the following year created a new kingdom called Ōu Lò (aka Âu Lạc) with its capital at Phục An (aka Cổ Loa) that ruled over both the Ōu Yuè and Lò Yuè (aka Âu Việt and Lạc Việt). Ōu Lò fell to the Qín general Zhào Tuó (aka Triệu Đà) in 207 BC and the lowlands of northern Việt Nam began a process of Sinification.

Although the Zhào Tuó referred to the people of Ōu Lò as naked—"those of the Ou Luo (Au Lac) naked kingdoms of the west also call me king"[26]—it is quite obvious that they were not. Archaeologists have found only a few pieces of cloth in Đông Sơn era burial sites and our knowledge of styles of ancient dress styles in northern Việt Nam comes mainly from human figures depicted on bronze objects.[27] There are a variety of dress styles depicted on these bronzes. Some of the dress of these figures is related to their activity or status, while it is also possible that some of the variation reflects the dress styles of different peoples. In regard to this last point, while most of the figures depicted on the bronzes appear to represent Ōu Yuè and Lò Yuè peoples there are also some figures that seem to represent other peoples.

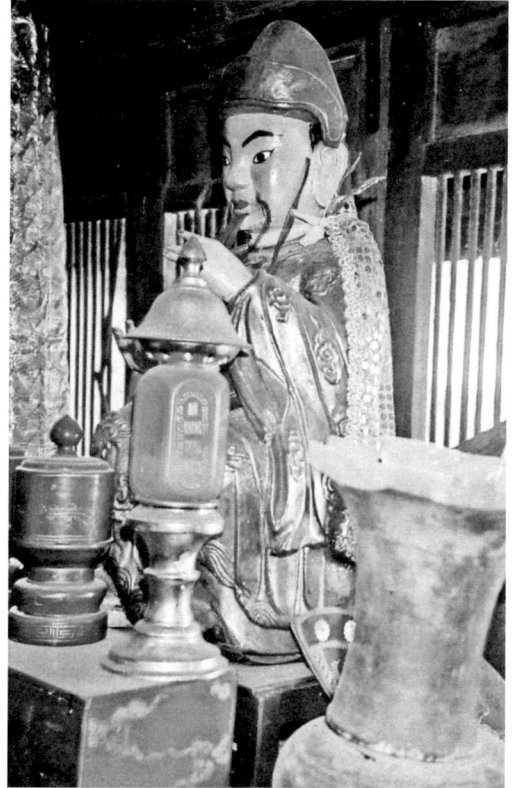 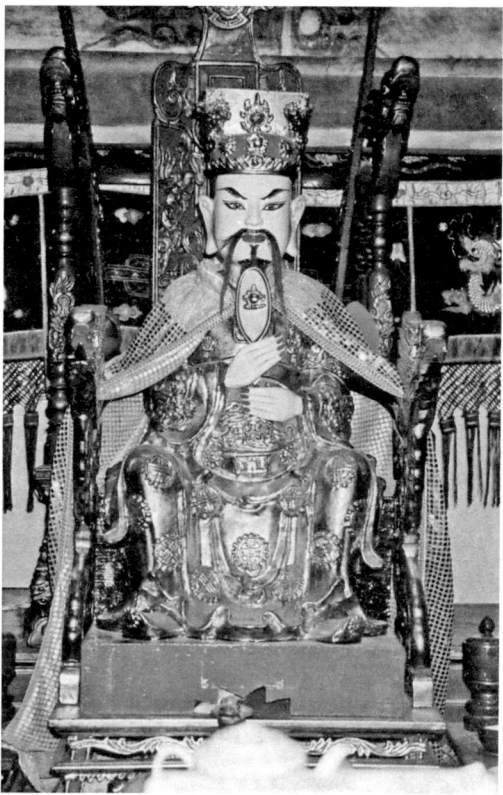

Left: **Image of Thục Phán, Cuông temple, Nghệ An Province.** *Right:* **Image of General Lò, commander of Thục Phán's army at Cuông temple, Nghệ An Province.**

Lê Ngọc Thắng compares the Ōu Lò/Âu Lạc figures depicted on ancient bronzes found in Thanh Hóa and Nghệ An provinces with modern Thái dress.[28] He points out that these noble women on Đông Sơn bronzes knotted their hair on top of their heads and covered it with a headcloth in much the same fashion as modern Thái women. Such women on the bronzes are also shown wearing blouses that open at least part of the way down the front (possibly indicating that they are pullover blouses), decorated tubeskirts, and decorated sashes surrounding the waistbands of the skirts. This style of dress is similar to the dress of modern Thái women and can be associated with the Lò Yuè. There is some variety in the blouses on the bronzes. Some blouses have long sleeves and others short sleeves. They are usually pullover blouses with a rounded or a V-shaped opening. Lí women of Hăinán Island wear pullover blouses with V-shaped openings and Thái women wear pullover long-coats with V-shaped openings. There are also bare-breasted women depicted on the bronzes and in the past this was common practice for women from throughout the region, in the case of Thái women especially those who were not of the noble class. There are also female figures on the bronzes shown at festivals wearing what appear to be full

1. Ancient Clothing

skirts rather than tubeskirts. These skirts resemble those worn by Tày and Nùng women and thus probably can be associated with the Ōu Yuè.

Male figures on Đông Sơn bronzes are depicted wearing loincloths. Some of these are narrow and others fairly wide with decorated ends hanging down the front and in some instances down the back as well. Among the best-known examples of such figures are those found on bronze daggers from the Làng Vạc archaeological site near the Cả River in Nghê An Province that depict bare-chested men wearing loincloths with patterns, long plaited hair, and headbands.[29] Among Tai-Kadai peoples, only Lí men on Hǎinán Island continued to wear loincloths into modern times. Other Tai-Kadai males adopted Chinese influenced styles of dress long ago and ceased to wear older styles of clothing. Male figures on the bronzes are usually bare-chested, but sometimes they are shown wearing a pullover shirt or a blanket wrapped over their shoulders. They are also often depicted with tattoos, another tradition that disappeared long ago among Tai-Kadai peoples with the exception of the Lí who continued to have tattoos in modern times.

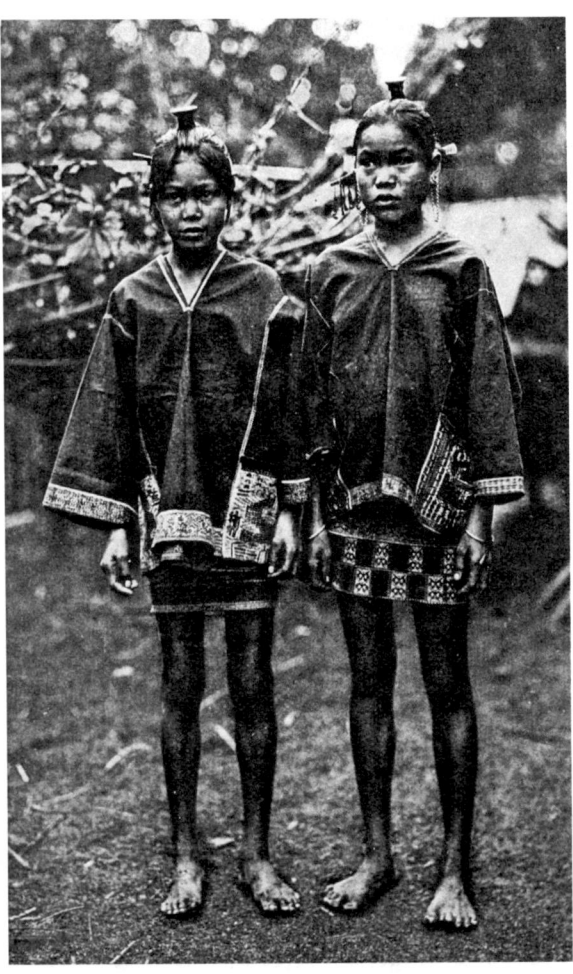

Lí women wearing pullover blouses and tubeskirts, Hǎinán Island (from Stübel, *Die Li-Stämme der Insel Hainan*, fig. 25).

Decorative patterns that are depicted on clothing on Đông Sơn bronzes include dots, round shapes, and parallel lines. The techniques used to produce these patterns likely include the warp ikat, supplementary warp, and supplementary weft techniques. These are techniques employed by modern Thái weavers and by the Lí. Chinese written sources use the term "spotted cloth" for patterning on clothing from the Nán Yuè region that may have been produced by the ikat technique, but may also refer to tritik dyeing.[30] While Thái weavers commonly used both warp and weft ikat techniques, tritik is rarely employed by Tai-Kadai peoples in modern times, being used in Việt Nam only by the Thù Lao sub-group of Tày in Lào

Cai Province on headcloths.[31] The Thù Lao people are the northernmost sub-group of Tày and live in the frontier region between Nán Yuè and Yèláng. Historical and contemporary evidence from existing Tai groups in Việt Nam and China indicates that only groups that trace their past to the coastal region of Nán Yuè such as the Lí, Thái, and others speaking Southwestern Tai languages have traditions of weaving ikat-patterned textiles. Modern Tày and Nùng, descendants of the Ōu Yuè, do not seem to have such a tradition of weaving ikat-patterned cloth. Tày and Nùng clothing tends to be fairly plain with supplementary weft patterning found on some special purpose textiles and the Thù Lao use the tritik technique only to decorate their headcloths. As will be discussed in the next section, the tritik technique seems to be more closely associated with the decorative traditions of the highland Yèláng region than with coastal Nán Yuè.

The patterns found on the clothing depicted on Đông Sơn bronzes are relatively simple and likely do not represent the full repertoire of patterns found on actual clothing. Some indication of other patterns that may have been woven is provided by a look at other images found on the bronzes, but not on the images of clothing on the bronzes, and that also appear on modern Thái textiles.[32] We discussed the gray heron above, which is undoubtedly the most famous motif associated with Đông Sơn bronzes. Other common motifs include a variety of geometric patterns (such as the hook and rhomb) and depictions of animals such as the spotted deer. The spotted deer appears on artifacts associated with Liángzhǔ Culture and dated about 3,000 BC from the Guangfulin site in Shanghai.[33] It is a popular figure in Tai legends and was associated with the Tai fire god.

Images on bronze cannot tell us what material the clothing is made from, nor the colors used. Chinese written sources and ethnographic research indicates that the materials employed are likely to have included silk cotton tree fiber/kapok and silk, and perhaps other fibers such as banana. In the case of silk, as was discussed above, it is primarily associated with the Lò Yuè and this is reflected in its widespread use among peoples speaking Southwestern Tai languages in modern times. Other Tai groups also have traditions of making silk, although they do not seem to have used it for cloth to the extent of the Southwestern Tai groups. Dark blue is the most common color employed on modern Tai-Kadai textiles and clothing, but the Thái in particular have a wide repertoire of natural dyes and produce an array of other colors as well and it is likely that many of these colors were found on Đông Sơn era clothing. Among the dyes that appear to have an ancient history of use in the Nán Yuè region are blues from *Persicaria tinctoria* and *Wrightia laevis* dyes, brown from the dye yam (*Dioscorea cirrhosa* Lour.), red from lac insect colonies (*Kerria chinensis*), and black from *Diospyros mollis* fruit.

Some Kadai groups also produce textiles and have dress styles that appear to reflect Tai influence. The Lí (aka Hlai) of Hǎinán Island are especially useful for shedding light on the early Tai textile and clothing traditions because of their relative isolation.[34] Isolated from other Tai-Kadai peoples on Hǎinán Island, they alone among

1. Ancient Clothing

Tai-Kadai peoples were still weaving cloth on a foot-braced back-strap loom in the 20th century and still wore styles of clothing reminiscent of those depicted on ancient bronzes from the region. At the time of Stübel's research in the 1930s, some Lí men still wore loincloths.[35] Men often went bare-chested, but sometimes they would wear shirts or vests, but these usually were clearly of Chinese-style.[36] Lí women in the 1930s wore tubeskirts that reached to the knees, went bare-chested or wore either pullover or Chinese style blouses, and sometimes wore headcloths.[37] Lí textiles at the time were often made of kapok and only sometimes of cotton. In terms of decorative techniques, the Lí weave warp ikat patterns in a series of simple narrow dashes and in wider bands of geometric and figurative patterning and produce a variety of supplementary warp and supplementary weft decorative patterns.

Ancient Bronze Age Yúnnán

Our next clothing tradition comes from a region that the Chinese called Nán Zong and its people as Nán Man or Southwestern Barbarians.[38] This was a region that included parts of the modern Chinese provinces of Yúnnán, Guìzhōu, Guǎngxī, and Sìchuān. We will focus on ancient Yúnnán in this section and ancient Guìzhōu in the next. Ancient Yúnnán included the kingdom of Diān, the Tai *mường* of Ai Lào in the south, and the kingdom of Gouding in the southeast, while Guìzhōu included a tribal confederacy known as Yèláng, which will be discussed in the next section. These were Bronze Age polities that had cultural and commercial links with the Đông Sơn cultural area as well as with Shǔ in Sìchuān.[39] Following the Hàn conquest of the region in 109 BC much of the area was divided into commanderies. In Yúnnán these included Yizhōu and Yongchang, which was located between the Mekong (aka Láncāng) and Salween (aka Nù) rivers in the south. The commandery of Zongke was located in Guìzhōu. Ai Lào remained independent until AD 69, when it became part of Yongchang. The kingdom of Gouding also remained independent for a time.[40] The people of this region today include a variety of Mon-Khmer, Tibeto-Burman, Hmong-Mien, and Tai-Kadai speaking minority groups. It should be noted that only a few of the peoples associated with these areas and polities lived in ancient northern Việt Nam, although some of them moved there in later times.

The ancient kingdom of Diān (aka Tien), the Heavenly kingdom, was located in the vicinity of Lake Diān (aka Diānchí) and modern Kūnmíng in Yúnnán. When the kingdom of Shǔ invaded Yúnnán in the 300s BC the region was inhabited primarily by a variety of peoples speaking Mon-Khmer and Tibeto-Burman languages. After Shǔ was conquered by Qín in 316 BC Shǔ's political control in Yúnnán ended and the independent kingdom of Diān was established in 310 BC. Ancestors of peoples speaking Southwestern Tai discussed in the previous section appear to have arrived in southern Yúnnán during this period. Early Chinese sources refer to the people of the kingdom of Diān in general as Diǎn Yuè ("Heavenly Yuè") and more specifically to

Ancient Bronze Age Yúnnán

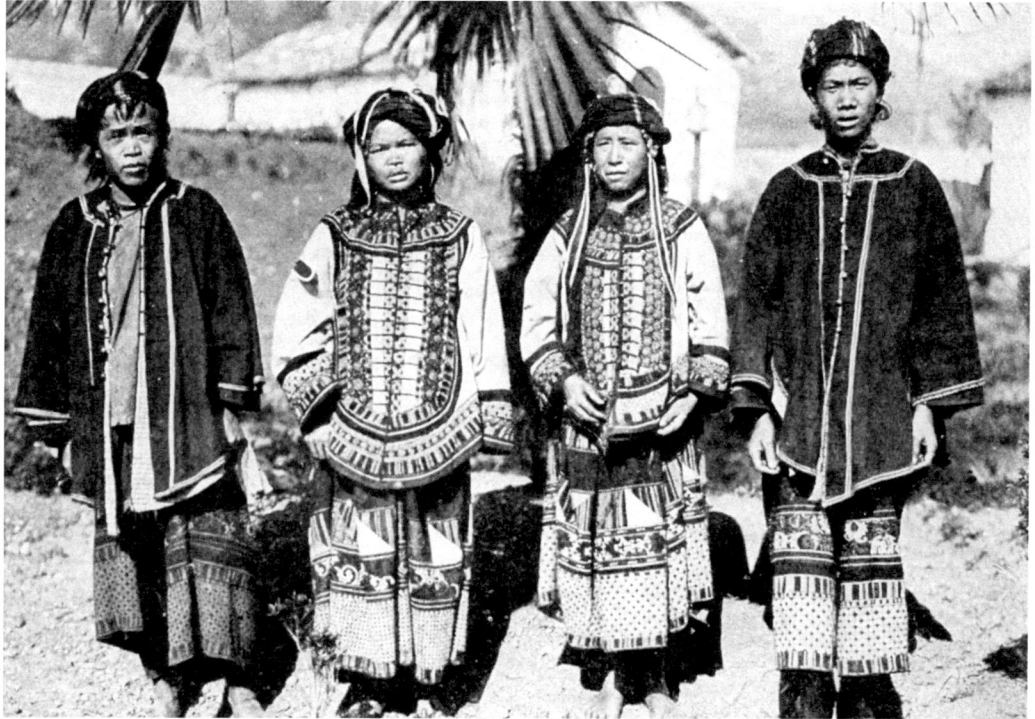

Lô Lô men and women (from Bonifacy, *Les Groupes Ethniques du Bassin de la Rivière Claire*, plate 21, fig. 1).

the Tai in Yúnnán as Pai Man (White Barbarians) or sometimes Pai I and the Mon-Khmer and Tibeto-Burman peoples as Wu Man (Black Barbarians).[41] The Hàn conquest initiated a process of cultural change in Yúnnán, but Chinese control over the area varied over the centuries. The independent kingdom of Nán Chào (aka Nán Zhào) was established in Yúnnán in AD 649, after a period of political fragmentation, and it remained an important regional power until the early AD 900s. Nán Chào exerted control over much of eastern Yúnnán and for a brief period also controlled parts of northern Việt Nam.

The kingdom of Diăn produced an amazing array of bronze objects, including many images of people. As with the human figures on Đông Sơn bronzes, those on Diăn bronzes represent people of different statuses, people engaged in different activities, and people from different ethnic or tribal groups. However, there are many more types of distinctive people engaged in a greater range of activities on the Diăn bronzes than on the Đông Sơn ones, giving us a better picture of life in ancient Yúnnán. While there are some similarities between the clothing styles of people on Diăn and Đông Sơn bronzes there are also significant differences. Rather than the bare-chested, tattooed, loincloth wearing men of the Đông Sơn bronzes, the men on Diăn bronzes are shown wearing such clothing as trousers and a variety of shirts, tunics,

1. Ancient Clothing

capes, and gowns. Many of the women on Diăn bronzes wear tunics or gowns and long full-skirts rather than tubeskirts.

Wang Ningsheng has surveyed some 300 human figures found on Diăn bronzes and divided them into four basic styles that he argues represent distinct ethnic groups.[42] Wang undertakes to link these ancient distinct styles with contemporary ethnic groups. Wang's Group I is described as the majority population, including the ruler. People of this group are characterized as wearing "a bun bound with a band, and a coat without buttons." Men's tunics or gowns often have "a tail-shaped cloth" and men also sometimes wear a "felt cloak and belt or girdle decorated with jade."[43] Wang says that these are probably the Me-Mo (aka Mi-Mo) people described in the *Shiji* ("Records of the Grand Historian") as living around Lake Diăn and, while noting that the hair style of these figures is not found among any contemporary peoples in Yúnnán, identifies these people possibly as being ancestors of the Wă.[44] Wang's Group II wears its "hair in plaits" and its style of dress bears similarities with the modern Yí (aka Lô Lô).[45] Group III wears its "hair in a knot-bun on the top of the head" and women are often depicted wearing a long and tight skirt. This group appears to represent ancestors of the modern Dăi.[46] Group IV wears "their hair in a snail-shaped bun" and Wang speculates that this group may be ancestors of the Hmông.[47]

Linking these human figures with contemporary ethnic groups is a difficult task. In the case of Wang's Group I, for example, that such figures represent the dominant, ruling peoples of ancient Diăn is undoubtedly true, but rather than being ancestors of the modern Wă, a Northern Mon-Khmer speaking group that lives in southwestern Yúnnán and adjacent areas of northern Myanmar and Thailand and that does not appear to be descended from the rulers of ancient Diăn, it is likely that these figures represent an ethnically mixed elite comprised of people speaking Tibeto-Burman languages as well

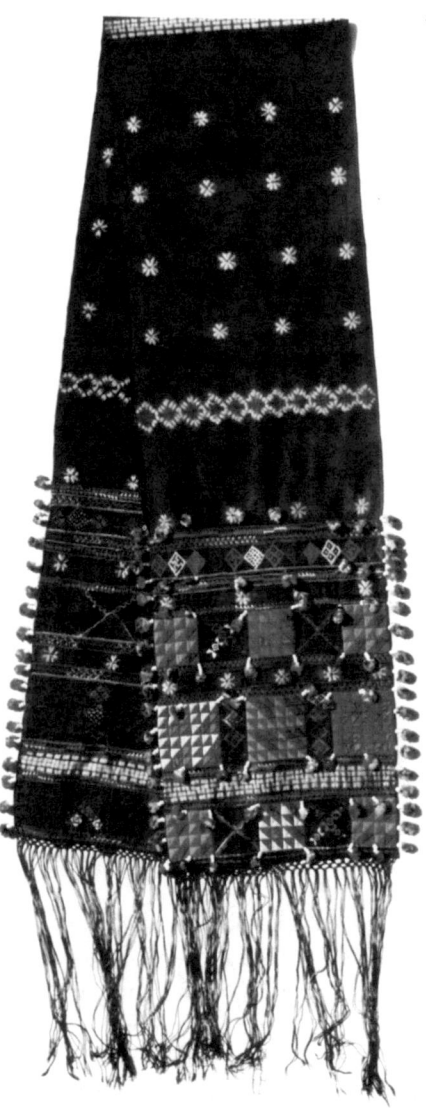

Flowery Lô Lô woman's headcloth decorated with appliqué and tritik, Mèo Vạc District, Hà Giang Province.

as perhaps Tai and Hmông. Thus, we are probably dealing with the dress fashion of a ruling class rather than a style of dress linked to a particular ethnic group. Wang is on firmer ground in the case of Groups II and III, while the identity of Group IV is fairly speculative. It is also likely that some of the bronze figures might be linked to other ethnic groups. Thus, the tunics and short trousers worn by some figures are reminiscent of the dress of Karen groups in Myanmar, whose ancestors originally lived in Yúnnán.[48] For our purposes, there are two particularly relevant styles. One feature is the full-skirts worn by some of the female figures that constitute an important characteristic of a style of dress found widely among peoples in Yúnnán and Guìzhōu and the border region of northern Việt Nam, including speakers of Central and Northern Tai languages. The second is the tubeskirt style associated with peoples speaking Southwestern Tai languages in Yúnnán that is clearly linked to the ancient dress style of the ancestors of the Southwestern Tai peoples in Việt Nam.

Yúnnán today is a region inhabited by quite a number of different peoples with many different styles of dress. There are several Mon-Khmer peoples in western Yúnnán, but none of these are found in Việt Nam. Large numbers of Tibeto-Burman peoples are scattered throughout the province, though in lesser numbers in the eastern part. The majority of people speaking Tibeto-Burman languages in Yúnnán speak languages belonging to the Lolo group. These include the Yí, Bái, Hāní, and Lāhù. Related Lolo speaking groups in northern Việt Nam include Lô Lô (called Yí in China), Hà Nhì, and La Hủ. The Hāní and Lāhù appear to have lived in southern Yúnnán in ancient times, with the Hà Nhì living to the east of the La Hủ not too far from the border with Việt Nam. The Yí lived mainly further west in central and northern Yúnnán. Some Hāní and Yí moved into northwestern Việt Nam during the Nán Chào period, the Hāní settling in northern Lào Cai Province in the 700s and the Yí coming to northern Việt Nam in 862 when Nán Chào invaded the area. However, the invaders were driven out in 866 and all Tibeto-Burman speaking peoples appear to have left Vietnamese territory at that time.[49] The ancestors of Lô Lô living in Việt Nam today arrived in the 1400s and 1700s, those of the Hà Nhì now living in Việt Nam arrived around 1700, and those of the La Hủ began arriving in northern Việt Nam in the mid–1800s and especially after a bout of Chinese repression in 1887.[50]

Not only is the dress of each of these groups distinctive, but there is also a great deal of variation within each group. Also, the Chinese have influenced the dress of many of these groups over the centuries. Nevertheless, there are many dress elements that appear to hark back to ancient times, such as the long pleated skirts commonly worn by Yi women and the short skirts worn by many Hāní women in China. Lô Lô women in Việt Nam wore long pleated skirts in the past, but most now wear baggy trousers and a rectangular piece of cloth as a back-panel or apron.[51] The Xá Phó (aka Phù Lá Lão, their language is Laghuu) are a small group living in northwestern Việt Nam that is related to the Muji in Yúnnán (a group that is categorized as Yí by the Chinese) with a distinctive style of female dress that includes a pullover blouse and a skirt that is stitched together but tailored in the fashion of a full skirt rather than

1. Ancient Clothing

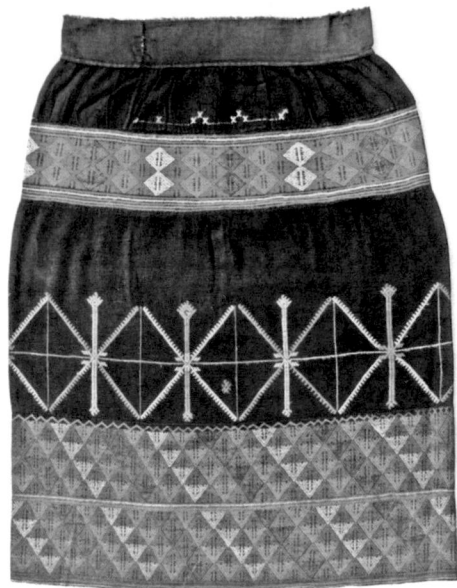

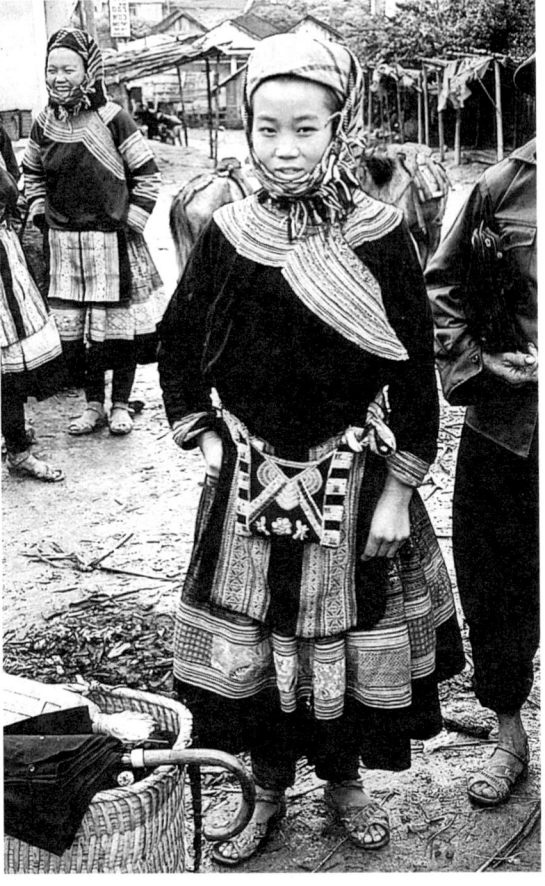

Above: Phù Lá (Xá Phó sub-group) skirt, Sa Pa District, Lào Cai Province. *Right:* Flowery Hmông woman wearing pleated skirt at Bắc Hà market, Lào Cai Province.

a straight tube.[52] In historical times all of these groups have made their clothing from cotton, and in fact many of these people were well known for growing cotton in the past. However, it is likely that they used kapok in ancient times. As for decorative techniques, none of these groups generally employs any sophisticated weaving techniques. Although their clothing is sometimes quite colorful, decoration is done by embroidery and appliqué. Also, while dark blue or black are the dominant colors, some of them (e.g., Xá Phó) have rich traditions of using a variety of natural dyes to produce a wide range of colors.

Yúnnán is also home to a large number of Hmông. There were Hmông among the Nán Chào troops that invaded Việt Nam in 862, but they too left in 866. The modern arrival of the Hmong in Việt Nam began in the late 1700s in response to increased Chinese control over the southern regions, which will be discussed below in relation to Guìzhōu, from where many of the Hmông in Việt Nam migrated.

There are two distinct groups of Tai in Yúnnán. One is comprised of people that today speak Southwestern Tai languages and the Chinese categorize them as Dǎi. The other is comprised of people that today speak Central Tai languages and the Chinese categorize them as Zhuàng. As was discussed above, these two groups have different migratory histories and different traditions of dress. The Dăi live in highland valleys across southern Yúnnán from the Jīnpíng Miáo, Yáo, and Dăi Autonomous County that is part of the Hónghé Hāní and Yí Autonomous Prefecture in the east, through Sipsong Panna (called Xīshuāngbănnà by the Chinese), and west as far as the Déhóng Dăi and Jĭngpō Autonomous Prefecture. In ancient times the area included Ai Lào and Yongchang. The Tai groups living here today includes various sub-groups of Thái (as they are called in Việt Nam) live in the eastern part of this area from Jīnpíng Miáo, Yáo, and Dăi Autonomous County in Hónghé Hāní and Yí Autonomous Prefecture near the Red River west to Jiāngchéng Hāní and Yí Autonomous County in Pu-er Prefectural Level City. These Thái include both Black Tái and White Tái, both of which are related to the Thái in northwestern Việt Nam. The Tai group known as Lự (aka Lü) live in Sipsong Panna (Xīshuāngbănnà) and, as mentioned previously there are also Lự living in northwestern Việt Nam. A group of Lự settled in the vicinity of Mường Thanh (near Điện Biên Phủ) in the early AD 600s and their descendants still live in northwestern Việt Nam.[53]

The textiles and dress of the Thái and Lự in Việt Nam will be discussed at greater length in a later chapter. Essentially Thái and Lự males have adapted Chinese style clothing, while females have retained a distinctive style of dress with links to the ancient Lò Yuè and to their ancestors in southern Yúnnán. It is interesting to note, however, that while women from both groups wear tubeskirts there is one basic difference between those of the Thái and Lự. The Thái make the bodies of their skirts from a single piece of cloth with a single vertical seam. Thus, the warp threads run horizontally on the skirt when it is worn.

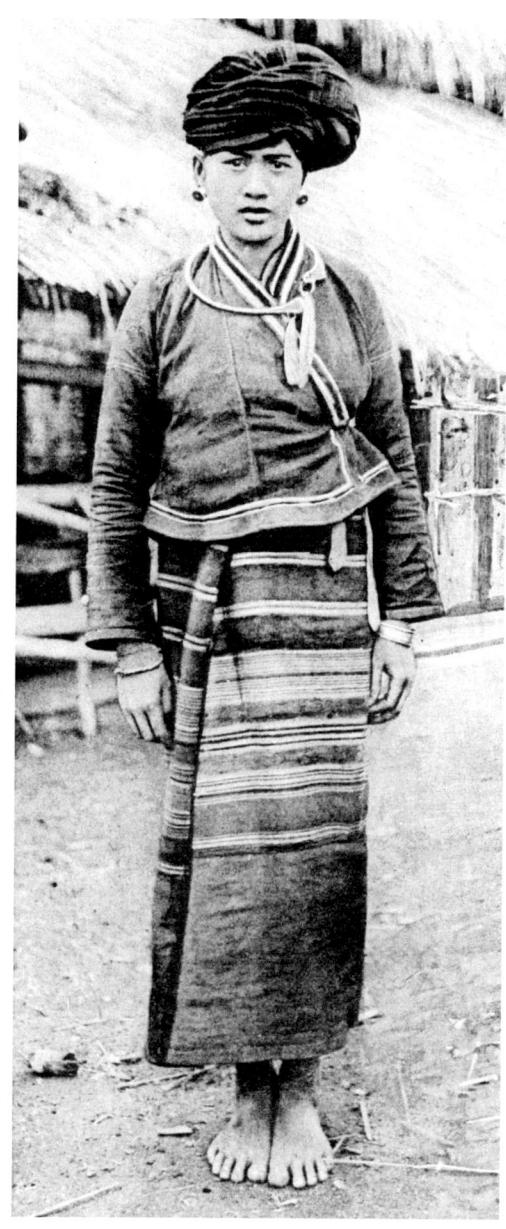

Lự woman, Lai Châu Province (from Abadie, *Les Races du Haut-Tonkin*, pl. 28, fig. 26).

1. Ancient Clothing

In contrast, the Lự make the bodies of their tubeskirts from two separate pieces of matching cloth that are joined with two vertical seams. In this case, the warp threads run vertically when the skirt is worn.

The Tai of Ai Lào were famous for their weaving in ancient times and their textiles received far more attention than is usual in early Chinese sources discussing barbarians.[54] Their textiles were exported over an extensive area. The Hàn Imperial envoy Zhāng Qiān encountered textiles from Ai Lào in Daxia (Bactria) in 122 BC that he was told had been brought overland from Shendu (India).[55] Traders from Shǔ, who were also active throughout southern China and northern Việt Nam, brought these textiles to India. There has been some debate about what these Ai Lào textiles were made of—silk or kapok—and this relates to an understanding of the type of fabrics woven in ancient Yúnnán and the cultural association of the Ai Lào with the other Tai in northern Việt Nam. In support of the notion that the cloth in question was made from kapok fiber, Laufer cites a Chinese passage from the AD 400s, "None of the Man tribes in the kingdom of Nan-cao [Nán Chào] rear silkworms, but they merely obtain seeds of the *so-lo* (*sa-la) tree, the interior of which is white and contains a floss that can be wrought like silk and spun into cloth; it bears the name *so-lo lun twan*," and identifies *so-lo* as the *Bombax malabaricum*, from which tree cotton/kapok is produced.[56] He adds that the *Bombax malabaricum* tree is widely grown in Guìzhōu, where it is used to make thread for cloth and that the Lô Lô use a similar word, "sa-la," for cotton. These passages certainly highlight the widespread use of silk cotton/kapok to make cloth in ancient Nán Zong, but I believe that it would be a mistake to rule out the cloth being made of silk. It is true that the various Mon-Khmer, Tibeto-Burman, and Hmong-Mien peoples in the region that comprise the vast majority of non-Hàn peoples living there, have no tradition of making silk cloth. However, reflecting their origins in Nán Yuè, the ancestors of all of the peoples speaking Southwestern Tai languages did weave silk and this includes the Tai of southern Yúnnán.

The Zhuàng (who speak Central Tai languages) in Yúnnán live mainly in Wénshān Zhuàng and Miáo Autonomous Prefecture in the southeastern corner of Yúnnán and immediately to the north of Hà Giang Province in Việt Nam. These Zhuàng are related to the Tày and Nùng in Việt Nam. Wénshān Prefecture is home to about 85 percent of Yunnan's Zhuàng and was the locale of the ancient Kingdom of Gouding and effectively the northwest frontier of the Ōu Yuè.[57] The Wénshān region has a long history of cultural, commercial, and political connections with most neighboring areas. In the AD 600s it came under the domination of Nán Chào and later was controlled by Yǒngzhōu in Húnán. The ten sub-groups of Zhuàng in Wénshān Prefecture can be divided into three main groups: the Nòng (Nùng in Việt Nam), Sha (aka Yei Zhuàng, Qiūběi Sha), and Tù (aka Tù Zhuàng, Tuliao, Pu-lao, and called Thù Lao in Việt Nam). We discussed the Tù/Thù Lao previously in relation to their tritik-patterned headcloths. There are four Tù sub-groups in Wénshān Prefecture and they can be distinguished by the style of the women's headdresses: piled, flat, pointed, and slanted.[58] Women belonging to all of these sub-groups wear long full-skirts (and now sometimes trousers instead of skirts in Chinese style). Most Tày in Việt Nam live in Cao Bằng and Lạng Sơn provinces, where there have been Tày living since ancient times. However, there are also Tày of the Thù Lao sub-group in Lào Cài Province that came from Wénshān Prefecture. Zhuàng women in Wénshān Prefecture sometimes wear their skirts bunched in the back that Wang and Johnson say, "reflects traditional bird worship."[59]

Mention should also be made of bast fiber weaving by the Zhuàng in Wénshān Prefecture. For the most part Southwestern and Central Tai peoples weave only cotton and silk cloth (and formerly kapok). However, Wang and Johnson mention the Zhuàng in Wénshān Prefecture weaving *"paeng'vae,"* which they describe as a thick type of cloth woven using "grass leaves" for the weft and hemp fibers for the warp.[60] The Gēlǎo weave a similar type of cloth using cogon grass (*Imperata cylindrica*) for the weft and hemp for the warp and this may be the same type of cloth as the Wénshān Zhuàng *paeng'vae*.

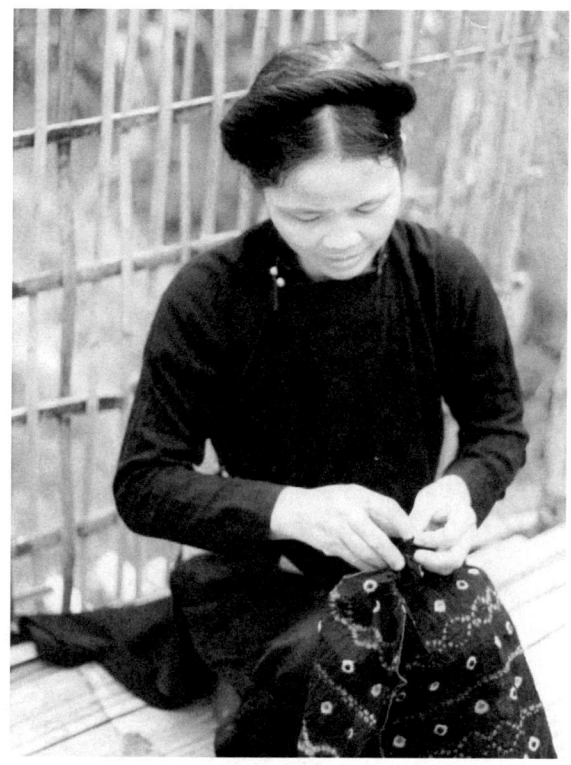

Tày (Thù Lao sub-group) woman holding a tritik patterned man's headcloth (*khăn lai*), Sa Pa District, Lào Cai Province.

An assortment of peoples speaking Kadai languages lives in southeast Yúnnán. These include Bùlǎng (aka Buyang), Laji (La Chí in Việt Nam), Gēlǎo (Cờ Lao in Việt Nam), and Qabiao (aka Pubiao, Pu Péo in Việt Nam). These are small groups that are generally classified as Zhuàng by the Chinese and people belonging to the last three of these groups are found both in China and in Việt Nam's Hà Giang Province. The dress styles of each of these groups are quite distinct. We will discuss the Gēlǎo/Cờ Lao in the next section since they are found mainly in Guìzhōu. In Việt Nam the Qabiao are called Pu Péo and are also sometimes referred to as La Qua (aka Laqua) or Pen ti/Ben ti Lô Lô, meaning aboriginal Lô Lô. The latter term refers to the fact that they are commonly viewed as being the aboriginal inhabitants of the Wénshān/Hà Giang region.[61] While Pu Péo males wear Chinese inspired trousers and shirts, females wear distinctive dress. This includes a long pleated skirt with front and rear aprons, and inner blouse, an outer blouse, and a headcloth. Their clothing is made of dark blue or black cotton cloth that is decorated with colorful appliqué and embroidered

1. Ancient Clothing

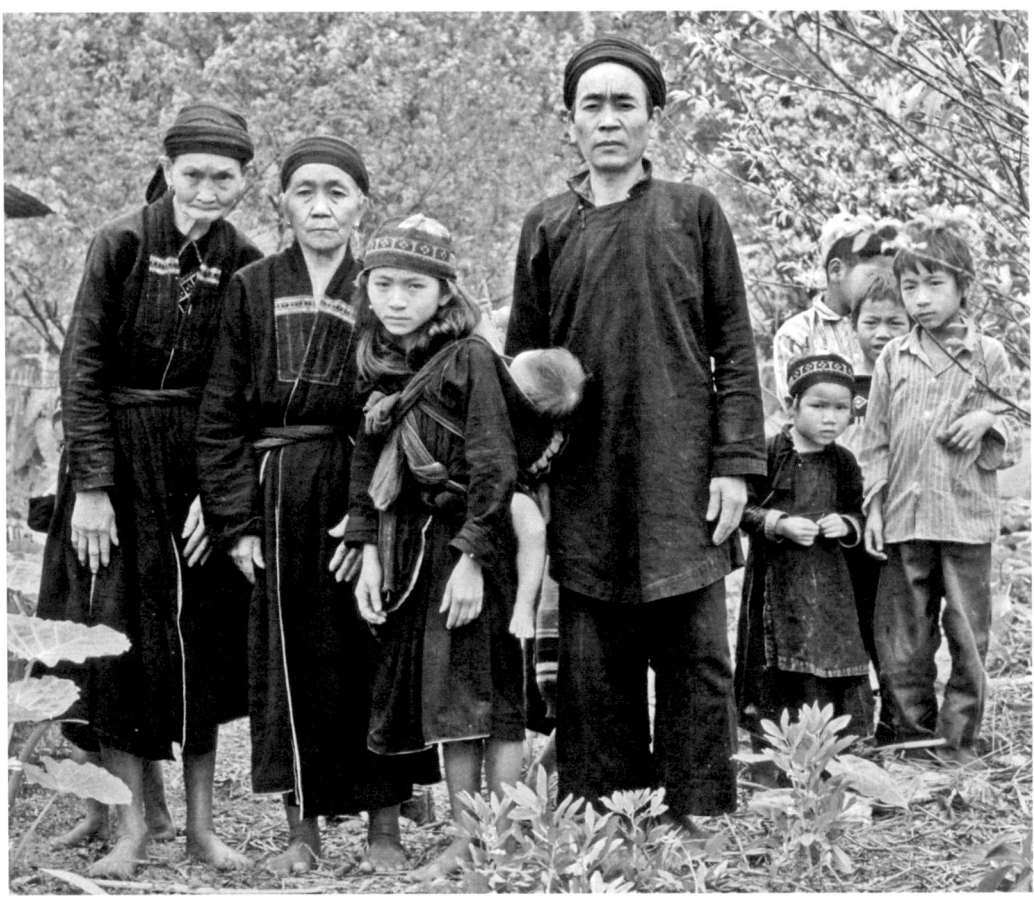

La Chí family, Bắc Quang District, Hà Giang Province.

patterning. The La Chí wear dark blue or black cotton clothing with little by way of decoration. Men wear trousers, a Chinese-style five-panel tunic that fastens on the left, and a headcloth. Women wear a skirt that is similar to that worn by the Tày (or these days often trousers instead), a bodice, and a long-coat that opens down the front and has a small amount of embroidery as decoration.[62]

Ancient Bronze Age Guìzhōu

Yèláng was a tribal alliance located between the kingdoms of Diǎn to the west and Nán Yuè to the east between at least 600 BC and 100 BC with its center on the Yúnguì Plateau in western Guìzhōu Province and extending into parts of neighboring eastern Yúnnán (an area that included the kingdom of Gouding).[63] The region had political and commercial links with Shǔ prior to the 300s BC and after, when it also developed ties to Nam Cường, Ōu Lò, and Diǎn. The Chinese sometimes treated the region as part of Bai Yuè and at other times emphasized its links to Shǔ and Yúnnán. After the fall of the Hàn Dynasty various Chinese states, beginning with Shǔ Hàn in Sìchuān, exerted nominal control over the region. Even more than northern Việt Nam, although the Chinese certainly influenced local cultures, the actual Chinese presence in Guìzhōu was very limited until the time of the Táng Dynasty.

Modern Guìzhōu is ethnically diverse with a population, including large numbers of Hmông, Northern Tai-speaking Bùyī (aka Bouyei and Bố Y in Việt Nam), Kam-Sui speaking Dòng and Shuǐ (aka Sui), Kadai speaking Gēlǎo (Cờ Lao in Việt Nam), and Tibeto-Burman speaking Tǔjiā (descendants of the ancient Bā) and Yí. Other groups present in the province include Central Tai-speaking Zhuàng; Kam-Sui speaking Máonán, Mùlǎo, and Mak; Yáo; and Tibeto-Burman speaking Bái. The presence of most of these peoples in Guìzhōu dates back to ancient times, but as with the peoples from Yúnnán they arrived in northern Việt Nam more recently, largely in response to increased Chinese control over the region during the Qīng Dynasty period.

The Míng had incorporated Guìzhōu into China in 1413, but control had remained nominal. In 1725, however, the Qīng replaced local chiefs with imperial appointees and in general the Chinese presence in the area grew appreciably. Problems created by the increased Chinese presence and political control resulted in the outbreak of several rebellions by local peoples. The Hmông were at the forefront of several of these, including the Miáo Rebellions of 1735–36, 1795–1806, and 1854–73 that resulted in considerable loss of life.[64] The Nanlong Rebellion in 1797 was of a more multi-ethnic character, with the Bùyī playing a major role, but also involving Hmông and Yáo.[65] The suppression of these revolts and generally adverse conditions faced by many people in Guìzhōu led some to leave and move to northern Việt Nam.

The archaeological record of Bronze Age Guìzhōu provides less information on ancient textiles and dress styles than do bronze artifacts from Yúnnán.[66] The Bronze Age artifacts from sites such as Jīgōngshān and Kele (4th to 1st Centuries BC) in northwestern Guìzhōu and Tonggushān (5th to 1st Centuries BC) in southwestern Guìzhōu indicate cultural connections to neighboring areas in Sìchuān, Yúnnán, and Việt Nam.[67] There are relatively few human figures depicted on the bronze objects from such sites and it is difficult to get much of a picture of the local textile and dress traditions from the material available. Written sources are not much better. The brief account of Yèláng in the *Sima Qian* notes only "chiefs wear their hair in mallet-shaped fashion."[68] However, by knowing who lived there and comparing textiles and dress styles from related peoples from neighboring areas and of their descendants, augmented by what we know about the region later, it is possible to gain an idea of the ancient textiles and dress in Guìzhōu.

The batik decorative technique is perhaps the most noteworthy characteristic of Guìzhōu textiles. It is found, for example, on the skirts of Hmông, Bùyī, and Gēlǎo women. The history of batik is controversial, but it was widely used in Southeast Asia and East Asia by the AD 600s to 900s. In China, paintings by famed Táng Dynasty

1. Ancient Clothing

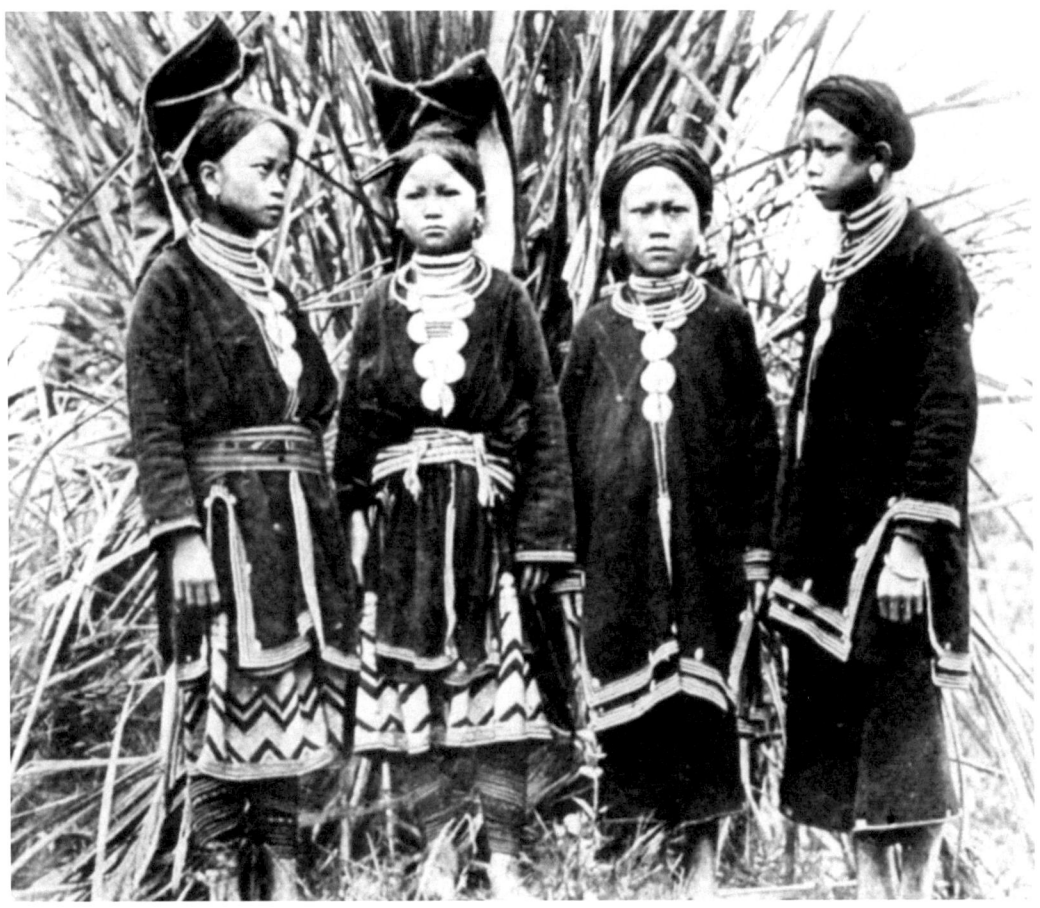

Dao Tiền women wearing batik patterned wrap-around skirts (from Bonifacy, *Les Groupes Ethniques du Bassin de la Rivière Claire*, pl. 19 fig. 2).

painter Zhāng Xuān (l. 713–755) at Dūnhuáng's Mògāo caves in Gānsù Province depict figures wearing clothing that appears to feature batik patterns. Huang Shoubao comments in relation to such images, "Historical data indicate that the wax dyeing art in the central part of China has come from the mountainous regions of Southwest China."[69] Citing a passage in the *Annals of Chi (Guizhou)* that mentions, "Cloth is painted with wax and dyed," he argues that its origins can be traced back to well before the time of the Táng Dynasty to the ethnic groups in Guìzhōu such as the Hmông, Bùyī, and Gēlǎo.[70] Batik from Guìzhōu is made using wax and blue dye with no other colors being employed.

Hmông comprise the largest ethnic group in Guìzhōu Province at present. Recent genetic research has linked the ancestors of the Hmông to Dàxī Culture (4500–3000 BC) that was located in the middle Yangtze River region stretching from western Húběi Province to eastern Sìchuān Province and the Hmông presence in Guìzhōu

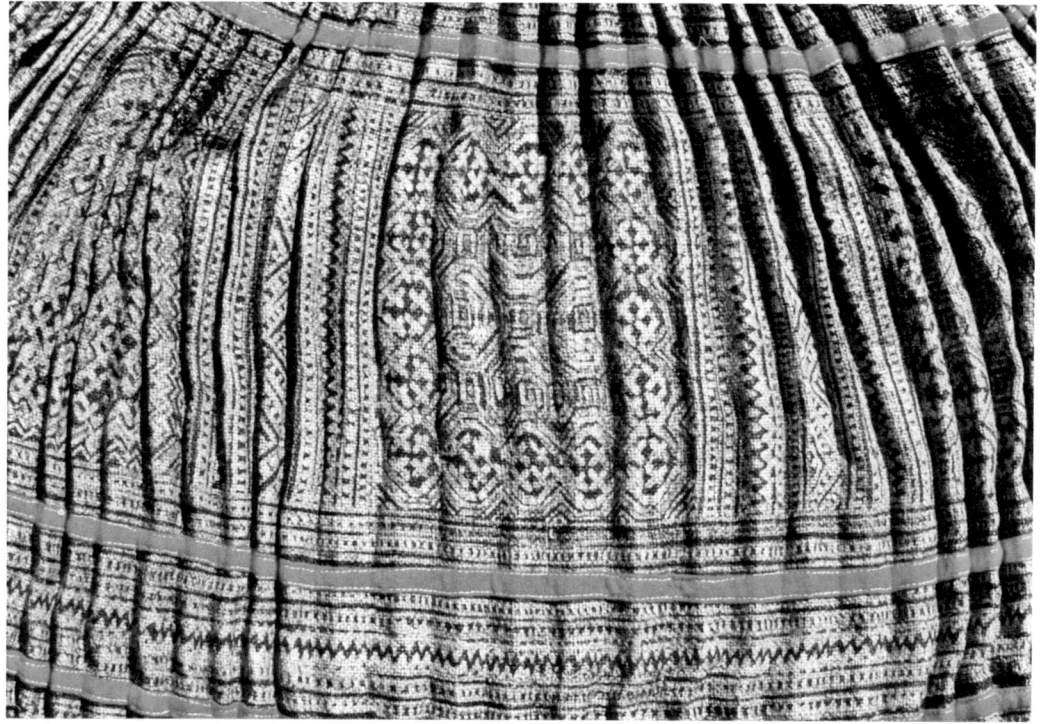

Detail of batik patterning on hemp cloth portion of a Flowery Hmông pleated skirt, Lào Cai Province.

appears to be quite ancient.[71] As for Việt Nam, Hmông (primarily White Hmông) began arriving in northern Hà Giang Province in the late 18th century and their number increased dramatically in the 1860s when they invaded the lowlands of northern Việt Nam. The invasion was stopped, but Hmông remained in the highlands of Hà Giang and Lào Cai provinces. Other groups of Hmông continued to move across the border and gradually to scatter across the highlands of northern Việt Nam.[72]

While Hmông men commonly wear Chinese-inspired clothing or generic modern clothing, women usually dress in a style of dress that retains elements with considerable antiquity. This is especially the case with the short pleated wrap-around skirts that they wear, as well as the front-opening blouses, aprons, and decorative sashes. Trần Thị Thu Thủy records a Flowery Hmông folktale that relates the skirts' pleats to the sky god and the earth's uneven terrain.[73] Although some Hmông in Việt Nam grow cotton (especially those living near Tày and Nùng) and some of their clothing is made of cotton cloth, hemp is the principal plant that Hmông cultivate for making cloth and it is likely that most of their clothing was made from in the past. Of all the highland peoples in southern China and northern Việt Nam, in fact, the Hmông are perhaps those most closely identified with the production of hemp cloth. Hmông clothing is often decorated, with embroidery, batik, and appliqué being the principal techniques employed. Not all Hmông skirts have batik (White Hmông often wear a plain white pleated skirt), but many do. In Việt Nam, the central portion of most pleated skirts worn by the Flowery Hmông, Black Hmông, and Red Hmông in the past was commonly made from a strip of hemp cloth decorated with batik patterns. Hmông batik features a wide variety of geometric and abstract figures and many of these resemble patterns seen on ancient bronzes.

As for the peoples that speak Mienic languages and are collectively called Yáo in China and Dao in Việt Nam, while belonging to the Khố Bạch group of Kim Mun branch (e.g., the Dao Quần Trắng) did come from China to settle in Quảng Ninh Province in the 1200s,[74] and a few Dao arrived in Việt Nam in the 1500s and 1600s,[75] most came in the 19th century at the same time as the Hmông and also gradually spread throughout the highlands of northern Việt Nam.[76] In China most people speaking Mienic languages, classified ethnically as Yáo, live in Guǎngxī Province, but there are also Yáo in Guìzhōu, as well as in Guǎngdōng and Yúnnán provinces. There is considerable variation in Yáo dress depending on sub-group and locale. Basically, however, males tend to wear some sort Chinese-style shirt and trousers. Likewise, while there are many differences in details, such as the styles of headcloth worn, most women wear a tunic and trousers. They make their clothing from plain cotton cloth that is dyed dark indigo blue or black. Most decoration entails the use of embroidery or sometimes appliqué. In Việt Nam most Dao women wear the tunic and trousers combination. The Dao Tiền are the sole exception, their women wearing a front-opening tunic and a short wrap-around skirt that is decorated with batik patterning.[77] The batik patterns include zigzag or wavy lines and rows of small disks with spokes. The patterns are drawn with beeswax using a boar's tusk and sometimes with the assistance of small frames made of pieces of bamboo.

Bouyei is a Northern Tai language that is more closely tied to the Northern Zhuang than Southern Zhuang. People speaking Bouyei are called Bùyī in China and Bố Y in Việt Nam. The Bùyī is the second largest ethnic group in Guìzhōu Province. Their ancestors are commonly considered to be the first Tai to have settled in Guìzhōu, probably around the same time that the ancestors of the Zhuàng/Tày and Thái were moving into Guǎngdōng and northern Việt Nam. There are several distinct sub-groups of Bùyī in China and in Việt Nam speakers of Bouyei are treated as two distinct ethnic groups, the Bố Y and Giáy. There are also the Tu Dí that are recognized as a distinct sub-group of Bố Y.[78] The first Bouyei migrants from Guìzhōu settled in Hà Giang Province following the Nanlong Rebellion. Others, the ancestors of the Giáy and Tu Dí, followed in the 1830s.

Many Bùyī in Guìzhōu wear relatively modern styles of clothing, but women in more remote areas continue to wear distinctive traditional dress.[79] This consists of a blouse with wide long sleeves that opens down the front and fastens on the lower right side, a long pleated full-skirt, an apron, a sash, and a headcloth. The body of the blouse is made of dark blue or black cotton cloth with strips of batik and supplementary weft patterned cloth added around the neck and front opening and on the sleeves. There is usually one relatively wide piece of cloth with blue and white spiral patterns attached near the top of the sleeve, a narrower piece of colorful supplementary weft patterned silk cloth attached further down the sleeve, and a narrow piece of blue and white batik patterned cloth near the end. The edging around the neck and front opening is comprised of a mixture of pieces of batik and supplementary weft patterned cloth. The apron has a plain dark blue or black center surrounded by a strips of supplementary weft patterned cloth and sometimes an outer edge of lighter blue cloth. The skirts may have an upper section with blue and white batik patterning and a lower part that is plain or they may be almost entirely covered with blue and white batik patterning. A variety of batik patterns appear in the upper part of the skirt, including spirals, circles, and zigzag lines. If most of the skirt is covered with batik patterning then the area below this multi-patterned upper part is covered with rhomb shaped patterns that resemble cross-hatching.

The Zhuàng in Guìzhōu are related to the Tày and Nùng in northern Việt Nam and, although the Tày in particular have a long history of residing in the highlands of northern Việt Nam, some Zhuàng migrated to northern Việt Nam more recently. This is especially true of those that are identified as Nùng in Việt Nam. Most Nùng in Việt Nam live in Cao Bằng and Lạng Sơn provinces, having migrated there in the late 18th and 19th centuries primarily from southwestern Guǎngxī as part of the general movement of local peoples fleeing Chinese rule.[80] The Nùng Dín, however, live in Hà Giang and Bắc Kạn provinces and seem to have come to Việt Nam from Guǎngxī between the 8th to 10th centuries.[81] Although all Nùng women wore long full-skirts (sometimes with pleats) in the past, they are commonly only worn by Nùng Dín women at present and other sub-groups of Nùng in Việt Nam wear Chinese inspired blouses and trousers (Nùng men wearing Chinese inspired shirts and trousers). Nùng Dín women wear a long plain warp-around full-skirt that is often

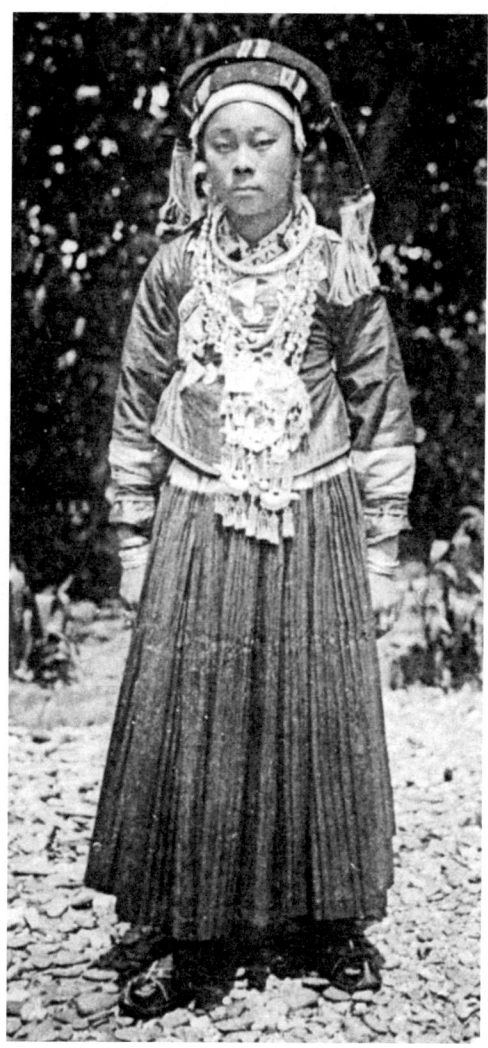

Nùng woman wearing pleated skirt (from Abadie, *Les Races du Haut-Tonkin*, pl. 23, fig 36).

lined. The outer part is made of fine, dark indigo blue cotton cloth and the lining of coarser cotton cloth that is dyed a lighter blue. The skirt is bunched at the back over the tie string in a similar manner as skirts worn by Zhuàng women in Wénshān Prefecture. The bunch is called a *u*, and the Nùng Dín are sometimes called Nùng U.

The Gēlǎo (Cờ Lao in Việt Nam) are one of the largest groups of people speaking a Kadai language in China. They live mainly in western Guìzhōu (where they are considered to be indigenous) and also western Guǎngxī, southeast Yúnnán, and southern Sìchuān provinces. There are only a couple of thousand Cờ Lao in Việt Nam living in northern Hà Giang Province.[82] Many Gēlǎo have been highly acculturated and wear Chinese inspired dress, however, some still weave traditional cloth and wear traditional clothing. In addition to weaving cotton cloth, the Gēlǎo also weave "five-coloured cloth made of silk, hemp and cotton" as well as blankets from cogon grass (*Imperata cylindrica*), hemp, or mulberry tree bark.[83] Traditional Gēlǎo female dress includes a long plain skirt, blouse, and short-sleeved vest. The skirts and blouses are largely plain, but are often decorated with narrow bands of batik and embroidery near the edges. Cờ Lao women in Việt Nam wore such skirts in the past, but French accounts in the early 20th century already describe them as wearing trousers.[84]

Nán Yuè and Chinese Ruled Việt Nam

A Qín army led by general Zhào Tuó (Triệu Đà in Vietnamese) defeated Thục Phán and conquered Ōu Lò in 207 BC. After the Qín Dynasty collapsed in 206 BC, Zhào Tuó established the independent kingdom of Nán Yuè (aka Nam Việt) in 204 BC.[85] Zhào Tuó (r. 204–136 BC) established his capital at Pānyú in Guǎngzhōu and divided it into commanderies. Ōu Lò was divided into two commanderies: Giao-chỉ (aka Jiāozhǐ) in the north and Cửu Chân (aka Jiuzhen) in the south (the latter including the present provinces of Nghệ An, Thanh Hóa, and Hà Tĩnh). These commanderies were administered by a combination of Chinese and local Tai feudal lords, who appear to have undergone a degree of Sinification. The adoption of Chinese culture by the lowland Tai was related to a policy of Harmonizing and Gathering the Hundred Yuè Tribes through which Zhào Tuó and subsequent rulers of Nán Yuè created a syncretic culture that was a blend of Chinese and Tai cultures. That this was far from a one-way affair is apparent in a comment by Herold Wiens that Zhào Tuó "had married a Yueh wife and tied in his fortune with high clan leaders of the Yueh, and in fact virtually 'turned native' in his culture."[86]

Western Hàn Emperor Gāo (aka Gāozǔ) sent Lu Jia (who was from Chǔ) as an emissary to Zhào Tuó in 196 BC. In response to Lu Jia's threat of an attack, Zhào Tuó acquiesced to become a vassal of the Hàn emperor. Lu Jia also accused Zhào Tuó of forsaking his cultural roots and casting aside the dress of his homeland for wearing his hair in a bun in the local fashion. The emissary was in effect accusing Zhào Tuó of behaving and dressing like a barbarian rather than a civilized person. In fact, Zhào

Tuó had not completely adopted local dress and imposed a policy of requiring local nobles to wear Qín-Hàn dynastic style clothing. The extent to which this edict was adhered to is difficult to tell, but there is evidence of at least some Nán Yuè nobility wearing Chinese style silk robes, sometimes with brocade patterns.

Relations with the Hàn Empire were far from smooth. Thus, Zhào Tuó proclaimed himself emperor after the Western Hàn Empress Lü Zhi (aka Lǚ Hòu) put an embargo on trade with Nán Yuè.[87] The Chinese were able to increase their influence over Nán Yuè after Zhào Tuó's death in 136 BC. In particular, when the kingdom of Mǐn Yuè attacked the kingdom of Nán Yuè the new emperor of Nán Yuè Zhào Mò (aka Zhào Wén Dì, Triệu Mạt in Vietnamese; r. 136–124 BC) was forced to ask the Hàn for help in warding off the attack. In return for helping out the Hàn emperor asked that the young Crown Prince Zhào Yīngqí (Triệu Anh Tề in Vietnamese) to live at the Western Hàn court, where he was to spend a good deal of his life.

A picture of elite Nán Yuè culture emerges from Emperor Zhào Mò's tomb, which was discovered in 1983 and is now housed in Guǎngdōng's Museum of the Mausoleum of the Nán Yuè King. The tomb contains a murals and a large number of local and imported artifacts. There are Đông Sơn style bronzes that include images of people wearing typical Đông Sơn dress. Silk textiles were found in the tomb, many of supplementary weft (brocade) patterning. There are also bronze object that were used for printing patterns on cloth. The emperor's jade and silk tunic is the most dramatic object from the tomb. Significantly it is quite different from any Qín or Hàn garments, being made of pieces of jade that are held together with silk thread and the front opening has distinctive fasteners that are also not found on Qín or Hàn garments. In addition, the emperor's suit of armor features patches with geometric patterns that are not found on Qín or Hàn objects. Images of Zhào Mò's wife show her wearing a long robe of a style that looks more Chinese than Tai.

Zhào Yīngqí had a son, Zhào Xīng (Triệu Hưng in Vietnamese), by a Chinese woman named Cù Thị while living with the Hàn. Zhào Yīngqí returned to Pānyú with his family in 124 BC when his father died and assumed the throne. Zhào Yīngqí's reign was brief and when he died in 115 BC his son was only six years old. Emperor Wǔ of Hàn (aka Wǔdì) brought Empress Dowager Cù Thị and Zhào Xīng to his court, where Cù Thị was beheaded and in 112 BC he sent an army south to conquer Nán Yuè. The Western Hàn army succeeded in conquering Nán Yuè the following year, although sporadic resistance continued for some time, culminating in a revolt led by the Trưng sisters—Trưng Trắc (Zhēng Cè in Chinese) and Trưng Nhị (Zhēng Èr in Chinese)—that was crushed in AD 43 by the Eastern Hàn general Mǎ Yuán (aka Fubo Jiangjun, Mã Viện in Vietnamese).[88]

Following the end of the rebellion the Eastern Hàn initiated construction of a major highway in order to facilitate communication with the south along with other infrastructure projects in Jiāozhǐ (Giao-chỉ in Vietnamese).[89] Mǎ Yuán also initiated a period of cultural repression to suppress local cultures and promote Hàn culture. This was symbolized by the melting of numerous bronze drums to make a large bronze column at Ái Nam Quan, a pass located on Jiāozhǐ's northern border (in modern times on the border between Lạng Sơn Province and Guangxi, and once known as Zhèn Nán Guān, "South Suppression Pass"). Zhào Tuó's Nán Yuè kingdom lasted only about a century, but Weins argues that during this time the various Zhuàng peoples living in kingdom were able to preserve much of their culture and "evolved into a coherent and well-defined cultural group."[90] While a sense of being a unified group of Tai people persisted following Mǎ Yuán's assimilation campaign, clearly at least among lowland peoples the cultural balance began to favor Hàn culture over Tai culture to a greater extent than was true previously. Schafer comments on the impact of Mǎ Yuán's campaign, "the soldiers were followed by colonists and their magistrates, bringing all the paraphernalia of official culture with them."[91]

Probably the most often-cited description of the dress of the people of ancient Jiāozhǐ (Giao-chỉ) is that by Nguyễn Văn Huyên (who served as Việt Nam's minister of education from 1946 until 1975) in his 1944 *La civilization Annamite*, which was subsequently published in English as *The Ancient Civilization on Vietnam* in 1995: "men and women were all clothed with a short vest, buttoned at the front, without any splits on the sides; trousers did not exist. Men used a band of cloth to gird his waist first, it then passed between the legs and was tied at the belly. This garment is called khố (loin cloth). Women wore around their waist a kind of pagne (type of poncho) called mấn and had a large hat on their head."[92] This description was taken from Trịnh Hoài Đức's *Gia Định thành thông chí* that was published in 1820 and that then appeared in a French edition in 1863, translated by Louis-Gabriel Aubaret.[93] The original passage by Trịnh Hoài Đức is a little more nuanced than Nguyễn Văn Huyên's. Prior to the above description of the male loincloth and female skirt, he says that the "mandarins" wear a high hat called "high mountain" and wear a flowing gown without buttons. He says that women wore a short vest without vents/slits on the sides and fasten it (Aubaret translates this as buttons) in the front. In addition, the Aubaret version of Trịnh Hoài Đức's passage refers to the mấn simply as a "kind of pagne," which can be translated as a type of skirt, with no mention of it being a "type of poncho." The loincloth and skirt described by the authors fit with the general picture of common Lò Yuè dress, while Trịnh Hoài Đức's (Aubaret's) description indicates that those of high status wore flowing gowns, with high status women adding a vest. Such gowns appear to be something worn by the Chinese rulers and probably by Sinified local elites.

The process of Sinification of local groups of Bai Yuè, especially in the lowlands, did not end after the fall of the Hàn Dynasty in AD 220. In the north of the Bai Yuè region those that the Chinese called Shǎn Yuè ("Mountain Yuè") resisted efforts by Sūn Quán (aka Emperor Dà of Wú; r. 229–252) to assert his control over the region for about a decade before being pacified. In the case of Jiāozhǐ (Giao Chỉ), the local governor Shì Xiè, who had been appointed by Hàn in AD 187, pledged his loyalty to Sūn Quán and remained in his post until he died in AD 226. Sūn Quán gave the governor considerable autonomy, treating Jiāozhǐ more or less as a vassal state. Shì Xiè was Chinese, however, and continued to promote Sinification as well as the spread of Buddhism. The process of Sinification continued in southeastern China and northern Việt Nam during the Jìn Dynasty (AD 265–420), especially after Sīmǎ Ruì (aka Jìn Yuán Dì) founded the Eastern Jìn Dynasty in AD 317 and established his capital at Jiànkāng (modern Nánjīng), the former capital of Wú. This began a period of large-scale migration of Hàn people south of the Yangtze River and had the effect of moving a major center of Chinese culture closer to northern Việt Nam. Despite some migration of Hàn Chinese to the lowlands of northern Việt Nam and increasing Sinification the bulk of the population in northern Việt Nam remained ethnically distinct non-Chinese, primarily Tày/Zhuàng.

Chinese control over northern Việt Nam passed to a variety of dynastic rulers during the Southern and Northern Dynasties period (420–589) and in general weakened until the region gained a degree of independence between 544 and 603. A military overseer named Lý Nam Đế led a revolt against the Southern Liáng governor of Jiāozhǐ in 540 and established an independent kingdom named Vạn Xuân in 544. The governor at the time, Hsiao Tzu, was a nephew of the Southern Liáng emperor and Lý Nam Đế himself was Chinese. However, many of those who took part in the revolt were not Chinese, including many non-Chinese holding lower level administrative posts. The Suí Dynasty reestablished control over northern Việt Nam in 603 and moved the capital of Jiāozhǐ from Long Biên (which continued to serve as an important port in later centuries) to nearby Sòngpíng (Tống Bình in Vietnamese, located in Từ Liêm and Hoài Đức districts of Hà Nội).

The period of Chinese rule under the Táng Dynasty (618–690, 705–907) had a major impact on the society and culture of northern Việt Nam and more than at any time over the previous centuries can be said to have laid the basis for modern Vietnamese society. The Táng *dào* (circuit) of Lǐng Nán (aka Lingnan), with its capital at Guǎngzhōu, encompassed an area that included eastern Guǎngdōng, Guǎngxī, Hǎinán, and northern Việt Nam. Under the Táng northern Việt Nam became an integral part of the Chinese empire more than over before. Wiens comments, "Ling-nan at this stage was being strongly impregnated with T'ang culture. Exiled scholars and literati were to be found everywhere, profoundly transforming the T'ai culture by a Han-Chinese superstructure it was the strong tide of northern T'ang civilization that made the Kuang-tung [Guangdong] Chinese of today regard themselves as T'ang-jen (T'ang people)."[94] This cultural transformation was accompanied by large-scale migration of Chinese people from the north to Lǐng Nán, including into the lowlands of northern Việt Nam. This included not only elite administrators, but also common soldiers and peasants. Schafer write about the "Creoles" of Nam Việt that emerged during the Táng Dynasty as the sons and grandsons of "banished northern Literati and upper-class immigrants fleeing the horrors of war and pillage which devastated the north in late T'ang times ... grew up as natives, accustomed to the sights and sounds of the far south."[95] As was mentioned previously, Táng-ruled northern Việt Nam also attracted Mon-Khmer migrants from the highlands southwest of the Red

1. Ancient Clothing

River lowlands and the mixture of these new Mon-Khmer and Chinese migrants with local Tai blended to create Kinh society. It was a society with a large dose of Chinese culture mixed with Tai and Mon-Khmer elements.

As we have seen, the dress of Nán Yuè elites was a mixture of Chinese and Tai styles. Direct Chinese rule over lowland northern Việt Nam for over 900 years (AD 40–938) resulted in increased Chinese influence on local clothing styles, especially among local elites. Even rebel leaders against Chinese rule generally are characterized as wearing Chinese-style clothing. Essentially this meant that they wore various styles of long silk gowns that that followed particular dynastic fashions. For this reason a brief overview of Chinese dress during this period is in order. First of all it is important to note that there were differences in the dress of elites and common people. Essentially elites wore colorful, decorated clothing made of silk, while commoners wore plain clothing that was usually made of hemp.[96] In the process of creating a unified China Emperor Qín Shǐhuáng promoted unitary styles of dress and during the Hàn Dynasty differences in the style of dress of elites came to be codified in relation to one's status. Such codification began in AD 59, when Emperor Míng instituted a number of Confucian rituals accompanied by decrees setting out distinct styles of dress for people of different ranks.[97] Such distinctions were indicated in particular by headgear and by a seal and ribbon that were carried by officials. The seal was placed in a leather pouch that was attached to a waistband with the ribbon attached to it hanging outside the pouch. The ribbons differed in size, color, and texture according to a person's status. The colors were reddish yellow for the emperor, red for princes, purple for nobles and generals, and blue or black for lower officials.[98] Most of the dress regulations imposed by the Chinese on northern Việt Nam pertained to the dress of officials. In terms of fashions, it is important to recognize that even with such regulations, Chinese dress was never completely uniform and that it was subject to change. External influences on Chinese dress became especially noticeable after Emperor Wǔ of Hàn (r. 141–87 BC) sent Zhāng Qiān as an envoy to the peoples living to the west of China. In addition, while new fashions became popular this did not mean that people stopped wearing old-fashioned clothing. This was especially true away from the capital.

When Zhào Tuó conquered northern Việt Nam elite Chinese fashion included older styles of dress from the Warring States (475–221 BC) period as well as newer Qín fashions. For formal wear, both men and women during the Warring States period commonly wore tight-fitting gowns that were folded to the right to form a V-shaped opening at the neck. It was common to wear three layers with each garment being exposed at the collar. The sleeves of the gowns tended to be fairly narrow and straight. The lower parts of the top two garments were worn so as to spread out "like a bell."[99] The outer gown had a curved front that was fastened towards the bottom right side and a low V-neck opening that allowed the other two layers to be seen. This outer gown usually was covered in decorative patterning with one set of patterns covering most of the material and bands with other patterns along the edges. The middle gown was made of a different color of fabric that was covered in different patterns. It extended beyond the outer gown at the sleeves, hem, and collar so that the contrasting fabric was exposed. The inner gown was made of plain white fabric with a narrow piece of it being exposed at the collar.

Elite women during the Warring States period sometimes would wear a blouse/jacket and a long full-skirt. The blouses reached to the waist, had relatively straight and narrow long sleeves, and opened in the front with a flap being fastened on the right to form a V-shaped collar. A blouse found in an Hàn Dynasty tomb from Gānsù Province is made of light blue silk with long cuffs made of white silk added.[100] The silk material of the blouse and the skirt that accompanied it were covered with decorations.

These types of garments were worn during the Qín and Hàn dynasties, even though they were old fashioned. In fact, although the blouse/jacket and skirt combination declined in popularity briefly after the fall of the Eastern Hàn Dynasty, it returned to fashion during the Jìn and Northern Wèi dynasties and continued to be worn, with variations in details, until the time of the Qīng Dynasty.[101] New styles of formal gowns appeared during the Hàn Dynasty with wider sleeves. There were two styles of sleeves, one that became progressively wider towards the end and another that had relatively straight sleeves that tended to be a little wider than the older style and narrow cuffs made of a different material. While some gowns continued to have a front flap that was fastened to the lower right, a newer style featured a much longer flap that was wrapped more than once around the wearer. These gowns often had a cloth belt to hold them in place.[102] Men also took to wearing a rectangular piece of decorative cloth (*jin xian guan*) around the mid-section of the gown. While formal gowns usually were lined, everyday wear included unlined gowns. Non-elite men generally wore fairly plain shirt-jackets and trousers and sometimes an apron. Elite women sometimes wore a long full-skirt skirt made of four pieces of white silk cloth underneath their gown. These skirts had a waistband that allowed them to tie the skirt. They wore crotchless pants underneath the skirt.[103] Non-elite women during the Hàn Dynasty wore plainer versions of the blouse/jacket and long skirt combination. The skirts generally were plain, but they also wore a decorated sash around their waist.

Shǔ, and especially the city of Chéngdū, was known to the Chinese for its production of silk cloth, including silk brocade cloth (sometimes referred to as Shǔ cloth or Shǔ brocade), since the Spring and Autumn Period (770–476 BC) and was exporting such cloth to China by the time of the Warring States Period (475–221 BC). The importance of Shǔ's silk and silk brocade industry increased under the Western Hàn Dynasty (206 BC–AD 23), and was exported not only throughout China but also south to Yúnnán, Myanmar, India-Pakistan, and on to the Middle East. Shǔ weavers produced a variety of textures of silk in a wide range of colors and patterns. A study of texts and fabrics indicates that "the chief patterns on these fabrics were the *xie* (a one-legged dragon-like monster from ancient fables), trees, animals within square frames and pairs of birds in linked rings" as well as patterns imported from Central and West Asia including "the incarnation of the celestial ruler, lotus flowers, and birds and animals linked with strings of pearls."[104] As was mentioned above, traders from Shǔ were active over an extensive area at this time and earlier. Silk from Shǔ came to be worn by elites throughout the Hàn Empire and the emperor appointed an official, the Jin Guan, in Chéngdū to oversee production.

Color became an important aspect of courtly dress under the Qín emperor. Influenced by *wǔxíng* (five elements/phases), the emperor identified with the Water element, which is associated with black. Accordingly, courtly dress favored black to symbolize the power of water.[105] *Wǔxíng* became even more important under the Hàn. The Hàn identified with fire and red and the color red was associated with virtue. Eastern Hàn (AD 25–220) Dynasty officials were required to wear clothing of different colors according to the season as prescribed by *wǔxíng*: green in spring, red in summer, yellow in late summer, white in autumn, and black in winter. *Wǔxíng* also proved important later as yellow colored clothing came to be reserved for emperors or other high-ranking officials. The legendary Yellow Emperor (aka Huángdì) was linked to the earth element and its corresponding color yellow and the Yellow Dragon (*huáng long*).[106] The Yellow Dragon motif, of course, also came to be featured on imperial clothing.

Chinese fashion changed in a number of ways during the Six Dynasties Period (220–589). Women's multi-layered costumes commonly included a decorative piece of cloth secured at the waist and hanging down the front over the gown apron-like. Elite women of the Northern Wèi and Jìn dynastic periods often added decorative pointed strips of cloth were sometimes added beneath this and there were long ribbons that hung down from the waist of their skirt. The style is sometimes referred to as a "swallowtail" costume.[107] Later the ribbons fell out of fashion and the decorative hem enlarged. In addition to such formal wear, elite women are also depicted and described wearing an unlined blouse, long skirt, and apron combination. The blouse, which is made of patterned cloth, features sleeves that become quite wide at the cuff and a V-neck opened that is usually lined with a decorative strip of cloth. A white breastcloth can be seen worn underneath. The apron has a waistband and lower section made of patterned cloth. There are a number of different styles of long skirt featuring a wide array of colors.

The Vietnamese word *áo*, as in *áo dài*, is derived from Middle Chinese, the word appearing in the *Qièyùn*, a Suí Dynasty rime dictionary that was published in AD 601. The Suí Dynasty word is sometimes translated as "padded coat," but might also be viewed as referring to an upper garment with lining. In Vietnamese *áo* can refer to a blouse, shirt, jacket, case, or cover. It is a word that also later enters into many languages of minority peoples in Việt Nam, especially those with no tradition of wearing such an upper garment, when referring to various types of upper garment. Southwest and Central Tai languages use *sửa* (*xứa*, *slửa* in some Tai languages) rather than *áo* to refer to a shirt or blouse.[108] It appears to be quite an old Tai word pre-dating the

Vietnamese *áo*. In Vietnamese and Tai languages these words also are used when referring to shirts and blouses as well as to longer garments. A further descriptive term is typically added to make it clear what type of garment is being referred to, especially when referring to longer garments. Thus, in Black Tái the long garment is called an *sửa hí,* meaning a long shirt/blouse. Various authors have used robe, gown, or tunic when describing these garments in English. I do not find that such terms adequately describe many of these garments and shall use long shirt or long blouse as distinct from the normal shorter shirt/blouse when discussing such garments.

Chinese fashion underwent further changes during the Táng Dynasty in part reflecting the more cosmopolitan nature of its culture as a result of extensive interaction with the world beyond China. In the course of a very busy year, the second Suí Dynasty emperor Yang (aka Yang Guang, r. 604–18) issued a decree in 605 that set forth his dynasty's rules for dress for all government officials. This meant that government officers in northern Việt Nam wore the same clothing as officials in other parts of the empire when performing official duties. Official dress basically consisted of elaborate headgear, gowns that opened in the front and had large sleeves, and often a decorative apron. During the reign of Emperor Yang of Suí, non-official elite dress was quite varied and fashions often changed. The women of Emperor Yang's court "indulged themselves in dress and vied with one another in adornment ... and wearing gorgeous costumes, so that their appearance became more and more colorful. The ordinary women followed suit, and this situation prevailed even in the Tang Dynasty."[109]

Emperor Gaozu of Táng (r. 618–26) issued a decree in 621 setting out official dress regulations for officials that remained substantially in force for the remainder of the Táng era. Emperor Tàizōng of Táng (r, 626–49) made an important addition in 630 when he issued regulations establishing particular colors of gowns to be worn by officials depending on their rank. With yellow or gold reserved for the emperor, purple was for the 3rd and 4th ranks, bright red for the 5th rank, green for the 6th and 7th ranks, and blue for the 8th and 9th ranks. In addition to headgear that was often extravagant, official men's wear under the Táng Dynasty continued to include a gown that opened down the front and with large sleeves and a decorative apron in the front. Everyday wear for men commonly included fairly plain gowns with rounded collars and narrow sleeves. Elite women in Sui and early Táng dynastic periods tended to wear a short blouse/jacket and a long skirt that fastened under the armpit with a sash around the waist that hung down the front of the skirt. There were front opening blouses that were fastened at the lower right-hand side as well as pullover blouses. There were also blouses with narrow sleeves as well as ones with very wide ones. Collar styles also varied. Sometimes a short-sleeved pullover vest was worn over the long-sleeved blouse. Women also sometimes wore gowns with wide sleeves over their skirts and over time these tended to become looser fitting. There were also a wide variety of skirt styles. One particularly colorful type of skirt was known as the one-hundred-bird feather skirt. Elite Táng women also wore shawls and later capes.[110]

1. Ancient Clothing

The silk brocade weavers of Shǔ responded to the growing market in Táng China with a greater variety of patterns and colors in their wares. The growth of international trade meant that their cloth was also exported in large quantities beyond China, east to Japan and west as far as Constantinople.

Chămpa

In ancient times central and southern Việt Nam was inhabited by a variety of peoples speaking Malayo-Polynesian and Mon-Khmer languages. Mon-Khmer peoples migrated down the Mekong River. The ancestors of some of those speaking Katuic and Bahnaric languages gradually migrated east into the highlands that straddle Laos and central Việt Nam. These include the ancestors of the Ba Na, who at some point also settled in the coastal lowlands of Việt Nam in Quảng Ngãi and Bình Định provinces.[111] Others, the ancestors of the Khmer, continued south to Cambodia and later out into the Mekong Delta. Peoples speaking a Malayic Malayo-Polynesian language began migrating from western Borneo to Việt Nam, Peninsular Malaysia, and Sumatra some time between 1000 BC and 600 BC. The Malayo-Chamic peoples appear to have settled initially along the coast of either what is now Bình Định Province or Bình Thuận Province and then spread out across the coastal regions of central and southern Việt Nam, interacting with the Bahnaric and Katuic speaking peoples in the vicinity and assimilating some of them living in the lowlands in the process.[112] In the south the Chăm also migrated up the Mekong River at least as far as Champasak Province in southern Laos. In the north they settled as far as the vicinity of Ngang Pass that forms the border between Quảng Bình and Hà Tĩnh provinces. Peoples speaking Malayo-Chamic languages in Việt Nam

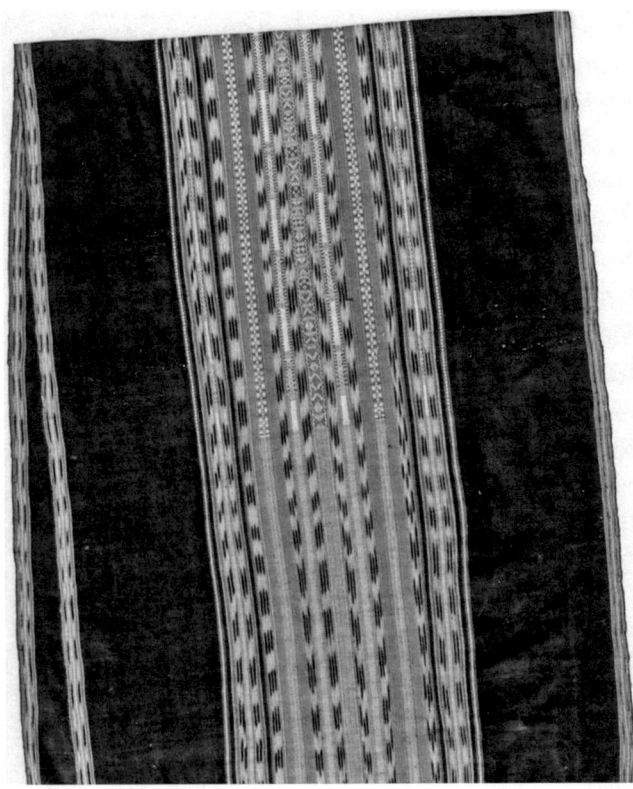

Hroi blanket, Đồng Xuân District, Phú Yên Province.

today include the lowland Chăm and the Ra Glai, Chu Ru, Gia Rai, Ê Đê, and Hroi in the adjacent highlands.

The early Malayo-Chamic peoples in Việt Nam are associated with Sa Huỳnh Culture. Sa Huỳnh Culture is named after an archaeological site in Quảng Ngãi Province, but archaeological sites associated with Sa Huỳnh Culture have been discovered throughout the coastal lowlands from Đồng Nai Province in the south to Quảng Bình Province in the north. It can be divided into an Early Sa Huỳnh period dating from roughly 1500 to 700 BC and a Late Sa Huỳnh period dating from around 700 BC to 0 BC. Peter Bellwood has referred to Late Sa Huỳnh as the "mature form" of this culture.[113] It is during this period that beads made of materials such as banded agate and carnelian that are probably imported from South Asia appear (such material arriving in Southeast Asia as early as 400 BC) as well as imported bronze objects.[114] Other evidence of trade between the Sa Huỳnh people and neighboring areas comes in the form of "the discovery of almost identical nobbed pennanular stone earrings (the so-called *lingling-o*) and of a special kind of earring of pendant with two animal heads (presumably deer) in a number of sites in Thailand, Vietnam, Palawan, and Sarawak."[115] Taiwan can be added to this list and "Vietnam" refers to the Đông Sơn cultural region in the north.[116]

Despite the close proximity of Sa Huỳnh and Đông Sơn cultures and some evidence of cultural contact until recently scholars wondered about the scarcity of artifacts from the respective cultures in each other's sites and the scarcity of Đông Sơn bronze drums in Sa Huỳnh sites in particular.[117] Recent archaeological work, however, has turned up many more Đông Sơn bronze artifacts in the south, especially in the Central Highlands where extensive caches of Đông Sơn bronze drums have been discovered, and pointed to greater contact between the two culture areas than was perceived previously. One important element of Đông Sơn influence on Sa Huỳnh culture (as well as on other Malayo-Polynesian cultures) is to be found in iconography. In regards to ceramics, Solheim notes, "Many of the elements of pottery decoration and the zoomorphic and anthropomorphic representation of the pottery are also found on the 'Đôngson' drums."[118] Of particular interest here is the question of Đông Sơn Tai influence on the Sa Huỳnh Malayo-Chamic peoples in terms of weaving.

It is doubtful that the earliest Malayo-Chamic migrants from Borneo knew how to weave and instead the Early Sa Huỳnh people probably made clothing from bark-cloth. By the Late Sa Huỳnh period, however, it appears that they did know how to weave. Solheim refers to "Cloth impressions" found on several artifacts and notes that Parmentier (who excavated in the area in the 1920s) mentioned two pieces showing traces of linen, one coarse weave and the other fine, and that Colani (who visited the sites in 1934), described cloth impressions on iron and pottery as well as a piece of "fossilized cloth of a simple overunder weave" made of "thread about 0.5 mm thick."[119] The "linen" he refers to is some kind of bast fiber and not actually linen. It seems likely that Sa Huỳnh weaving began as a result of contact with Đông Sơn culture either directly or indirectly through some of the Mon-Khmer groups living in the

1. Ancient Clothing

region and, thus, that weaving technology diffused from the Tai in the north to the Sa Huỳnh area.[120] Such scant archaeological evidence of weaving does not tell us very much about Sa Huỳnh textiles and weaving and tells us nothing about how they dressed. Based on later evidence from ethnic groups living in the region, however, it is likely that Sa Huỳnh men wore loincloths and women short wrap-around skirts and both may have worn some sort of pullover shirt/blouse.

The kingdom of Fù Nán (aka, Funan, Phù Nam) was founded in the Mekong Delta region around AD 68. The identity of the people associated with Fù Nán has been subject to dispute with the most likely candidates including ancestors of the Chăm or "proto–Mon."[121] A combination of the two is also a possibility. Excavations of the Fù Nán port of Óc Eo have served to highlight that Fù Nán was actively engaged in maritime trade between India and China and that its cultural orientation was towards India. Writing was in Sanskrit using Brahmi script and numerous Buddhist and Hindu artifacts have been found in sites associated with Fù Nán. Emissaries were sent back and forth between the rulers of Fù Nán and various Chinese states, starting with the kingdom of Wú in the late 220s and until the time of the Southern Liáng Dynasty in the 500s, when Fù Nán ceased to exist as an independent state. This reflects the increased importance of maritime trade for the Chinese following the fall of the Hàn Dynasty. Cotton fabrics from India were among the goods that Fù Nán is reported to have shipped to China.[122] Fù Nán ceased to exist as an independent entity in the mid–500s as the Khmer kingdom of Chēnlà (aka Zhēnlà) in Cambodia and Chăm kingdom of Chămpa in central Việt Nam emerged as the dominant powers in the region.

Accounts by some of the Chinese emissaries to Fù Nán found their way into later official dynastic histories and these give us some idea about the people of Fù Nán and their dress. Clothing in fact figures in the founding myth of Fù Nán as recorded in AD 635 in the *Liáng Shū* ("Book of Liáng"). The story refers to a foreigner named Hùntián who came to Fù Nán from a country to the south named Jiào (the identity of Jiáo is not known). He married the local queen named Liǔyè. She is described as being naked and Hùntián not being happy about this folded a piece of cloth to make a pullover blouse, which he had her wear.[123] Chinese writers at the time tended to use the term naked rather loosely when referring to anyone that wore less clothing than people in China. One envoy wrote, "The Fu Nan people are dark and ugly, with curly hair, no clothes or footwares…. The Fu Nan people have the custom of being naked and tattooed, their hair kept long at the back and they wear no clothes, on the upper part or lower part."[124] The description in the *Nán Qí Shū* ("Book of Southern Qí") written by Xiāo Zìxiǎn during the Southern Qí Dynasty (479–502) is undoubtedly more accurate: Regarding goods, they have gold, silver, and silk. The sons of rich families cut brocade to make loin-cloth, women pull a cloth over their head to make clothes. Normal people cover their body with a meager piece of cloth.[125] The mention of silk in this account should not be taken to mean necessarily that the people of Fù Nán were weaving their own silk cloth at this time since elite people in Fù Nán, made wealthy by international trade, might well have worn imported silk cloth.

Chămpa

Although Ngang Pass formed the effective southern boundary of the commandery of Cửu Chân (aka Nhật Nam, Rìnán, Jiuzhen), the Chinese sought to extend their control beyond the pass into the lowlands of Quảng Bình, Quảng Trị, and Thừa Thiên–Huế provinces, and perhaps even south of Hải Vân Pass into Quảng Nam Province. This was beyond traditional Tai territory and was inhabited primarily by Chăm. The Hàn characterized this area as "a dangerous and impenetrable area whose population was ... so wild 'that they knew only hunting and fishing and did not know how to till the soil.'"[126] Indeed, even recently small bands of nomadic hunters and gatherers categorized by Vietnamese as Chứt have inhabited the adjacent highlands of this region. However, this area also was the northern frontier of the Chăm, who lived primarily south of Hải Vân Pass, and the Chinese seem to have pushed into Chăm territory. The Chinese push to the south into central Việt Nam eventually elicited a backlash when a man from Xianglin (Tượng Lâm in Vietnamese, in modern Quảng Nam Province) named Khu Liên (aka Sri Mara, Qū Lián) led a revolt against the Chinese in AD 192 and established a kingdom in what the Chinese referred to as Lin Yi (Lin District), effectively putting an end to a Chinese presence south of Ngang Pass.

Another political entity known as Chămpa (aka Chăm Pa, Champapura, Lâm Ấp, Zhànchéng) emerged between Fù Nán and Lin Yi during the 300s and by the early 600s it had encapsulated Lin Yi and effectively controlled the coastal lowlands from Ngang Pass to Bà Rịa–Vũng Tàu Province and the Đồng Nai River in the south, with its influence reaching along the Mekong as far as Champasak in southern Laos.[127] Chămpa also had a presence in parts of the Central Highlands.[128] Early sources commonly point to the Chăm being divided into two regional clans. The Areca Palm Clan was located in northern Chăm territory roughly from Quảng Bình Province to Phú Yên Province and the Areca Palm Clan in the south from Khánh Hòa Province to Đồng Nai Province.[129] It is unclear whether these clans began as two separate groups of Chăm or later separated into two distinct groups as well as whether there were important cultural differences between the two clans in ancient times. Maspero makes the interesting point that the Areca Palm Clan "boasted greater purity of race," highlighting the mixture of Mon-Khmer and Malayo-Polynesian peoples that was taking place.[130]

Chămpa reached its greatest extent roughly from the 600s until the late 900s. During this time Chămpa was divided into five regions: Indrapura (Quảng Bình, Quảng Trị, and Thừa Thiên–Huế provinces), Amaravati (Quảng Nam and Quảng Ngãi provinces), Vijaya (Bình Định and Phú Yên provinces), Kauthara (Khánh Hòa Province), and Panduraga (Ninh Thuận Province and south into Đồng Nai Province). The Areca Palm Clan ruled over the three northern provinces and the Coconut Palm Clan over the southern two. Simhapura (located in the Trà Kiệu valley to the southwest of Đà Nẵng in Quảng Nam Province) became Chămpa's first capital in the late 300s. The capital was moved to Indrapura in 854 (near Đồng Dương, also in Quảng Nam Province) and after Chămpa lost some of its northern territory to Đại Việt in

1. Ancient Clothing

1069 the capital was moved south to Vijaya in Bình Định Province. Lê Hoàn of Đại Việt sacked Indrapura in 982 and, as was common in those days, took a number of skilled Chăm back to his capital of Hoa Lư, including musicians and dancers. Additional Chăm artists and artisans were taken to Đại Việt following subsequent campaigns. Prior to the sacking of Indrapura there were already some Chăm merchants living in ports along the maritime sea route between India and China such as Guǎngzhōu. After the sacking of Indrapura additional Chăm (probably merchants) left. Thus, the *Sòng Shū* mentions Chăm arriving on Hǎinán Island in 986 and another group went to Guǎngzhōu in 988.[131] Still others headed off to the Malay Peninsula and northern Sumatra (Aceh).[132]

Like Fù Nán, Chămpa was influenced by Indian culture. This included the adoption of Hindu and Buddhist religious beliefs and practices and the use of Sanskrit and Brami script. Chămpa was also actively engaged in maritime trade between India and China, gradually taking over from Fù Nán. The port of Đại Chiêm (aka Lâm Ấp Phố, modern Hội An), located east of Simhapura and Indrapura at the mouth of the Thu Bồn River became the most important port between India and China and the source of considerable wealth for Chămpa. Such trade eventually included the export and import of textiles and not only played a role in introducing Indian-inspired dress fashions to Chăm society but also may have been instrumental in introducing Indian varieties of cotton to Chămpa.

Chămpa was a multi-ethnic kingdom that included the majority Chăm as well as other Malayo-Chamic and Mon-Khmer peoples, many of the latter gradually becoming assimilated as Chăm.[133] Factors such as warfare within the Chamic population and later the Kinh push to the south resulted in migration of some Chamic groups into the adjacent highlands.[134] These include the ancestors of the Hroi, Gia Rai, Ê Đê, Ra Glai, and Chu Ru. The Hroi (aka Haroi) live in western Bình Định and Phú Yên provinces in close proximity to the Mon-Khmer speaking Ba Na. The Gia Rai live mainly in Gia Lai and Kon Tum provinces, with some living further south in Đắk Lắk Province and Cambodia's Ratanakiri Province. The Ê Đê live mainly in Đắk Lắk Province, with some also in western Phú Yên and Khánh Hoà provinces. The Ra Glai live in western Khánh Hoà, Binh Thuận, and Ninh Thuận provinces as well and adjacent parts of Lâm Đồng Province. The Chu Ru live in Lâm Đồng and Binh Thuận provinces.

The Chăm of Chămpa referred to the Chamic and Mon-Khmer peoples living in the adjacent highlands as "mlecchas" (savages) or "kiratas" (hill people).[135] The highland Chamic peoples effectively formed a wedge between northern and southern Bahnaric Mon-Khmer speaking groups. These highland Chamic peoples can help to shed light on the ancient textile and dress traditions of the Chamic peoples in general, especially in regard to the period prior to Indian influence and the earliest Chinese accounts of Chămpa. The Ra Glai, who lived in the lowlands prior to moving into the highlands of Khánh Hoà and Ninh Thuận provinces, never wove and only made barkcloth and cloth from plaited bast fibers as well as obtaining cloth from the Chăm

Chămpa

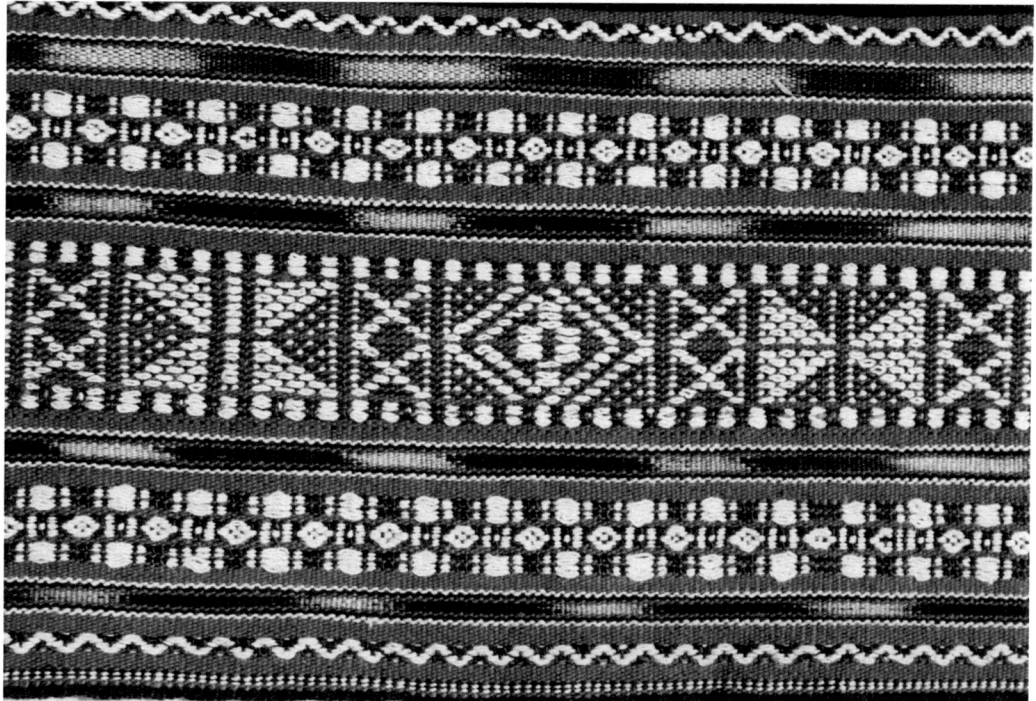

Detail of warp ikat and alternating warp float patterning on Hroi textile, Phú Yên Province.

through trade.[136] It can be argued that they represent an early non-weaving, bark-cloth making tradition among the Chamic peoples. Weaving was not well developed among the Chu Ru, who also commonly traded with Chăm and others to obtain cloth.[137]

The Gia Rai and Ê Đê have similar weaving and dress traditions. Bast fibers were sometimes used to weave cloth in the past, but most cloth is made of cotton. They weave

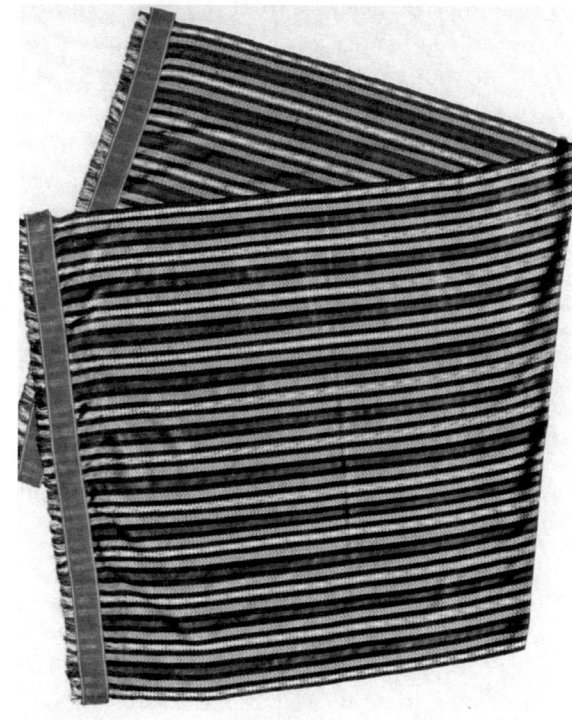

Chăm wrap-around skirt with weft directional bands near ends, Mỹ Nghiệp village, Ninh Phước District, Ninh Thuận Province.

1. Ancient Clothing

on what Vietnamese refer to as an Indonesian back-strap loom (which is also used by modern Chăm). Dark blue or black are the dominant colors, with decorative highlights in white, red, and yellow being common. Alternating warp float and supplementary weft are the main decorative techniques, with supplementary warp and warp ikat being rare. In fact, only the Bih (a distinctive sub-group of Ê Đê) employ the warp ikat technique.[138] Traditional Gia Rai and Ê Đê male clothing consists of a loincloth and sometimes a pullover long-sleeved shirt. There are distinct styles of loincloths and shirts that represent differences in status. Essentially those worn by most men are plainer than those worn by higher status men and the loincloths of high status are also longer and wider. In particular, high status male attire features a distinctive band near the ends with supplementary weft patterning (called *kteh* in Ê Đê). Traditional female attire consists of a relatively long wrap-around skirt made of two pieces of cloth and sometimes a long-sleeved pullover blouse. Both men and women also may wrap themselves in a blanket during cold weather. This style of dress is quite different from that associated with modern Chăm and its general features may represent an older style of dress that was common to Chamic people prior to the migration of the Gia Rai-Ê Đê into the highlands and the development of a more Hinduized culture among the lowland Chăm.

The Hroi, who live north of the Gia Rai and Ê Đê, and their textiles and dress are somewhat different than those of the Gia Rai and Ê Đê and more like those of the Ba Na. In ancient times the Ba Na lived north of Cù Mông Pass in Bình Định Province and the Hroi lived south of the pass in the lowlands of Phú Yên Province. The Ba Na occupied the adjacent highlands much earlier than the Hroi, who only moved there in the 1600s.[139] It is important to note, however, that there are Chămpa sites located in the highlands area occupied by the Ba Na and that even today Ba Na sometimes visit lowland markets, indicating that even after the Ba Na moved into the highlands they were not completely isolated from Chămpa.

Traditional Hroi and Ba Na male clothing consists of a loincloth and sometimes a pullover shirt. While the high status loincloth is similar to that worn by the Gia Rai and Ê Đê, the more common variety is different. In particular it commonly includes warp directional stripes with warp ikat dashes.[140] Traditional Hroi and Ba Na female clothing consists of a wrap-around skirt and a long-sleeved pullover blouse. The skirt consists of a rectangular body and a waistband that is longer than the body is wide. Sometimes an additional smaller rectangular piece of cloth is attached to the center of the body. Blankets are also sometimes worn during cold weather. Hroi and Ba Na female clothing in particular is covered more extensively with decorative features than those of the Gia Rai and Ê Đê and in general Hroi women's skirts and blouses more elaborately decorated than those of the Ba Na.[141] Moreover, Hroi and Ba Na textiles feature extensive use of warp ikat patterning in the form of warp directional dashes. It is difficult to know whether the Hroi influenced the Ba Na or the other way around in regard to weaving techniques and dress style, but it is likely that this is a local style of weaving and dress that developed in the course of interaction between the two groups that is distinct from the Gia Rai-Ê Đê style to the south. Like the Gia Rai-Ê Đê style, it is also a style that is distinct from that of modern Chăm and one that may represent an older dress tradition.

Northern Bahnaric peoples with a history of contact with the Chăm include the Hrê (aka Davak) and Ba Na. The Hrê, have a long history of living in the western parts of Quảng Ngãi and Bình Định provinces and were sometimes referred to as Chăm Rê in the past.[142] The Ba Na at one time lived along the coast of Quảng Ngãi and Bình Định provinces, but now live only in the highlands to the south of the Hrê, mainly in Kon Tum Province, with some also found in western Quảng Ngãi and Bình Định provinces. Southern Bahnaric peoples with a history of contact with the Chăm include the Mnông, Cơ Ho, and Mạ. The Mnông live south of the Ê Đê in Đắk Lắk, Lâm Đồng, and Bình Phước provinces. The Cơ Ho and Mạ live south of the Mnông in Lâm Đồng Province and have a long history of contact with the Chăm and possibly with Fù Nán as well.[143]

Beyond men wearing loincloths and women wrap-around skirts, the weaving and dress traditions of the Southern Bahnaric Mnông, Cơ Ho, and Mạ are quite different in many details from those of neighboring Chamic peoples and probably reflect a distinct tradition with different roots. Nevertheless, there are some elements that do indicate Chamic or perhaps a common Đông Sơn influence, especially among those Bahnaric groups living closest to the Chamic groups. Thus, most Mnông, Cơ Ho, and Mạ men wear loincloths that are very different from those worn by the Gia Rai and Ê Đê. They are decorated differently and, although they often have a weft directional decorative band at the ends, they are narrower and decorated differently than Gia Rai and Ê Đê high status loincloths. However, the Eastern Mnông Gar, Rlâm, Kuênh, and Chil sub-groups that live in Đắk Lắk Province's Lắk, Krông Bông, and Krông Buk districts have many cultural elements similar to the neighboring Ê Đê, including styles of dress. High status men from these sub-groups often wear long-sleeved pullover shirts similar to those of the Ê Đê and women from these groups sometimes wear long wrap-around skirts similar to those of the Ê Đê rather than the normal shorter wrap-around skirt that is worn by women from other Mnông sub-groups.[144] The most common element of dress of Cơ Ho, and Mạ that appears to be indicative of Chăm influence are women's wrap-around skirts and especially the decorative weft directional bands at the ends of the skirts.[145]

Evidence of the textiles and dress of the Chăm from the Chămpa period comes primarily from Chinese written accounts. The earliest Chinese accounts are found in the *Liáng Shū* ("Book of Liáng"), which was completed in 635, and the *Suí Shū* ("Book of Suí"), which was completed in 636. Later accounts are found in such works as the *Jiù Táng Shū* ("Old Book of Táng"), which was completed in 945, and the *Xīn Táng Shū* ("New Book of Táng"), which was completed in 1060. Mǎ Duānlín's encyclopedia, *Wénxiàn Tōngkǎo*, published in 1317, is another later source. These were among the sources examined by Georges Maspero when compiling his *Le Royaume de Champa* in the early 20th century.[146] A few issues should be considered in relation

1. Ancient Clothing

to the Chinese sources. One is that they do not cover the earliest period of Chăm settlement and of Chămpa's founding and thus only describe the situation centuries after a Hinduized culture had become well entrenched. Another is that the Chinese providing these early accounts did not visit all of Chămpa and thus the accounts tend to focus on Chăm society in and around the capitals of Simhapura and Indrapura and the port of Đại Chiêm.

Mention should also be made of human figures that appear on ancient Chăm sculptures, carvings, and bronzes. Care needs to be taken when using these as evidence of early Chăm dress since many of them appear to be highly stylized Indian-influenced figures often copied from elsewhere that may not shed too much light on what Chăm people wore at the time. Both male and female figures generally are bare-breasted, often with necklaces or other jewelry worn around the neck and forearms. The lower body is covered with some sort of long skirt, sarong, or *sampot* (a rectangular wrap-around hip-cloth) with folds or pleats at the center of the front and sometimes pleating throughout. Some female figures are shown wearing a double skirt. There is no patterning visible on most of these garments, because of wear or because there were no patterns on the images to begin with. In the case of those that do depict patterns, there are a variety of geometric patterns, including rhombs and star shapes, as well as floral patterns (especially four-petal flowers).

The early Chinese sources mention that the Chăm grew mulberry trees to feed silkworms and that they also made kapok cloth from the silk cotton tree: "During its blossoming, its flowers are similar to goose feathers. They are emptied and spun to make cloth, which, if well cleaned and whitened, can scarcely be distinguished from cotton. It is dyed. They make cloth with five colors and speckled cloth with it."[147] While some accounts clearly refer to cloth being made from the silk cotton tree, others refer to cotton, especially in reference to the fine cotton clothing worn by royalty. Use of the term cotton certainly may refer to cloth made from *Gossypium* varieties of cotton in some instances, but the term is often used loosely and may sometimes refer to kapok. As for silk, there are few details about silk production in Chămpa in terms of where it was produced, methods of production, and types of silk produced. In addition, it is quite possible that at least some of the silk garments described as being worn by the king and other notables may have been made from imported silk.

Both the *Liáng Shū* and the *Suí Shū* describe common attire of men and women as consisting of "a piece of cotton ... which they wind around their body from right to left and covers it from the waist to the feet" and "a thick robe" during the winter.[148] Wearing a wrap-around skirt/hip-cloth and robe describes a style of dress that is generally like that of Chăm in modern times, but the details are too vague to provide a better idea of any particular similarities. Nor should use of the term cotton here be seen as necessarily referring to *Gossypium* varieties of cotton rather than kapok. Unfortunately, there is no indication of the color of the cloth that they wear or whether it is decorated or not. However, the *Liáng Shū* adds that a bride wears "a cotton robe made of strips of cloth assembled in the manner of a well grid."[149] Thus, at least on special occasions it appear as if women at least wear decorated clothing, even if the nature of such decoration is not clear; a "well grid" perhaps indicating some sort of checked pattern.

A good deal more attention is paid to the dress of the king and other nobles in early written sources. These sources mention that the king wore one type of attire when taking part in ceremonies and another when holding audiences. His dress for audiences included a robe that Maspero describes from a passage in the *Xīn Táng Shū* ("New Book of Táng") as being made of "very fine white cotton, sometime embroidered with braids or adorned with gold fringe."[150] Schafer's description of the royal dress based on the *Xīn Táng Shū* is somewhat different, and a little more precise: "The king's dress is of *bagtak* or *kārpasa* [cotton goods], draped slanting from his upper arm," adding "His wife is costumed in a short skirt of 'morning-cloud' pink *kārpasa*."[151] He also mentions that the king of Chămpa sent a mission to the Suí court in 630 and among the gifts for the emperor were "a many colored sash" and "'sunrise clouds' pink cotton."[152] For formal ceremonial occasions the king is described as wearing "a robe of damask with golden flowers on a black or green background" that is fastened by "links" made of "thin gold" and "adorned with pearls"[153] Around his waist on such occasions he is described as wearing "a gold belt enriched with precious stones."[154] These Chinese accounts also mention a royal "sarong formed by open crosspieces, with a gilded ribbon and lozenges connected by twists of black silk."[155]

In regards to the actual weaving, Maspero comments "The women wove silk and cotton; the cloth enclosed in the Treasury of the ancient kings show that the Cham had acquired great skills. They knew how to mix gold thread into the weft and weave, without wrong or right side out, a different pattern on each side."[156] The early Chinese accounts do not go into detail about the patterns found on royal clothing, but a later description of a royal *"sampot"* or "loincloth" [i.e. hip-cloth] says that it was decorated with "a wide series of parallel patterns in white and black

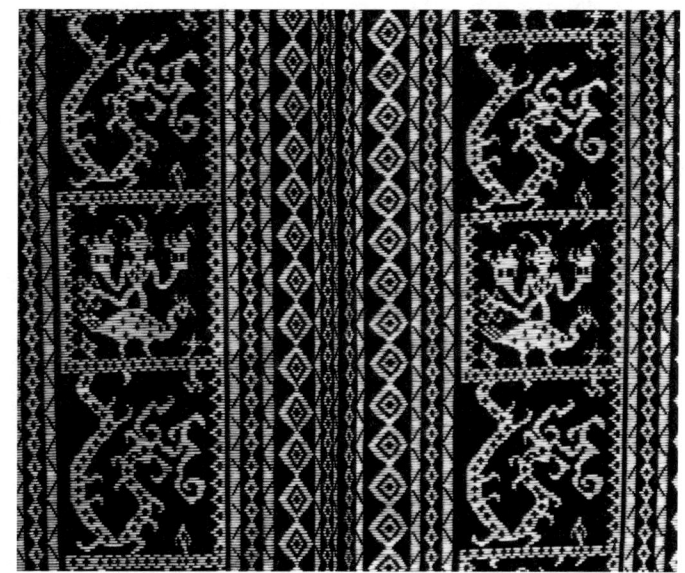

Detail of Chăm blanket showing dancing Śiva on peacock and dragon motifs woven using supplementary weft technique, Mỹ Nghiệp village, Ninh Phước District, Ninh Thuận Province.

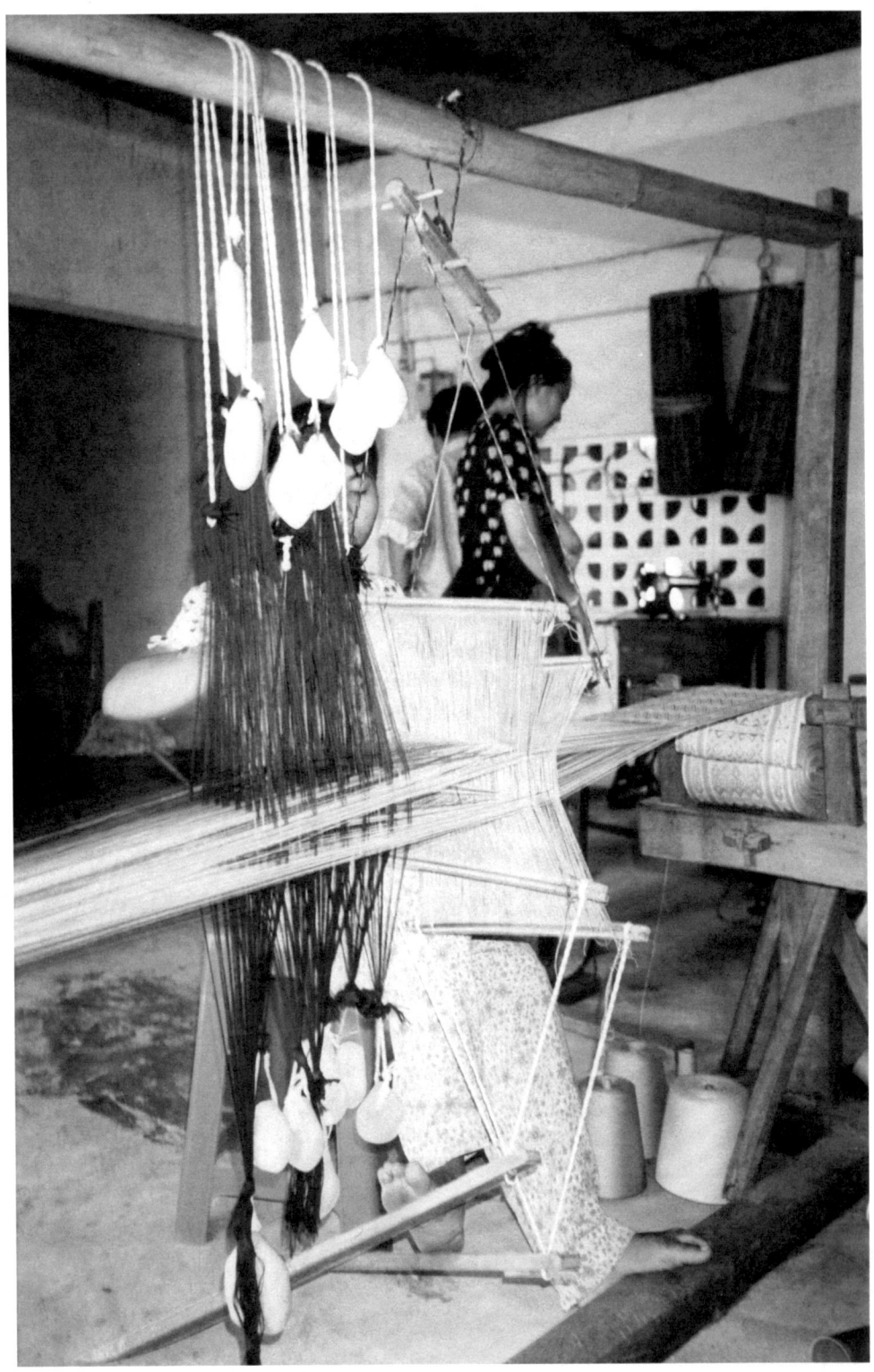

silk, filigreed with gold on a red background depicting *garuts* in dance or prayer postures and other fantastic animals."[157] Such decorations are described as being woven onto separate pieces of cloth that are attached to the garment.[158] What are called *"garuts"* in this passage may refer to Garuda, but it is more likely to refer to images of Śiva (Shiva), a popular figure in Chăm iconography and featured on existing royal textiles.

The type or types of looms that the ancient Chăm used are not described in the early Chinese texts and we are not fortunate enough to have any bronze or carved images of Chăm women weaving. Contemporary and recent historical evidence points to two types of loom having been used by the Chăm in the past. Most cloth is woven on what Vietnamese refer to as the Indonesian type of back-strap loom. It is possible that the ancient Malayo-Chamic people initially wove on a foot-braced back-strap loom, which is the type used by most Mon-Khmer groups in the Central Highlands, but there is no evidence of such a loom being used by any Chamic groups in Việt Nam to weave regular cloth. Highland Chamic groups and the modern Chăm use an Indonesian style back-strap loom. The Chăm weave wide pieces of cloth, such as plain white cotton cloth and decorative skirt cloth, on this type of loom. The narrow pieces of cloth that are used as sashes and to decorate the edges of fancy clothing are woven on a different type of loom, one that is unique to the Chăm, but similar to one employed by Balinese, who are also Hindu, to weave narrow strips of cloth.

This is a long and narrow frame loom called a *tano pa cako* or *tanung munim jih talah* in Cham. The distinctive characteristics of this type of loom include the use of weights that are attached to the bar and threads used to produce supplementary warp and supplementary weft patterns. While the Indonesian style back-strap loom is part of the common cultural heritage of all Chamic peoples and is likely to have been used by them in ancient times, the narrow frame loom is used only by the Chăm and thus, was probably developed later to produce decorative clothing for Hinduized elites (as in Bali).

Opposite: **Chăm woman weaving on a long and narrow frame loom called a *tano pa cako* or *tanung munim jih talah*, Mỹ Nghiệp village, Ninh Phước District, Ninh Thuận Province.**

2

Feudal Việt Nam

The period covered in this chapter begins with the end of Chinese rule in the north around 900 and the beginning of French rule during the latter half of the 1800s. During a good deal of this time Việt Nam was divided between Đại Việt, Chămpa, and the Khmer Empire as well as there being a good deal of highland territory that was under no central political control. From an ethnic and cultural perspective it is important to recognize that the Kinh population that had developed in Chinese controlled northern Việt Nam under the Táng Dynasty did not account for a majority of the population living within the territory occupied by modern Việt Nam until near the end of this period. The Kinh assumed their majority status largely as a result of Đại Việt's gradual conquest of Chămpa and the resultant decline of the Chăm population through death or assimilation. It is also important, as we shall see, to recognize the extent to which China continued to exert considerable cultural influence on Việt Nam throughout this period.

Đại Việt

The emergence of an independent Việt Nam, known for most of its history as Đại Việt, begins in the waning years of the Táng Dynasty, when the local military governor abandoned Tĩnh Hải *quân* (as the region was then known) in 880 and a local lord from Hải Dương (located with the metropolitan area of modern Hà Nội) named Khúc Thừa Dụ assumed the title of military governor and set about to rule it in effect as an autonomous territory. The Southern Hàn reestablished direct rule in 930, but in 938 Ngô Quyền, who had been born in the Ba Vì district (also in Hà Nội) the son of a Táng Dynasty official, defeated the Southern Hàn and proclaimed himself emperor and established his capital Cổ Loa the following year. After a period of considerable instability, another local named Đinh Bộ Lĩnh (aka Đinh Tiên Hoàng), from Hoa Lư in Ninh Bình Province, proclaimed himself emperor in 968. The Sòng invaded in 979, but Lê Hoàn from Ái Châu (modern Thanh Hóa Province) defeated the Sòng army and became emperor in 980, laying the groundwork for rule by the Early Lê Dynasty (980–1009).

The clothing of lowland northern Việt Nam during this period continued to reflect Chinese influence. This was related to a significant number of ethnic Chinese

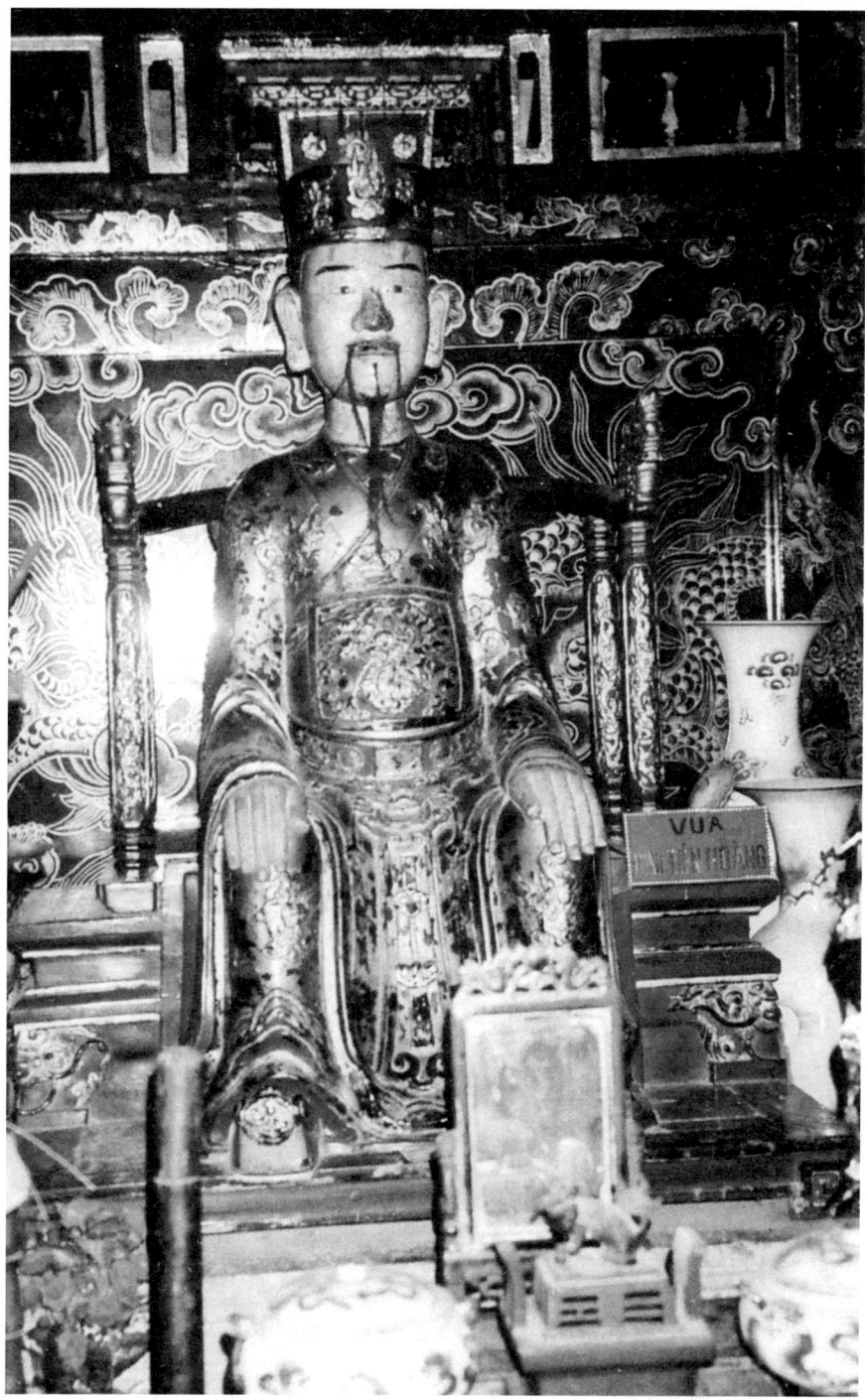

Statue of Đinh Bộ Lĩnh, Hoa Lư Citadel, Ninh Bình Province.

2. Feudal Việt Nam

having settled in the region under the Táng Dynasty, the acculturation of non-Chinese people under Táng rule, as well as clothing regulations for those working for the government. Even as Táng authority weakened the power of cultural perceptions that identified Chinese-style dress with civilization and high status remained strong not only among elites, but it also percolated downwards as something to be emulated, albeit in modified form. This meant that government officials dressed more or less in accordance with regulations such as those issued by Emperor Gaozu of Táng in 621 and Emperor Tàizōng in 630 that were discussed above. This included silk gowns with large sleeves in colors denoting rank for men performing government duties and an outer gown and long skirt for women with materials and colors also reflecting relative status. Commoners wore plain clothing that was usually made out of cotton. Commoner male attire included a hip-wrapper (often referred to as a loincloth) and sometimes a long-sleeved tunic or gown. Commoner women wore a long wrap-around skirt, breastcloth, and sometimes a long-sleeved gown or tunic. It is unclear when such dress came to be worn among Kinh commoners, but certainly by the time of the Táng Dynasty and possibly during the Six Dynasties Period.

The early rulers of Đại Việt may have been locally born, but this did not mean that their perceptions of appropriate dress were significantly different from that of the Chinese from the north. Thus, Ngô Quyền (r. 939–944) issued a decree regulating the color of clothing and many subsequent rulers issued similar decrees.[1] As in China, the color of clothing was an important marker of relative status in Đại Việt. While the precise colors worn by elites varied over time, basically elites wore colorful clothing, whereas common people wore either dark blue or brown clothing. As for materials, common people usually wore clothing made of rough cotton or lesser quality silk, while the elite mainly wore clothes made of fine silk or sometimes fine cotton. This is not to say that there were no differences between dress in early Đại Việt and China. Reminiscent of the account of Zhào Tuó going native in his style of dress, a Chinese description of the court of Lê Hoàn (r. 980–1005) mentions that the emperor sometimes wore only a loincloth with his chest and feet bare, as did many in his palace.[2] The precise meaning of loincloth in this instance is unclear. It might have been a narrow long strip of cloth wrapped around the waist with one end hanging over the loins, but it might also have been a rectangular piece of cloth wrapped around the waist and worn like a sarong and sometimes called a hip-wrapper. To the Chinese the implication was that Lê Hoàn and the other men in his court sometimes dressed like barbarians. Other differences between the Kinh and Chinese highlighted by the Chinese included women in Đại Việt often having dyed teeth as a result of chewing betel nut and men favoring tattoos on their bodies.

Đại Việt's emergence as a distinct feudal society took place under the Lý Dynasty (1009–1225). Its founder, Lý Thái Tổ (aka Lý Công Uẩn, r. 1009–28) moved the capital to Đại La in 1010, which he named Thăng Long (modern day Hà Nội) and undertook a number of reforms aimed at creating a new state, including creation of a new tax system that included a tax collected on mulberry trees on the royal estates surrounding his capital. Also of note, the Sòng court recognized Lý Thái Tổ's kingdom as a vassal rather than continuing to view it as an integral part of China.

In general the Chinese-style loose-fitting gown continued to be the main article of formal clothing worn by the nobility in Đại Việt during the time of the Lý Dynasty, although there were differences in length, width, style of sleeves and other details over time and according to rank. As in China, noble men also wore distinctive hats that served to mark their particular status, as well as other items to mark high status such as shoes with curved toes and socks, and fancy belts. Women usually wore a breastcloth and long wrap-around skirt underneath their gown.

Lý Thái Tông (aka Lý Phật Mã, r. 1028–54) issued a decree regulating official dress in 1029. The decree stated that those of the 5th rank and higher alone could wear clothing made of the highest grade of silk with brocade (*lụa gấm*) and only those of 9th grade and up could wear clothing made of satin (*lụa vóc*). Moreover, the silk that officials wore had to be domestically produced rather than imported form China.[3] Lý Thánh Tông (aka Lý Nhật Tôn, r. 1054–72), known for his promotion of Confucianism and the arts, created stricter rules for courtly in a decree issued in 1059.[4] He decreed that when a mandarin met with the king he had to wear an *áo bào tía* (purple gown), a four-corner/four-ear hat, socks, shoes with curved toes, and a belt made of leather. The decree also stated that soldiers meeting the emperor had to wear a long tunic with tight sleeves that reached to the knees underneath armor decorated with particular patterns, a hat that covered the ears, and curved shoes.

The family of Trần Thái Tông (aka Trần Cảnh), the founder of the Trần Dynasty (1225–1400), came from Fújiàn and settled in Nam Định, where they grew rich and powerful. The Chinese roots of the Trần rulers were apparent in the ability of many of them to speak Chinese. The dynasty is best known for having to confront three Mongol invasions in 1257, 1284, and 1287 and for its wars with Chămpa. Trần Thuận Tông (aka Trần Ngung, r. 1388–1398) was only a youth when he became the second to last emperor of the Trần Dynasty and the government was largely in the hands of advisors, including Hồ Quý Ly who became regent in 1399 (he had the capital moved to Tây Đô in Thanh Hóa Province). A decree was issued during his reign in 1395 assigning specific colors for the clothing of those serving in the government.[5] The color purple was reserved for those of the 1st rank, deep pink for the 2nd rank, light pink for the 3rd rank, dark green for the 4th and 5th ranks, grass green for the 6th and 7th ranks, blue for the 8th and 9th ranks, and servants were to wear white. Servants carrying the king's litter were to go bare-chested and wear only a plain white loincloth. Soldiers at court were to wear blue gowns with loose sleeves. Female commoners were not allowed to wear green, red, yellow, or purple clothing. In any event, most common people wore black or brown clothing. Particular types of headgear were also assigned to each rank. Male commoners at this time generally wore brown trousers and either went bare-chested or wore a black four-panel tunic with a round collar. Some people did, however, wear a silk scarf. Most common people went bare foot, but some wore leather shoes.

2. Feudal Việt Nam

Hồ Quý Ly seized power in 1400. The Hồ clan's ancestors had come from Zhèjiāng in the 900s during the relatively instable Five Dynasties and Ten Kingdoms Period and settled in Thanh Hóa Province (hence the move of the capital). Despite his ancestors coming from China, once in power Hồ Quý Ly's son Hồ Hán Thương (who assumed the throne in 1400 after his father abdicated) instituted wide-ranging reforms that included the promotion of local culture over Chinese culture. Hồ Hán Thương did not last long as emperor and in 1406 the Yǒnglè Emperor's army invaded and put an end to the Hồ Dynasty the following year, sending the former emperor into exile in Guǎngxī.

Míng rule of northern Việt Nam, which once again became a province of China, lasted roughly twenty years. The Míng instituted a policy of enforced Northernization (i.e., Sinification) that met with some success in the lowlands, but faced stiff opposition from northern highland groups such as the Mường and from the Kinh living to the south of the Red River area. Dress was included in the Northernization campaign and efforts were made to force people to change their style of dress. Both men and women were not to cut their hair. Women were supposed to wear a short blouse and long trousers in Míng style rather than skirts and to dress according to their rank under the Míng dress code. Female commoners were supposed to wear a loose blouse, long trousers (again, rather than skirts), a black silk scarf, and cloth or leather shoes. In particular they were not to expose their legs and they were not to wear yellow or purple clothing.

A revolt against the Míng that was eventually to prove successful broke out in Thanh Hóa Province in 1418 led by Lê Lợi (aka Lê Thái Tổ). Lê Lợi was supported by the Trịnh and Nguyễn lords and was able to defeat the Míng in 1427. Popular opposition to Míng rule included not only refusing to wear Míng style clothing, but some females used breastcloths (*yếm*), which were banned, as rebel banners. The breastcloth had become a common part of Kinh female dress over the centuries and by this time it was viewed as indigenous Vietnamese female attire both by the Kinh and the Míng.

Míng policies concerning dress in Việt Nam reflect policies that had been instituted several years earlier in China as the Míng sought to purge China of foreign influences associated with the Yuán Dynasty. The Liáo, Jīn, and Yuán dynasties were periods in which people from non-Hàn tribes (Khitan, Jurchen/Nuzhen, and Mongol) had dominated China. They adopted Chinese dress to some extent, but modified it to their own tastes (e.g., favoring tighter sleeves on gowns) as well as introducing elements of their own styles of dress.[6] The Míng abolished Yuán rules for dress and restored styles associated with the pre-tribal dynasties (e.g., Táng and Hàn). These styles of dress were codified in considerable detail in 1393 in the *Míng Hui Dian* ("The Collected Statutes of the Ming Dynasty").[7] Formal wear for officials included a wide-sleeved gown that fastened on the right in Hàn Dynasty tradition with the color and patterns of the gown reflecting a person's rank. They also introduced an embroidered square that was attached on the chest of the gowns designating the status and rank of the wearer, with different birds for each civil rank and different beasts for each military rank.[8] In addition there were regulations for commoners that included prohibitions on their wearing clothing decorated with gold embroidery and certain colors such as yellow.

Lê Lợi founded the Later Lê Dynasty (1428–1788) and came to be known as Lê Thái Tổ. Although courtly dress continued to resemble that of the Míng, the early Lê emperors saw to it that there were differences in order to create a distinct style of courtly dress.[9] In 1429 Lê Thái Tổ ordered high-ranking civil officials and military officers to wear a red gown. Lê Thái Tông (r, 1433–42) issued a decree concerning the type of hats to be worn by various officials in 1434.[10] Lê Thánh Tông (r. 1460–97) issued six additional dress regulations, starting with one in 1466 concerned with the colors of the silk gown worn by various officials: military and civil officials of the 1st to 3rd rank were to wear pink, 4th and 5th dark green, and others blue. He issued several other decrees dealing with minor items of dress.[11] Thus, in 1469 he decreed that high-ranking officers guarding the palace were to wear a particular type of red hat and in 1486 he issued another order that high-ranking officers were to wear a type of hat with wings like those of a dragonfly when meeting with the king.[12]

Lê Thánh Tông issued a more far-reaching decree in 1488 that overhauled courtly dress and also included regulations for commoners.[13] These regulations for courtly wear were quite detailed. Thus, the distance that the hems were to be from the ground and the width of sleeves of each type of gown was specified. There were also regulations for the type of dress to be worn on particular occasions, such as when meeting the Míng ambassador. Commoners were forbidden to wear yellow or gold colored clothing and curved shoes and could not wear clothing with the dragon or phoenix motifs. Popular motifs on elite clothing at this time included those known as the longevity motif, letter of the king's stamp motif, and auspicious wedding characters motif, as well as depictions of dragons and phoenix. Also, only monks were allowed to shave their heads.

Lê Hiến Tông (r. 1497–1504) in general followed his father's policies with some modifications. In regard to dress, in 1499 he issued a regulation requiring changes in the fabric of palace dress according to season (lighter silk in the hot season and heavier silk in the cold season).[14] In 1500 he modified official dress and included regulations concerning decorative patterns that were to be worn according to a person's rank.[15] Thus, those of the 3rd rank and above were to wear a purple gown with appropriate motifs according to their rank, military officers of the 4th and 5th rank to wear a particular type of white hat, and civil officers of the 4th and 5th rank to wear a particular type of hat and a blue over-gown fastened with a sash made of dark brown rough silk. Various types of silk were also specified according to rank and occasion.

Following Lê Hiến Tông's death the country entered a period of political turmoil. Mạc Đăng Dung seized power in 1527 and established the Mạc Dynasty. A civil war broke out in 1533, however, when the Trịnh and Nguyễn lords of Thanh Hóa Province who backed a new Lê ruler. The Mạc were forced out of the lowlands in 1592 and held out in the highlands east of the Red River in Cao Bằng and Lạng Sơn until 1677. The Mạc rulers instituted a wide range of economic reforms aimed at improving the economy, including promotion of craft production and foreign trade. The former included widespread expansion of silk production and the latter primarily development of the export market for raw silk and silk cloth, mainly to Japan.[16] These were important developments that had an impact on silk production in northern Việt Nam long after the Mạc were gone.

After the Mạc rulers were pushed into the highlands in 1592 the Lê Dynasty was restored to power. Although Lê emperors served as heads of the government in Thăng Long (Hà Nội) until 1789, actual power was largely in the hands of the Trịnh lords north of Ngang Pass and in the hands of the Nguyễn lords south of the pass. Thus, the Nguyễn lords ruled over the southern frontier occupying territory that formerly had been part of the kingdom of Chămpa and the Trịnh lords ruled over the Đại Việt heartland.

The post–1592 Lê emperors may not have wielded much power, but they were able to issue decrees about dress. In 1653, Lê Thần Tông (r. 1619–43, 1649–62) ordered that over-gowns of officials should be of different lengths and sleeves of widths according to rank.[17] In 1664, during the reign of the child-emperor Lê Huyền Tông (b. 1654, r. 1662–71), new regulations were issued concerning the type of cloth and size of sleeves for outer-gowns and specifying that gowns worn by common people must have narrower sleeves than those worn by officials.[18] The following year a decree was issued forbidding women to wear trousers and requiring them to wear a new style of skirt called a *váy thúng* (*thúng* being a type of basket). Essentially, trousers were seen as Chinese, while the *váy thúng* was viewed as national dress. Under Lê Dụ Tông (r. 1705–29) there were frequent debates about the details of official dress and new regulations were issued every few years. Decrees in 1714 and 1725 in particular dealt with the tailoring of over-gowns according to rank and other aspects of the dress of civil officials and military officers.[19]

During the 1600s and 1700s men in the countryside sometimes (especially when working) wore hip-wrappers and went bare-chested and at other times wore trousers and a shirt. Brown was the most common color. More formal male attire included a loose-fitting four-panel gown called *áo giao lãnh* (aka *áo giao lĩnh* or *áo đối lĩnh*). It opened down the front and was fastened on the side, had loose sleeves, slits down the sides, a round collar, and reached to the ankles. It was undecorated and usually dyed black. Men also often wore a headcloth, a tight-fitting skullcap, or a broad lotus leaf hat. Women usually wore skirts and a breastcloth (leaving their arms bare), although blouses and trousers were also worn. Skirts were white, dark blue, or brown and the breastcloths usually were white. Blouses were not common in the countryside. More formal female dress included a loose-fitting four-panel gown like those worn by men and also called *áo giao lãnh*, *áo giao lĩnh*, or *áo đối lĩnh*. They were usually worn with a sash around the waist. Such garments were undecorated and dyed dark blue, brown, or black and the sash was either white or the same color as the gown.

The Nguyễn lords played an important role in promoting the spread of Chinese-style clothing to central and southern Việt Nam. The Nguyễn presence in central Việt Nam began in 1558 when Nguyễn Hoàng was sent to serve as governor over the province of Ô Châu (roughly the former Chămpa province of Indrapura and the modern provinces of Quảng Bình, Thừa Thiên-Huế, and Quảng Nam). Small numbers of Kinh had been migrating beyond Hải Vân Pass into northern Chămpa since the early 1300s during the Trần Dynasty.[20] After the destruction of Vijaya in 1471 more Kinh settled in the northern part of Vijaya, especially in the vicinity of the Thu Bồn River in Quảng Nam Province. The numbers increased from the mid–1500s onwards as the Nguyễn lords asserted control over the area. They brought with them officers, soldiers, and craftsmen initially primarily from Thanh Hóa Province, but later Kinh migrated into Nguyễn territory (generally referred to as Đàng Trong) from the densely populated Red River Delta area as well.[21] A 1741 list of craftsmen in Hội An mentions "dye-workers" among the specialties.[22]

Ruling Đàng Trong from their citadel of Phú Xuân (modern Huế) from 1602 the Nguyễn lords gradually extended their control over all of the territory formerly ruled by the Chăm and Khmer in central and southern Việt Nam. Then, after defeating the Tây Sơn rebels, the Nguyễn lords led by Nguyễn Phúc Ánh (aka Gia Long) became rulers of all of Việt Nam in 1802. In addition to bringing Kinh people south into the newly conquered lands, the Nguyễn lords allowed Chinese refugees who fled south after the fall of the Míng Dynasty in 1644 to settle in the area, creating a Kinh society that was a blend of Kinh, Chinese, and Chăm and in various ways distinct from Kinh society in the north.

The Kinh and Chinese brought their own styles of dress with them to Đàng Trong and local styles of dress persisted despite pressures favoring assimilation. This situation began to change in 1739 when Nguyễn Phúc Khoát (r. 1738–65) proclaimed that people under his rule were to wear what in effect was Míng-style Chinese clothing.[23] The purpose of this proclamation was to have people dress differently than those living under the rival Trịnh lords. Accordingly, the Kinh gown and skirt with ties that was commonly worn in the north was to be replaced by trousers and a gown with Chinese-style fasteners. The new fashion included a four-panel gown that contemporary writer Lê Quý Đôn described as a *áo dài* (long blouse or tunic), but that was still loose fitting like *áo giao lãnh*.

Hội An re-emerged as a major trading port in the 1600s under the Nguyễns. It was an especially important port for Japanese traders, for whom it served as a major source of silk in particular.[24] The Chăm may have already produced silk in of Quảng Nam Province and silk production in the region increased markedly under the Nguyễns, now being largely in the hands of Kinh immigrants from the Red River Delta area. Raw silk was produced mainly in the coastal districts of Thăng Bình and Điện Bàn with commercial silk weaving being concentrated in Hội An. Silk exports to Japan from Hội An included yellow raw silk, spun silk fabric, and damask silk.[25] The term yellow silk refers to the color of the yarn as distinct from white silk. Silk worms in Việt Nam generally spun their cocoons in the hot summer months and the thread was a yellow color as a result. In contrast, Chinese silk worms usually spun their cocoons in the cooler winter months and the thread was white. The Japanese preferred white silk and it fetched a higher price, but the Chinese market was restricted at this time and access to the Japanese market was easier. One of the main reasons for the Nguyễn lord's promotion of silk exports was to allow them to purchase modern European weapons that could be used in their war with the Trịnh lords.[26]

The success of the Nguyễn lords in developing Hội An as a port and generating money to buy arms from the sale of silk prompted the rival Trịnh lords to try to do the same in the north.[27] As was mentioned above, silk production was already well developed in the Red River Delta region. Raw silk was produced in many areas and silk cloth was woven commercially in and around Thăng Long in state-owned factories that produced cloth for the court and to be sent as tribute to China. Now the Trịnh lords sought to increase production and to sell raw silk and silk cloth to foreign merchants for export to Japan. A temporary anchorage was established for merchant vessels at Doméa (in Tiên Lãng District, Hải Phòng City) in the early 1600s and merchants were allowed to reside in Thăng Long.[28] Japanese merchants were not particularly attracted by the prospect of obtaining silk from northern Việt Nam, preferring to stick to Hội An, where the Nguyễn lords had created a more favorable environment for foreign traders and the Japanese had a virtual monopoly on local silk and also had access to a wide range of other desirable local and regional goods like aloe wood (*Aguilaria malaccensis*).[29]

The Trịnh lords succeeded mainly in attracting merchants from other countries that had been able to gain only a smaller portion of the silk available through Hội An. These were mainly Chinese, but also Dutch and other Europeans. As for the types of silk exported from northern Việt Nam, they included yellow silk, spun silk fabric, damask silk, thin damask silk, and *ba xi* silk (described as "A kind of thin, hard-wearing woven silk, used for making trousers").[30] The number of Chinese living in Thăng Long (many of them engaged in the silk trade) increased after the fall of the Míng Dynasty to the point that in the 1660s the Lê began to place restrictions on them, including a regulation in 1666 ordering "that Chinese who wanted to live permanently in Tonkin had to register as a member of Vietnamese families and adopt Vietnamese customs which would involve changing their hairstyle, the way of dress, and the like."[31] This was a very different attitude towards the Chinese than the one espoused by the Nguyễn lords. Chinese merchants were forced out of Thăng Long altogether in the 1680s and only Dutch and English ones were allowed to remain, but by then the silk trade in northern Việt Nam was in sharp decline as a result of increasingly hostile attitude towards commerce by the Lê-Trịnh administration after the final defeat of the Mạc and competition from Bengali silk.[32] This did not mean that domestic production ceased in the north, only that it decreased and the focus was more on selling to the domestic market.

Chămpa

After the loss of northern territory to Đại Việt in 1069 Chămpa's capital was moved south to Vijaya. The port of Đại Chiêm in Quảng Nam Province was now under Đại Việt's control and Sri Boney in Bình Định Province (north of Quy Nhơn) became Chămpa's major port. Most foreigners living in Chămpa at this time (mainly traders) lived in Sri Boney.[33] The defeat and destruction of Vijaya in 1471 by Lê Thánh Tông effectively put an end to Chămpa's existence as a powerful and wealthy trading state.[34] Cù Mông Pass between Bình Định and Phú Yên provinces became Chămpa's northern border. Next Chămpa lost Kauthara to the Nguyễn lords, starting with Aya Ru (Phú Yên) in 1611 and then Aya Trang (Khanh Hòa) in 1653. Panduranga was all that remained of Chămpa, surviving as a poor, relatively isolated kingdom that became a protectorate of the Nguyễn lords in 1720 and then was abolished completely in 1832. The capital of Panduranga was located at Panrang (modern Phan Rang) and it served as the center of what remained of Chămpa's feudal society until 1832.

The gradual conquest by Đại Việt had an important cultural impact on central Việt Nam as the territory occupied by the Chăm decreased and the Chăm population dwindled as a result of war, slaughter by the Kinh conquerors, migration, and assimilation. Despite such demographic changes and the loss of the territory to Chămpa, this does not mean that there were no Chăm in what had formerly been the northern part of Chămpa. Thus, Wheeler argues that Chăm were the main inhabitants of the area south of the Thu Bồn River in Quảng Nam Province in 1500s and that there were still quite a few Chăm in Quảng Nam Province in the 1600s, even though Kinh migration into the area was starting to tip the demographic balance.[35] The remaining Chăm of Panduranga gradually became a minority in this region (that eventually became Ninh Thuận and Bình Thuận provinces) as a result of migration into the area by Kinh and Chinese. Chinese migration to southern Việt Nam increased after the fall of the Míng Dynasty in 1644, when many supporters of the Míng fled to Nguyễn territory where they were welcomed and settled across former Chăm and Khmer territory.

Mă Huān, the Muslim translator from Zhèjiāng who accompanied Admiral Zhèng Hé on three of his voyages, provides a brief account of Chămpa in 1413 that includes a description of the clothing worn by the people. He describes the king as wearing "a long robe of foreign cloth with small designs [worked in] threads of five colors, and round the lower part [of his body] a kerchief of colored silk and he has bare feet."[36] In a footnote, the translator of this passage, J.V.G. Mills, says that the Chinese term for this "kerchief" is Shou chin or "hand cloth" and compares it to "the Malay sarong."[37] Turning to the "chiefs" he says that they wear hats decorated with "gold and coloured ornamentation; [and] differences in [the hats denote] the gradations of rank" and that the "coloured robes which they wear are not more than knee-length, and round the lower part [of the body they wear] a multi-coloured kerchief of foreign cloth."[38] He adds, "As to the colour of their clothing: white clothes are forbidden, and only the king can wear them; for the populace, black, yellow, and purple coloured [clothes] are all allowed to be worn; [but] to wear white clothing is a capital offence."[39] As for the common people: "On the upper part [of the body] they wear a short sleeveless shirt, and round the lower part a coloured silk kerchief. All [go] bare-footed."[40] In regard to foreign cloth, he mentions that Chămpa imports "hemp-silk" and "silk-gauze" cloth from China,[41] the former in fact referring to cloth made of ramie and silk.

It is useful to look at documents relating to trade with Chămpa in the 1500s and 1600s to get an idea about the types of fabrics produced by and available to the Chăm after the fall of Vijaya. Tomé Pires mentions that Chămpa imported some "cloth from Bengal, large and small sinabafos, panchavilizes, and a few Kling cloths."[42] The passage refers to various types of Indian cotton cloth. Pires also mentions that "with the merchandise of the country and with the cloth produced in the country for their clothes they go to Siam and Cochin China,"[43] but he does not specify what type of cloth this is. A list of trade commodities from the 1600s mentions Chămpa exporting kapok, but not silk.[44] The Chăm certainly were producing silk cloth at this time, but it appears to have been mainly for domestic consumption. It is unclear whether they were producing raw silk or importing it from neighboring areas.

When the Buddhist Abbot Shilian Dashan visited the island of Cù lao Chàm near Hội An in 1695 the people that he encountered appear to have been Chăm and not Kinh (he refers to them as Man rather than as Yuè).[45] Shilian Dashan describes the men that he encountered as "naked and hair disheveled, with only a cloth for their fronts" and notes that they "blacken their teeth."[46] This does not fit with earlier Chinese descriptions of Chăm men wearing hip-wrappers, but could fit with Mă Huān's "kerchief" and is in keeping with the tradition of wearing loincloths among nearby highland peoples and, thus, might be a survival of this older dress tradition. It is important, however, to keep in mind that these were men working on an offshore island that Shilian Dashan encountered and their style of dress might not have reflected common Chăm dress style in Quảng Nam Province at the time. It is perhaps relevant to note that it was after the Nguyễn conquest of Aya Trang (Khanh Hòa Province) that the Hroi moved from the lowlands of Phú Yên Province into the adjacent highlands and Hroi men certainly do wear loincloths.

Mekong Delta Khmer and Chăm

Until the arrival of the Nguyễn lords in the late 1600s the history of the Mekong Delta region (*Đồng bằng Sông Cửu Long* in Vietnamese, Nine Dragons River Delta) is not well documented. Likewise, the composition of its population during this period is far from clear, beyond the fact that at various times it included Chăm and Khmer peoples. The Cham appear to have arrived in the area prior to the Khmer, but the extent of their presence is not known.

The Khmer are a Mon-Khmer speaking people whose ancestors migrated down the Mekong River and settled in the flatlands south of Laos in what today is Stung Treng Province in northern Cambodia. A number of small chieftanships had emerged here by the AD 400s and around 550 the area was unified as a larger kingdom called Chēnlà (aka Zhēnlà) by the Chinese that was a vassal of Fù Nán.[47] By the early 600s Chēnlà had become ascendant over Fù Nán and, thus over at least parts of the Mekong Delta. Around 707 Chēnlà itself divided into an inland realm in the west commonly known as Land Chēnlà and an eastern realm known as Water Chēnlà (aka Shuī Zhēnlà).[48] The identity of the people occupying Water Chēnlà is subject to debate. Khmer may have settled in the Mekong Delta at this time, but this is far from certain. There does appear, however, to have been cultural interaction between the Khmer and Chăm.

A new Khmer political entity emerged in Cambodia in 802 with the founding of the Khmer Empire (aka Kambujadesa) in Cambodia's Kampong Cham Province. The Khmer Empire expanded over the next couple of centuries and came to include the Mekong Delta. The extent of the Chăm presence beyond Đồng Nai Province during this early period is poorly understood. At some point there was a Chăm community called Baigaur located in the vicinity of modern Sài Gòn/Hồ Chí Minh City.[49] Under Khmer rule Baigaur became Prey Nokor (aka Kompong Krabei, Bến Nghé in Vietnamese),[50] which served as a minor trading center linked to international maritime commerce. Chămpa reasserted control over Baigaur/Prey Nakor in the late 1200s, but the history of the Khmer Empire's versus Chămpa's presence in the Mekong Delta region is unclear during this period. The power of the Khmer Empire came to an effective end with the sacking of Angkor by Siam in 1430. As Chămpa's own power declined the subsequent Khmer kingdoms eventually were able to reassert control over the Mekong Delta. After the founding of Oudon in 1601 Khmer polities were once again divided in a similar way as they had been during the time of Land Chēnlà and Water Chēnlà and there were two Khmer realms, that of the Mountain King in Oudon and that of the Water King in Prey Nokor.[51] By this time the population of the Mekong Delta region appear to have been composed primarily of Khmer (or at least people who have been assimilated and become Khmer). The descendants of these people are known as Khmer Krôm (aka Khơ Me Crôm). The region was gradually taken over by the Nguyễn lords, starting with Prey Nokor in 1698, and the remaining region in the 1750s to 1770s. Under the Nguyễn lords the demography of southern Việt Nam changed considerably as Kinh and Chinese migrants arrived and as local Khmer intermarried with these new settlers.

The Mekong Delta region under Khmer rule was far away from the center of power and relatively little is known about its population and their textiles and dress during this period. We are left having to assume that the Khmer living in the Mekong Delta region wove textiles and dressed more or less like other Khmer, minus the textiles and fashions associated with high-ranking elites.[52] Vickery cites records from the Chēnlà period that mention temples as being centers of weaving and that there were specialist weavers and spinners.[53] Types of cloth mentioned include a *canlek yugala* (double-length/width *yugala*) that was worn as a lower garment.[54] Vickery also points to the association of cloth-related terms used by the Khmer that are Malayo-Chamic in origin as "evidence of the ultimate foreign origin of this type of goods in pre–Angkor Cambodia."[55] One gets a sense that weaving was far less developed in Chēnlà at this time than was the case in Chămpa and that weaving and styles of dress were strongly influenced by the Chăm.

Our knowledge of Khmer textiles and dress during the era of the Khmer Empire comes primarily from two sources: human figures carved during the period and Zhōu Dáguān's account. Zhōu Dáguān visited the Cambodia 1296–7 as part of an official Chinese delegation sent by Temür Khan (aka Emperor Chéngzōng of Yuán).[56] Zhōu Dáguān arrived by sea first landing somewhere in the Mekong estuary and then travelled up-river to Angkor, where he spent most of his time. Thus, while he passed through the Mekong Delta region his account is based mainly on observations in and around Angkor.

According to Zhōu Dáguān, the Khmer only wove cloth made from the silk cotton tree (*Bombax ceiba* Linn., *Bombax malabaricum* DC.).[57] Local silk threads were obtained from Tai people that had settled in Khmer territory: "In recent years people from Siam have come to live in Cambodia, and unlike the locals they engage in silk production. The mulberry trees they grow and the silkworms they raise all come from Siam."[58] It appears that only the Tai wove silk cloth and Zhōu Dáguān states, "The only thing they [the local Khmer] can do is weave cotton from kapok." As for the nature of the silk cloth, he says they "weave the silk into clothes made of a black, patterned satiny silk."[59] His mention of black silk cloth is interesting since in modern times Tân Châu in An Giang Province, near Việt Nam's border with Cambodia, as was mentioned in the introduction, is famous for its black silk that is made using a dye from the fruit of the ebony tree *Diospyros mollis* fruit (mặc nưa, aka *mac leua*). This dye is widely used in Cambodia and neighboring parts of Southeast Asia for dyeing cotton and silk.[60] *Diospyros mun* A. Chev. ex Lecomte, another type of ebony tree, is also used for black dye in the region.[61] Zhōu Dáguān also mentions that the Khmer had hemp, but does not say that they used it to weave cloth.[62] He also indicates that the Khmer did not know how to spin thread, but only how to make kapok thread by using "their hands to gather the cloth into strands" (i.e., by hand splicing).[63] As for looms, he says that they used the Indonesian type of back-strap loom (like the Chăm): "they just wind one end of the cloth around their waist, hang the other end over a window, and use a bamboo tube as a shuttle."[64]

Zhōu Dáguān states that there are "many different grades of cloth," and in addition to that made domestically cloth is also imported from Siam, Chămpa, and from across "the Western Seas" (an unknown locale, but perhaps India).[65] He notes, the cloth imported from across the Western Seas "is often regarded as the best because it is so well-made and refined."[66] In his discussion of trade he notes that after gold and silver "Next they value items made of fine, double-threaded silk in various colors."[67]

Turning to styles of dress, Zhōu Dáguān says "From the king down, the men and women ... go naked to the waist, wrapped only in a cloth. When they are out and about they wind a larger piece of cloth over a small one."[68] He does not specify the type of material worn by particular classes of people, but a later account from the 1500s says "the nobles would wear silk or very fine cotton, while common folk wore coarse cotton" and this probably was true in Zhōu Dáguān's time as well.[69] Zhōu Dáguān does discuss dress restrictions associated with rank in terms of how textiles were decorated. He states, "Only the king can wear material with a full pattern of flowers on it.... Senior officials and relatives of the king can wear cloth with a scattered floral design, while junior officials and no others can wear cloth with a two-flower design. Among the ordinary people, only women can wear cloth with this design."[70] Some idea of what these patterns actually looked like will be discussed below in relation to carved human figures. Given that the Mekong Delta was a distant and not overly important frontier region of the empire, it is likely that the Khmer living there did not wear any of these fancier types of clothing and that most people wore a plain or at least fairly plain piece of kapok cloth wrapped around their waist.

Human figures carved in stone at Khmer sites help to flesh out our knowledge of the clothing that people wore, especially in regard to style of dress and decorative patterns. Such figures appear to be more useful in this regard than similar figure from Chămpa sites, but caution is still needed in interpreting images of dress on these figures as being entirely representative of what people actually wore. Green says that it is possible to identify "some fifteen distinct styles of hip-wrapper" on the Khmer figures and that over time the textiles are more decorated.[71] She argues that this is because "progressively more exotic fabrics had become available."[72] This is undoubtedly true, but it probably also reflects the presence of more skilled weavers coming to live in the empire who were able to produce more intricate types of cloth as well.

The earliest cloths depicted on carved Khmer figures have plain warp-directional stripes. Pleats appear in the 800s, but the cloth is still plain. These images are from the centuries prior to the Khmer Empire's height of power and wealth. Patterns begin to appear on textiles in the 1100s, once the empire had become more powerful and wealthy. The dominant pattern is the four-petal flower. Other patterns include intersecting circles, rhombuses with a dot in the center, and circles with radiating wavy lines. Some of these patterns, especially the intersecting circles (sometimes referred to as roundels), appear on Javanese, Indian, and Chinese textiles from the same period.

The dress and textiles of the Khmer Krôm during the feudal and early modern period is poorly documented. It can be assumed, however, that Khmer Krôm weaving and style of dress was more or less like that of Khmer living further to the west. That is, it consisted primarily of a relatively long piece of cloth wrapped around the hips and made of kapok, cotton, or silk. In his discussion about the products of Cochin China, which he treats as part of Cambodia, Tomé Pires says, "They have better, bigger and wider and finer taffeta of all kinds than there is anywhere else here.... They have the best raw silks in colours, which are in great abundance here, and all that they have in this way is fine and perfect."[73] Taffeta is an ambiguous term that might refer to silk, but could also refer to silk-like cloth. Unfortunately, he does not specify precisely where the taffeta and raw silk is made (i.e., in the Mekong Delta region, further inland in Cambodia, or elsewhere). However, the 1600s trade figures mentioned earlier for Đại Việt and Chămpa mention yellow silk, spun silk fabric, and damask silk as products exported from Cochin China and only cotton for Cambodia, indicating that at least by that time (and probably earlier) there was a significant silk industry in southern Việt Nam.[74] The silk industry within what is now Cambodia appears to be a relatively recent development. During the period of the Khmer Empire silk thread came primarily from what is now Thailand and southern Việt Nam and silk cloth was produced mainly by Siamese and, as will be discussed below, later Malay and Chăm living within the empire. In the case of southern Việt Nam within traditional Khmer territory sericulture is found in especially in Lương Hòa, Nguyệt Hòa, Cầu Ngang, and Trà Cú districts in Trà Vinh Province and in Dự Tâm district in An Giang Province and there are silk weaving centers in Tịnh Biên and Tri Tôn districts in An Giang province. Sericulture in some of these districts appears to date from before conquest by the Nguyễn lords of the area and subsequent arrival of Kinh and Chinese and to have been carried out by Khmer, but the silk industries that exist in this region at present are largely modern developments associated with Kinh and Chinese migration to the area.

The Nguyễn conquest of Kauthara in the 1600s also led to increased conversion of Chăm to Islam and some of the Muslim Chăm migrated to Cambodia after the king of Cambodia Ramadhipati I (aka Ramathibodey, r. 1642–59) married a Muslim woman, converted to Islam, and adopted the name Ibrahim. Even before this time, as was mentioned in the previous chapter, there was a long history of Chăm traders taking up residence abroad in a variety of trading centers. Initially such traders were Hindus, but by the 1400s most of them were Muslims. The Chăm Muslim refugees of the 1600s to some extent followed in the path of these expatriate merchants. There was another flight of Chăm Muslims to Cambodia and other locales after 1832. In Cambodia they settled primarily along the Mekong and Tonlé Sap rivers. This group is significant here because some of them subsequently returned to Việt Nam in the late 19th century, settling in An Giang and Tây Ninh provinces, especially around Châu Đốc.

There was an important addition to Khmer fashion and the textile repertoire during the reign of Ramadhipati I.[75] The king employed Chăm weavers in his court to produce large weft ikat patterned silk textiles for the court. This type of textile, known as a *sampot hol,* was similar to textiles woven in Sumatra, the Malay Peninsula, and southern Thailand, and was probably introduced from there, with local modifications especially in regards to motifs. Weaving and wearing this style of textile later spread from the palace into the countryside, where the Chăm featured prominently among those weaving such silk textiles. Away from the royal court the Chăm in Cambodia produced textiles for domestic use as well as for the wider Cambodian market.

The early history of such market production (i.e., prior to French rule) is not well understood, but as landless refugees the Chăm found that they often had to take up non-agricultural occupations to support themselves and this included Chăm men working as sailors and fishermen and women as weavers.[76]

As the Muslim Chăm who came to Cambodia as refugees mixed with local Malays and other Muslims and settled into their new life in Cambodia they developed a culture that was increasingly different from that of the Chăm back in Việt Nam. The blending of Malay and Chăm cultures resulted in it becoming common in Cambodia to refer to the two peoples collectively as Chăm-Malay. Linguists refer to the Cambodian Chăm as Western Chăm and those in coastal Việt Nam as Eastern Chăm. While the dress of the Western Chăm was still like that of the Eastern Chăm in general features, differences in the details gradually emerged. Muslim Chăm males in Cambodia generally wore a hip-wrapper or sarong that was made of cotton, but on special occasions they sometimes wore ones made of mixed cotton and silk. They also adopted the Malay fashion of wearing sarongs with checked patterning and sometimes with warp ikat patterns as well. Over the hip-cloth or sarong they might wear a typical Chăm gown. Women generally wore a skirt made of cotton cloth, but sometimes of silk. The silk skirts were either plain or decorated with patterns that included motifs that were popular in Cambodia such as a yellow/gold colored supplementary weft eight-pointed figure inside a rhomb, said to depict a type of fruit, and a variety of weft ikat motifs. In addition, although many Chăm women continued to weave on an Indonesian-style back-strap loom, gradually a variety of Malay-style frame loom became more popular. When some Western Chăm migrated to the Châu Đốc area in the 19th century they brought these new weaving and dress styles with them.

3

Modern Việt Nam

The history of modern Việt Nam can be divided roughly into three periods: Nguyễn Dynasty, French Colonial, and Independent. Each of these can be characterized by very different fashion trends shaped in part by prevailing attitudes towards the outside world. The Nguyễn rulers favored many aspects of Chinese culture and were cautious to outright hostile towards Western culture and this was reflected in dress during this period. The French promoted the values of Western civilization, but also were keen to keep a distance between the rulers and the ruled and thus promoted Western-oriented modernity in Việt Nam only up to a point and generally were content for most Vietnamese to retain traditions. Thus, while some Vietnamese adopted Western style dress under French rule, most continued to dress more or less as they had under the Nguyễn Dynasty. A big difference, however, was in what clothing was made of since industrially produced cloth and thread became much more readily available to almost everyone. With independence most aspects of the old feudal order was swept away. Although modernity has taken an increasingly strong hold on Vietnamese life since the 1950s many traditions have been maintained and some even revived. Again, this can be seen in dress where, although Western-inspired modern dress is widely worn now, new versions of older styles of dress are still popular and some are even gaining in popularity.

Nguyễn Dynasty

Shortly after Nguyễn Phúc Ánh unified Đại Việt and proclaimed himself Emperor Gia Long (r. 1802–20) in 1802 he moved national capital from Bắc Thành ("Northern Citadel"), as Hà Nội was then known, to Huế and changed the name of Bắc Thành back to the older Thăng Long ("Soaring Dragon"). Two years later, in 1804, he changed the name of the country to Việt Nam. Gia Long had been supported by a variety of foreigners in his bid to gain the throne and once in power was relatively open to foreign activities, especially during the early years of his reign. Mgr. Pierre Joseph Georges Pigneau (d. 1799) had been appointed Apostolic Vicar of Cochin China in 1774 and was a major force behind Nguyễn Phúc Ánh's successful campaign.[1] In addition, his army and navy included an assortment of foreigners form other Asian countries as well as about fourteen to fifteen "European adventurers" from France, England, and Ireland.[2]

Some of these "adventurers," such as Olivier de Puymanel (aka Nguyễn Văn Tín) who helped to train the army and oversaw building fortifications and Jean Baptiste Marie Dayot (aka Nguyễn Văn Trí) who commanded the navy, left once the fighting was over. Others, however, such as Philippe Vannier (aka Nguyễn Văn Chấn) and Jean-Baptiste Chaigneau (aka Nguyễn Văn Thắng) remained in Việt Nam after Gia Long became emperor. They married into prominent Catholic Vietnamese mandarin families, became mandarins themselves, and developed something of a bi-cultural lifestyle.[3] There is a portrait of Chaigneau wearing a military uniform consisting of a European-style blue jacket worn over Vietnamese military dress.[4] Crawfurd met both Vannier and Chaigneau during his visit to Việt Nam and noted that although they and other foreigners dressed like Vietnamese, the meal that he had at Chaigneau's home was "entirely French."[5]

The French and Chinese were the main beneficiaries of Gia Long's openness, the Chinese primarily in commerce and the French mainly as Catholic missionaries. Chinese merchants and traders were scattered throughout Việt Nam. Not only was maritime trade mainly in the hands of Chinese, even domestic trade was "almost exclusively in the hands of the Chinese residents."[6] There was an especially large concentration of them living at Faifo (Hội An), which John Crawfurd referred to it as "one of the principal seats of Chinese commerce."[7] As for the French, French and Spanish Catholic missionaries were allowed to operate almost freely in Việt Nam during Gia Long's reign. There were dozens of them in the country and over 300,000 converts, especially in northern Việt Nam.

During official events Emperor Gia Long wore a sky-blue colored dragon gown (*áo long cổn*) made of satin.[8] The body of the gown was decorated with embroidered motifs depicting a dragon, the sun, moon, stars, clouds, and water and waves. The sleeves were decorated with embroidered dragons. Underneath he wore a white shirt that was also decorated with embroidered dragons and clouds and a hip-wrapper (*xiêm*) made of gold colored satin with an embroidered hem. Courtly inspired fashion included various styles of five-paneled gowns (*áo ngũ thân*), which were loose fitting and featured wide sleeves. Prior to issuing a comprehensive new legal code (the *Bộ luật Gia Long*) in 1815 that was modeled on the legal code of the Qīng Dynasty in China, Gia Long issued an edict in 1806 establishing different styles of dress for civil officials and military officers that also drew heavily on practices in China.[9] It specified what was to be worn by civil officials and military officers depending on their rank and whether attending great ceremonies or normal ceremonies. There were distinctive hats, gowns, and hip-wrappers. Particular colors and decorative motifs were assigned to the gowns.

For great ceremonies civil officials of the 1st rank wore purple over-gowns (*áo ngũ thân*), while the lower ranks wore dark green and dark blue over-gowns. For normal ceremonies those of the 1st to 3rd rank wore blue, dark blue, and black gowns that were embroidered with flowers and had a white collar. Civil officers of the 4th to 6th rank wore an over-gown made of blue, dark green, and navy blue gauze. The gowns of civil officers of the 7th to 9th rank was similar, but with different embellishments. The color of the hip-wrapper (*xiêm*) worn by civil officers was flexible, though dark green was popular, and they were decorated with embroidery that commonly included images of birds (including herons) and flowers.

For great ceremonies, military officers of the 1st rank also wore gowns that were purple, while those of the lower ranks wore ones that were blue, dark blue, and dark green. They wore a hip-wrapper that was embroidered with images of various animal figures. For normal ceremonies military officers of the 1st to 3rd rank wore gowns that were blue, dark green, and dark blue and made of gauze and rough silk. These gowns also had white collars. The gowns of military officers of the 4th to 9th ranks were the same, but they wore different styles of hat. When not taking part in ceremonies high ranking military officers and soldiers in service to the king wore a gown that opened down the front, a white sash, trousers, and leggings. Ordinary soldiers wore brown gowns or shorter yellow or yellow-brown shirts that opened in the front and had narrow sleeves and high standing collars. They also wore blue or red hip-wrappers with sashes of matching colors.

Emperor Minh Mạng (aka Nguyễn Phúc Đảm, Nguyễn Phúc Kiểu, r. 1820–41) was a capable administrator who was also a Confucianist traditionalist and hostile to Christians. Even though he banned Christian missionaries from entering the country in 1825 and was generally hostile to Christians, foreign missionary activity did not cease during his reign. One interesting outcome of this hostility was that it sparked interest by the Bishop of Quy Nhơn in establishing a mission in the highlands away from the control of the Nguyễn government.[10] After some unsuccessful attempts in the 1840s, a mission was established successfully at Kon Tum in Ba Na territory in the 1850s. The Nguyễns had in fact sought to increase their influence in the highlands since the 1700s, but little had come of this beyond a

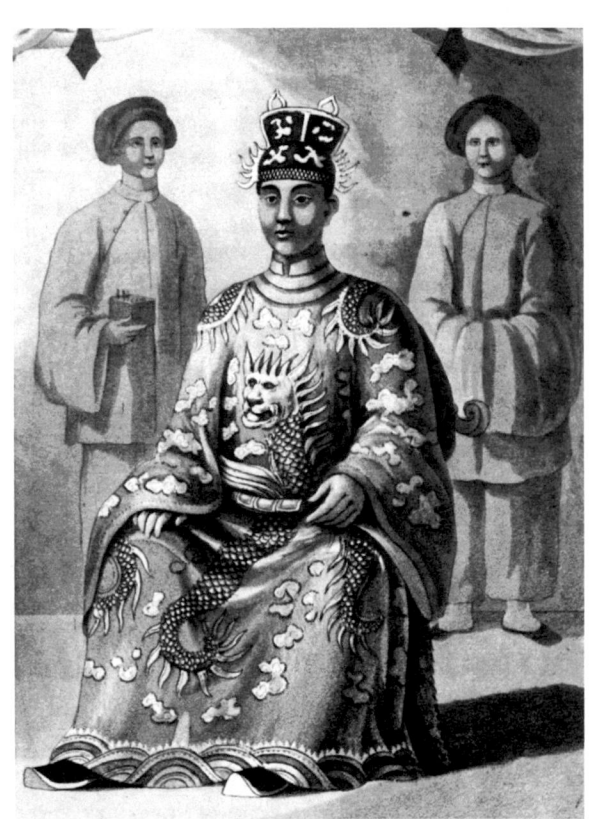

Drawing of Emperor Minh Mạng (from Crawfurd, *Journal of an Embassy to the Courts of Siam and Cochin-China*).

growing presence of Kinh traders in the highlands. Shortly after Minh Mạng was crowned in 1820 diplomatic relations were established between the Nguyễn court and the Gia Rai *P'tau Ia* ("King of Water"), who sent tribute and gifts to the emperor. Minh Mạng reciprocated in 1831 with gifts that included pieces of cloth.[11] Minh Mạng's antipathy to Christians and desire to curtail their activities carried over to the realm of foreign trade and in 1835 he issued an edict requiring European vessels to land and carry out trade at Cửa Hàn ("Hàn Port," aka Turon, Tourane, Đà Nẵng).

The Governor-General of India, Francis Edward Rawdon, Marquess of Hastings, sent John Crawfurd to visit Siam and Việt Nam in 1821. Crawfurd arrived in Việt Nam the following year and the account of his visit provides a good description of dress styles in the country at that time. He describes the common dress of most people as follows:

> The dress of both sexes is becoming,—and the same as the old costume of China, before the Chinese were compelled to adopt the fantastic one of their Tartar conquerors. Both sexes dress nearly alike. For the lower part of the body, the covering consists of a pair of loose trowsers, secured at the waist by a sash. The main portion of the dress consists of two or more loose frocks, reaching half-way down the thigh. This, for such matters as among other Eastern people is uniform and constant, overlaps to the right side, and is secured by five buttons and as many loops. Its sleeves are loose, and with persons not compelled to labour, they dangle a foot, or even a foot and a half, beyond the extremities of the fingers; but the lower orders, from necessity, wear them short....
>
> With the women, the inner frock reaches below the knee, and the outer down to the ankles. When Cochin Chinese is in full dress, as when he makes visits, or is engaged in the performance of religious rites, he always wears over the frock now mentioned a loose silk gown reaching to the ankles.... Both sexes wear turbans.... The form of this article of dress, which is always determinate, distinguishes the civil from the military order of public officers. The

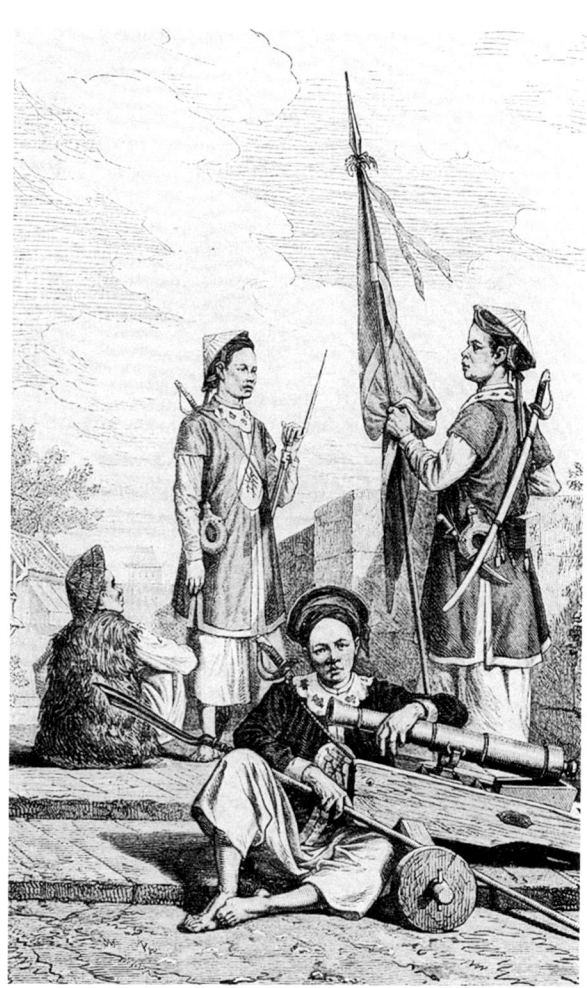

Drawing of Nguyễn Dynasty soldiers (from Jules Michel Brossard de Corbigny, "Une Ambassade Française à Hué en 1874," *Le Tour du Monde*, 35, 1878, 33–64).

lower orders, except when dressed, seldom wear these turbans. When abroad, both sexes wear varnished straw hats, little less than two feet in diameter, tied under the chin....

Men of all ranks, and women above the laboring class, always carry about them a pair of silken bags, or purses, strung together, and usually carried in the hand, or thrown over their shoulders. These are intended to carry betel, tobacco, and money. Women of the laboring class are forbidden to carry these; and men of the same order, when they meet a person of condition, must take them off their shoulders and conceal them as a mark of respect. These purses are generally of blue satin, and with the better classes often richly embroidered.[12]

He briefly describes the dress of court officials: "The Mandarins wore a cap and a peculiar uniform, and on a square piece of silk, on the breast of their gown, was embroidered the badge of their order. That of the military chief was a boar, and of the man of letters a stork."[13] His description is of *áo gấm* decorated with rank badges.

Crawfurd also describes the materials used to make their clothing:

The materials of dress consist of silk or cotton; the first being of more frequent use than I have observed in any other country. The inner frock is cotton of domestic manufacture, always unbleached; for, literally, there is not a rag of white linen in the kingdom. The outer frocks and gown, with the better ranks, are always of silk, or flowered gauze; and the latter is commonly Chinese manufacture. The trowsers, with the same class, are either plain silk, or crape of domestic fabric. The turban is crape, always black or blue, but most frequently the former; and is also a home fabric.... The lower orders are generally clad in cotton; but even among them, silk is not unfrequently seen.... At home, they wear their foul cotton shirts; and when they go abroad, without changing them, they clap over them their fine silk robes.[14]

Crawfurd's description of cotton production in Việt Nam was included in the introduction. He also comments, "They manufacture no fine cotton fabric, nor any thing indeed approaching to it, and they appear ignorant of the art of calico printing in any form."[15] As for silk, he remarks, "The art which they have carried to the greatest extent, is that of rearing silk-worm and weaving silk; but both the raw silk of Cochin China and its silk fabrics are of very inferior quality to those of China."[16]

As for colors, "Cloths, indeed, of a variety of colours, are not used in the dress of people, and are generally repugnant to their tastes" and "Their cotton dress is very generally dyed of a dark brown color, as if tanned. This colour is given to it by a tuberous root."[17] He adds, "The royal colour is yellow, or rather orange. The King's own standard is of this colour, but the national flag is white. Cloth, figured with an emblematic dragon, can only be worn by the highest class. White is considered mourning, and cotton only is used under such circumstances."[18]

He gives the following description of military uniforms:

The dress is the most liberal part of the military organization. The most essential portion of it consists of a loose convenient frock of strong English scarlet broadcloth, which reaches down to the knee. The head-dress is a small conical cap of basket-work, lackered over, ornamented at the peak with a plume of cocks' feathers, and tied under the chin.... The dress of the lower part of the body consists of a pair of loose drawers, reaching to below the knee.... The officers wear no uniform, but are clad in the ordinary dress of the country; consisting of loose silk robes, trowsers, and turbans.[19]

Prior to Gia Long's assuming the throne and during the early years of his reign uniforms had been more varied and were often made of locally manufactured cloth, but once the country became more stable and trade picked up uniforms became more standardized and imported cloth more widely used.

The mention of broadcloth above draws attention to the growing importance of imported cloth in Việt Nam. Most cloth was still domestically produced, but there was a growing market for particular types of imported cloth in the early 19th century. The English broadcloth that Crawfurd refers to was a dense wool fabric woven by the industrial mills of England. Chinese junks mainly from Guǎngzhōu picked it up in the British trading entrepôts along the Strait of Malacca. These same junks also picked up types of cotton fabrics that were not made in Việt Nam such as calico prints. Among the export items that they carried from the ports of Việt Nam was cotton and raw silk.[20] Chinese silk cloth was imported to Việt Nam primarily on junks sailing from Xiàmén (aka Amoy).

Crawfurd makes an interesting observation about the style of dress of foreigners living in Việt Nam at this time (mainly Chinese, but also a few Europeans and other Asians). He says, "Both the gentlemen and ladies dress in the Cochin Chinese fashion—a compliance with the customs of the country, indispensible to every stranger who takes up permanent residence in it. Even the Chinese, who are not very tractable in matters of this nature, are obliged to submit to it; for such is the vanity of the people, that the dress of a stranger, of whatever country, is considered by them as nothing less that ridiculous, and is sure to attract so much curiosity as to prove very inconvenient."[21] This would not have been much of a hardship for the Chinese since their typical dress was not much different from that of the Vietnamese, but for many others it meant adopting very different styles of dress than that they were accustomed to wearing.

Crawfurd describes Vietnamese women as wearing trousers. In fact, not all women did so at this time. This prompted Minh Mạng to issue a decree in 1828 yet again forbidding women to wear skirts and telling them to wear trousers.[22] Outside of the court the decree was not popular and even led to satirical poems. Such decrees and people's resistance to them meant that while some women wore trousers others wore skirts. In addition, while many women continued to wear breastcloths, some wore blouses. In general skirts and breastcloths were more popular in the north and trousers and blouses in the south where Nguyễn influence was stronger. As noted by Crawfurd, both men and women also wore robes/over-gowns. These were either four-panel or five-panel gowns. Men's gowns were called *áo the* and they were relatively loose fitting. Especially on formal occasions they were worn with a headcloth called *khăn đóng* (Crawfurd's "turban"). Women in the countryside and poorer women in towns wore a four-panel *áo tứ thân*, its two front panels being left loose and tied together when working and its back two panels made of narrower cloth and sewn together. The *áo tứ thân* was tighter and shorter than the older style of *áo giao lãnh*, which was still sometimes worn, especially at ceremonies and when preying. More affluent women living in towns usually wore a *áo ngũ thân*, with the two front panels sewn together, the two back panels sewn together, and an additional piece of cloth sewn inside the front panels as a petticoat/lining. The *áo ngũ thân* was stiffer and less suitable than the *áo tứ thân* for someone doing manual labor.

Subsequent Nguyễn rulers of independent Việt Nam essentially maintained Minh Mạng's domestic policies as well as those towards the outside world. They continued to persecute Christians and generally sought to restrict European influence, while looking more favorably upon cultural and commercial relations with China. There were few changes in dress in Việt Nam during this time. Vietnamese society was largely closed and inward looking. Virtually the only ones who had contact with the outside world and non-Vietnamese were resident ethnic Chinese merchants and a small number of Kinh Catholics. The Nguyễn Dynasty made no significant effort to modernize the country, economically or culturally. There were a few individuals that advocated such initiatives, but such suggestions were not received well and Việt Nam experienced nothing like China's Self-Strengthening Movement during the 19th century and had no rulers such as Siam's King Mongkut and King Chulalongkorn.

One change during latter part of Nguyễn rule in northern Việt Nam was a general decline in domestic silk and cotton production largely as a result of the considerable instability experienced in the area. This was related in large part to unsettled conditions in southern China that spilled over into Việt Nam, especially after the Black Flag army (*Quân cờ đen* in Vietnamese) moved into northern Việt Nam in 1865. As was noted earlier, these unsettled conditions also led to migration of people from several ethnic groups from southern China to northern Việt Nam from the time of the Nanlong Rebellion in Guìzhōu in 1797 onward.

French Colonial Period

The French conquest of Việt Nam took place in two stages, beginning with the conquest of southern Việt Nam between 1859 and 1867 and the founding of the colony of Cochin China (*Cochinchine* in French) in 1864. This was followed by the conquest of Annam and Tonkin in the early 1880s, culminating in a peace treaty in 1884 that established French rule over all of Việt Nam. The French administered Việt Nam as three distinct states within French Indochina (*Indochine française* in French): Tonkin, Annam, and Cochin China. Sài Gòn was the capital of French Indochina until 1902, when it was moved to Hà Nội.

Though it no longer governed the country, the French allowed the Nguyễn court to survive along with many parts of its feudal system since it did not interfere with the aims of the colonial state and was in fact viewed as helping to provide a degree of stability through a system of indirect rule. There was still an emperor and his court based in Huế, though he had little power, as well as mandarins scattered throughout Kinh society that continued to play a role in local administration. While his actions had to be approved by the colonial administration, so long as his actions did not interfere with the running of the colonial state, the emperor was "the supreme head of native affairs."[23] Surrounding the emperor in Huế was a ministerial council, another council made up of members of the royal family, and a variety of other entities such as the *Khâm thiên Giám* ("Astronomical Observatory") that was responsible for establishing the annual calendar for rites and other events dictated by astrological observations. Beyond the palace there was an array of civil and military officials drawn from the mandrinate that was still divided into nine ranks to look after native administration. However, the influence of the Nguyễn court over native affairs was strongest in Annam and weakest in Cochin China. Having been under French rule prior to Huế being conquered, the court had relatively little influence in Cochin China. The role of the court was reduced in Tonkin in 1897 and, although native administration was in the hands of mandarins, the French Resident appointed them.[24]

French colonialism led to a greater openness of Vietnamese society to the outside world and to the spread of modernity in Việt Nam in general, but both were limited in various ways by the structure of French colonial society. During the period of French rule there was an unprecedented growth of urbanization, creation of new educational institutions, significant conversion to Christianity, and economic changes in agriculture and industry as well as in trade relations. French rule also changed the ethnic composition of the country, especially with the creation of a new European elite and by encouraging higher levels of Chinese immigration than in the past.

Turning first to the ethnic composition of Việt Nam under French colonial rule, by the time that the French seized the country decades of Nguyễn rule had greatly reduced the number of people identified as members of ethnic minorities in the lowlands (mainly Chăm and Khmer) and the Kinh had become an overwhelming majority throughout the lowlands. In 1936–7 there were 16,461,000 Kinh out of a total population of 18,972,000 people in the three states that comprised French-ruled Việt Nam, or 86.76 percent of the population.[25] The Khmer and Chăm populations had begun to recover under French rule, but by the late 1930s there were still only 326,000 Khmer and 31,000 Chăm living in southern Việt Nam.[26]

The most significant change in the ethnic composition of Việt Nam under French rule was the arrival of large numbers of Chinese, primarily from the coastal regions of Fújiàn southward and including Hak-kâ, Cantonese (Yuè), Hokkien (Hok-kiàn, Fújiàn huà), Teochew (Cháozhōu, Cháozhōurén), and Hǎinánese. The French saw the Chinese as hardworking people who could help with the development of the colony as well as being useful intermediaries with the Kinh. As for the Chinese immigrants they were motivated by the relative stability of French Indochina compared with the numerous problems in China. The number of Chinese in Indochina reached 293,000 by 1912 and over the next couple of decades the number continued to grow, peaking at 419,000 in 1931 and then declining to 326,000 in 1936 as many returned to China because of the economic downturn in French Indochina brought on by the depression.[27] The majority of these Chinese settled in Cochin China and Cambodia rather then further north. Thus, in 1936 there were 171,000 Chinese in Cochin China,

3. Modern Việt Nam

106,000 in Cambodia, and only 35,000 in Tonkin, 11,000 in Annam, and 3,000 in Laos.[28] While many of these Chinese lived apart from the Kinh, forming a distinct ethnic group referred to as Hoa, there was considerable mixture. Such mixture reflected the fact that many of the migrants were men. While some of these men eventually brought brides form China others married local Kinh woman. This mixed group numbered around 62,000 in Cochin China, and 11,000 in Tonkin.[29]

Rather than assimilation, French colonial policy favored keeping ethnic groups apart and distinct. The French created what essentially were two separate administrations in Việt Nam, one for the French and another for the natives, the Kinh in particular. This separation was codified in the 1931 Civil Code of Tonkin, which was applied to Annam in 1936. Accordingly, the French colonial administration sought "not to encroach in any way on the fundamental institutions of Vietnamese society."[30] The French had veto power over any actions taken by native administrators, but this was rarely an issue. The fundamental elements of Kinh society such as those pertaining to family, clan, and commune were left largely intact and the villages and communes retained considerable autonomy. There were native schools that employed a

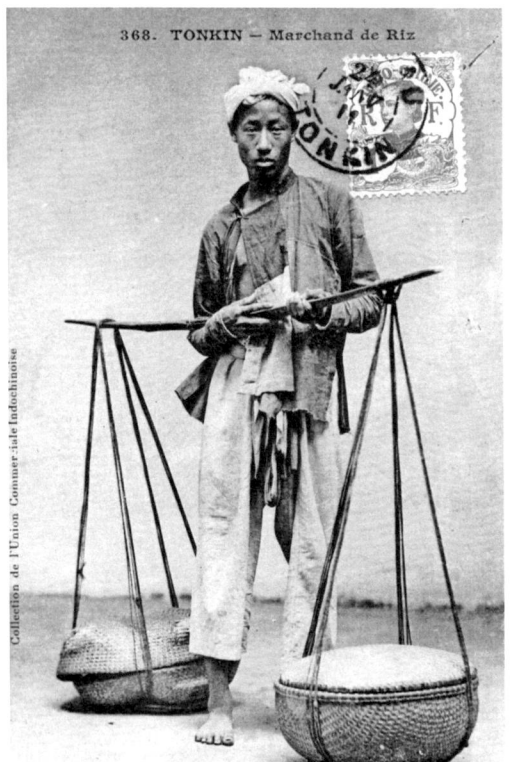 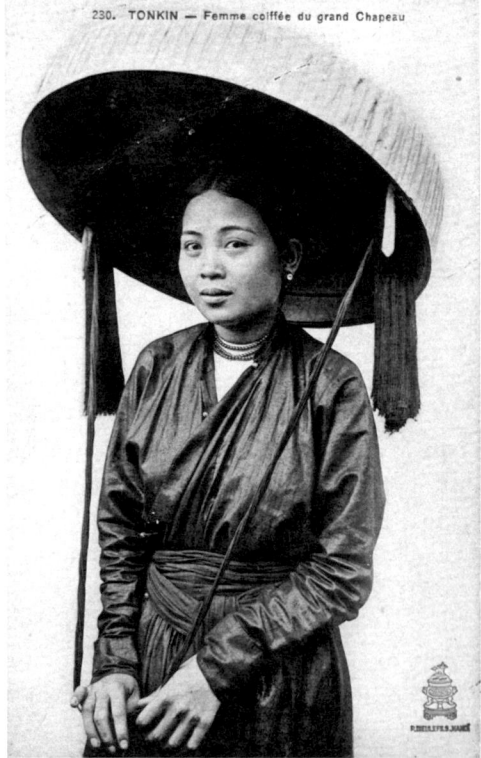

Left: Kinh man (early 20th century), Tonkin. *Right:* Kinh woman wearing *áo giao lãnh* and flat palm leaf hat (*nón quai thao*) that was commonly worn in Tonkin (early 20th century).

fairly traditional curriculum. This was true even of schools in cities such as Huế and Hà Nội.

Kinh society became increasingly diverse under French colonial rule as a result of different degrees of Western influence among various sectors of Kinh society. Western influence was most pronounced among elites and members of the new middle class, especially in the case of those living in urban areas, but it was also significant for a new class of working people employed in factories, plantations, and other segments of the local economy that had emerged under colonial rule. In addition, by the 1930s the feudal elite was no longer a particularly traditionalist sector of Kinh society. Like Emperor Bảo Đại some of them had gone to France to study when young and others went to schools in Việt Nam where they were exposed to Western culture. These included a number of *lycées* and *collèges* that were run along lines similar to such institutions in France. These included schools that were attended primarily by French students, but with small number of Kinh, as well as segregated schools attended exclusively by "natives." The latter were found in Hà Nội, Sài Gòn, Hải Phòng, Nam Định, Lạng Sơn, Thanh Hóa, Vinh, Huế, Quy Nhơn, Mỹ Tho, and Cần Thơ. The staff included a mixture of French and Kinh teachers, the latter being trained either in France or at the University of Hà Nội. In addition to such public schools, there were private Catholic schools, such as the Ecole Puginier in Hà Nội, the Ecole Taberd in Sài Gòn, and the Ecole Pellerin in Huế. There were also vocational and technical

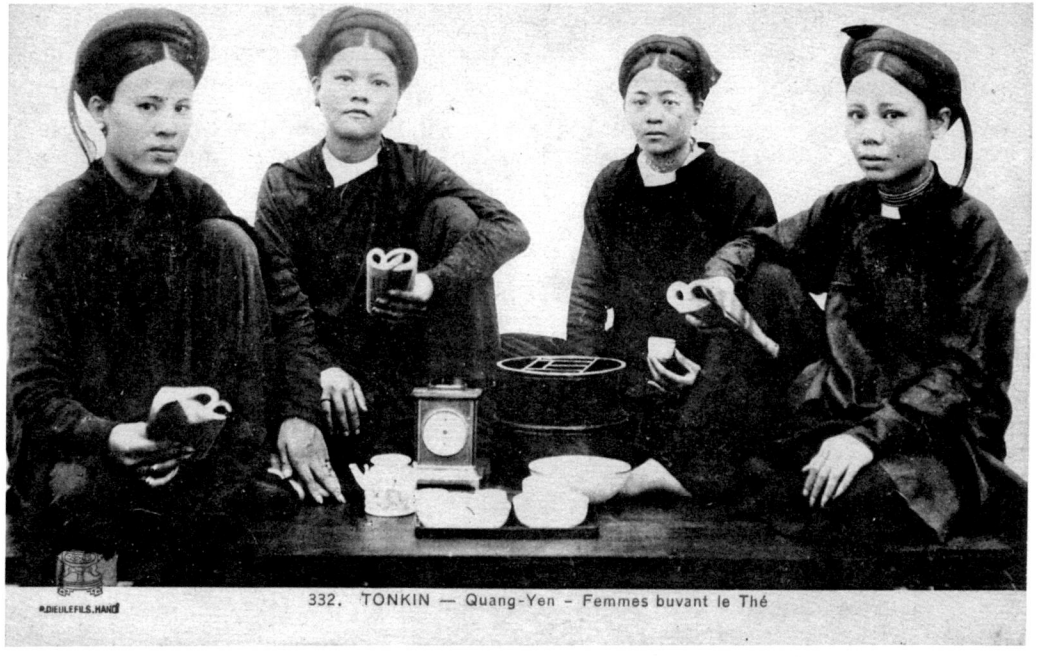

Kinh women (early 20th century) wearing *áo ngũ thân*, Quảng Yên town, Quảng Ninh Province.

schools in Hà Nội, Sài Gòn, Hải Phòng, and Huế. The University of Hà Nội was established in 1906 and in 1937 was attended by 87 French, 541 Kinh, and 3 Chinese students.[31]

Prior to French colonial rule urbanization had been minimal, restricted to a few small administrative and commercial centers. Under the French such towns grew in size. In the lowlands, the French substantially rebuilt and expanded the towns of Hà Nội, Sài Gòn, Hải Phòng, Nam Định, Bắc Ninh, Lạng Sơn, Vinh, Huế, Tourane (modern Đà Nẵng), Quy Nhơn, Nha Trang, Mỹ Tho, Cần Thơ, and Bạc Liêu. In the highlands they built the new towns of Đà Lạt, Chapa (modern Sa Pa), and Kon Tum. By 1936 there were thirteen towns with populations of over 20,000. These included Hà Nội (149,000), Sài Gòn (111,000) and Chợ Lớn (145,000), Hải Phòng (70,000), Huế (43,000), Cần Thơ (27,108), Nam Định (25,347), Vinh (25,000), and Tourane (23,000).[32]

Residence in such towns during the French period was highly segregated and most featured distinct European, native, and Chinese quarters. The larger towns in particular had a core administrative, commercial, and residential area built according to French plans and featuring a number of European-style and hybrid European-colonial style buildings and with roads and other infrastructure built along European lines. In contrast, the native parts of these towns were more Asian in character in terms of styles of architecture, infrastructure, and population. This was where Asians lived and where native businesses were located. In terms of the ethnic composition of these towns, natives (mainly Kinh) were the majority and Europeans by far the minority, with the number of Chinese tending to increase during the French period. Thus, the population of Hà Nội was 86,000 in 1913, including 80,000 natives, 4,000 Europeans and others, and 2,000 Chinese. By the mid–1920s Hà Nội's population had grown to 130,000, including 99,000 natives, 25,000 Chinese, and 6,000 Europeans and others. The population of Sài Gòn-Chợ Lớn (Chợ Lớn was not joined with Sài Gòn until 1932) was 181,000, including 96,000 natives, 85,000 Chinese, and only a small number of Europeans and others.[33] Despites such residential segregation there were settings where at least some Kinh and French did meet and interact at work and school.

Christianity also served to promote modernity and Kinh who converted to Christianity (mainly to Catholicism) commonly were given favorable treatment by colonial authorities. Catholics comprised as much as 10 percent of the population of Việt Nam by the 1930s. In addition to Catholic churches, as noted above, there were also Catholic elementary and secondary schools scattered throughout Việt Nam and many Kinh students sent to France attended Catholic schools there. Kinh Catholics tended to be concentrated in certain areas.[34] Thus, in Tonkin the main concentration of Kinh Catholics was near the coast to the south of the Red River. This area included the Vicarate Apostolic of Bùi Chu (est. 1848) in Nam Định Province and the Vicariate Apostolic of Coastal Tonkin (est. in 1901) in Ninh Bình Province. Both had Kinh bishops in the 1930s. Statistics for 1950 provide some indication of the number of

Catholics in these two vicarates: Bùi Chu, total population 697,009, Catholics 190,329 (27.3 percent), 182 priests; Coastal Tonkin, total population 250,000, Catholics 99,904 (40 percent), 163 priests.[35] There were many prominent Kinh Catholics in French Indochina. Emperor Bảo Đại's primary wife, Marie-Thérèse Nguyễn Hữu Thị Lan, was from a Catholic family. Ngô Đình Diệm's father, the mandarin Ngô Đình Khả, was also from an influential Catholic family (they had been converted in the 1600s). He served in the court of the Emperor Thành Thái as chamberlain, minister of rites, and keeper of the eunuchs. One of Ngô Đình Khả's son's, Ngô Đình Thục, studied philosophy and theology in Paris and Rome, and in 1938 became a bishop in Vĩnh Long in the Mekong Delta (he later became archbishop of Huế). Ngô Đình Diệm graduated from the School of Public Administration in Hà Nội and joined the civil service as a mandarin. He married the daughter of another prominent Catholic mandarin, Nguyễn Hữu Bài, who was head of the emperor's council of ministers.

The number of Kinh in modern occupations was relatively small as a percentage of the total Kinh population during the French period, but such people were a significant part of colonial society and their contribution to Vietnamese history far exceeded their number. Within French Indochina there were around 20,000 Kinh employed by the colonial government in various capacities in the 1930s. There were also a few thousand working in mines or on plantations. In addition, a

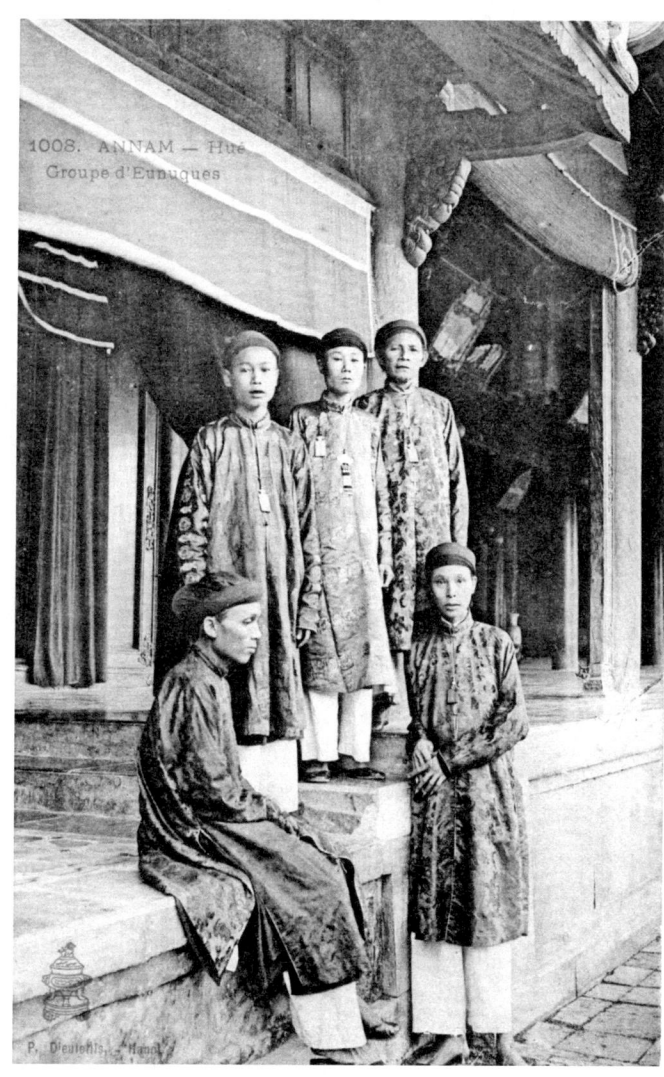

Palace eunuchs (early 20th century) wearing *áo gấm* and *khăn đóng*, Huế.

number of Kinh left Việt Nam for varying periods to work in France and elsewhere around the world (often as plantation and mine workers). The French employed around 140,000 Vietnamese in Europe during World War I as soldiers and laborers.

The period of French colonial rule saw a number of changes in clothing styles in Việt Nam, but there was also continuity. The most obvious impact was the introduction of European style clothing, but such clothing was not widely worn among Vietnamese. Urban elite and middle class males were the main groups of Kinh wearing European style clothing, and among them it was worn mainly as work clothing or when attending social functions associated with the French. There was also a consolidation of Chinese-style clothing's dominance among the Kinh population in general accompanied by the arrival of large number of migrants form China (especially in the south).

People in the Nguyễn court and mandarins outside of the court continued to wear Chinese-style gowns (including *áo long bào* or imperial gown with dragon design and *áo gấm bào* or imperial gown made of brocade) and other items of attire like those that had been worn before the French conquest for formal attire, but the style of dress of the emperors and other members of the nobility gradually changed over time. Although Emperor Thành Thái (r. 1889–1907) cut his hair in European style he normally wore traditional clothing for formal occasions as well as when away from the court. Emperor Duy Tân (r. 1907–16), however, sometimes wore Western-style suits, while retaining traditional imperial clothing for formal occasions. The clothing worn by Emperor Khải Định (r. 1916–25) was particularly varied. It included traditional imperial clothing, western clothing, as well as hybrid clothing. The latter included a coat tailored in European fashion that was made of blue silk and decorated with embroidered gold dragon and cloud motifs along with European-style medals and epaulets. Emperor Bảo Đại (r. 1926–45, Chief of State 1949–55), who had been educated in France when young,[36] also wore a mixture of styles of clothing and in later years he was often seen wearing Western style clothing. Empress Nam Phương (l. 1914–63, born Marie-Thérèse Nguyễn Hữu Thị Lan) was the daughter of a wealthy Catholic merchant and a naturalized French citizen who also had been educated in France. In photographs she is shown wearing Vietnamese style clothing including formal aristocratic attire as well as *áo dài* and Western style clothing.[37]

Outside of the court clothing styles began to change during the early decades of the 20th century. This was especially true among members of the small, but growing urban middle class. In the case of male attire, some middle class men began wearing European style clothing, but it was far more common for men to wear Chinese-style trousers and shirts (with wide sleeves and two pockets in the lower part). Wealthy and high status men often wore a gown that fastened on the right side as an outer garment, with tight sleeves being in fashion. These gowns usually reached to the knees in the south, while in the north they reached to mid-calf. As in the past, undecorated gowns were called *áo the* and those with brocade *áo gấm*. It was also still common to wear headcloths (*khăn đóng*) with gowns.

French Colonial Period

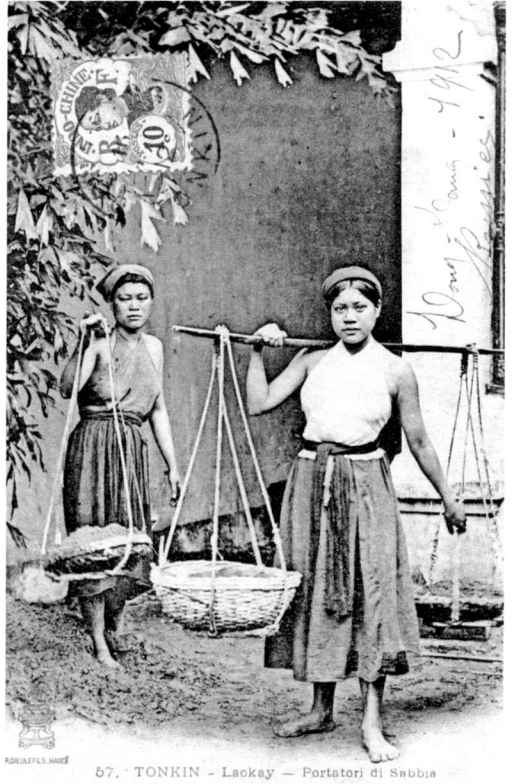 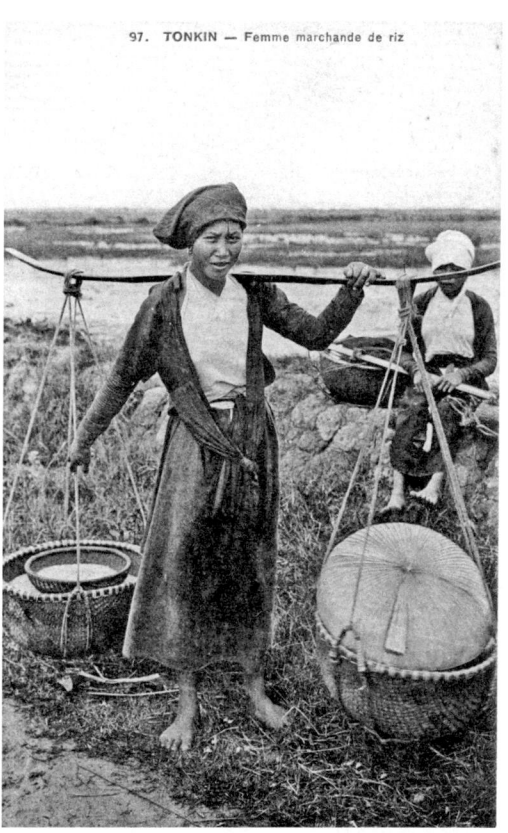

Left: Kinh women (early 20th century) wearing breastcloths (*yếm*) and skirts (*váy đụp*), Lào Cai Province. *Right:* Kinh women (early 20th century) in the countryside wearing breastcloths (*yếm*), skirts (*váy đụp*), and *áo tứ thân* tied for working.

During the French period women in rural southern Việt Nam almost universally wore Chinese-style black cotton trousers and a simple black cotton blouse, referred to as *áo bà ba*. Wearing cotton trousers and a blouse, called *áo cánh*, was also becoming more popular in the north, though the tailoring of the blouse was slightly different and they were dyed a variety of colors, including blue and green. However, many rural northern women continued to wear a four-panel *áo tứ thân* and breastcloth (*yếm*). While rural northern women often still wore skirts under their gowns, some wore trousers. Women in urban areas also often wore *áo bà ba* or *áo cánh*, although their trousers and blouses commonly were white cotton cloth or, if wealthier, made of silk or some imported fabric. Older affluent urban women also continued to wear *áo ngũ thân*, but new styles of *áo dài* had become popular among younger urban women by the late 1920s. These were modern tight-fitting garments made of new lightweight fabrics.

French influenced Vietnamese artists associated with the *École supérieure des beaux-arts de l'Indochine* (College of Fine Arts of Indochina, *Trường Mỹ thuật Đông Dương* in Vietnamese) in Hà Nội were responsible for the appearance of modern *áo dài*. The *École supérieure des beaux-arts de l'Indochine* was established in 1925, modeled on the *École des Beaux-Arts* in Paris, and continued to function until 1945. It was an interesting bi-cultural French-Kinh colonial institution that played a crucial role in the development of modern Vietnamese art that is characterized by blending of European, Chinese, and Vietnamese influences. After graduating from the college a number of its students went to Paris to exhibit their works or for further study. Two of its Kinh graduates, painter Lê Phổ (class of 1925–30) and Nguyễn Cát Tường (class of 1928–33), were the most influential in regard to creation of the modern *áo dài*. Nguyễn Cát Tường (aka Le Mur, the wall) and his associates in Hà Nội created the first modern version of the *áo dài* in 1930.[38] Called the *áo dài Le Mur*, it showed considerable Western influence, especially in the collar and puffed sleeves, It continued to be worn by some urban women until the early 1940s, but was criticized by many as not being decent and fit only for artistic types to wear. Lê Phổ went to Paris in 1930 for further study and then returned to Hà Nội in 1933 to join the faculty of the college. The following year, in 1934, he created another version of *áo dài*, called the *áo dài Lê Phổ*. It more closely resembled the traditional *áo tứ thân*, but was tight-fitting. He and members of the *Tự Lực văn đoàn* (Self-Strengthening/Self-Help literary group, f. 1932–3) avidly promoted this new style of *áo dài* in the mid–1930s.

Independent Việt Nam

The end of French colonial rule had a major impact on the types of clothing worn in Việt Nam. The end of the Nguyễn dynasty and other political changes put an end to the formal aspects of feudalism and the wearing of the various types of clothing associated with it at court. Away from the court wearing formal traditional attire for state functions and at work had already been in decline for decades and now it largely came to an end. Change in clothing styles for the Kinh population in general was more gradual and the simpler types of Chinese-style clothing continued to be widely worn for decades following independence.

The short-lived State of Việt Nam (*Quốc gia Việt Nam*, 1949–55) sought to retain some ties to Việt Nam's feudal past. Emperor Bảo Đại served as the Chief of State (*Quốc Trưởng* in Vietnamese). Prime Minister Trần Văn Hữu (1950–2), a wealthy landowner and French citizen from the south, was a monarchist who had been active in the movement aiming to restore Bảo Đại in the 1940s.[39] In 1952 he assigned dress comprised of a male gown (*áo dài chẽn*), white silk trousers, and a black headscarf for government officials attending events of a religious or historical character. However, in photographs Trần Văn Hữu himself is always shown wearing a Western-style suit rather than some form of national dress.

The division of Việt Nam into the communist Democratic Republic of Việt Nam

(*Việt Nam Dân chủ Cộng hòa*) in the north and non-communist Republic of Việt Nam (*Việt Nam Cộng Hòa*) in the south resulted not only in significant political and economic differences between the two regions but also to differences in styles of dress. Changes in dress were most noticeable for the Kinh population in the north. Members of the new communist political elite in the north such as Hồ Chí Minh and Phạm Văn Đồng followed contemporary communist fashion in China and favored wearing so-called Mao suits like Máo Zédōng. These were, in fact, a type of dress created during the early 20th century under the Republic of China that were a blend of Western and Eastern fashion. They were worn by Sun Yat-sen (aka Sūn Zhōngshān) and hence initially were often referred to as Zhongshan suits (*Zhōngshān zhuāng* in Chinese).

In the north wearing clothing associated with feudalism ceased and wearing robes such as the *áo tứ thân* and related garments was less common than in the past. The more modern versions of *áo dài* were no longer so commonly worn by urban women in the north, even in Hà Nội. Such *áo dài* were relegated largely to something to be worn occasionally by women attending official functions as a means of demonstrating national dress, especially when travelling abroad. Western style clothing was also more widely worn by urban women than before, especially by younger people. In the northern countryside many Kinh women continued to wear *áo cánh* with trousers becoming increasingly common rather than skirts. Some men in the north continued to wear Chinese style shirts and trousers, but wearing Western style trousers and shirts became much more common.

One important issue influencing dress in the north during the early years of independence was the general scarcity of commercial cloth with which to make clothing and the limited range of types and colors of cloth available as a result of government policy and this scarcity. Thus, industrial textile production in the north in 1939 had been 55.5 million meters, but the textile mills of Nam Định had been largely destroyed in the fighting immediately after the end of World War II and the French engineers running the mills had left and in 1955 production was only 8.5 million meters.[40] Thanks in part to aid from the Soviet Union industrial production gradually increased during the latter part of the 1950s and early 1960s and by 1965 had reached 134 million meters.[41] Fall characterizes female dress in the north in the mid–1960s as follows:

> Western observers report that the regime has begun to feel secure enough to allow its female citizens to divest themselves of the Chinese-style uniforms in which they had been clad for some years and to revert to the far more form-flattering Vietnamese national costume. Although the everyday street scene still is dominated by black, white, and faded blue, which seem to be the only colors in which textiles are now produced, expensive and colorful older dresses are being worn again on holidays.[42]

Attitudes towards dress were more liberal in the Republic of Việt Nam than in the north and cloth was more readily available in terms of quantities and varieties. The textile industry in the south that was concentrated in the Sài Gòn-Chợ Lớn area did not suffer such extensive damage as did the industry in the north and production increased sharply during the late 1950s and early 1960s, largely as a result of aid from the United States: from 35 million meters in 1939 to 144 million meters in 1965.[43] One important difference between the textiles produced in the south and the north was that the textile mills in the south produced a wider variety of types of cloth in more colors and featuring a far greater variety of patterns than in the north. In addition, government policy and market demands in the south continued to encourage the production of silk brocade to a much greater extent than in the north.

As during the French period, people's dress in the south varied depending on social class and place of residence (i.e., rural versus urban). The urban elite tended to be strongly attached to French culture. Among men, Western style suits were commonly worn in public (white jackets being especially popular), but more traditionally oriented national clothing was also worn on occasions linked to Vietnamese culture. Although he dismissed Emperor Bảo Đại from office, President Ngô Đình Diệm (1955–63) was from a prominent mandarin family and wore Western suits and national dress depending on the occasion. Elite women sometimes wore Western style clothing, including imports from France, but national dress was more commonly worn. The particular features of such national dress underwent changes over the years, however. Ngô Đình Nhu's wife Trần Lệ Xuân (the so-called First Lady of South Việt Nam) created a new style of *áo dài* in 1958 that featured a boat-shaped (*cổ khoét*) neck rather an upraised collar and decorative patterns on the body such as images of bamboo.[44] Trần Lệ Xuân referred to her creation as *áo dài cổ thuyền,* but it was more commonly known as *áo dài Trần Lệ Xuân* or *áo dài Bà Nhu.* There was some criticism of the *áo dài cổ thuyền* for not adhering to traditional aesthetics, but variations of this style of *áo dài* have remained popular. There was further innovation in tailoring in 1960, when the Dung tailor shop created the *áo dài với tay raglan.* It featured a distinctive sleeve with no seam on the shoulder that was designed to overcome wrinkles in the armpit and had buttons from the neck to the armpit and down to the hip, permitting the outer garment to be tighter while also allowing comfortable movement of the arms. This subsequently became the established manner of tailoring modern *áo dài.*

Urban middle class Vietnamese in the south tended not to have such strong ties to France and French culture as did the elite, but their dress styles in general followed those of the elite. Middle class men usually wore Western style clothing in public except for when attending events linked to Vietnamese culture, when they also usually wore some type of national dress. In the case of middle class women in the south, contemporary versions of the modern *áo dài* remained popular. Female students commonly wore *áo dài*, with other women wearing them mainly for special occasions. A style of *áo dài* known as the *áo dài chít eo* or *áo dài mini* became popular with students in the 1960s. It was very tight, emphasizing the breasts, short (reaching to the knees), and had narrow panels. Another innovation of these modern *áo dài* was that women wore bras rather than breastcloths underneath them.

Independent Việt Nam

The dress of lower class Vietnamese in the south was mixed. Some lower class men wore Western style clothing at work, but many continued to wear Chinese style clothing. Western style clothing was also slowly becoming more popular dress for younger men. Western clothing was not widely worn by lower class women at this time.

Dress of people living in rural villages remained much the same as it had during the French period with men wearing Chinese style cotton trousers and shirts and women black cotton trousers and blouses (*áo bà ba*). Men holding government positions or serving on village councils would "don white shirts, light trousers and, perhaps, shoes while on routine duty and wear suits and ties when receiving a government official from outside the village. At other times, however, they much prefer to wear Vietnamese dress."[45] The only distinguishing feature of such dress worn by men of this status was that sometimes their clothing was made of silk rather than cotton. Some younger men also had begun to wear Western style clothing.

The *áo dài* and other types of traditional clothing were largely out of fashion among Kinh people from 1975 until the late 1980s. After the fall of Sài Gòn in 1975 the new government banned wearing clothing such as the *áo dài* that were associated with the former government.[46] Such restrictions on dress were lifted as part of the Đổi Mới (*Chính sách Đổi Mới* in Vietnamese) reforms in the late 1980s. This was followed by a revival in the popularity of the *áo dài*. Initially this was in part a result of government efforts to promote the *áo dài* as a national dress for all Vietnamese

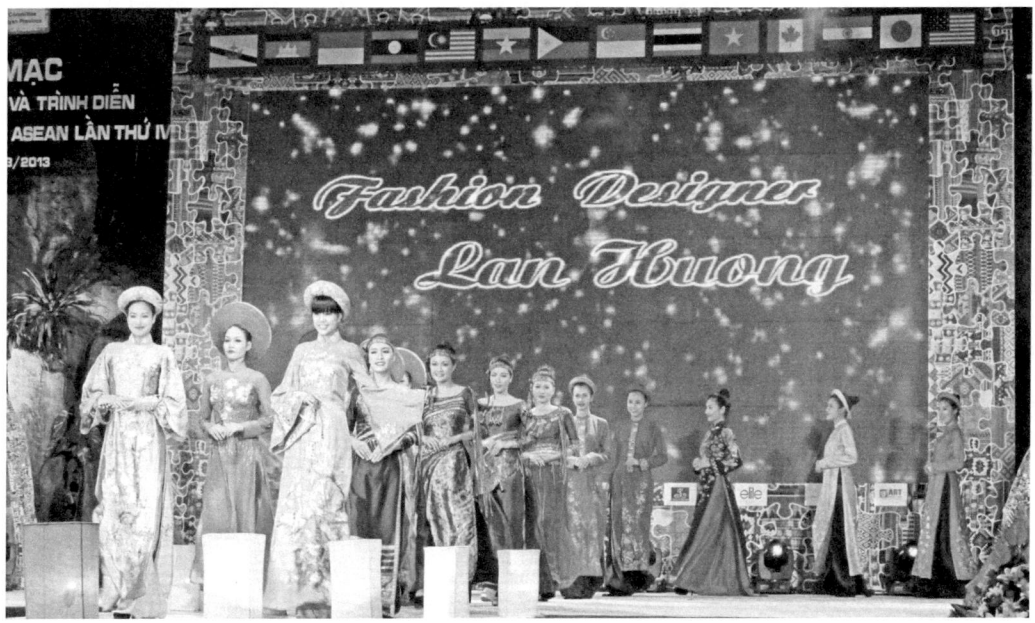

Fashion show by contemporary *áo dài* designer Lan Hương.

women. Such efforts included the use of popular media and public events such as the sponsoring the first post-war *áo dài* competition by the women's magazine *Báo Phụ Nữ Việt Nam* in 1989.[47]

Since then the *áo dài* emerged as a national symbol of Việt Nam and become popular even as everyday wear among Vietnamese women.[48] While the *áo dài* remains essentially a style of dress associated with the majority Kinh its general popularity has also meant that it is sometimes worn by non-Kinh women for special occasions and on an everyday basis. Finally, *áo dài* fashions have been constantly changing for the past couple of decades with fashion designers constantly employing new patterns and occasionally employing minor stylistic innovations as well. While everyday male dress in Việt Nam overwhelmingly favors Western style clothing, in recent years men have begun on occasion to wear modern versions of traditional supplementary weft (brocade) patterned silk over-gowns/robes (*áo gấm*) and headcloths (*khăn đóng*) for weddings and other special occasions.

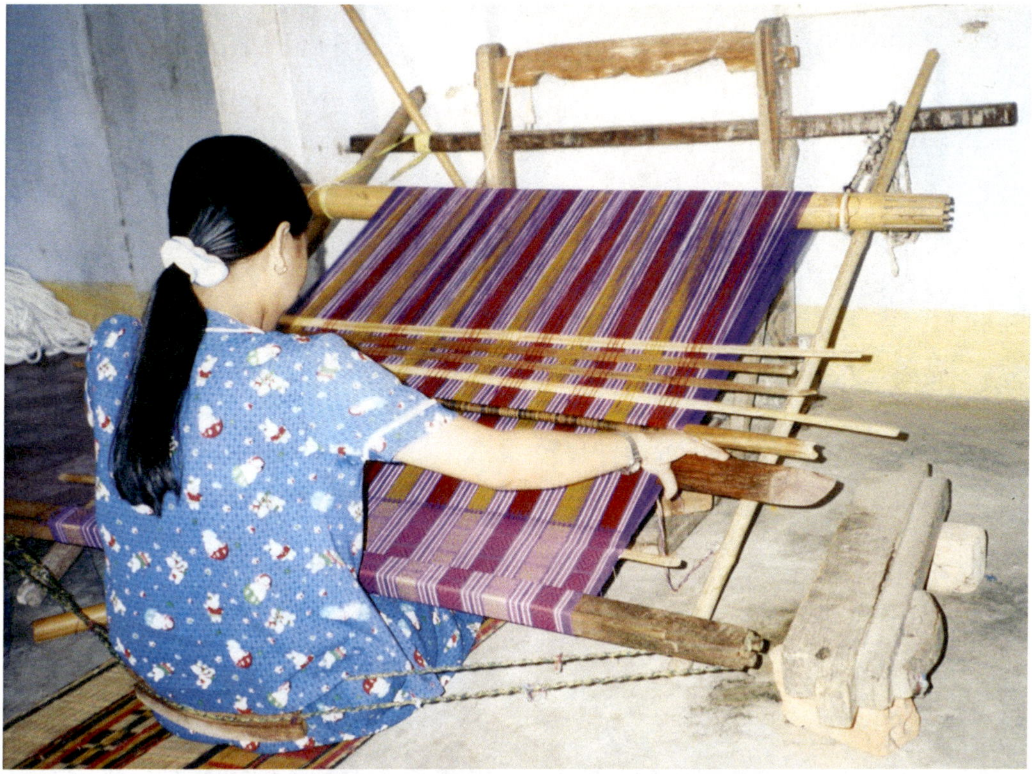

Top: Chăm woman weaving on a backstrap loom, Mỹ Nghiệp village, Ninh Phước District, Ninh Thuận Province. *Bottom:* Detail showing hook and rhomb motif on Chăm textile woven with silk thread using supplementary weft technique, Mỹ Nghiệp village, Ninh Phước District, Ninh Thuận Province.

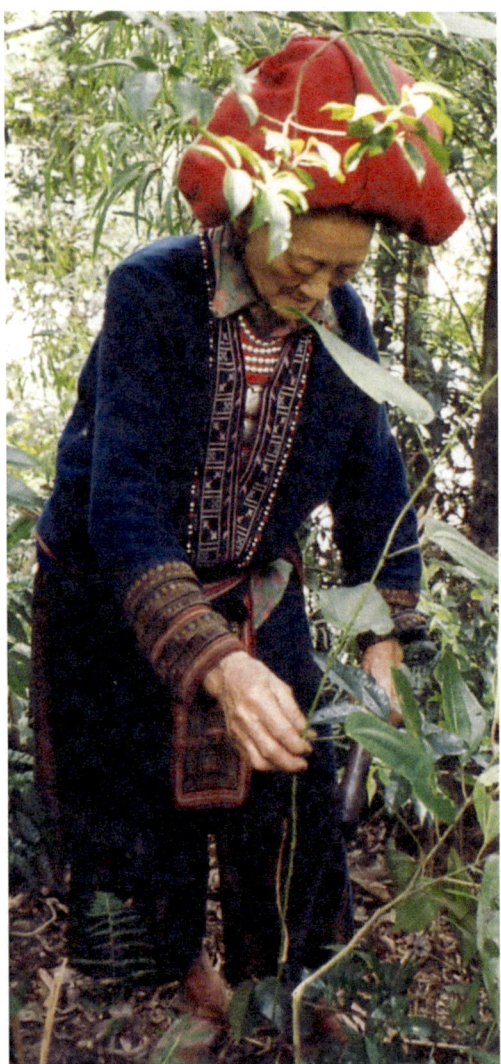
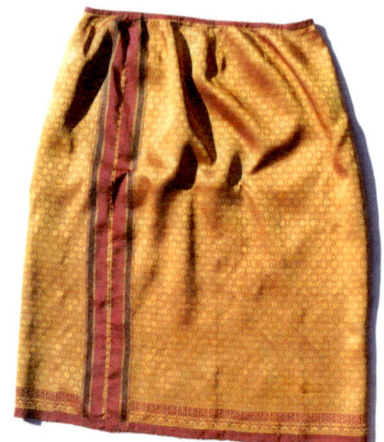
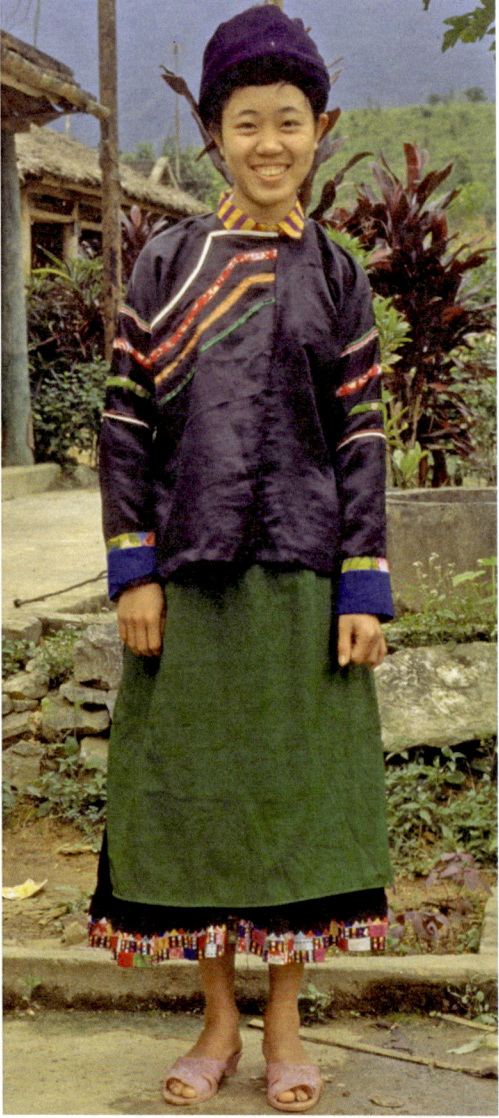

Top, left: Dao Đỏ (Red Dao) woman gathering dye yam (*Dioscorea cirrhosa* Lour.) roots, Sa Pa District, Lào Cai Province.
Top, right: Chăm tubeskirt with supplementary weft floral patterning, Tân Châu District, An Giang Province.

Right: Pu Péo woman wearing pleated skirt with appliqué and aprons, Bắc Quang District, Hà Giang Province.

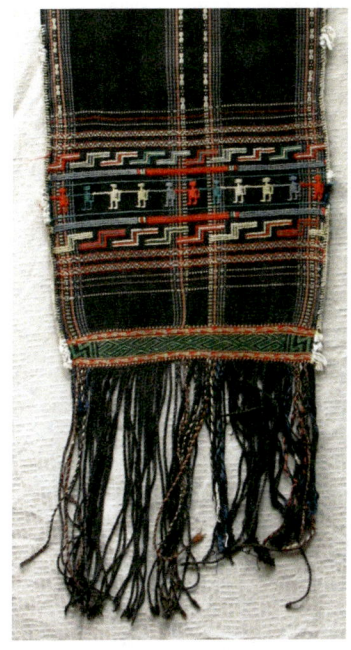
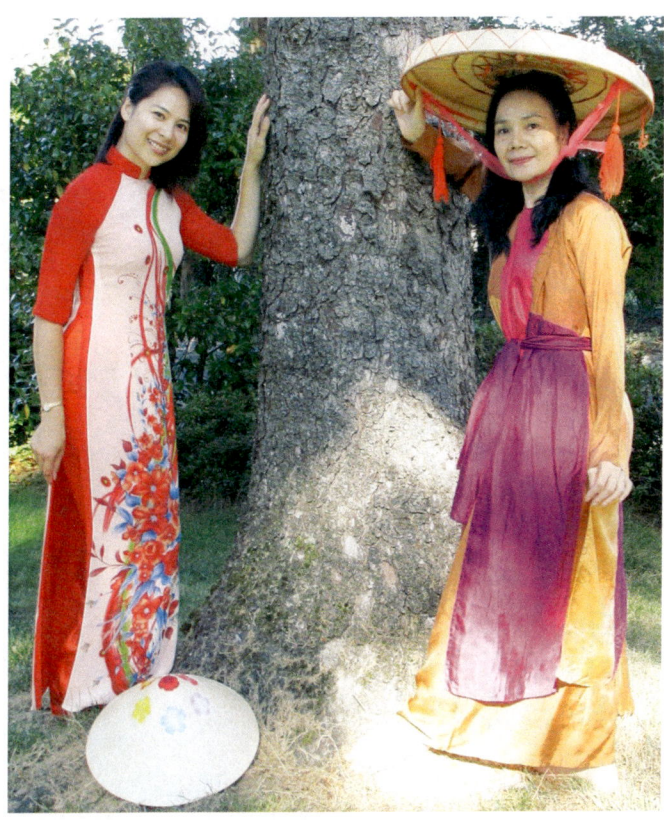

Above: Detail of Mnông-Xtiêng loincloth showing supplementary weft bands at ends, Bù Đăng District, Bình Phước Province. *Right:* Contemporary *áo dài* and *áo tứ thân*.

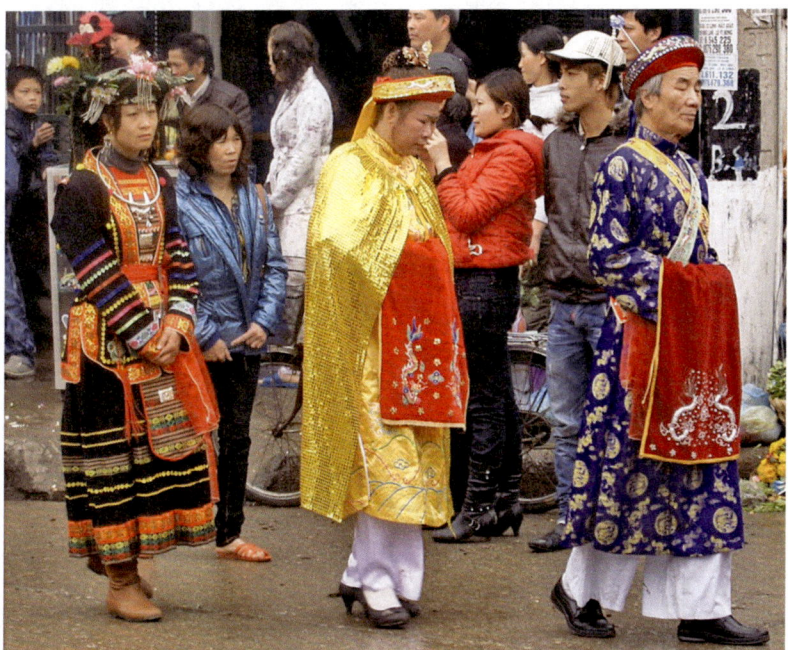

Man (right) wearing a contemporary *áo gấm* and *khăn đóng* in parade, Lạng Sơn City. Woman in the center wearing a long coat loosely based on tradition, followed by a woman from the Hmông ethnic group.

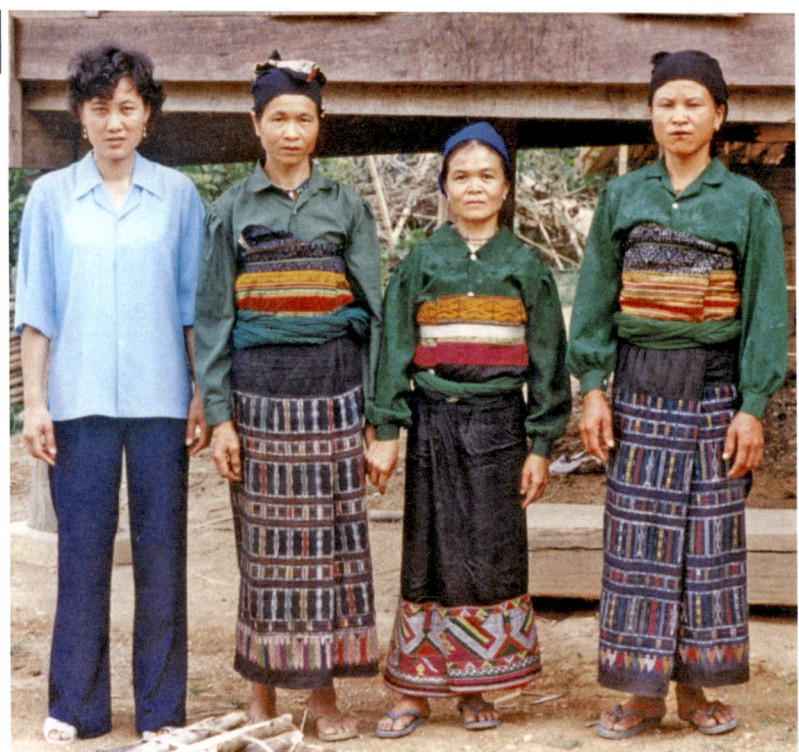

Thái (Tái Dăm/Black Tai subgroup) women, Quan Sơn District, Thanh Hóa Province.

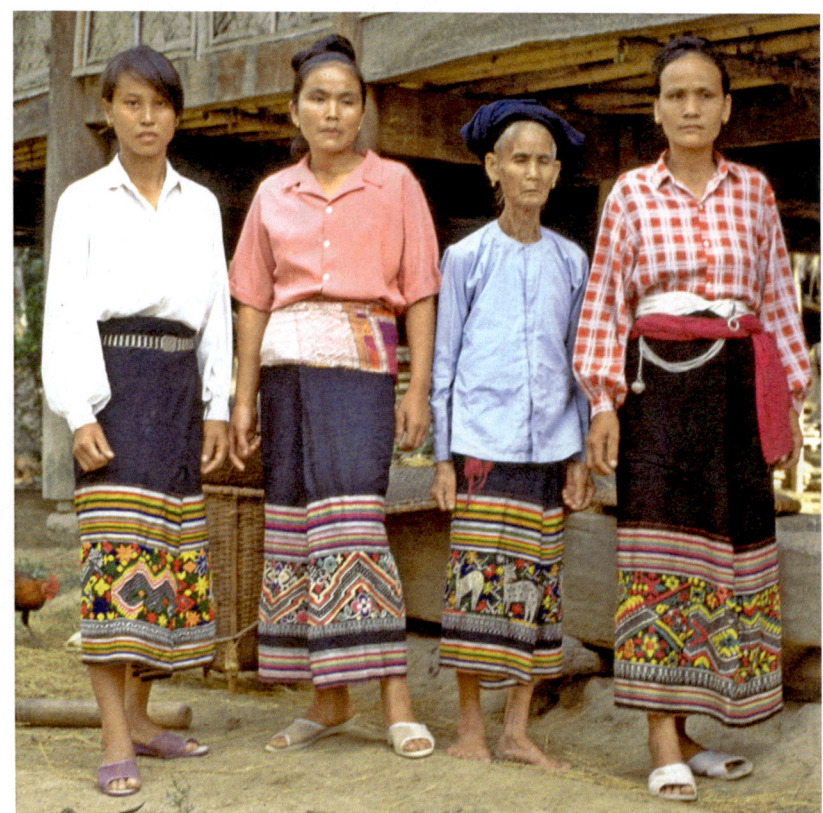

Thái (Tái Mường subgroup) women, Tương Dương District, Nghệ An Province.

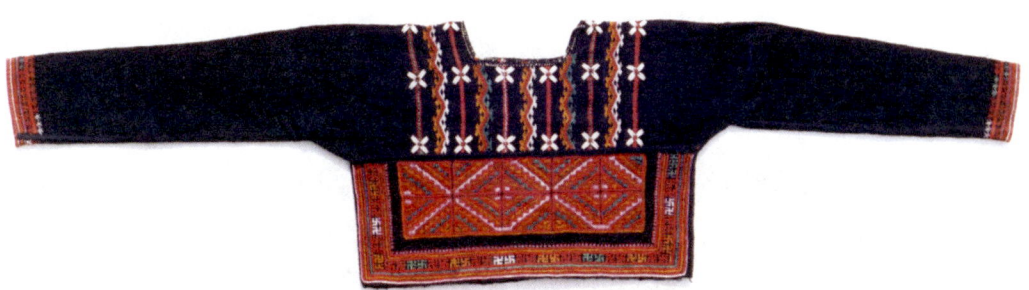

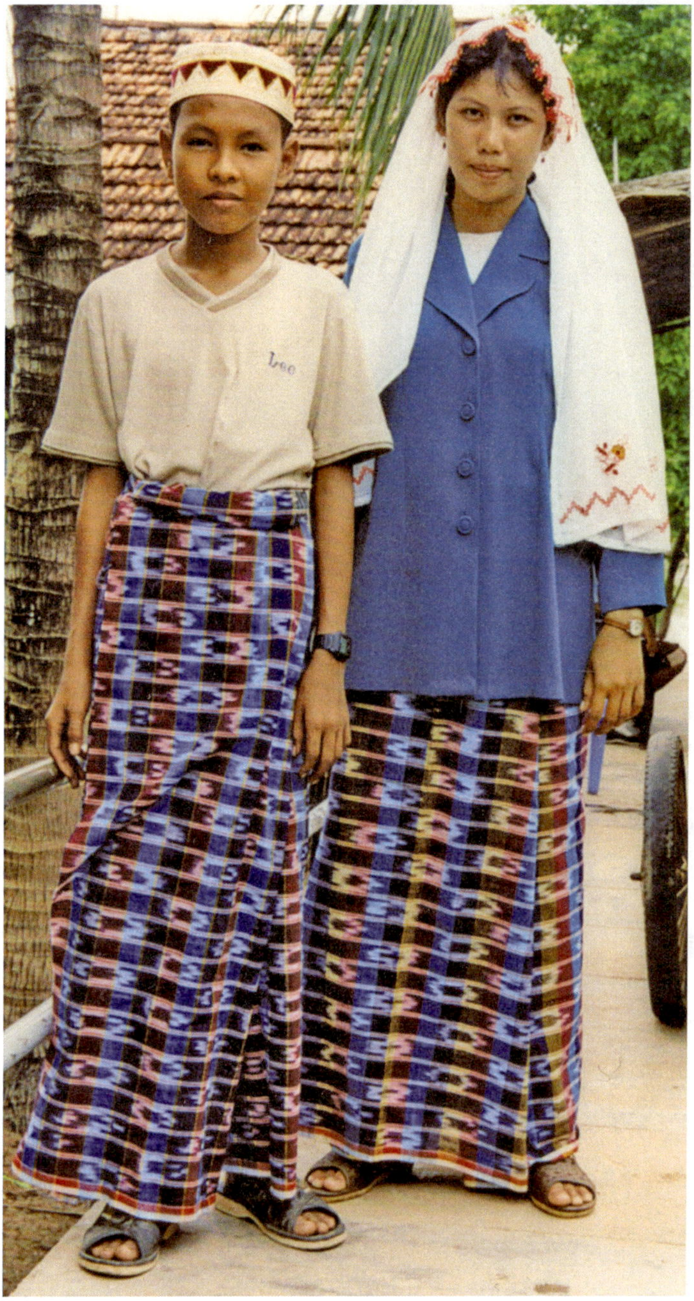

Above: Phù Lá (Xá Phó sub-group) blouse, Sa Pa District, Lào Cai Province.

Left: Two young Chăm wearing contemporary cotton sarongs with warp ikat patterning, An Phú District, An Giang Province.

C6

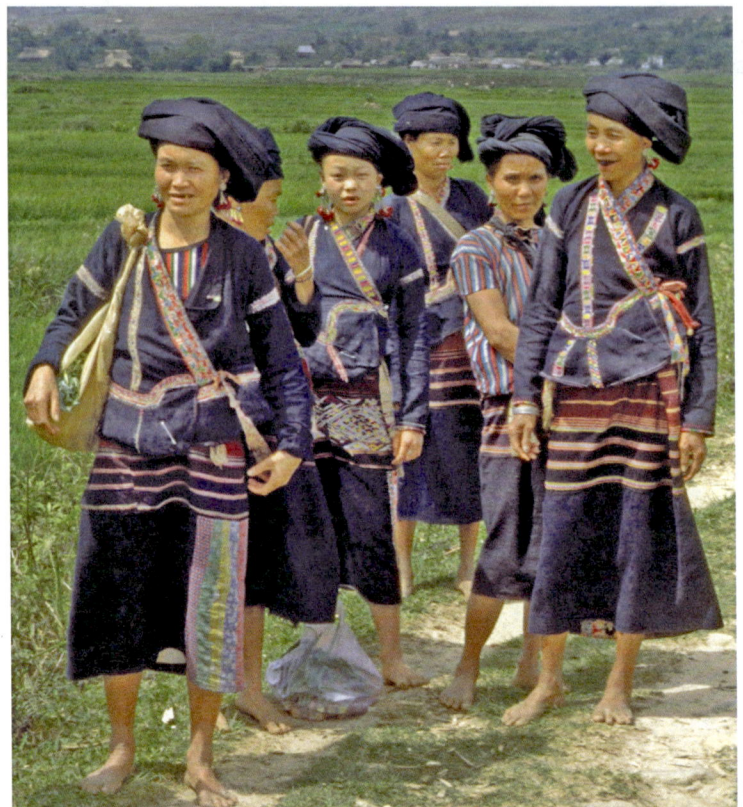

Group of Lào women, Bình Lư District, Lai Châu Province.

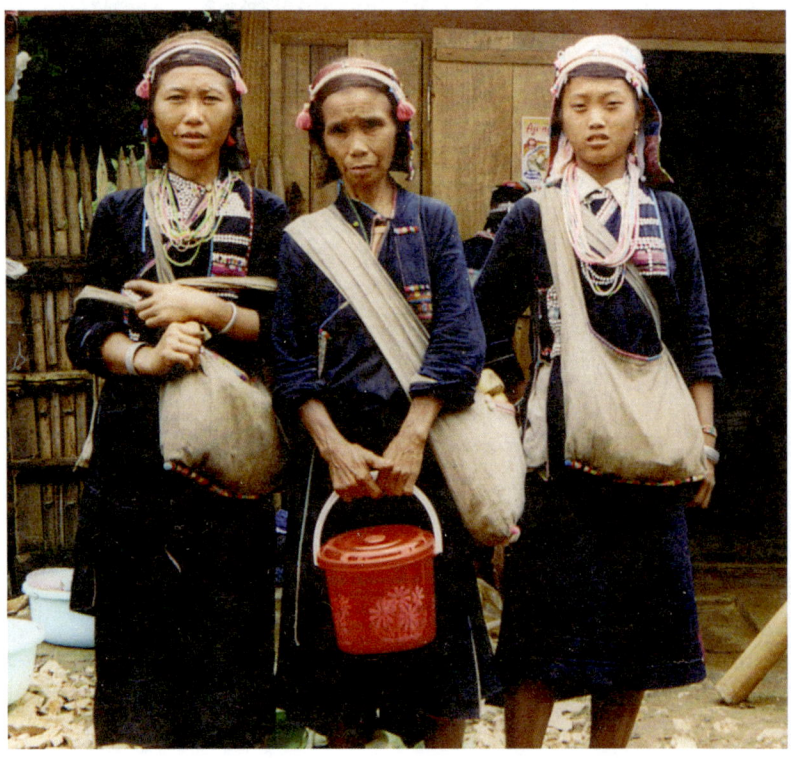

Hà Nhì women, Phong Thổ District Lai Châu Province.

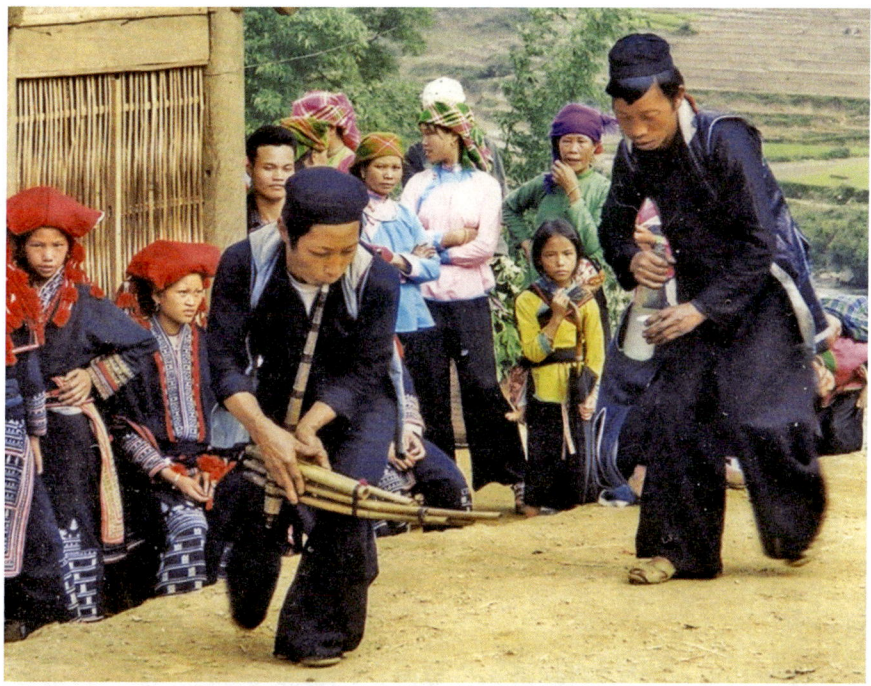

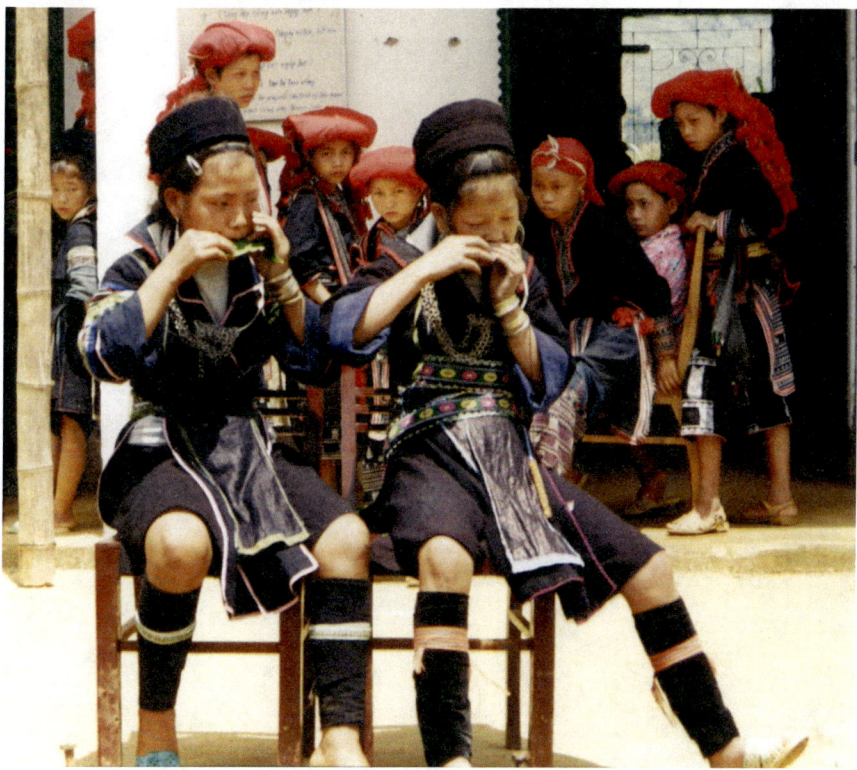

Top: Hmông (Black Hmông) men giving a *khèn* (bamboo flute) performance, Tả Van commune, Sa Pa District, Lào Cai Province (Giáy and Dao Đỏ/Red Dao in background). *Bottom:* Hmông (Black Hmông) girls giving a leaf blowing performance, Tả Van commune, Sa Pa District, Lào Cai Province (Dao Đỏ/Red Dao in background).

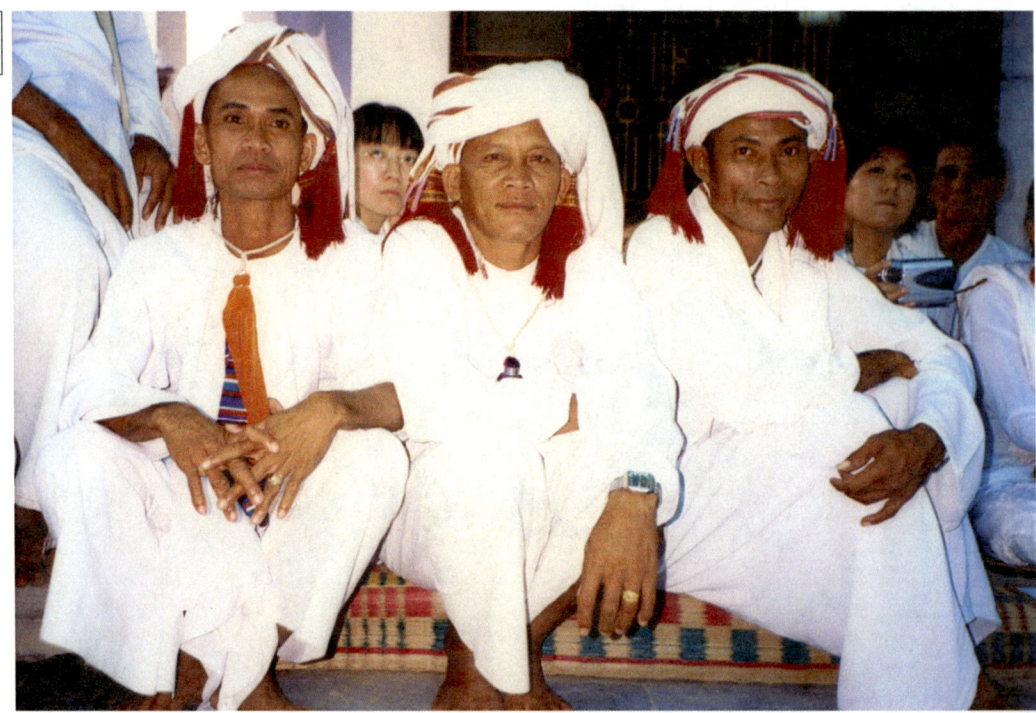

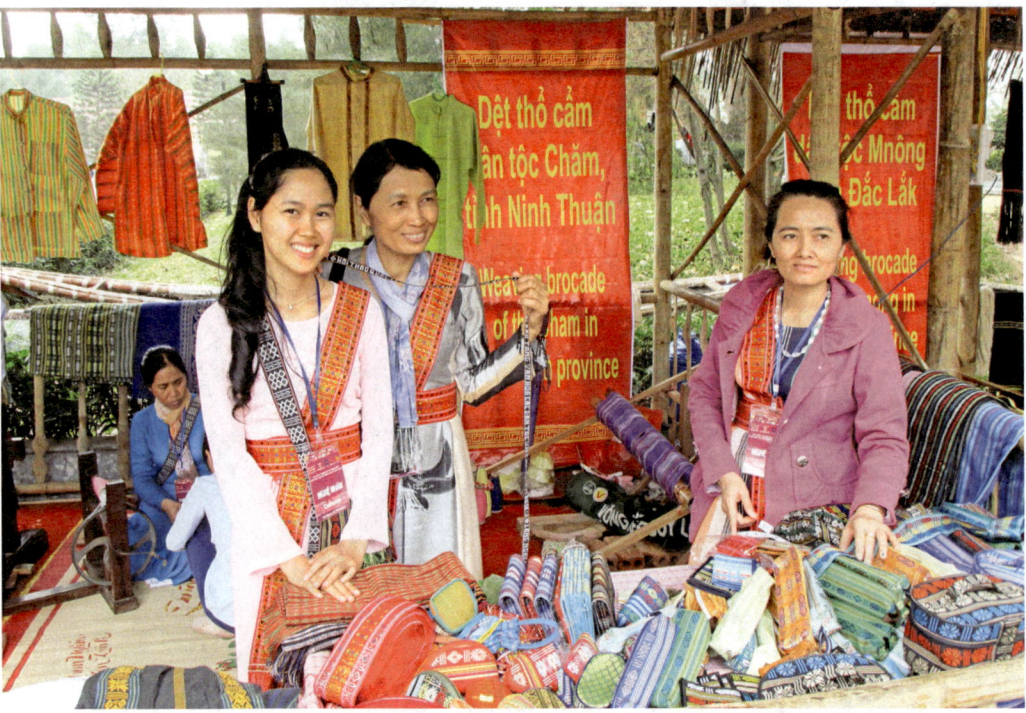

Top: Chăm men in religious dress for a community meeting, Ninh Hải District, Ninh Thuận Province. *Bottom:* Chăm women from Mỹ Nghiệp village, Ninh Phước District, Ninh Thuận Province, selling hand-woven textiles at a textile bazaar sponsored by the Museum of the Cultures of Vietnam's Ethnic Groups, Thái Nguyên City, during the 4th ASEAN Traditional Textile Arts Community Symposium in 2013.

4

Ethnic Minorities in Northern Việt Nam

Ethnic minorities account for only about 14 percent of Việt Nam's population, but as we have seen are a very important part of the history of dress and textiles in Việt Nam as a whole. However, the dress and textiles of these groups should not simply be seen as survivals of ancient traditions. True, many aspects of weaving and dress among Việt Nam's ethnic minorities are closely related to ancient traditions, but they have also evolved and changed over time.

By the time the French took over in Việt Nam almost all of the people living in the lowlands had been assimilated into Kinh society. The main exceptions were the Chăm and Khmer in the south. In the north the Lê Dynasty rulers of Đại Việt had established a degree of indirect rule over the Tày-Nùng in the northeastern highlands in the 1400s and 1500s by sending mandarins into the area. These mandarins took Tày wives and over time formed a local Kinh-Tày elite called "Thổ-ti" that pursued a policy of assimilating the Tày into Kinh culture.[1] This policy continued under the Nguyễn Dynasty. Neither the Lê or Nguyễn dynasties exerted much influence over the northwestern highlands. Some elites in these regions paid tribute to the Kinh rulers, but this was essentially a symbolic gesture and such tribute was often also sent to the rulers of Siam.

The initial French presence in the northwestern and central highlands consisted mainly of a series of military and exploratory expeditions to formally establish its rule over the regions and to determine what was there. The French gradually established a system of indirect rule over these areas under local chiefs or feudal lords who were advised by a small number of French officers. A handful of administrative centers were created in the northern highlands with French and Kinh administrators and occasionally French missionaries and Kinh traders in residence. Thus, the French established a military post and Catholic mission at Chapa (modern Sa Pa) in Lào Cai Province near a Black Hmông village in the late 19th century. A permanent French civilian resident was based there in 1909 and it began to develop as a resort hill station as well as a local administrative and commercial center. This early period of French rule had little impact on local dress and textiles in these regions beyond making imported thread and cloth a little more available. French colonial silver coins that were popular to decorate women's clothing also became increasingly available.

4. Ethnic Minorities in Northern Việt Nam

The French presence in the highlands increased in the 1920s and 1930s. New all weather and dry season roads were build connecting many of the highland areas with the lowlands.[2] This led to greater exposure to the outside world for highlanders, but such exposure was mainly for elites and was still relatively limited. Dress and textiles styles changed little for most people, but imported items continued to become more readily available. Highlanders employed by the colonial government and some elites, however, did begin to wear Western style clothing by the 1940s.

The anti-colonial war in northern Việt Nam during the 1940s and early 1950s and the war between the communist Democratic Republic Việt Nam in the north and non-communist Republic of Việt Nam in the south in the 1960s and early 1970s had a profound impact on highland ethnic groups. In the northeastern and northwestern highlands the old Tày and Thái feudal structures were eliminated and many member of the feudal elite were killed or fled. The communist government in the north established the Thái-Mèo Autonomous Zone (*Khu tự trị Thái-Mèo* in Vietnamese) in the northwest in 1955 (it became the Tây Bắc Autonomous Zone in 1962) and the Việt Bắc Autonomous Zone (*Khu tự trị Việt Bắc* in Vietnamese) in the northeast in 1957. These were abolished in 1978 after the end of the war with the south. These autonomous zones were not very autonomous, but they did provide for a transition period from the old order to the new. Wartime and post-war conditions in the north meant that imported thread and cloth that had been available during the French period was no longer easily obtained. Since the elites that had been the main consumers of these materials were largely dead or gone this did not have much of an impact for those who had survived the war. French silver coins also were no longer available for import into the highlands and impoverished conditions meant that aluminum came to replace silver for decoration. Another change was that the communists established weaving cooperatives in some highland communities to produce cloth. Such cooperatives were established in Hòa Bình to weave cloth for the Mường. These cooperatives produced Mường-style cloth, but with some modifications and generally with a simplified range of patterns.[3]

Việt Nam's economy has grown considerably since the advent of the Đổi Mới reforms in 1986, but the growth has been uneven, with the highland areas lagging far behind the rest of the country in terms of incomes and infrastructure. The result has been that while in general poverty has been reduced in the country, minority peoples in the highlands have benefitted less from the growth than the population as a whole. However, even where there has been economic growth in the highlands it has tended to benefit recent migrants from the lowlands more than highland minority peoples.[4]

Economic liberalization in Việt Nam has been accompanied by a relaxation of overt assimilationist policies aimed at minority peoples and even a somewhat favorable attitude towards cultural revival.[5] At the same time, however, the impact of economic growth and exposure to the outside world has undermined traditional textile production activities and wearing traditional dress by minority peoples. Thread making has almost entirely vanished with a few notable exceptions (e.g., hemp thread continues to be made in some Hmông communities). The use of natural dyes has also declined considerably. Weaving by hand continues in poorer more isolated minority communities, but also has declined overall. Generic Western-style clothing is now easily available in most highland minority areas and is now widely worn by most minority men and by many women on an everyday basis. At the same time, more liberal cultural policies and greater wealth has meant that at least some minority groups have been able to maintain aspects of their dress traditions, while others have been able to revive aspects that had been lost.

Ethno-linguistically we can divide northern Việt Nam's ethnic minorities into those speaking Tai-Kadai, Mon-Khmer, Hmong-Mien, Tibeto-Burman, and Sinitic languages. We discussed the Sinitic or Chinese groups in the last chapter. In this chapter we will look at the textiles and dress of these minority groups, with an emphasis on the contemporary situation.

Kadai Groups

The Kadai (aka Kadaic, Kra-Dai) languages constitute a sub-family of the Tai-Kadai language family. People living in Việt Nam speak languages belonging to the Kra branch, which includes a total of seven languages spoken by people living in the border region of southeastern China and northern Việt Nam.[6] There are four ethnic groups speaking Kadai languages in Việt Nam: the Cờ Lao, La Chí, La Ha, and Pu Péo. As was mentioned previously the ancestors of these people lived in northern Việt Nam in ancient times and can be considered indigenous to the region. Today these are very small ethnic groups as a result of assimilation and depopulation in the past.

Cờ Lao. There are about 1,500 Cờ Lao living in Hà Giang Province. Cờ Lao males do not wear distinctive dress. Cờ Lao women wear either trousers or a knee-length skirt.[7] The clothing is made of plain dark colored (usually black) cotton. For upper garments they wear either a five-paneled cotton gown that reaches to the knees fastens on the right or a shorter five-panel blouse that also fastens on the right. They sometimes wear two blouses, with the outer one having shorter sleeves than the inner one. The blouses are made of black or blue cotton cloth (shades of blue vary) that are decorated with narrow strips of different colored or colorfully patterned cloth on the sleeves and along the top of the front flap. The Cờ Lao do not grow cotton and at present do not weave. They trade with neighboring groups for cotton hand-woven cloth and also use commercial cloth.

La Chí. At present there are about 8,000 La Chí living in Hà Giang and Lào Cai provinces. We discussed La Chí dress briefly in the section on ancient Yúnnán. The La Chí grow cotton and weave plain cloth, which they dye dark blue or black. Decorative features are made using purple silk thread for embroidery and by attaching strips of plain white or patterned commercial cotton cloth. Men wear a long-sleeved tunic that reaches to mid-calf and fastens on the right, trousers, and a headcloth. All of these are plain. Male religious specialists wear a larger version of this tunic when performing rites or ceremonies. Women wear a gown that reaches to below the knees and opens down the front.[8] It has small decorative rectangles on the sides of the front opening near the top and the inside hems of the bottom and side vents are lined with light colored commercial cotton cloth. Underneath this they wear a breastcloth that is decorated with simple embroidery in the center and with narrow strips of colorful commercial cotton cloth forming a triangle at the end of the strings used to fasten the cloth around the neck. They wear either a plain tubeskirt, often with a strip of lighter colored cloth lining the lower hem, or trousers. The skirt is similar to the style worn by Tày women. They wear a headcloth that has a few rows of embroidery at the ends. They also sometimes wear leggings made of plain triangular pieces of cloth with the inner edge of the top lined with a narrow strip of plain white cotton cloth.

La Ha. There are only around 1,400 La Ha living in Yên Bái and Sơn La provinces. They have been largely assimilated by neighboring Black Tái and no longer have a distinctive style of dress and have adopted Black Tái dress. They grow cotton, but do not weave and trade the cotton with neighboring Thái for woven cloth.[9]

Pu Péo. There are about 400 Pu Péo living in Đồng Văn District of Hà Giang Province. We also briefly discussed traditional Pu Péo dress in the section on ancient Yúnnán. Most Pu Péo wear generic modern clothing on an everyday basis at present, but women often still wear traditional dress for special occasions such as weddings.[10] The Pu Péo obtain cloth from neighboring peoples or use commercial cloth. Decoration is largely in the form of appliqué. This dress includes an ankle-length full-skirt. The body is made of plain black or dark blue cloth and it is decorated with a band of fine colorful appliqué at the bottom. Aprons are worn over the front and back of the skirt. These are made of plain rectangular pieces of cloth of a lighter color than the skirt, such as green or light blue. In the past they wore two long-sleeved blouses, but women rarely wear the outer blouse any longer. One style of blouse opens down the front and the other is a five-panel blouse that fastens on the right. The front-opening blouse probably represents an older tradition and the one that fastens on the right more recent Chinese influence. The blouses are made of black or dark blue cloth. In the case of the front-opening blouse and there are strips of appliqué around the collar, down the front, and across the bottom, with the lower part of the sleeves decorated with a couple of bands of plain cloth and a few narrow strips of decorative cloth. The blouses that fasten on the right tend to be plainer with strips of decorative cloth attached around the collar, across the front flap, and on the sleeves. The headcloth is made of a piece of black or dark blue cloth with a little embroidered patterning at the ends.

Tai Groups

Groups of people speaking Tai languages constitute the largest portion of the ethnic minority population in Việt Nam. Most of these people speak Central and

Tai Groups

Southwestern Tai languages and, as was discussed in the first chapter, those speaking Central Tai languages are descendants of the Ōu Lò (aka Âu Lạc) and those speaking Southwestern Tai languages are descendants of the Lò Yuè (Lạc Việt). As was also discussed in that chapter, the Northern Tai speaking groups migrated from Guìzhōu during the late 18th and early 19th centuries. Central Tai speaking groups in Việt Nam include the Tày and Nùng. Southwestern Tai speaking groups include the Thái, Lào, and Lự.

Tày. There are over 1.7 million Tày and they are the largest minority group in Việt Nam. The Tày live across the highlands of northern Việt Nam from Lào Cai Province in the west to Quảng Ninh Province in the east with most of them concentrated in Cao Bằng, Lạng Sơn, and Bắc Kạn provinces. Many Tày no longer wear traditional clothing, especially those living in towns. Most Tày people simply regard themselves as Tày, but there are several small sub-groups. These include the Ngạn, Thù Lao, Pa Dí, and Phén.

Tày clothing traditionally was made of cotton, which was dyed dark blue. Silk was used only for a limited range of items; i.e., to make special decorated mosquito nets and blankets, decorated baby carrier, and special shirts for small children. In the past most Tày villages grew both *Gossypium arboretum* and *Gossypium herbaceum* cotton and produced silk. There was some local trade in cotton between areas with a surplus and those that were not able to produce sufficient quantities for local consumption. Commercial threads and dyes became increasingly available in the Tày area starting in the late 19th century under French colonial rule and today only a few communities still grow cotton and local silk production has almost disappeared. The Tày weave on a frame loom, but by the latter part of the 20th century weaving by hand had become quite scarce. In the late 1990s and early 2000s there were efforts to revive weaving in a few communities, especially in in Hòa An District in Cao Bằng Province. Brightly colored supplementary weft patterned shoulderbags produced for the tourist market are the main items produced as a result of such efforts at reviving hand weaving.

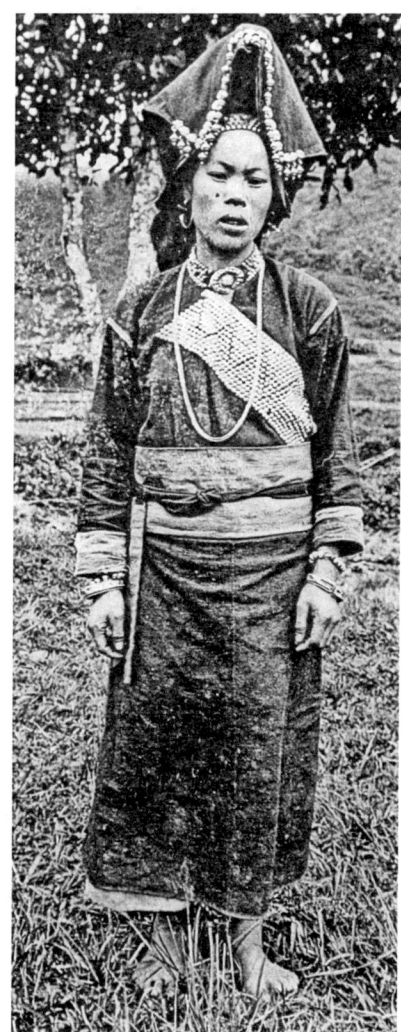

Tày (Pa Dí sub-group) woman, Lào Cai Province (from Abadie, *Les Races du Haut-Tonkin*, pl. 30, fig. 234).

4. Ethnic Minorities in Northern Việt Nam

Traditional Tày male and female clothing generally was made of cotton, dyed dark blue, and left undecorated, but with the decline of hand-weaving commercial materials came to be widely used during the latter half of the 20th century. Tày men adopted Chinese-style clothing long ago and this can be considered their traditional clothing. This includes loose-fitting trousers, a long-sleeved tunic that reaches almost to the knees and fastens on the right or less often a shorter long-sleeved shirt that opens down the front and is fastened with knotted ties, and a headcloth.[11] During the Nguyễn Dynasty period wealthy men and government officials wore clothing made of black silk rather than dark blue cotton.[12] Traditional female dress included a tubeskirt, a long-sleeved five-panel gown, a white breastcloth, a sash worn around the waist, a headcloth, and sometimes leggings.[13] The gown worn by women differed from men's long-shirts in some features: the collar is round and not standing and the sleeves and body are narrower. Tubeskirts represented an older style of dress that was gradually giving way to trousers by the late 19th century and in recent decades generally only older women in remote areas wear tubeskirts. Gowns also became less popular as everyday wear during the latter half of the 20th century and were supplanted by tailored front opening shorter blouses, with gowns being reserved for special occasions. The blouses are often made of light blue material.

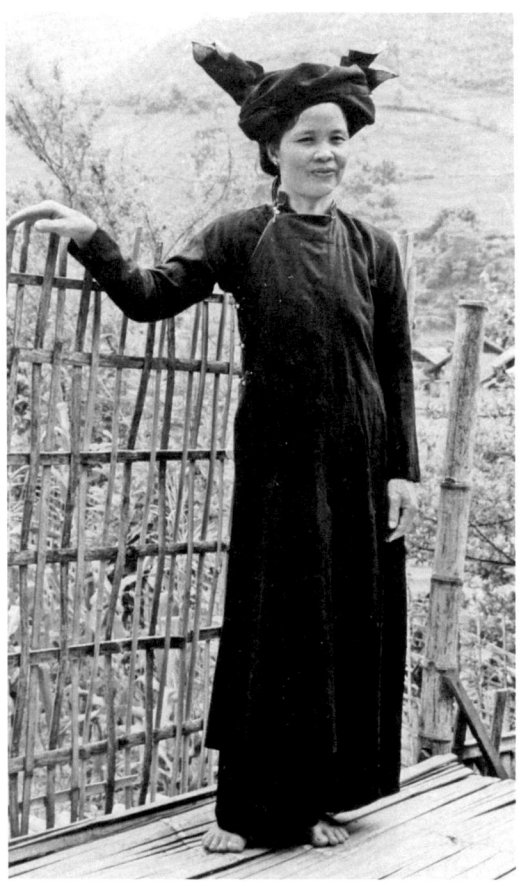

Tày (Thù Lao sub-group) woman wearing a tritik patterned headcloth, Sa Pa District, Lào Cai Province.

There are some regional and sub-group differences in traditional dress. Tày women in the west (i.e., Hà Giang, Tuyên Quang, Lào Cai, and Yên Bái) tend to wear gowns with the cloth of the upper part being a different shade than the lower part. The gown worn by Pa Dí women is a little looser than usual, the sleeves are made of two parts with the lower part being made of a lighter colored material (often white) and sometimes decorated with embroidery, and the front flap is often decorated with a wide band of silver or silver colored metal disks.[14] They also commonly wear a headcloth made of two pieces, a pointed cap with a rectangular piece of cloth placed on top.

Phén women wear a short white blouse. We discussed the tritik-patterned headcloths of the Thù Lao earlier.

The Tày make long pieces of cloth that are made into family altar screens, curtains for sleeping areas, blankets, and baby carriers.[15] These pieces of cloth may be fairly simple with check patterns or may have colored supplementary weft weave patterning. Traditionally these decorated textiles had a cotton ground with the decorations woven with silk, but today commercial cotton thread or wool yarn are commonly used. Patterns include various geometric figures as well as more realistic depictions of animals. As the weaving of supplementary weft patterned textiles declined during the 20th century people used patterned commercial textiles as replacements. Thus, so-called "peacock cloth" imported from China (cloth with flowers and peacocks on a red ground) became widely used as altar cloths.

There are also specialized items worn by male and female priests.[16] Male priests wear special hats and gowns that open down the front and are decorated with embroidered images of dragons, horses, and other figures. Female priests wear special hats and gowns. The gowns worn by female priests usually are made of plain cloth, with red or light blue being popular colors.

Nùng. There are almost 1 million Nùng in Việt Nam. The Nùng live in the same general area of northern Việt Nam as the Tày, with most Nùng living in Cao Bằng and Lạng Sơn provinces. There are about twenty sub-groups of Nùng, including the Nùng Phàn Slình, Nùng Dín, Nùng Cháo, Nùng Inh, and Nùng An. As was mentioned in the first chapter, the Nùng Dín migrated to Hà Giang and Bắc Kạn provinces between the 8th to 10th centuries, while other Nùng migrated to Việt Nam in the late 18th and 19th centuries.

Like the Tày, Nùng clothing is traditionally made of cotton that is dyed dark blue. However, the Nùng dye their cotton a greater variety of shades of blue than the Tày. Different tints of blue are obtained by such means as soaking the indigo-dyed cloth in mud, dye yam (*Dioscorea cirrhosa* Lour., *củ nâu* in Vietnamese), or lac (*Kerria chinensis*, *cánh kiến* in Vietnamese). The Nùng weave on a combination backstrap and frame loom. Most villages

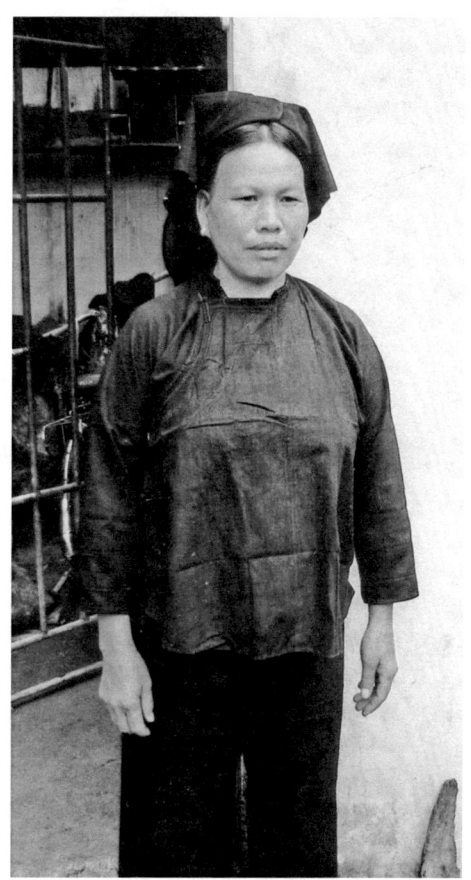

Nùng Phàn Slình (Hua Lài sub-group) woman, Lạng Sơn Province.

4. Ethnic Minorities in Northern Việt Nam

grew cotton in the past, but produced little silk. If they needed silk they usually obtained it from the Tày. Weaving and dyeing was more widespread among the Nùng than the Tày during the 20th century, but also began to decline after 1954 as did growing cotton.

Nùng men traditionally usually wore a Chinese-style long-sleeved front-opening shirt and baggy trousers, but most Nùng men now wear generic modern clothing except on special occasions.[17] The traditional dress of Nùng women included a long pleated full-skirt, long-sleeved five-panel blouse that fastens on the right, a sash, and headcloth.[18] Trousers had begun to replace skirts by the early 20th century and are almost universally worn by Nùng women now, except for Nùng Dín women, who still usually wear skirts.[19] While some Nùng women still wear traditional headcloths, many now wear the generic headcloths that have become popular in the highlands that are made commercial patterned wool in a variety of colors. There are differences in the style of dress of some sub-groups. Nùng Phàn Slình women usually wear a headcloth that is white with a wide band with narrow plain stripes and narrow stripes with colored supplementary weft geometric patterning.[20] However, those of the Nùng Phàn Slình sub-group known as Nùng Hua Lài (aka Nùng Thu Lài) used to wear a headcloth decorated with small tritik dots, but these are rarely made today. There are also differences in the styles of women's blouses and sashes, with some sub-groups adding distinctive features.[21] Thus, Nùng Giang and Nùng Lòi women decorate the top edge of the front flap and the cuffs of their blouses with strips of cloth, but the strips on Nùng Lòi blouses are narrower than those on Nùng Giang blouses. Nùng An men are the only ones that traditionally wore a five-paneled shirt that fastened on the right rather than a front-opening shirt. Nùng priests also traditionally wore special hats and robes similar to those worn by Tày priests, but these are rarely worn any longer.

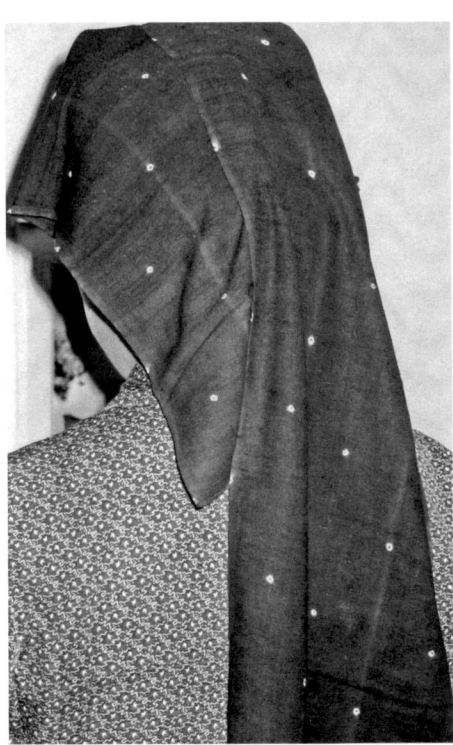

Nùng Phàn Slình (Hua Lài sub-group) tritik patterned headcloth, Lạng Sơn Province.

Thái. The Thái ethnic group in Việt Nam includes several sub-groups that can roughly be divided into a northern group in Điện Biên Province and Sơn La Province and a southern group in Hòa Bình, Thanh Hóa, and Nghệ An provinces.[22] Traditionally Thái identified primarily with their *mường* (aka *mueang, muang*) or principality rather than with a broader ethnic sub-category or political entity. That said, in general they were also divided into Tái Dăm (i.e., Black Tái) and Tái Dón (i.e., White Tái, aka Tái Khao). This distinction remained important in the northern area that at one time was part of a loose confederation of *mường* known as Sípsong Châu Tái. Within this region, Tái Dón live in northern Điện Biên Province and Tái Dăm in southern Điện Biên Province and Sơn La Province. The Thái originally settled in this area in the 800s, moving west from the vicinity of the Red River around the time that Nán Chào invaded northern Việt Nam, and then in the early 1300s some of these Thái began moving south first to western Hòa Bình Province and then into the western parts of Thanh Hóa and Nghệ An provinces. While these Thái retained the black and white distinction in practice it became very mixed and Thái in the southern area are often identified by regional sub-categories. Essentially the Thái in the southern area can be divided into Tái Mai Châu, the Tái Dăm of Thanh Hóa Province, and the Tái Mường and Tái Thanh of Nghệ An Province. In general, the Thái remained more isolated from the Chinese and Kinh feudal states that ruled in the lowlands of northern Việt Nam than the Tày and were less influenced by their cultures. Thus, their culture has retained more of the cultural heritage of the ancient Lò Yuè than the Tày have of the ancient Ōu Yuè.

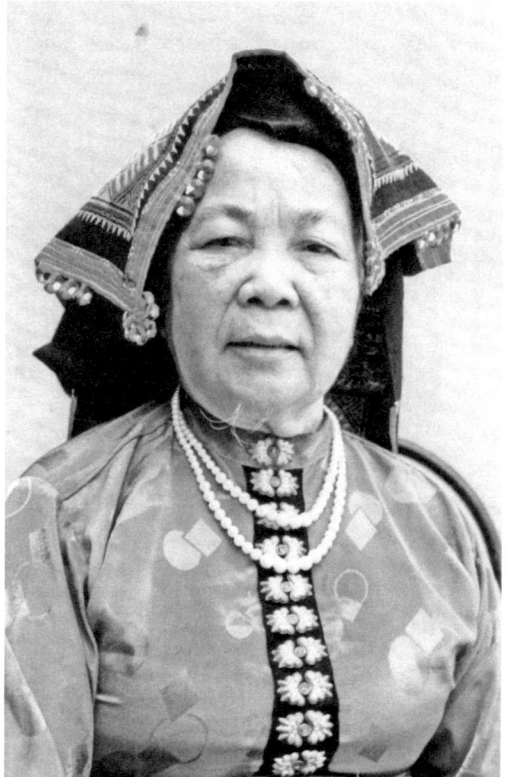

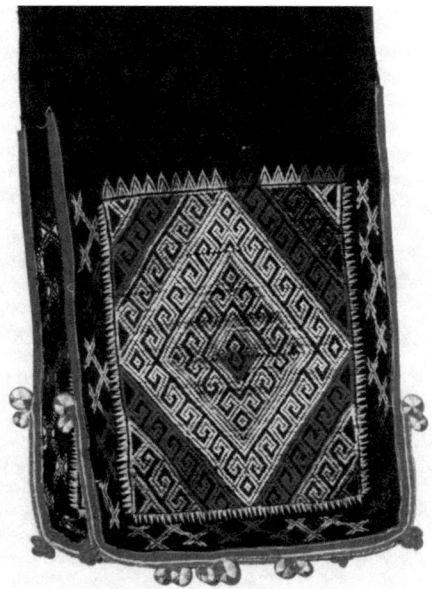

Left: Thái (Tái Dăm/Black Tái sub-group) woman from Thuận Châu District, Sơn La Province. *Right:* End portion of a Thái (Tái Dăm/Black Tái sub-group) woman's headcloth (*khăn piêu*), Yên Châu District, Sơn La Province.

4. Ethnic Minorities in Northern Việt Nam

The Thái grew mainly *Gossypium arboeum* cotton, although other varieties of cotton were also grown. They also produced silk. Growing cotton and producing silk declined markedly during the latter half of the 20th century, but small amounts of cotton are still grown and some Thái communities still produce silk. Thái clothing traditionally was predominantly dyed dark blue or sometimes almost black by adding dye yam (*củ nâu, mák bau* in Tái Dăm). Natural dyes began to be replaced by aniline dyes by the 1970s and are rarely used today. Handspun cotton and silk thread also increasingly came to be replaced by commercial thread, including sometimes by pre-dyed thread. The Thái weave on a frame loom. Weaving has declined in many Thái communities in recent decades and the use of commercial cloth and commercial clothing has become more widespread. Even where Thái women still wear traditionally tailored clothing often the clothing is made from commercial cloth. In other instances it is made from hand-woven cloth that is obtained from weaving villages or from Thái across the border in Laos. Most clothing is plain, except for special occasion tubeskirts and Tái Dăm women's headcloths. Decorative techniques used for these tubeskirts include warp ikat, supplementary warp, weft ikat, and supplementary weft. The use of the warp ikat and supplementary warp techniques along with a preference for decorating within relatively narrow bands can be seen as a legacy of an earlier time when Thái women wove on a foot-braced back-strap loom. Weaving patterned skirt cloth virtually disappeared among Thái in the northern area by the mid–20th century and little patterned cloth is still woven in the northern area today.

It is important to realize that the present Thái sub-groups share a common textile

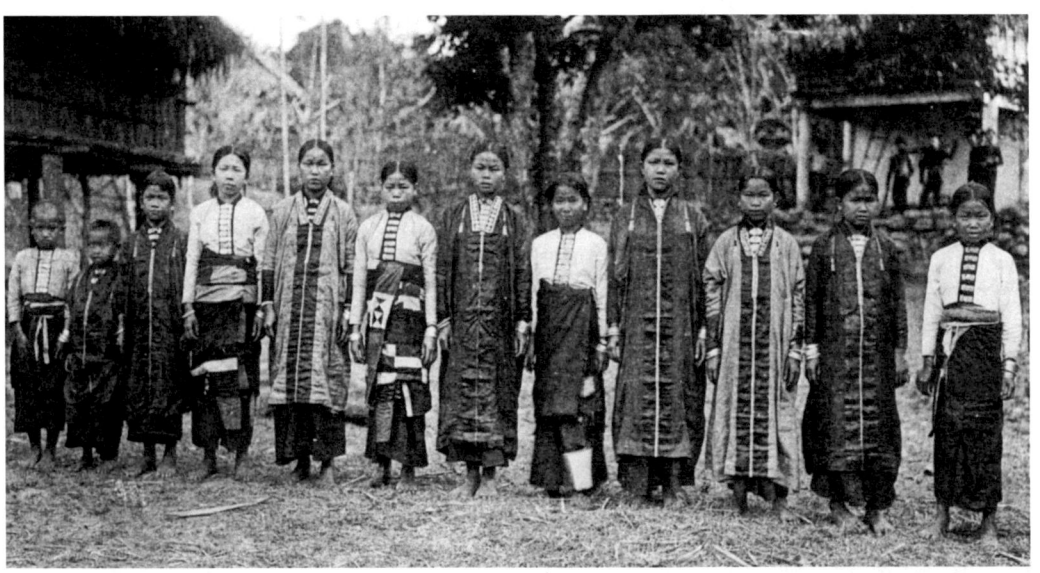

Group of Thái (Táy Dón/White Tái sub-group) women dressed for Tết, Phong Thổ (Tam Đường), Lai Châu Province (from Abadie, *Les Races du Haut-Tonkin*, pl. 17, fig. 17).

and dress heritage. After they moved apart, however, over time some aspects of these traditions disappeared, others were modified, and there were new creations as well. That said, the Thái have been fairly conservative when it comes to their dress. One reason for this relates to an emphasis on mastery of technique rather than innovating. In the case of decorating textiles, for example, for a woman to deviate from existing patterns is considered to have damaged a beautiful thing.[23] Religious beliefs associated with death and funerals also play a role in that it is believed necessary to dress the deceased in a certain manner to prepare them to meet their ancestors and so that the ancestors will recognize them and for those attending funerals to dress in a certain way.[24]

Thái males long ago adopted Chinese influenced styles of dress and this can be considered their traditional dress. This includes a long-sleeve shirt with ties in the front, long trousers, and sometimes a headcloth.[25] Men also occasionally wear a five-panel gown that fastens on the right side. All of these garments are usually made of cotton and dyed dark blue or black. As with the Tày, wealthy Thái men and government officials in the past often wore gowns and trousers made of black silk. The White Tái ruler Đèo Văn Tri (aka Cam Oum, d. 1908) wore a Chinese-style

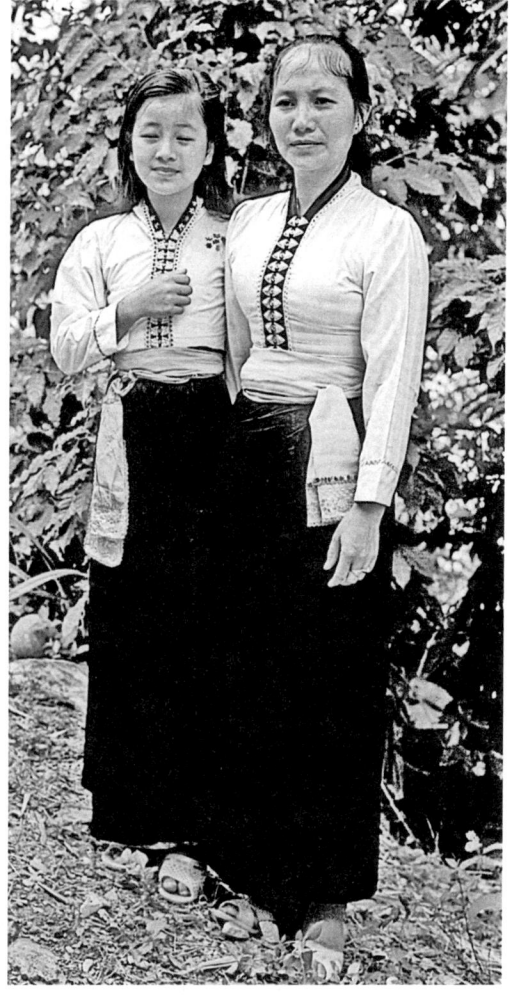

Contemporary Thái (Táy Dón/White Tái sub-group) women, Lai Châu town, Lai Châu Province.

mandarin's gown. There is also a pullover style of shirt (and blouse) that is sometimes worn or hung at funerals and probably reflects an older dress tradition.[26]

Thái women's attire is more complex and it is here that regional and sub-group differences can be most readily seen. A complete Thái woman's wardrobe includes a long-sleeved front-opening blouse, a pullover gown, a tubeskirt, a sash, and a headcloth.

Tailoring of the blouses varies between some sub-groups and there are different ways of fastening them. Tái Dăm and Táy Dón women in the northern area commonly wear long-sleeved short-blouses, with each group wearing a distinctive style.[27] In the past Tái Dăm women wore dark blue or black blouses and Táy Dón women wore white blouses white (sometimes edged with strips of different colored cloth), but at present women from both groups commonly wear blouses made of commercial cloth that is other colors such as light blue, pink, or green. The tailoring of the blouses sometimes differs. Tái Dăm blouses are always closed at the neck, while Táy Dón blouses sometimes have a V-neck cut. In the past there were three styles of fastening blouses. Most blouses were fastened with knotted cloth ties or small round metal buttons, while the blouses of noble women were fastened with clasps made of silver called *mák pém*.[28] These are sometimes referred to as butterfly buttons, but literally *mák* refers to fruit, a flower, or a branch, while *pém* means to attach. The clasp or knotted tie on the left side is referred to as male and the one on the right side as female—a designation that some associate with female fertility. Also, there should always be an odd number of clasps, button, or ties since odd numbers are associated with living things and are a symbol of imperfection and the need to develop, while even numbers are associated with the dead. The silversmiths able to make *mák pém* were found only in a few communities in the northern region and after 1954 production of *mák pém* virtually ceased and Thái women gradually sold off their silver until few *mák pém* were left in the northern region. Instead, women wore commercially made aluminum copies of *mák pém*. In recent years as the Thái in the northwest have become wealthier as a result of national economic reforms there has been a revival of making silver *mák pém* in a couple of communities.

The southern Thái region was further removed from the center of Thái feudal culture in the north. There were fewer Thái nobles and silversmiths and blouses with *mák pém* were not worn. Following an older Tai tradition most Thái women in the southern area in the past did not wear blouses and simply covered their breasts with the upper part of their tubeskirts or they wore sleeveless pullover blouses with rounded collars.[29] Only wealthy women or women of the noble class wore long-sleeved blouses similar to those worn in the northern area, but with small round metal buttons rather than *mák pém*. These blouses were referred to as *sửa Lò* in the past in reference to their being a style of blouse formerly worn by noble women of the Lò clan. Both types of short blouse were made of dark blue or black cotton and both were rarely worn by the mid–20th century. Today Thái women in the southern area usually wear generic blouses made of commercial cloth.

Thái women have a tradition of wearing a range of styles of tubeskirt, but most varieties are only worn in the southern area at present.[30] In the northern area Tái Dăm and Tái Dón women wear a tubeskirt (*sin*) with a plain black or dark blue body that reaches to the ankles and a waistband that is usually made from a piece of cloth that is predominantly red. A strip of plain red cloth is also attached inside the hem. The body of the tubeskirt was usually made of cotton, but in the past wealthy women sometimes would wear skirts made of silk. A sash (*sai eo*) is tied around the top of the skirt. It is normally plain green and made of silk. The ends of the sash may be decorated with pieces of red cloth or embroidery. Wealthy women in particular in the past always wore three silver chains around their waist. A variety of small silver objects usually are attached to these chains as further decoration. In the past Thái noble women in particular in the northern area wore tubeskirts with decorative patterning on special occasions, especially for funerals, but weaving and wearing these types of skirt had ceased by the mid–20th century and they continued to be woven and worn only in the southern area.

Mention should be made of the Tái Dăm of Mường Vat (modern Yên Châu District in Sơn La Province) since the women wear tubeskirts that are different from those worn by other Tái Dăm.[31] Their tubeskirts are a little shorter than those commonly worn by other Thái women and have a plain dark blue or black waistband and hempiece. The skirt body has narrow light blue and black stripes or black and red ones. The Tái Dăm in Thailand whose ancestors migrated there in the 19th century also wear this type of tubeskirt.

The more varied repertoire of Thái tubeskirts worn in the southern area reflects a survival of older pan–Thái traditions as well as distinctive regional variations. Such variation is found in the three components of the tubeskirts: the waistband or "head" (*hua*) of the skirt, the body of the skirt, and the hem-piece or "foot" (*tin*) of the skirt. Sometimes the waistband is made of a plain piece of cloth, sometimes it is made of a strip of a type of cloth with bands of weft ikat and supplementary weft patterning that is also used for blankets and other items, and sometimes there are waistbands made of special narrow pieces of cloth with supplementary warp patterning that are woven specifically for use as waistbands. In the past these special waistbands were worn primarily by noblewomen and were seen as a way of demonstrating a woman's skill at weaving.[32] Formerly it was normal to attach three of these waistbands to the top of a skirt, but sometimes there would only be one or two. Dozens of different geometric and representational motifs appear on these waistbands, including many depicting animals as well as dragons. The dragon motif in particular in the past was reserved for noble women and today is the most popular motif found on these textiles.

Skirt-cloth is woven in a long roll up to 20 meters in length, which is then cut into segments to make individual skirt bodies. There are seven basic types of skirt body: (1) plain dark blue or black cotton cloth; (2) cotton cloth woven with a few different colors of warp threads to produce narrow stripes and sometimes with simple warp ikat dashes or embroidered decorative patterns; (3) like #2 but with weft ikat patterns scattered about the cloth (*mí* is the Thai word for weft ikat); (4) cloth with a ground of stripes like #2 with additional warp directional bands of supplementary warp patterning using white thread (often silk)[33]; (5) cloth with silk warp directional supplementary warp stripes that frame rows of small rectangles with alternating weft ikat and silk supplementary weft patterning (sometimes depicting human figures); (6) a simpler version of #5 lacking the weft ikat patterning; and (7) silk cloth with wide weft directional bands of weft ikat patterning, sometimes with red and dark blue backgrounds, and narrower weft directional bands with supplementary weft geometric patterns.

A skirt made with the last type of body is called a *sin mí* and in the past such skirts with particular motifs were worn at funerals by noble women.[34] These skirts featured depictions of a funeral hut (*thiêng hèo*) and an artificial ceremonial tree (*co hèo*) in the dark blue weft ikat bands and of either a dragon or grey heron in the red colored bands. In ancient Thái belief a man's soul was carried to heaven when he dies by a grey heron and a woman's soul by a dragon. At funerals, women of the maternal side of the deceased wore skirts with dragon motifs and women of the paternal side wore skirts with grey heron motifs.

The Tái Mường in Nghệ An Province make two additional types of silk skirt cloth. One features a variety of patterns, including depictions of human and animal figures that are woven using a continuous supplementary weft weave with a double layer of weft threads to create patterns that appear in a different color on the reverse side of the material.[35] Thái call this the *màn* technique and the Tái Mường use it to weave cloth for skirts (called *sin màn*) and coffin screens.[36] The other type of cloth is a variation of the seventh type discussed above with wide bands that feature large supplementary weft rhomb and hook patterns in both the red and blue ground bands or, when intended for funeral wear, the rhomb and hook motif in the red band and a weft ikat representation of the funeral hut and artificial tree in the blue band.[37] Skirts made using this type of cloth are called *sin bók*, *bók* being Thái for flower.

Most Thái skirts either do not have a separate hem-piece or they have one made of a narrow piece of dark blue or black cloth. Only the Tái Mường in Nghệ An Province have skirts with separate patterned hem-pieces. These feature colorful embroidered patterns. In the past silk thread was used, but now it is common to use commercial thread made from various materials. Since these patterns are produced by embroidery there is scope for considerable individual variation. Dragons are especially popular, but in recent years there has been considerable innovation.[38]

In the past Thái women in the northern area in particular often wore gowns (*sửa nhính hí*) on special occasions or at home during cold weather. The basic difference between men's gowns and women's gowns is that men's have five panels and fasten on the right side whereas women's normally are pullovers that open almost to the waist. Women's gowns are mostly made of plain black cotton or silk cloth. Additional pieces of cloth often are attached inside the collar and along the inside of the hem. Táy Dón gowns are decorated with embroidery and appliqué along the collar and upper part of the front opening, long triangular pieces of decorative cloth reaching from the upper part of mid-shoulder downward, and sometimes with embroidery at the ends of the sleeves.[39] In addition to their tubeskirts being different Tái Dăm women of Mường Vạt also formerly wore a distinctive colorful gown that was worn when attending special ceremonies. They are also pullovers, but they have shorter sleeves than those worn by other Thái. Most of the body is made of plain black or dark blue cotton cloth, but a large portion of the center is covered with vertical strips of bright colored plain cloth (red, yellow, and other colors) and similar slightly narrower strips are place horizontally across towards the bottom. There are also thin appliqué stripes within the dark area. A separate piece of colorful silk cloth with supplementary weft patterning is attached to the bottom and a large part of the sleeve is made of plain bright (often red) cloth.[40]

Thái women in Hòa Bình and Thanh Hóa provinces also wear a type of gown called *sửa tin sao*.[41] These gowns are worn by a woman at the funeral of her husband's parents and by priests at the funeral when praying. It has short sleeves, opens down the front, and is tailored loosely and worn as an over-gown. The upper part traditionally was made of gauze-like silk and a decorative piece of silk cloth that is cut from a long roll of cloth with supplementary weft patterning called a *phải sao*. These gowns are not worn very often any longer and the gauze-like silk cloth is no longer woven so that some other type of cloth has to be substituted (often a bright piece of commercial cloth).

Thai women usually wear a headcloth. In the northern area Táy Dón women wear ones made of plain white cotton, while Tái Dăm women wear black or dark blue ones. For everyday wear these generally are made of plain cotton cloth and Táy Dón only wear plain headcloths and sometimes wear a large hat instead of a headcloth.[42] Tái Dăm women wear a dark blue or black headcloth (*piêu* or *khăn piêu*) with decorated ends. All of the Tái Dăm headcloths have certain features in common, but until recently there were regional differences.[43] Overall, there has been a tendency to add more and more colorful embellishments in recent years. In the past headcloths from Mường Vat were the most colorful, but they no longer are exceptional. The middle part of the headcloth is left plain. Strips of plain red cloth are used as edging at the ends. Pieces of twisted red cloth are placed at the corners to form the headcloth's "ears." The headcloth's "fingerprints" are attached in the center of the ends and on each side near the end of the cloth. These are small round pieces with a hole in the center made of various colors of thread (usually silk). The number of "fingerprints" varies, but it is customary to have an odd number. The central parts of the ends of these headcloths are decorated with patterning that includes various geometric or representational patterns and groups of three parallel lines in a variety of colors. In the past these patterns were woven into the cloth using a supplementary weft technique, but now they are embroidered.

Thái women in Thanh Hóa and Nghệ An provinces wear a style of decorative headcloth for special occasions that is not found in the northern area. This is called a *khăn Tái* ("Tái headcloth") and they are rarely worn at present.[44] The common version of this type of headcloth is made of two pieces of cloth. The smaller one is a piece of silk cloth with a red or rust red ground and colorful supplementary weft patterning and often a braided fringe. More recent pieces using aniline dyes may have other colors for the ground. This is attached to a much longer piece of black or dark blue cotton cloth that is either plain or decorated with a few woven or embroidered patterns at one end. In the past women commonly gave these headcloths along with decorative silk sashes as gifts to their daughters and daughters-in-law at weddings.

Prior to 1954 Táy Dón women often wore a decorative hipcloth over their

4. Ethnic Minorities in Northern Việt Nam

tubeskirt on special occasions. It is about one-quarter to one-third the length of the skirt and is made of a variety of colored pieces of cloth.[45]

The Thái produce textiles to be used for a variety of other purposes as well. These include blankets, cotton checked sheets,[46] mosquito nets with decorated tops,[47] curtains to divide areas in the house, bed covers, face towels/handkerchiefs,[48] bath towels, decorated pillow covers, and decorative baby carriers. Blankets are made by sewing two pieces of cloth with supplementary weft patterning together and using pieces of plain cloth as edging and backing. With one type of blanket the decorative cloth has a plain white cotton ground and blue or black supplementary weft decorative patterning also woven with cotton thread.[49] The decorative cloth of the other type has red silk (or sometimes cotton) warp threads and supplementary weft patterning using a variety of colors of silk thread.[50]

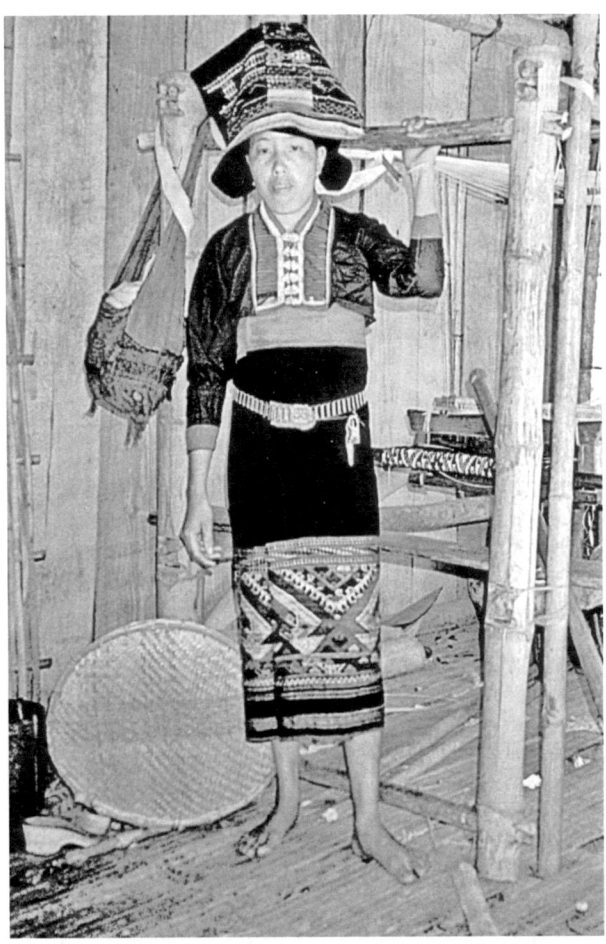

Lào (Lào Nọi sub-group) woman, Điện Biên District, Điện Biên Province.

Lào. The ancestors of the Lào lived in southern Yúnnán and then migrated south to settle in the vicinity of the Mã River in Điện Biên Province and western Sơn La Province. Some subsequently moved on to Laos and northeastern Thailand, but a few remained in northwestern Việt Nam. Among those remaining in Việt Nam some stayed in the Mã River while others moved north to Bình Lư (Phong Thổ District, Lai Châu Province) in the late 1700s along with a group of Lự from Điện Biên Province. I refer to the Lào that remained in the Mã River area as southern Lào and those that moved to Bình Lư as northern Lào. In the case of the Lào that migrated towards Laos members of one sub-group of Lào, the Lào Khrang settled in Xieng Khouang and Huaphanh provinces in Laos and a small number of them migrated to Kỳ Sơn District in the far west of Nghệ An Province during the 20th century. At present there are a total of about 15,000 Lào in Việt Nam.

The northern Lào adopted the dress of the Lự living there and this will be discussed in the next section. The Lào Khrang brought with them the dress style of Lào Khrang in Laos. This includes silk tubeskirts that have a body featuring weft ikat patterning and a separate hem-piece with supplementary weft patterning.[51]

The southern Lào live close to the Tái Dăm and were integrated into Thái feudal society and adopted many aspects of Tái Dăm culture, while retaining their own language and a distinctive style of female dress. These Lào were well known in the past for making handicrafts such as pottery, textiles, and silver jewelry. Southern Lào men often worked as traders in the past carrying such goods by overland on horseback or down rivers by boat to neighboring peoples and territories in Việt Nam and Laos.

In the past the southern Lào grew cotton and produced silk, but it is now common to use commercial threads as well as aniline rather than natural dyes. Southern Lào men formerly wore the standard highlands style of Chinese-inspired shirts and trousers and at present many wear generic commercial clothing. Most southern Lào women, however, continue to wear distinctive clothing that is often made of locally woven material. Southern Lào female clothing includes a blouse, tubeskirt, and headcloth. The blouse has long sleeves and opens down the front, but it is relatively short so that the waistband of the skirt is visible. Sometimes the blouse is fastened using *mák pém*. Formerly these were made of silver, but now they are aluminum. The blouse is made from plain cloth, usually dyed dark blue, with a lighter colored decorative panel attached around the collar and down the sides of the front opening. This is made of a piece of light colored cloth and narrow strips of brightly colored or patterned cloth are usually added around the edges.[52]

Southern Lào tubeskirts have one or two waistbands, a body, and sometimes a separate hem-piece. The waistbands may be made of plain cotton cloth or of silk cloth with plain weft directional stripes. There can be a single waistband made of either cotton or silk cloth or two waistbands made of both types (with the cotton piece placed above the silk one). The southern Lào weave the cloth for a skirt body so that the weft directional decorative features appear horizontally when worn. The cloth is cut into two pieces that are then stitched together down the sides. This is different than Thái skirts that have bodies made of a single piece of cloth that is formed into a tube and stitched together in one place only.

The southern Lào have several varieties of tubeskirt body.[53] One simple type is like those woven by the Thái and is a dark brownish color with thin weft directional lines (rather than warp directional). Sometimes these have ikat dashes, but by the 1990s only a few older women still made these ikat-patterned cloths. Another type features a wide decorative section with supplementary weft patterning, usually covering the lower part of the skirt body, but sometimes encompassing a larger portion. The upper part may have plain thin stripes like the first type of skirt-cloth or it may feature decorative stripes with colorful supplementary weft weave patterns and sometimes there are also separate narrow bands with tapestry weave patterns. The area in between these stripes may be left plain or occasionally it is covered with blue and white weft ikat dashes. There is a wide range of geometric and representational supplementary weft patterns. The southern Lào are the only group in Việt Nam to employ the tapestry technique and it is likely that they learned it from the Burmese who invaded the area in the late 1700s.[54] Sometimes a separate decorative hem-piece with colorful supplementary weft patterning is attached to the first type of skirt body.

Southern Lào women wear a simple style of headcloth on an everyday basis and a more decorative one on special occasions.[55] The everyday one is made of a piece of cotton cloth that is dyed dark blue or black that is either left plain or decorated at the ends with a little embroidery using silk thread or with narrow pieces of colorful commercial cloth. The special occasion headcloths may be made of cotton or silk and dyed red or black. The middle of the headcloth is left plain while the ends are decorated with supplementary weft patterning. If the central part becomes worn or soiled the ends will be cut off and attached to a new piece of plain cloth.

Lự. There are relatively large numbers of Lự (aka Tai Lü, Thai Lue, Lữ) living in southern Yúnnán and adjacent areas of northern Myanmar, Thailand, and Laos and there are around 6,000 of them living in northwestern Việt Nam. The Lự in Việt Nam came from southern Yúnnán and Phôngsali Province in northern Laos and settled in Điện Biên Province in the early 600s.[56] Like the Lào they later came under control of the Tái Dăm. When the Burmese invaded the area in the late 1700s most of the Lự, along with some Lào, moved north to Bình Lư.

Lự male attire in Việt Nam is a variation of the Chinese-inspired highlands male dress that includes a dark blue or black cotton shirt and trousers and sometimes a dark blue or black cotton headcloth.[57] In the past it was common for men to wear an inner shirt and an outer shirt. What distinguishes the clothing of these Lự men from that of other Tai-speaking men is the decoration on Lự men's shirts and trousers, whereas other Tai men's clothing is left plain, the outer shirts of Lự men have thin strips of the embroidery around the collar, down part of the sides, and across the pockets. The trousers have narrow bands of embroidery at the bottom of the trouser legs.

Lự women wear a headcloth, blouse, and one or two tubeskirts.[58] The blouse has narrow long sleeves and fastens on the right. Normally it is made of black cotton cloth, but on festive occasions some women wear blouses made of silk. The blouses commonly are decorated in a variety of ways with appliqué, strips of colorful cloth, embroidery, and round (these are sometimes French Indochinese coins) and triangular shaped pieces of silver (or silver-colored metal) along the collar and down the front flap, around the waist, on the upper and lower parts of the sleeves, and sometimes elsewhere as well. The headcloth is much longer than those worn by other Tai women. It is made of black cotton cloth that is largely left plain except for several thin stripes at the ends. The headcloth is folded and then sewn together at the ends. There is fringe at each end and it is common to attach tassels of colorful thread and beads at one end.

There are two styles of tubeskirt: a simple one that is worn while working and as an underskirt and a fancier one that is worn on special occasions over the simple skirt. The simple everyday skirt is comprised of three parts. The waistband is made of a single piece of plain brown or rust colored cotton cloth. The body of the skirt is made of two pieces of cloth that are stitched together down the sides of the skirt. The body is usually woven with cotton thread, but silk thread is used as well sometimes. The top half of the body is divided into an upper part with plain wide brown or rust colored horizontal stripes that are divided by thin white and brown or rust colored stripes and a lower part with plain wide black horizontal stripes that are divided by thin white and rust colored stripes. The hem-piece is roughly the same length as the body and is made of plain black cotton cloth. There is a decorative panel attached to the hem-piece made of an odd number (often seven) of vertical stripes that are made from strips of patterned commercial cotton cloth. In addition, a narrow strip of patterned commercial cloth is attached along the bottom of the hem. The fancier skirt is basically the same as the simple skirt except that the lower section of the body features three bands with colorful supplementary weft patterning woven using silk thread. There is a wide central band and narrower bands above and below it.

Other Lự textiles include towels/handkerchiefs similar to those made by the Thái and cotton blankets. The blankets are made by sewing two pieces of cloth together. They have a white ground and indigo or rust colored supplementary weft patterning. Unlike the Thai, the Lự do not add pieces of plain white cloth as edging and backing.

Bố Y and Giáy. As was discussed in the first chapter, the sub-groups of Bùyī (Bouyei) that migrated from Guìzhōu to northern Việt Nam are treated as two separate ethnic groups in Việt Nam, the Bố Y and Giáy, and the Tu Dí are treated as a distinct sub-group of the Bố Y. There are a little over 2,000 Bố Y in Việt Nam (about equally divided between Bố Y and Tu Dí) and about 60,000 Giáy. The Bố Y live in Hà Giang Province's Quản Bạ District, the Tu Dí in Lào Cai Province (mainly in Mường Khương District, with a few also found in Bảo Yên and Bát Xát districts), and the Giáy are found in several districts in Cao Bằng, Hà Giang, Lào Cai, and Lai Châu provinces.

While some Bố Y grow cotton and weave their own cloth, most Giáy and Tu Dí make their clothing from commercial cloth. Modern Bố Y males in Việt Nam wear Chinese-style shirts and trousers. Some Bố Y women in Hà Giang Province's Quản Bạ District continue to wear traditional dress as is worn in remote areas of Guìzhōu (discussed in Chapter 1), but since the 1940s most have come to wear Chinese-style five-panel blouses and trousers like neighboring Nùng and Hoa.[59]

The Giáy have completely adopted Chinese-style dress.[60] In the past Giáy women wore a five-panel tunic that had wide sleeves and vents on the sides and a full skirt that reached to the knees, but these were no longer worn by the 1970s. Weaving had also largely ceased by that time and is now very rare. Contemporary Giáy female clothing consists of a tight-sleeved five-panel blouse that is made of commercial cloth. Colors of the body of the blouse vary and normally strips of cloth of a contrasting color are added around the collar, across the front flap, and at the cuffs.

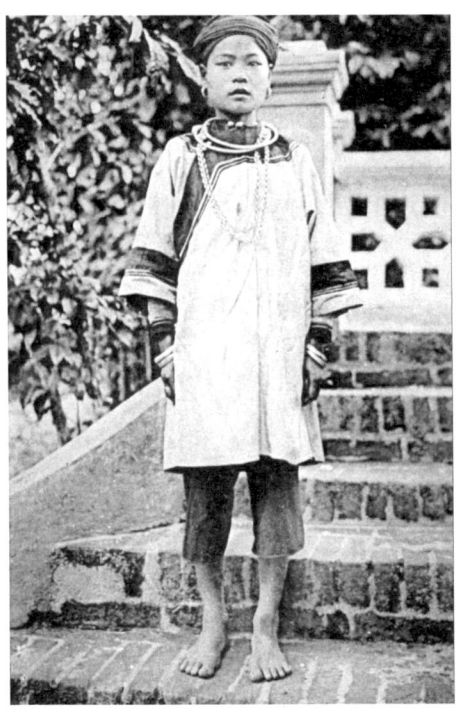
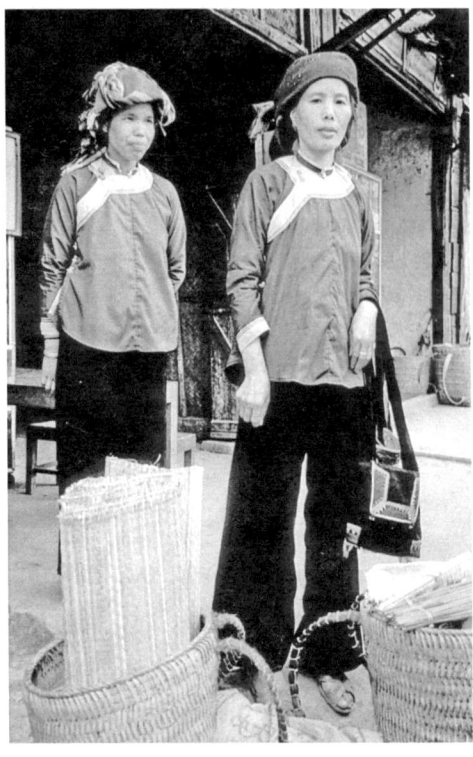
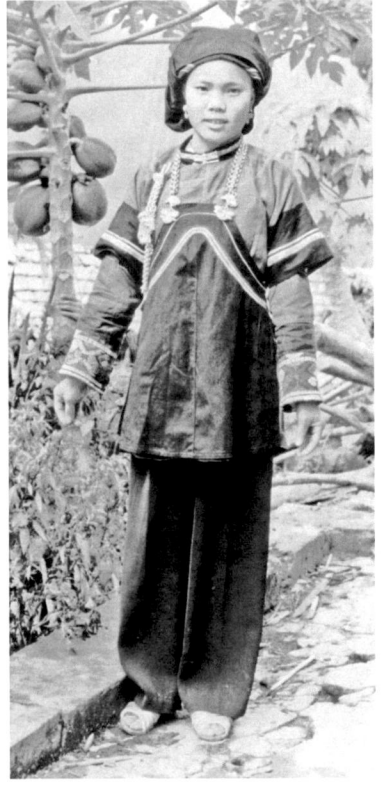

Left, top: **Giáy woman (from Abadie, *Les Races du Haut-Tonkin*, pl. 23, fig. 64).** *Right:* **Modern Giay women, Tả Van commune, Sa Pa District, Lào Cai Province.** *Left, bottom:* **Tu Dí woman, Mường Khương District, Lào Cai Province.**

The Tu Dí have also adopted Chinese-style dress. Tu Dí women formerly wore full skirts, but trousers had replaced them by the mid–20th century. In fact, the Tu Dí had adopted many elements of Chinese culture by the 19th century.[61] In the past Tu Dí women were well known for their abilities at making thread, weaving, and embroidery. They still embroider, but now usually use commercial cloth and thread. Tu Dí women wear a Chinese-style five-panel blouse that fastens on the right, but that differs from those worn by many other groups in the way the sleeves are made.[62] The blouse has segmented sleeves composed of a relatively wide short sleeve and then a separate narrower sleeve-piece with embroidery at the end that is attached inside the short sleeve. Tu Dí women also still wear aprons. These are relatively plain with a few pieces of decorative cloth added near the top.

Cao Lan. People speaking Cao Lan are included in the Sán Chay ethnic category in Việt Nam along with the Chinese-speaking Sán Chỉ. This unusual situation is a result of the their ancestors migrating together from China some time in the 1600s. The ancestors of the Cao Lan originally lived in the Húnán, Guǎngdōng, Guǎngxī border region and spoke a Northern Tai language. They then moved south to settle among the Zhuàng in Guǎngxī before finally settling in northern Việt Nam.[63] As a result the Tai that they speak can be categorized as Northern Tai, but it contains Central Tai elements.[64] There are about 170,000 Cao Lan living mainly in Tuyên Quang, Thái Nguyên, and Bắc Giang provinces. The Cao Lan dress like Kinh or Tày.

Mon-Khmer Groups

The Lò Yuè and Hàn assimilated the Mon-Khmer people that lived in the lowlands of northern Việt Nam in antiquity and their descendants eventually became Kinh. Today there are two distinct groups of Mon-Khmer speaking minority peoples in northern Việt Nam. One is comprised of the Vietic speaking Mường and Thổ. Vietic languages belong to the Northeastern Môn-Khmer sub-family and are related to the Katuic languages. The ancestors of these people migrated down the Mekong River, settled in Laos, and then later migrated east into Việt Nam. The Mường and Thổ are commonly viewed as ancestors of the Kinh that remained in the highlands rather than moving into the lowlands to eventually become Kinh. The second is comprised of ethnic groups that speak languages belonging to the Northern Mon-Khmer sub-family. Northern Mon-Khmer languages are spoken along the border region of southern China and the northern parts of Việt Nam, Laos, Thailand, and Myanmar. The ancestors of the Northern Mon-Khmer groups in Việt Nam lived in the highlands prior to the arrival of the Thái. After the Thái settled in the highlands many of these Northern Mon-Khmer were assimilated into Thái society, but some retained distinct identities, although with cultures that were noticeably influenced by the Thái. The Tái Mười of Nghệ An are an example of a group of Northern Mon-Khmer people that adopted Thái language and culture, including styles of dress, to the point of identifying themselves as a Thái sub-group.[65] Contemporary Northern Mon-Khmer groups in Việt Nam include the Khơ Mú, Xinh Mun, Kháng, Mảng, and Ơ Đu.

Thổ. Thổ is an ethnic category for seven different small closely related Vietic groups: the Họ, Kẹo, Mọn, Cuối, Đan Lai, Ly Hà, and Tày Poọng. There are about 75,000 Thổ living mainly in Nghệ An Province with a few also found in Thanh Hóa Province. They grow hemp, which is used to make such things as nets, hammocks, and bags, but they do not weave. Thổ men presently wear generic modern clothing, while Thổ women dress like neighboring Mường or Thái from with whom they trade for cloth.[66]

Mường. There are around 1.3 million Mường living mainly in Hòa Bình and Thanh Hòa provinces, with some also in Nghệ An Province. Mường culture, including their styles of dress has been strongly influenced by Thái culture.[67] In the past many Mường households grew cotton, produced silk, and wove in frame looms similar to those used by the Thái. During the French colonial period, although home-based weaving was still important the Mường made greater use of commercial cloth for their clothing than many of the other highlands peoples. Most of this commercial cloth was produced in the lowlands, but the Mường also purchased Chinese silk imported from China and cotton imported from Japan. Male clothing in particular usually was made from commercial cloth.

By the time of the French colonial period Mường males were wearing clothing like that worn by Thái and Kinh males. This included Thái/Kinh versions of Chinese-style trousers and shirts and sometimes a Kinh-style long shirt. They often wore a headcloth. These were undecorated and usually were white or brown, although where Thái influence was especially noticeable they often were dark blue. Prior to 1954, like their Thái counterparts, Mường males of noble status or that held government posts often dressed like their Kinh counterparts.

Traditional Mường female attire is similar to that of neighboring southern Thái and includes a tubeskirt, breastcloth, blouse, gown, sash, and headcloth. The body of the tubeskirt is made of plain dark blue or black cotton or silk (sometimes the material is a combination of the two). Before 1954 high status Mường women often wore clothing made of satins and brocades on special occasions. Mường skirts are commonly tailored to be a little looser than Thái tubeskirts.[68] A thin strip of red, green, or sometimes blue or yellow cloth is added inside the hem. Like southern Thái tubeskirts the Mường add up to three waistbands that are decorated with supplementary warp patterning. Everyday skirts as were worn by most women would have only two bands, while skirts with three bands were worn by noble women on an everyday basis and sometimes by others on special occasions. The Mường followed Thái practice and reserved the dragon motif on waistbands for noble women.

The breastcloth worn by Mường women is similar to those worn by Kinh women, but shorter, reaching only to just below the breasts rather than down to the navel. The blouse is made of plain white or brown cotton cloth. The sash is usually made of plain green silk cloth. The headcloth is relatively short and is made of plain white, dark blue, or black cotton cloth. The gown opens in the front. Women sometimes wear a plain white gown under a dark colored one. In the past noble women might wear an over-gown on special occasions. Sometimes these were made of red silk or of silk with brocade patterning. A plain white sash is worn around the gown.

Khơ Mú. There are over 600,000 Khơ Mú (aka Khmu) living in Laos and about 73,000 in Việt Nam. Most Khơ Mú in Việt Nam live in Nghệ An Province, but there are small groups of them scattered across the northwestern highlands. Only a few Khơ Mú communities in Việt Nam have traditions of weaving. These Khơ Mú weave narrow pieces of rough cotton cloth on a backstrap loom.[69] The Khơ Mú generally obtain cloth from neighboring Thái and dress like the particular sub-group of Thái that lives near them.[70]

Xinh Mun. There are around 24,000 Xinh Mun (aka Con Pua, Puộc, Pụa) living in Điện Biên and Sơn La provinces. In the past they occupied a low status in the Tái Dăm feudal system. It was never common for Xinh Mun to weave and for the most part they obtain cloth from neighboring Thái and they dress like the Tái Dăm.[71]

Kháng. There are about 14,000 Kháng and they live to the east of the Xinh Mun Điện Biên and Sơn La provinces. The Kháng grow cotton, which they exchange with the Thái for cloth. The Kháng also occasionally weave on a backstrap loom. Kháng clothing is made of plain dark blue or black cotton cloth. Kháng men dress like Thái men. Kháng women also traditionally dress like Thái, except that sometimes they would wear Chinese-style trousers instead of a tubeskirt. In the past Kháng women often wore tunics, but this is no longer common.[72]

Mảng. There are around 4,500 Mảng in Lai Châu Province in Việt Nam and a few across the border in Yúnnán. The Mảng are well known for making rattan baskets and stools, which they trade with Táy Dón for cotton cloth.[73] Mảng men wear common highlands male attire or, these days, commercial Western-style clothing. Mảng women wear a plain dark blue of black wrap-around skirt and a blouse that is similar to those worn by neighboring Táy Dón women. They also wear a sort of apron around the center of their body (covering an area roughly from below the breasts to the middle of the thighs) that is secured by tied at the waist. It is made of two pieces of white cotton cloth that is plain except for some decorative embroidery using red thread along the edges and seam. In addition they sometimes wear white leggings with embroidery near the edges like those worn by neighboring Dao.

Ơ Đu. The Ơ Đu is a small group of only about 600 that live in Nghệ An Province's Tương Dương District (there are also a few living across the border in Laos). Some Ơ Đu wove in the past, but in general they obtain cloth from neighboring Thái. Men tend to dress like Thái or to wear generic clothing. Women generally wear Tái Mường style skirts, but occasionally wear Tái Thanh style ones.[74]

Hmong-Mien Groups

As was mentioned in the first chapter, for the most part peoples speaking Hmong-Mien languages began to arrive in Việt Nam in the late 18th century with most coming during the latter half of the 19th century. They settled mainly at high elevations, far away from the reaches of government authorities, initially in Hà Giang and Lào Cai provinces and gradually spread across the highlands to the east and west. These highland regions are no longer as isolated as they were in the 19th century. Sa Pa District in Lào Cai Province, where a large number of Black Hmông and Red Dao live in particular attracts tens of thousands of domestic and international tourists every year and this has created a commercial market for Black Hmông and Red Dao textiles.[75]

Hmông. There are about 1.1 million Hmông in Việt Nam today and most still

4. Ethnic Minorities in Northern Việt Nam

live at high elevations. The largest number of Hmông live in Hà Giang and Lào Cai provinces, with smaller numbers being found in all of the northern highland provinces as far south as Nghệ An Province. Some also moved to the Central Highlands during the latter half of the 20th century. As was mentioned in Chapter 1 there are five main sub-groups in Việt Nam. In order of relative size they are the Flowery Hmông (aka Hmông Hoa, Hmông Lenh), White Hmông (aka Hmông Trắng, Hmông Do, includes Striped Hmông), Black Hmông (aka Hmông Đen, Hmông Du), Red Hmông (aka, Hmông Đỏ Hmông Si, Hmông Su), and Blue Hmông (aka Hmông Xanh, Hmông Njua, includes Chinese Hmông/Hmông Sua).

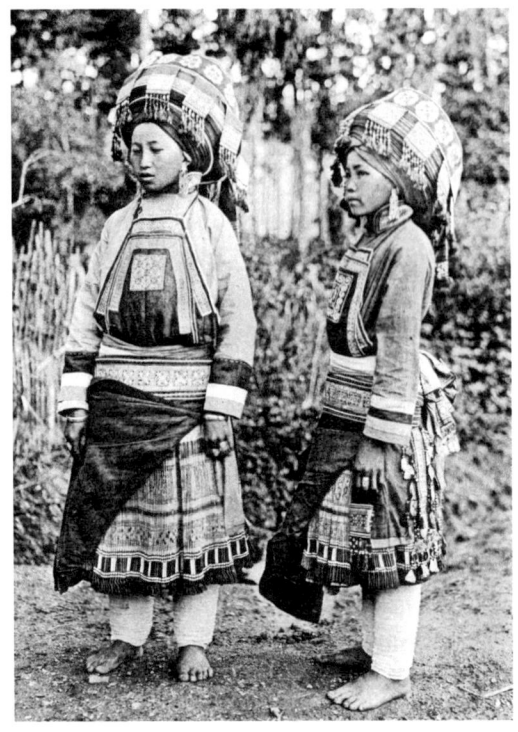

Hmông (White Hmông sub-group) women (from Abadie, *Les Races du Haut-Tonkin*, pl. 35, fig. 46).

Since the Hmông live at high altitudes they are able to grow little or no cotton and mainly must obtain cotton thread or cloth through trade. They are, however, able to grow hemp, which is used to make thread for cloth. The use of hemp cloth by the Hmông has declined in many areas in recent years as commercial thread has become more readily available, but hemp cloth continues to be made in several areas. It is used especially in making women's skirts. The Hmông weave on a type of combination frame and backstrap loom.

Hmông male attire consists of trousers, a shirt, and a headcloth. There is no specific difference between the dress of men from the various sub-groups. The trousers have a wide waist and are folded when worn. In the past it was common to hold the trousers in place with a belt made of woven cloth. Men often wear both a plain white under-shirt and a dark blue or black outer-shirt. The outer-shirt has long sleeves and fastens to the right side. The outer-shirt does not fully cover the stomach and is shorter than shirts worn by highland men from other ethnic groups. It is also shorter than the under-shirt. Male headcloths are made of plain dark blue or black cloth. They are not worn everyday, but only on special occasions. Since the French colonial period Hmông men also sometimes wear dark colored caps.

Hmông women wear a long-sleeved blouse, short wrap-around pleated skirt, sash, apron, headcloth, and leggings. The attire of females from each Hmông sub-group differs in some features and most of the names commonly used by others to identify the Hmong sub-groups are related to the predominant color of female skirts.

White Hmông women wear a long-sleeved blouse that opens in the front and sometimes a breastcloth underneath the blouse.[76] The breastcloth is usually made of plain white cloth. The blouse is made of plain dark blue or black cloth and decorated with strips of different colored cloth around the collar, front opening, across the bottom, around the upper part of the sleeves, and at the end of the sleeves. Blouses also sometimes have what French authors commonly refer to as a "marine" collar (i.e., a collar resembling a sailor's). In the case of the common blouses this collar is made of a narrow piece of plain cloth that is of a different color than the body. With fancier blouses wider pieces of colorful cloth with embroidery and other decorative features are used. The blouses of the Striped Hmong sub-group differ in the manner of decorating the sleeves with a series of stripes that are a contrasting color with the body of the blouse.

The pleated skirts of White Hmông women are made of plain white cloth. The common version of the apron is made of plain dark blue or black cloth, while fancier versions are made of several pieces of differently colored cloth forming a series of rectangles. White Hmông women employ a variety of types of cloth for their sashes. The leggings are usually made of dark blue or black cloth. The headcloth is made from a long piece of dark blue or black cloth that is folded and wrapped around the head a number of times. Most of the headcloth is plain with small decorative pieces of differently colored cloth attached along the end. It has become common in recent year for Striped Hmông women to wear trousers instead of skirts.[77]

A Flowery Hmông female is easy to distinguish from a White Hmông.[78] The Flowery Hmông blouse fastens on the right side and never has a "marine" collar. The blouse is made of dark blue or black cloth and may be lined with plain white cloth. Strips of decorative cloth are attached around the collar, along the front flap, on the ends of the sleeves, and sometimes around the upper part of the sleeves as well. As with White Hmông blouses, the decorative cloth used on common Flowery Hmông blouses is narrower and has fewer decorative features than that used for fancier versions. In general, however, Flowery Hmông women's blouses are more extensively decorated than those of White Hmông

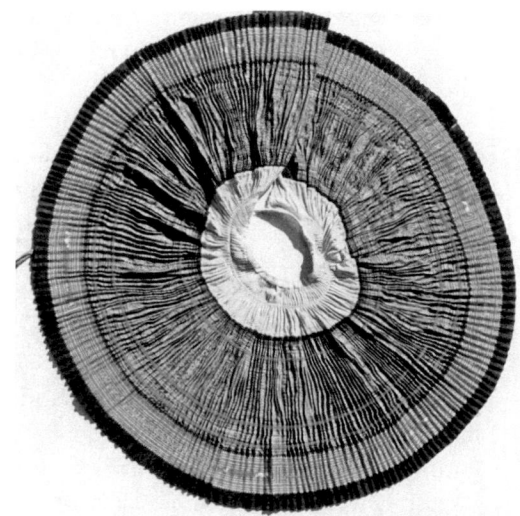

Hmông (Flowery Hmông sub-group) pleated wrap-around skirt (central portion made of batik patterned hemp cloth), Lào Cai Province.

women. Also, the Flowery Hmông sometimes use cloth decorated with batik patterning on their blouses, something that is not found on White Hmông blouses. When the weather is cold Flowery Hmông sometimes also wear a sleeveless jacket over their blouse that is made of plain dark blue or black cloth.

The Flowery Hmông pleated wrap-around skirt is made of four pieces of cloth and it is quite different looking than White Hmông skirts. The waistband is made from plain dark blue or black cloth. The upper part of the skirt body is made from a piece of cloth that is decorated with blue and white batik patterning. The lower part of the skirt body is made from a piece of cloth that is decorated with multi-colored embroidery and appliqué and sometimes also with blue and white batik. The hem is made from a narrow piece of black or dark blue cloth.

Flowery Hmông aprons may be made solely of rectangular pieces of plain cloth or may include two decorated pieces of cloth over the plain cloth. Whereas White Hmông aprons layer single rectangular pieces of cloth, Flowery Hmông aprons feature two parallel pieces of cloth.

There are two types of Flowery Hmông sash. One type a made from an undecorated piece of dark blue cloth. The other type is made from a shorter piece of cloth and features a section at each end that is decorated with embroidery and long fringe. Flowery Hmông leggings are made of white, blue or black cloth. The Flowery Hmông headcloth is made from a long piece of plain dark blue or black cloth.

The Black Hmông in Việt Nam live mainly in the far west of Lào Cai Province. A French source from the early 20th century describes Black Hmông women wearing a short black pleated skirt, dark blue blouse edged with light blue and with sleeves that end with light blue facing and white edging, an embroidered breastcloth, a sash of light color with long fringe hanging down the rear, a light blue headcloth, and leggings.[79]

Reference to the skirt being short reflects the fact that generally Black Hmông skirts usually are shorter than those worn by White Hmông and Flowery Hmông. This type of skirt is dark, but in fact not completely black. It has a plain dark blue or black waistband and a body with blue and white batik and appliqué patterning. The colors tend to be darker than those used by the Flowery Hmông. Also the Black Hmông skirt is made of two pieces of cloth, whereas the Flowery Hmông skirt is made of three pieces and also has embroidered patterning. The Black Hmông in Mù Cang Chải District, Yên Bái Province, have two styles of skirt. One is like the type worn by other Black Hmông women and a second type has a body that is white with narrow dark blue or black stripes.[80] Black Hmông women sometimes wear a black apron. They also sometimes wear a relatively long dark blue sleeveless vest that opens down the front. For the most part, Black Hmông clothing is more somber than that worn by other Hmông sub-groups. In recent years Black Hmông women increasingly wear black trousers. These are shorter than men's trousers. They also wear woolen scarves imported from China as headcloths. These have become popular throughout the highland border area.

The Red Hmông are commonly treated as a sub-group of Flowery Hmông in Việt Nam even though they speak a language categorized as belonging to the Xianxi branch of Hmong and the Flowery Hmông speak a language that belongs to the Chuan-qiandian branch. Red Hmông women in Lai Châu Province wear blouses that are similar to those worn by the White Hmông, but wrap-around skirts similar to those worn by the Flowery Hmông.[81] The Red Hmông skirts are also made of three pieces of cloth and tend to differ from Flowery Hmông skirts in decorative details, especially the lower part that is made of plain black cloth with embroidered patterning and rectangular pieces of cloth, and in the predominance of red.

There are relatively few Blue Hmông in Việt Nam, where the live in a few communes in Lai Châu and Lào Cai provinces. Traditionally Blue Hmông women wear a wrap-around pleated skirt made of two pieces of cloth similar to those of the Black Hmông and a blouse that is fastened on the left side with a single string.[82]

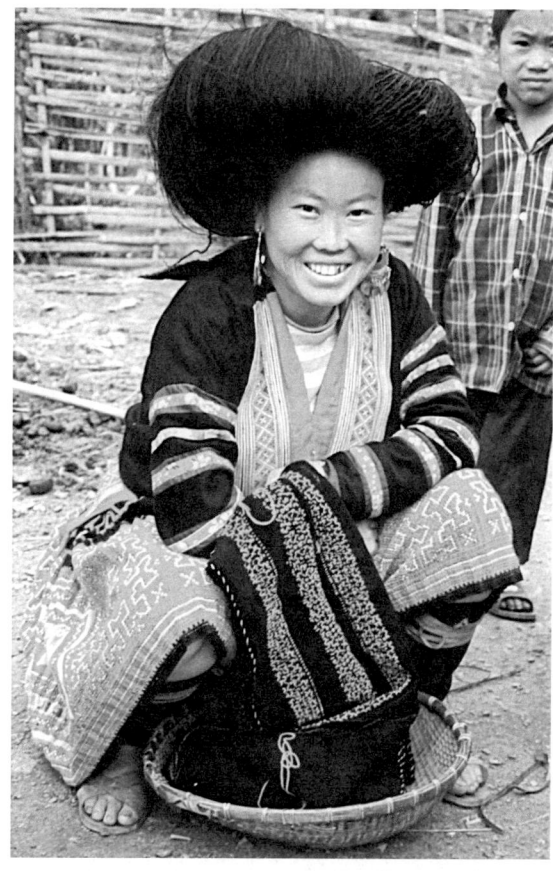

Hmông (Red Hmông sub-group) woman, Mường Chà District (formerly Mường Lay), Điện Biên Province.

The blouse is decorated with pieces of white or colored cloth. The upper part of the skirt is made of dark blue cloth and the lower piece has blue and white batik patterning and thin strips of cloth and dark embroidery.[83] Some Blue Hmông women now wear trousers instead of skirts.

Since the late 1980s the Hmông in Việt Nam have had much greater access to commercial cloth and decorations for their clothing than previously. While the basic design of their clothing has not changed, the materials used have. When making their skirts many Hmông women now use cloth made of commercial cotton or synthetic fiber rather than hand-woven hemp cloth. Making hemp thread and weaving hemp cloth on traditional looms is a time-consuming process that meant Hmông families had little clothing. Essentially, a person got a new set of clothes at New Year. The use of commercial cloth has meant that they now have more items of clothing than in the past and women spend less time making clothing. The new clothing is far less

4. Ethnic Minorities in Northern Việt Nam

durable than the older type of clothing, but it is also easier to replace. Hmông skirts are still decorated as in the past, but now strips of commercial cotton or synthetic fiber cloth with printed patterns made to resemble the Hmông batik ones are available from China, where it is made for the Chinese Hmông market. In addition a wide variety of decorative items are imported from China for clothing ranging from pompoms made of synthetic fiber to narrow strips of colorful patterned cloth.

Pà Thẻn. The Pà Thẻn (aka Pa Hng, Pá Hưng) speak a Hmong language that is sometimes categorized as belonging to a separate branch of the Hmong-Mien family. In China they live primarily in Guìzhōu and Húnán and were sometimes referred to as Màn Pà Seng or Eight Surname Yao and other ethnic groups tend to categorize them as a sub-group of Iu Mien. Some of them migrated to Việt Nam along with groups of Iu Mien in the late 18th or 19th centuries and scattered along the Gâm River in Hà Giang and Tuyên Quang provinces, where today there are about 7,000 of them living in several districts.

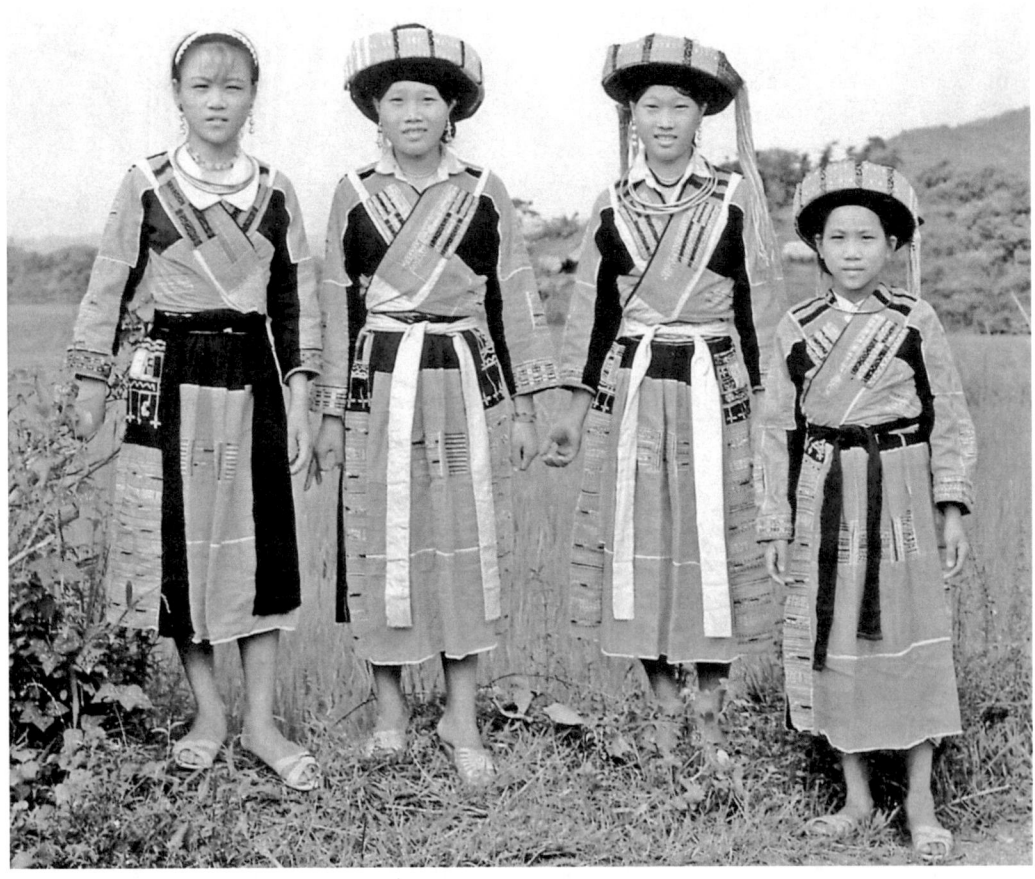

Group of Pà Thẻn women, Bắc Quang District, Hà Giang Province.

The Pà Thẻn traditionally grew cotton and wove narrow strips of cloth on a small frame loom.[84] They weave plain cotton cloth as well as cloth with a cotton ground and supplementary weft patterning using silk threads.[85] The patterns are mostly geometric such as triangles, rhombs, and floral shapes, but occasionally there are representations of human and animal figures. They assemble these narrow pieces of cloth to make their clothing. Pà Thẻn women have a reputation as good weavers and there is a history of the Pà Thẻn exchanging textiles to obtain other items in trade.

Pà Thẻn men in Việt Nam tended to dress in Chinese fashion like neighboring Tày-Nùng men. The dress of Pà Thẻn women, however, is unique.[86] They wear a long-sleeved blouse that is folded to the right and closed by tucking it into their skirt leaving a shallow V-opening at the neck. The blouse is made of several plain pieces of red, dark blue or black, and, sometimes white cloth. Small rectangular pieces of cloth with supplementary weft patterning are then attached at the cuffs and near the V of the opening. They wear a skirt that reaches to mid-calf. It is made of long strips of dark blue or black cloth and the hem is edged with a thin strip of plain red cloth. A sash made of plain cloth is worn around the waist. It is often white, but can be another color. Women wear either one or two aprons over their skirts. These are mainly made of plain red cloth along with some pieces of dark blue or black cloth, and it is common to add a few long strips of cloth with supplementary weft patterning. There are two parts to the headcloth. There is an inner part made of plain dark blue or black cloth that is folded and then tightly wound around the head. A long strip of decorative cloth with supplementary weft patterning is then wrapped around the outside.

Dao. There are about 470,000 people in Việt Nam speaking Mienic languages. The Vietnamese refer to them as Dao and in the past they were commonly called Mán. Elsewhere they are sometimes called Yao. The Dao in Việt Nam speak two different Mienic languages: Iu Mien and Kim Mun. Most Dao speak Iu Mien. Iu Mien speakers can be divided into the Đại Bản and Tiểu Bản groups. Most Iu Mien belong to the Đại Bản group and only one sub-group, the Dao Tiền, are categorized as Tiểu Bản. Đại Bản sub-groups are comprised of the Dao Đỏ, Dao Thanh Phán, and Dao Quần Chẹt. There are two groups of Kim Mun speakers, the Khố Bạch and the Lán Tiền. The Khố Bạch group is comprised of the Dao Quần Trắng and Dao Thanh Y sub-groups and the Lán Tiền group includes the Lán Tiền. The reason for mentioning all of these sub-groups is that many of them have distinctive styles of dress. In addition, there are often regional differences within sub-groups. Moreover, like the Hmông, many Dao sub-group names refer to the dress of the women. For example, Dao Quần Trắng means Dao with white trousers and Dao Quần Chẹt means Dao with tight trousers.

Some Dao communities in Việt Nam have traditions of growing cotton and weaving their own cotton cloth, but not all. Many Dao communities in Lào Cai Province have traditions of trading for cloth with people living at lower elevations. Also, some

4. Ethnic Minorities in Northern Việt Nam

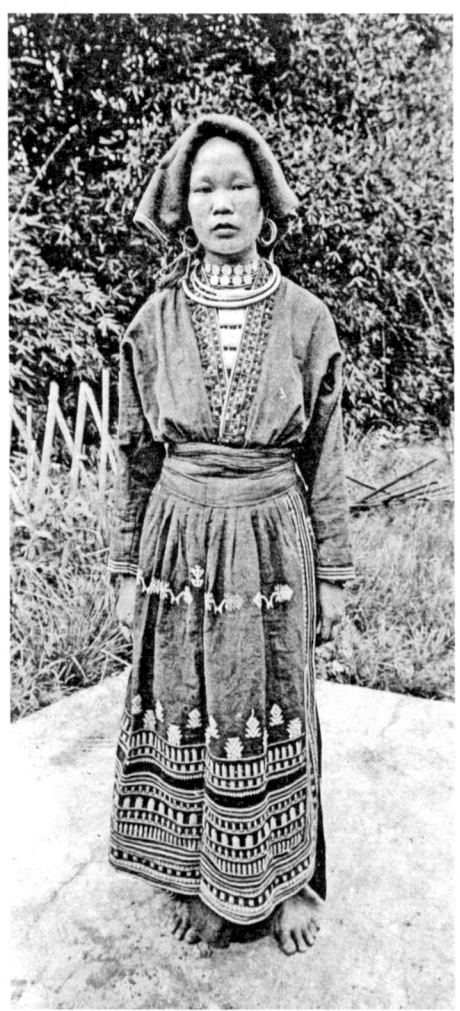

Dao (Thanh Phán sub-group) woman, Bắc Hà District, Lào Cai Province (from Abadie, *Les Races du Haut-Tonkin*, pl. 32, fig. 421).

Dao Đỏ and Dao Lô Gang (a sub-group of the Dao Thanh Phán) communities that grow cotton do not weave, but trade it for woven cloth. Overall growing cotton does not seem to have ever been widespread among the Dao and today much of the clothing that they wear is made from commercial cloth. During the French colonial period wealthy Dao sometimes wore clothing made of silk that they obtained through trade, including imported Chinese silk satin.[87]

Dao cloth usually is dyed dark blue and the natural dye repertoire of the Dao is not very extensive. Traditional Dao dress is strongly influenced by the Chinese. It can be viewed essentially as an older style of Chinese dress with variations that are particular to the Dao. This is especially true of the manner in which the Dao decorate their clothing. The Dao decorate their clothing largely with embroidery and by attaching various decorative items. While the embroidery technique reflects Chinese influence, the particular patterns tend to be distinct. Most colors found on Dao clothing besides dark blue are associated with embroidery. The Dao sometimes use colored silk thread that they obtain through trade for embroidery, but in recent years they have mainly used commercial cotton thread and wool yarn. Many of the other items that they use to decorate their clothing are also obtained through trade. In the past various decorative objects were made of silver in some Dao communities, but this ceased decades ago and now these objects are made from aluminum or other less expensive metals. In addition to clothing intended for everyday wear, many Dao sub-groups produce a variety of textiles to be worn on special occasions or by religious specialists. Dao religious beliefs include ancestor worship and Taoist elements, along with belief in numerous spirits and priests are quite important in their society.

We turn first to the Đại Bản sub-groups, starting with the Dao Đỏ (Red Dao) and Dao Thanh Phán (aka Man Ta Pan, Black Dao; and including local groups such as the Dao Lô Gang).[88] The Dao Đỏ are the Dao that tourists encounter when visiting

Hmong-Mien Groups

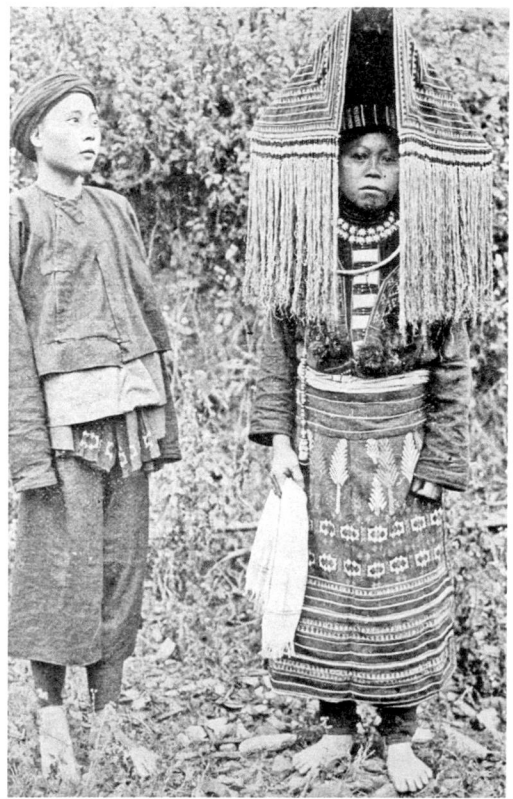
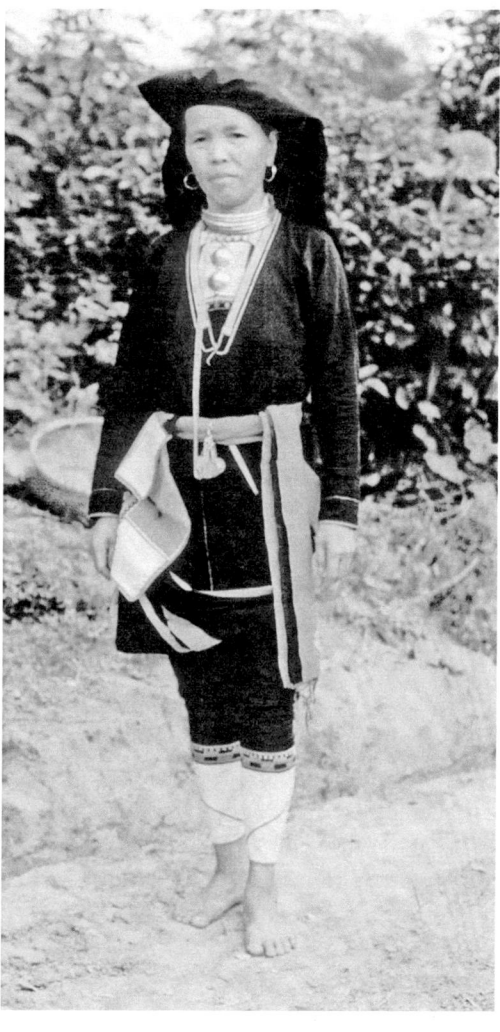

Left: Dao (Thanh Phán sub-group) couple in wedding dress (from Bonifacy, *Les Groupes Ethniques du Bassin de la Rivière Claire*, pl. 14, fig. 2). *Right:* Dao (Quần Chẹt sub-group) woman, Sơn Dương District, Tuyên Quang Province.

Sa Pa, but there are other Dao Đỏ scattered across the northern highlands. The name Dao Thanh Phán appears to be a Vietnamese version of the Chinese name for them, Man Ta Pan, meaning Man with large trousers.[89] The Red Dao and Black Dao distinction refers to the color of the headdresses worn by women of the respective sub-groups. There are regional differences in the dress of both groups. Thus, the Dao Thanh Phán living from Phong Thổ District in Lai Châu Province in the west to the western part of Cao Bằng Province in the east dress more or less alike, but those living further east in Bắc Giang and Quảng Ninh provinces dress like the nearby Dao Lô Gang and Dao Quần Chẹt sub-groups.

Dao Đỏ and Dao Thanh Phán men have the same style of traditional dress and it is increasingly common for them to wear generic Western-style clothing on an everyday basis. Their traditional clothing includes trousers, a long-sleeved shirt, a sash, and a headcloth. During the French colonial period wearing a French-style beret became popular and these are still worn by some men. Their traditional clothing is made of dark blue cotton cloth. The trousers have a wide waist and are folded and tucked. Men sometimes wear a sash around their waist that is made from a folded piece of cloth and decorated with embroidery at the ends. The shirt has long sleeves and opens down the front. It is fastened on the right side with ties or small metal balls that are attached to a narrow flap. The outer edges of the front flap are decorated with narrow strips of colored cloth. The ends of the sleeves are decorated with several rows of embroidery. At the center of the back of the shirt there is usually a rectangle with embroidered patterning that represents the seal of the Iu Mien's ancestral king, Bàn Vương. Headcloths are made from long pieces of cloth that are plain except for some embroidery at the ends.

Dao Đỏ and Dao Thanh Phán women's dress includes trousers, tunic, breastcloth, headcloth, sash, leggings, and sometimes an apron. Women's trousers are made of dark blue cotton and are extensively decorated with embroidered patterns. The traditional style of trousers is for them to have a baggy waist and to be secured by folding and tucking, but drawstrings have become increasingly common. Now leggings for everyday wear are made of dark blue cotton cloth that may be decorated with some embroidered patterning, while special leggings worn by brides are made of white cotton cloth with extensive embroidered patterning. The tunic opens down the front, is worn so as to open only slightly near the neck, and has vents on the sides. It is decorated with appliqué and embroidery around the collar, along the upper part of the front opening, and sometimes there is embroidery at the ends of the sleeves and in a small rectangular area behind the collar as well. The front opening also may be decorated with a row of red pompoms on each side. There is usually an embroidered rectangle representing Bàn Vương on the back just below the collar and the portion of the back is extensively decorated with embroidered patterning. The breastcloth may be made of plain cotton cloth or from cloth that is decorated around the neck and down the front with embroidery. In the past Dao Thanh Phán women attached a row of rectangular silver plates to the center of the breastcloth (the number of these reflecting the individual's wealth). It has become increasingly common for Dao Đỏ and Dao Thanh Phán women to wear a commercial blouse under their tunic rather than a traditional breastcloth. Sashes are made from a piece of plain cotton cloth that is folded and decorated at the ends with fringe, beads, and sometimes with embroidery. Everyday aprons are relatively plain, while the special occasion version is larger and features extensive embroidered patterning. On special occasions, such as weddings, women commonly will wear two aprons, one in front and another in back.

As was mentioned above, Dao Đỏ and Dao Thanh Phán women wear different colors of headcloth. The Dao Thanh Phán headcloth is made from dark blue cotton cloth. Sometimes these are quite large.[90] There are a variety of regional styles of headcloth worn by Dao Đỏ women. In the Sa Pa area they wear a headcloth made of a rectangular piece of plain red cotton cloth with tassels made of red thread and decorated with beads and small silver coins attached to two of the corners. The headcloth is folded to lie flat on the head and so that these decorative items hang down the back of the head.⁹¹ In Cao Bằng Province Dao Đỏ women sometimes wear a long piece of plain dark blue cloth that is folded and then tightly wound around their head. A shorter narrow decorative piece of cloth with a predominant red coloring is than fastened around the outside. Pà Thẻn women wear a similar style of headcloth (see the previous section).⁹² In Lai Châu Province's Phong Thổ District they form the red cloth into a cone and secure the lower part of the cone with a wide metal band that formerly was made of silver, but is now usually made of some silver-colored metal.⁹³ Brides traditionally wore a special headdress comprised of a rectangular piece of cloth (*dom paa*) decorated with embroidery

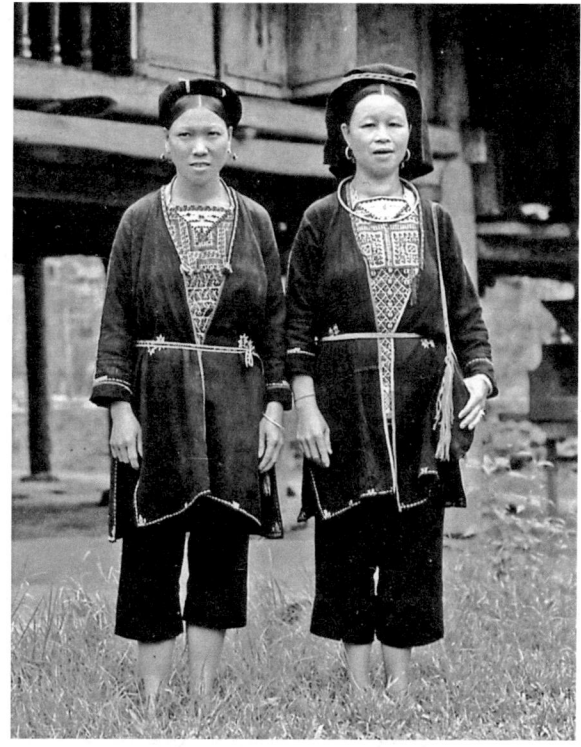

Dao (Quần Trắng sub-group) women, Tuyên Quang Province.

and sometime appliqué mounted on a frame made of wood and bamboo. These bridal headcloths are no longer made in all Dao Đỏ and Dao Thanh Phán communities and in some it has become common practice to use an umbrella instead of the traditional frame.⁹⁴

The Dao Lô Gang is a small sub-group of Dao Thanh Phán that live in Yên Sơn District of Tuyên Quang Province and Bắc Sơn District of Lạng Sơn Province.⁹⁵ The dress of Dao Lô Gang women is similar to that worn by other Dao Thanh Phán except for their headcloths. Also there tends to be less embroidery. The headcloth of Dao Lô Gang women in Lạng Sơn Province is made of a square piece of dark blue or black cloth that is edged with red cloth and worn folded in layers. Those in Tuyên Quang Province wear a headcloth made of a long piece of dark blue or black cloth with two sticks placed so as to make two points near the temples.

The Dao Quần Chẹt live in several different provinces scattered throughout the northern highlands as far south as Nghệ An Province. Despite this geographical spread there is no significant regional difference in their dress, with the exception of the Dao Sơn Đầu sub-group that live on Mẫu Sơn Mountain in Lạng Sơn Province.⁹⁶ Dao Quần Chẹt men wear a distinctive shirt. It is made of the usual dark blue or black cotton cloth, but features three pockets that are decorated. Traditionally the upper pocket has a red hem with white rhomb-shaped embroidered patterns and the center of the pocket has an embroidered square with the sun motif in the center that is surrounded with stars and other patterns. The two lower pockets are decorated in a similar fashion, but include a greater variety of patterns. In recent years it has become increasingly common for men to wear shirts with simpler decorative embroidery.

As the name indicates Dao Quần Chẹt women wear tight trousers. These trousers are made of dark blue or black cotton cloth and are largely left plain except for a narrow band of embroidered patterning near the bottom. The trousers reach to just below the knees and they wear plain white leggings that are wrapped tightly over the lower part of their legs. They wear a tunic made of dark blue or black cotton cloth that opens down the front and has vents on the sides. The left panel is fastened across the right one to form a V-neck opening. The collar and upper part of the neck opening are decorated with thin strips of colored cloth. Three thin strips of plain red and white cloth are sewn across the bottom of the front panels and usually there are three rows of embroidery above these. The embroidered motifs are fairly standardized: small square called pig cages on the lowest row, motifs representing trees in the middle row, and cross-like figures representing waterwheels on the top row. Five thin strips of plain red and white cloth and two sections with embroidery decorate the bottom of the back panels. There are more motifs on the back than the front, including ones depicting birds perched on trees and another representing the sun. The breastcloth worn under the blouse is made of dark blue or black cloth with embroidery and some metal decorations. The latter were made of silver in the past, but now are usually made of tin or aluminum. Dao Quần Chẹt women wear three styles of headcloth. One of these is made of a plain piece of dark blue cloth and it is worn underneath another headcloth with decorations. The everyday decorated headcloth is long and has embroidered patterning in the center and near the ends. The embroidery in the center features the sun motif, while the embroidery near the ends includes a variety of patterns such as those depicting pine trees and waterwheels. A woman wears another style of decorated headcloth when she marries. This one is square and covered with geometric embroidered patterns. Plain strips of red, white, and black cloth are sewn along the edges and rows of pompoms, pieces of colorful cloth cut into triangles, and strands of beads are attached along the edges and across the center. Glass beads were popular in the past, but today plastic ones are more common.

The dress of Dao Tiền women, which has been briefly discussed already, is quite different from that of other Dao in that they alone have a tradition of wearing skirts and of employing the batik technique. The Dao Tiền ("Dao with coins") include two regional sub-groups, the Southwestern Dao Tiền that live in Sơn La and Hòa Bình provinces and the Northern Dao Tiền that live in Cao Bằng and adjacent provinces.

Dao Tiền men's traditional dress includes dark blue cotton trousers that are decorated with embroidery at the bottom of each leg and a dark blue cotton long-sleeved tunic that reaches to the knees and opens in the front.[97] The tunic is decorated with small, embroidered patterns near the edges of the bottom of the front and at the ends of the sleeves. In the past it was common for there to be three or more large silver disks that are split to function as fasteners attached to the upper part of the front opening of the tunic, but these are now rarely worn. The embroidery often includes a motif that looks like a dog with a human head. This is the mythical dragon-dog Phan Hu that is a founding ancestor of the Iu Mien.[98] A small rectangular piece of cloth hangs down the back of the tunic. It is embroidered at the top and seven copper coins (*sapèques*) are suspended from the cloth. The coins represent the vital spirits. Men wear a sash around their waist that is usually made from a piece of cloth that is of a lighter color than the shirt. They also wear a dark blue headcloth and, sometimes, dark blue leggings.

Dao Tiền women wear a tunic that is similar to that worn by men except that it has nine rather than seven coins attached to the back and usually it has more embroidered patterning.[99] It is common for everyday tunic worn by both men and women to have less embroidery than those worn for weddings. In addition, brides and grooms wear two tunics, the outer one being slightly shorter than the inner one. Women wear a white breastcloth under their blouse. The short wrap-around skirt that they wear is dark blue and features rows of blue and white batik patterns across the lower half. This batik patterning includes a wide band with zigzags and above this, two narrow lines of small disk-shaped patterns. Dao Tiền women may wear a headcloth made of plain dark blue cloth or, primarily on special occasions, one that is made of plain white cotton cloth with an embroidered decorative square in the center near each end. Over this they may place a second piece of plain red cloth that often has small silver coins attached along with other items for decoration.

Unlike the Iu Mien and Làn Tiến that first came to Việt Nam in the 18th or 19th centuries, Dao of the Khố Bạch group of Kim Mun first arrived in Quảng Ninh Province from China in the 1200s. From there some moved Lạng Sơn Province and then further south to Thái Nguyên Province before finally settling down in Tuyên Quang Province. Today there are Dao belonging to the Thanh Y sub-group in a few districts in Quảng Ninh and Lạng Sơn provinces as well as in Tuyên Quang, Hà Giang, and Yên Bái provinces. Those belonging to the Quần Trắng sub-group live in Tuyên Quang, Hà Giang, and Yên Bái provinces.

An account of the Dao Thanh Y in the early 20th century describes men dressing like neighboring Tày and Nùng (i.e., in Chinese fashion).[100] While Dao Thanh Y men in some remote areas still dress in this fashion, most now wear generic Western-style clothing.

Dao Thanh Y females wear skullcap, headcloth, tunic, breastcloth, either long or short trousers, a sash, and leggings.[101] The skullcap is made of frame of hemp or loofah fibers that is covered by dark blue or black cloth.[102] The center of the cap is often decorated with a metal disk in the shape of a ten-pointed star with the rest of the area covered with rows of round metal disks or embroidery and a long fringe is attached, which is twisted around the head and allowed to hang loosely down the front or back. An additional small square piece of cloth is worn over the cap. It is made of white cotton cloth with embroidery using dark blue and red thread. This embroidery features a large eight-pointed star in the center surrounded by rows of small patterns including swastikas and two rows Chinese characters, one signifying "birth, preservation, fate and eternity" and the second "longevity as long as the mountains of the South; happiness as huge as the Eastern Sea."[103]

The Dao Thanh Y tunic is made of dark blue or black cotton cloth. The right front panel is shorter than the left one. The long panel is placed over the short one and the blouse is secured with a sash. Formerly the ends of the sleeves were decorated with embroidery, but now they are decorated with strips of commercial cloth. It has what one French author referred to as a "seaman's collar" that is decorated with embroidery.[104] The front panels are often edged with strips of colored cloth along the front opening and vents. The breastcloth is made of two pieces of cloth. The upper piece is white and has some embroidery. The lower part is dark blue or black. A curved collar with strands of beads is attached to the top of the breastcloth. In the past the beads were glass, but now they are usually plastic. Also formerly there were silver decorations attached to the breastcloth, but these are rarely seen now. Dao Thnh Y women in Quảng Ninh and western Lạng Sơn provinces wear short trousers, while elsewhere they wear long ones. In the past the cuffs of the trousers were decorated with embroidery, but now they are usually left plain. The leggings are made of plain triangular pieces of dark blue or black cloth. They are held in place by strings that often are decorated with beads or fringe.

Although they are called "Dao with white trousers," at least since the mid–20th century Dao Quần Trắng women wear plain dark blue trousers for everyday wear and plain white ones are worn only for weddings.[105] It is possible that they wore white trousers on an everyday basis previously, but this is unclear.[106] They also wear a front-opening tunic that reaches to just above the knees. It has vents on the sides and is closed so as the form a large V-shaped area reaching almost to the waist.[107] it is made of dark blue cotton cloth and is relatively plain. There are thin lines of decorative embroidery using silk thread across the shoulders on the cuffs, down the center of the back where the two panels are joined, along the vent openings, and across the bottom of the back. Pairs of small eight-pointed star figures are embroidered at the waist on each front panel and a large one at the waist in the back.[108] Thin strips of decorative cloth may be attached to the lower edges of the front panels as well. The tunic is secured with a narrow sash or belt.[109] The breastcloth worn by Dao Quần Trắng women is quite distinctive.[110] It is relatively large and covers the entire chest. It is made of white cotton cloth an area with embroidered patterning across the top and down the center. Red and black are the main colors of thread used. The lower part of the breastcloth is edged with strips of red and black cloth. Everyday headcloths are made of a square piece of dark blue or black cloth that is usually edged with strips of plain red, light blue cloth and has string attached to two corners to secure the cloth. Another style of headcloth is made of a dark blue pieces of cotton cloth covered

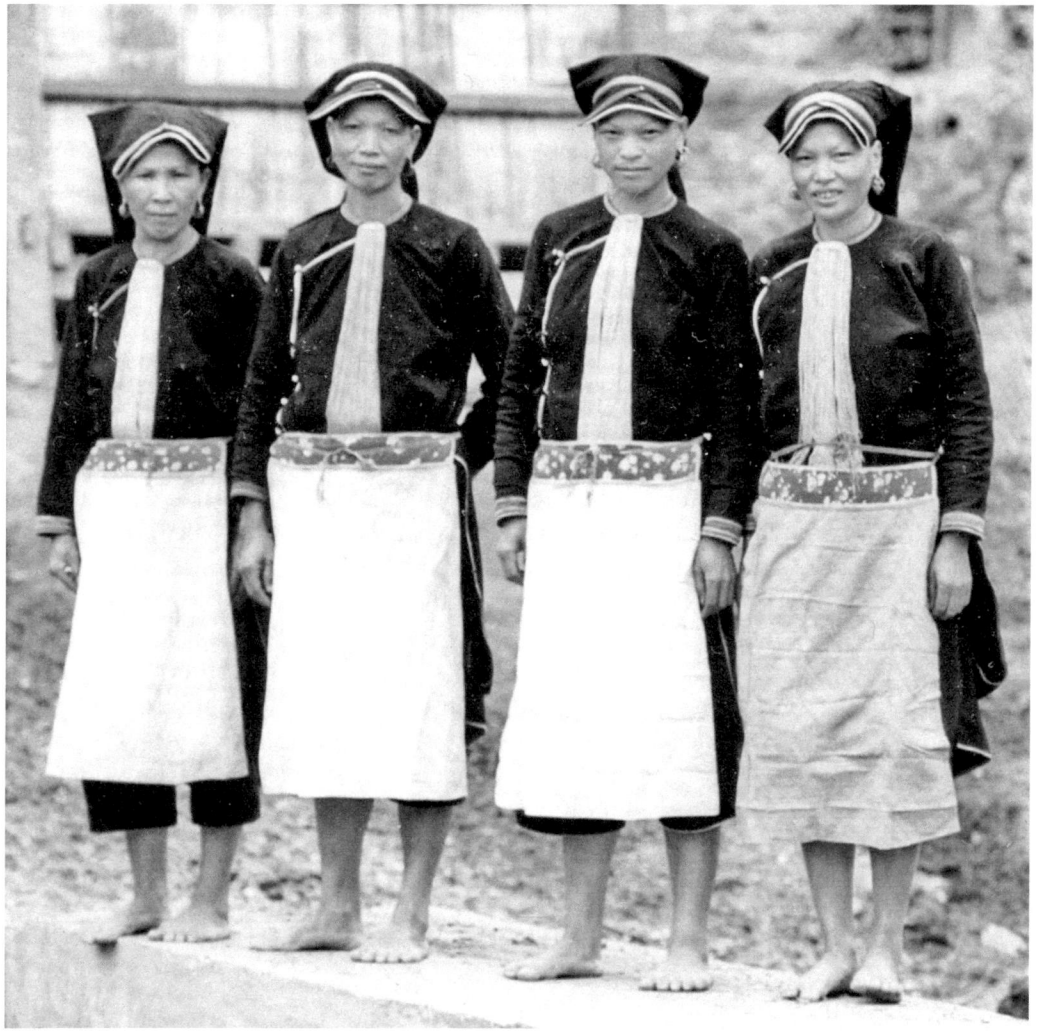

Group of Làn Tiẻn (Làn Tiẻn sub-group), Phong Thổ District, Lai Châu Province.

with embroidery, edged with narrow strips of red and white cloth, with fringe attached to one corner, and one or two strings that are used to secure the headcloth. The embroidery is done with red and white thread and commonly features a large eight-pointed star in the center that is surrounded by smaller eight-pointed stars.[111] Sometimes they wear leggings that are made of triangular pieces of plain black or dark blue cloth.

Làn Tiẻn (aka Lan Tin, Lenten, Mán Lantien, Dao Chàm) sometimes refer to themselves as Kim Mun. The name Làn Tiẻn in Chinese means indigo, hence the name Dao Chàm ('Indigo Dao') for them in Vietnamese. There are three sub-groups of Làn Tiẻn. One sub-group is called Làn Tiẻn and lives in the further west in Phong

Thổ District of Lai Châu Province (e.g., in Hoang Thèn commune) than a second sub-group called Dao Đầu Bằng that lives further east in Phong Thổ District in the vicinity of Bình Lư. The third sub-group is called Dao Tuyển and lives east of the Red River in Bắc Hà and Mường Khương districts of Lào Cai Province.

The Làn Tiẻn grow cotton, but not all communities produce their own thread or cloth.[112] The Dao Đầu Bằng of Bình Lư, for instance, trade with neighboring Táy Dón for cotton cloth and have a preference for cloth that is a good deal thicker than that used by other Làn Tiẻn. They dye the cloth dark blue or sometime a lighter shade of blue. Their clothing is fairly plain and neither sub-group embroiders very much. Silk thread for embroidery is usually a light shade of purple and is obtained through trade. Most of the cloth is dyed a very dark shade of blue, although the Làn Tiẻn in western Phong Thổ District also leave some white and dye some a light shade of blue.

Làn Tiẻn men from all three sub-groups wear plain cotton trousers that reach below the knees and sometimes a pair of leggings as well. These are usually dyed dark blue, but Làn Tiẻn men in western Phong Thổ also wear trousers that are a light shade of blue. Boys wear a round cap that is made of dark blue cloth. The lower half is decorated with two narrow strips of purple colored cotton cloth. Sometimes three metal disks are attached to the front and pompoms to the top.[113] In the past it was common for men to wear a plain dark blue headcloth. Làn Tiẻn men traditionally wear a distinctive shirt that, as described by one early 20th century French author, is fastened "by means of braided frogs and small round silver, glass, or bone buttons."[114] There are in fact two styles of these shirts. One style has a front panel and fastens on the right.[115] There are two buttons to fasten the upper edge of the front panel and another one on the lower right side of the shirt by which the panel is also fastened. A few additional buttons are added above this one for decoration. Another style of shirt opens down the front and there are metal buttons and "braided frogs" on both sides of most of the front opening.[116] These buttons are purely decorative, however, and the shirt is closed with a sash. At present Dao Đầu Bằng men tend to wear the front-opening style of shirts and other Làn Tiẻn men the style that fastens on the right. Formerly local silversmiths made the silver buttons, but these days such buttons are made of aluminum.

There are some differences in female styles of dress between the three sub-groups.[117] In the past women from all three sub-groups wore relatively short trousers that left the lower part of the leg exposed and sometimes leggings. This is still the case with the Làn Tiẻn and Dao Đầu Bằng, but Dao Tuyển now often wear more generic looking longer dark colored trousers. The tunic that they wear is made of plain dark blue cloth. The tunic is relatively plain, with decoration consisting thin strips of cloth attached to the collar, cuffs, outer edges of the vents, and sometimes along the right edge of the left panel. The right front panel is considerably shorter than left front panel and the tunic is closed to the right side. Usually a metal clasp is attached to the front of the collar. In the past this was made of silver, but now it is made of aluminum. A long fringe is hung from each side of the clasp. Làn Tiẻn and

Dao Đầu Bằng women in Phong Thổ usually made this fringe from purple silk thread, but it is now common for those in Bắc Hà and Mường Khương, perhaps as a result of influence from the Flowery Hmông in the area, to use more colorful thread as well as plastic beads and other decorative items to make their fringe. Làn Tiẻn women in western Phong Thổ also wear a pair of aprons on the front and back. The body of these aprons is made of plain light blue cloth. These days a bright piece of patterned commercial cloth is added across the top.

Women from the Làn Tiẻn sub-group in Phong Thổ and the Dao Tuyển in Bắc Hà and Mường Khương wear a headcloth that is made of a plain dark blue square piece of cloth that sometimes is edged with narrow strips of different colored cloth. In Phong Thổ it is usually held in place by a thin strip of light purple colored cloth, but in Bắc Hà and Mường Khương it is common at present to add a variety of other decorative items and sometimes even one of the woolen headcloths that have become popular in the area. Dao Đầu Bằng women in the Bình Lư area wear a basket-shaped metal headpiece (formerly made of silver and now of aluminum) underneath a headcloth that is made from a plain long dark blue piece of cloth. The headpiece results in the headcloth being elevated and it is worn so that the ends of the cloth hand down at the sides of their heads.

The Dao Áo Dài sub-group lives mainly in Tuyên Quang Province, but are also found in surrounding areas. Dao Áo Dài women wear a long-blouse that is fastened on the side and the upper parts of the front panels along the opening are decorated with numerous red pompoms. They wear undecorated dark blue or black trousers.

Tibeto-Burman Groups

There are about 40,000 people speaking Tibeto-Burman languages living in the border region of northern Việt Nam from Bảo Lạc District in Cao Bằng Province in the east to Lai Chau Province's Mường Tè District in the east. They migrated to this area from southern Yúnnán and northern Laos and belong to six different ethnic groups: Lô Lô, Hà Nhì, La Hủ, Phù Lá, Cống, and Si La. While some Lô Lô and Hà Nhì came to northern Việt Nam in the mid–800s in the wake of the Nán Chào invasion most of these people subsequently left the area. Lô Lô crossed the border again following ethnic revolts against the Míng Dynasty in the mid–1460s. Lô Lô as well as Hà Nhì migrated to Việt Nam in the 1700s and early 1800s as a result of political instability in China. The Si La migrated from Laos in the mid–1800s and the La Hủ arrived to Việt Nam in the late 1800s. The Cống came from Laos more recently.

Hà Nhì. There are around 22,000 Hà Nhì living in Việt Nam's Lai Châu Province and they are divided into three sub-groups: Black Hà Nhì that live in Bình Lư and Bát Xát districts and Cồ Chồ Hà Nhì and Là Mi Hà Nhì that live in Mường Tè District.

The Black Hà Nhì live at such high elevations that they cannot grow cotton. Traditionally they traded forest products, dye plants, baskets, and domestic animals with neighboring Gíay and Dao for white cotton cloth, which they dyed a very dark shade of blue.[118] The Cồ Chồ Hà Nhì and La Mi Hà Nhì live at lower elevations and are able to grow cotton. In fact, they set aside their best land for cotton cultivation. They weave cloth that is about 8 inches wide on a small frame loom.

Hà Nhì men as wear typical dark colored highland men's attire.[119] Black Hà Nhì women wear a plain dark blue long-sleeved tunic that reaches to the knees and fastens on the right side. It is undecorated or if decorated it will have a few rows of small metal disks along the collar and front flap and around the sleeves. In the past these were made of silver, but now they are made of aluminum or some other inexpensive silver colored metal.[120] The dress of Cồ Chồ and La Mi Hà Nhì women is different and more colorful.[121] They wear a tunic that fastens on the right side. The body is dyed dark blue and the sleeves are covered with appliqué comprised of narrow strips of bright colored cloth. They often decorate their tunics with coins, crescent-shaped pieces of metal, and beads. They also wear a breastcloth, trousers, sash, and leggings. These items usually are undecorated. The headcloth or hat worn by Hà Nhì women is undoubtedly their most distinctive item of clothing. It consists of a rigid frame that is covered with a piece of dark blue cloth and decorated with round metal disks, colorful fringe, and other decorative items. Again, in the past the disks were silver, but now are made of a less expensive silver colored metal.

Lô Lô. There are around 4,500 Lô Lô (aka Màn Dì, Striped Màn) in Việt Nam. They are divided into two sub-groups, Black Lô Lô and Flowery Lô Lô (aka Variegated Lô Lô, White Lô Lô). The Flowery Lô Lô call themselves Màn Dì Qua or Màn Dì Pu and live in Hà Giang Province, most of them in Mèo Vạc District and a few in Đồng Văn District. Black Lô Lô that call themselves Màn Dì No live in Đồng Văn District and those that call themselves Màn Dì Mân Tê live in Bảo Lạc District in western Cao Bằng Province. There is also a small number of Black Lô Lô living in northern Lào Cai Province's Mường Khương District.

Some Lô Lô communities have traditions of growing cotton and weaving, but some do not grow cotton and trade with cloth. In the past even communities that weave sometimes would trade with neighboring Tày for cloth and all communities trade for silk thread. All of the clothing is made of dark blue or black cotton cloth. Everyday clothing is either completely plain or has only limited decorative features, such as narrow appliqué stripes on the sleeves of women's blouses. When clothing is decorated it consists of appliqué using small pieces of colored cotton cloth and embroidery using silk thread. Lô Lô also wear headcloths with dark blue and white tritik patterning like the headcloths worn by the Tày Thù Lao in Bắc Hà and Mường Khương districts and Tù Zhuàng in Wénshān Prefecture. Such cloth is sometimes obtained from the Tày through trade.

By the early 20th century some Lô Lô men dressed in Chinese-style shirts and trousers like neighboring Tày men, but it was still common for Lô Lô men to wear distinctive clothing.[122] Moreover, writing in the early 20th century Abadie noted even

Tibeto-Burman Groups

those who had adopted Chinese-style clothing "still preserve an example of their distinctive tribal costume and are dressed in it after death so that their ancestors can recognize them."[123] Their traditional clothing includes a tunic, trousers, headcloth, and sometimes leggings. Lô Lô style men's tunics are loose fitting. They open down the front, had wide sleeves, and reached to the upper thighs. The tunic is made of dark blue cloth with thin strips of light blue cloth around the collar and shoulders, down each side of the front opening, across the bottom, and at the cuffs. They are fastened with small round metal buttons. Their trousers are much more baggy than the trousers of most highland men and sometimes are extensively decorated with rows appliqué and embroidery. A sash is worn around the waist and it is sometimes decorated with appliqué at the ends. They also wear a headcloth made of a long piece of cloth that was folded and twisted tightly around the head. The body of the headcloth is made of a dark blue piece of cloth that was either left plain or decorated with small tritik patterns in rows, sometimes with long decorative fringe at the ends. The everyday dress of Lô Lô men today varies. Most men wear generic Western style clothing or Chinese-style highland shirts and trousers, but very baggy trousers and loose-fitting front-opening shirts are still popular for special occasions. The traditionally styled contemporary clothing is plain or sometimes the shirt has a little decoration and decorative fringe is added to the headcloth, but some men still wear special occasion clothing that is more extensively decorated.[124]

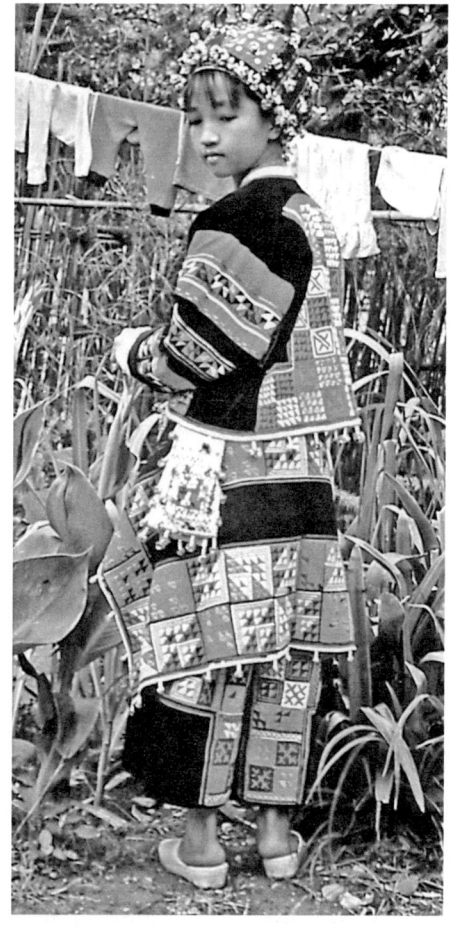

Lô Lô (Flowery Lô Lô sub-group) girl, Mèo Vạc District, Hà Giang Province.

The dress of Lô Lô women includes a long-sleeved front-opening blouse, a long wrap around skirt or long trousers, a short wrap-around back-panel over-skirt, sash, and a headlcloth.[125] Everyday clothing in the past included a plain dark blue skirt or baggy trousers, a plain dark blue back-panel over-skirt, a plain sash that was usually a light shade of blue, a dark blue blouse with narrow appliqué stripes on the sleeves, and a dark blue headcloth that sometimes had a little decoration.[126] The more extensively decorated clothing features appliqué and embroidery covering a large portion of the blouse, skirt or trousers, and back-panel over-skirt, and the ends of the headcloth and sash. The dress of Black Lô Lô and Flowery Lô Lô women differs in several details. Thus, in the past Flowery Lô Lô women wore blouses made of white cloth and Black Lô Lô women wore blouses made of dark blue cloth.[127]

La Hủ. There are about 10,000 La Hủ (aka Lahu) living in Mường Tè District, Lai Châu Province. There are three sub-groups of La Hủ in Việt Nam: Yellow La Hủ (La Hủ Sủ), Black La Hủ (La Hủ Na), and White La Hủ (La Hủ Phung). The La Hủ Su is the largest sub-group. The La Hủ in Việt Nam but trade handicrafts with Tái Dón and other neighboring ethnic groups for cloth. La Hủ men tend to dress in Chinese-style highland male clothing or these day to wear generic Western-style clothing. There does not appear to be any difference in the dress of La Hủ women belonging to the three sub-groups today. They wear a tunic, trousers, and headcloth. The tunic is made of dark blue or black cotton cloth, has narrow long sleeves, fastens on the right side, and reaches almost to the ankles. The collar and front flap are decorated with narrow strips of colorful cloth and a line of embroidery. The sleeves are made of a series of narrow strips of colorful cloth

Phù Lá. There are about 11,000 Phù Lá (aka Phula) in Việt Nam and a few hundred thousand of them scattered across southern Yúnnán.[128] There are six sub-groups of Phù Lá in Việt Nam from northern Yên Bái Province in the west to Xín Mần District in Hà Giang Province in the east. Most Phù Lá belong to the Phù Lá Hán and Xá Phó sub-groups. The Phù Lá Hán live just east of the Red River mainly in Lào Cai Province's Bắc Hà and Mường Khương districts. The Xá Phó live west of the Red River in Bát Xát and Sa Pa districts in Lào Cai Province, Sìn Hồ District in Lai Châu Province, Tuần Giáo District in Điện Biên Province, and Quỳnh Nhai District in Sơn La Province.

The Phù Lá Hán and Xá Phó sub-groups are sometimes treated as separate ethnic groups. This reflects significant cultural differences. In particular, while the Phù Lá Hán were more influenced by the Chinese, the Xá Phó were integrated into the Thái feudal system and adopted many aspects of Thái and Giáy culture.[129] The dress of the Phù Lá Hán exhibits strong Chinese influence and the Thái have influenced Xá Phó dress. Both sub-groups grew cotton and wove cotton cloth in the past. The cloth is fairly narrow. They made thread by hand splicing rather than using a spinning wheel. Today many Xá Phó communities still grow cotton, weave, and some even make their own thread. Silk thread obtained through trade was commonly used to embroider in the past, but now commercial wool thread is often used. In addition, the Xá Phó produce a wide range of colors using natural dyes and are well known for their skill at dyeing and making thread. The Phù Lá Hán have largely abandoned these traditional crafts and the use of commercial thread and cloth is widespread.

The shirt traditionally worn by Phù Lá men is distinctive. It opens down the front, has a round collar, and is fastened with a few buttons made of small silver balls. The edges of the front opening, front and back hem, seam on the back where the two panels are joined, center of the back, and cuffs are decorated with a few rows of embroidery and scattered pairs of Job's tears. The embroidery is mainly with red and white thread and the most common patterns include swastikas and rhombs. The trousers sometimes have embroidery featuring small swastikas around the hem. The headcloth is made of plain dark blue cloth that is tightly wrapped around the head with a large rim.[130] Such clothing is still worn by Xá Phó men, although on an everyday basis they may wear generic Western-style clothing. Phù Lá Hán men for the most part ceased to wear traditional dress during the 20th century. An account in the early 20th century noted, "in addition to the 'uniform' of this tribe, Fou La men indifferently wear Thai or Meo or even Chinese clothing."[131]

Phù Lá Hán women wear a five-panel blouse that fastens on the right side. It is usually made of dark blue or these days of black cloth, but sometimes of lighter blue cloth. There is a narrow collar that is sometimes decorated with embroidery. The manner of decorating these blouses appears to have changed from the early 20th century to the present.[132] Photographs from the early 20th century show blouses with decorative strips of cloth along the top of the front flap and another fairly wide piece of decorative cloth around the cuffs with the sleeves otherwise being plain. Present-day fashion favors sleeves that have one to three narrow decorative stripes at the cuffs and a wider decorative band composed a several pieces of colorful cloth nearer the shoulder. Phù Lá Hán women wear dark blue or black trousers that reach to mid-calf. Sometimes they are decorated with light blue or red and embroidery at the cuffs, but today they are usually left plain. Over the blouse and trousers they wear an apron that is held in place by two small chains. The chains used to be silver, but now they are usually made of some less expensive silver colored metal. In the past these aprons commonly reached to below the knees, but now they tend to reach only to the upper calf. The upper part of the apron is edged wit a strip of colorful cloth. Sometimes another narrower strip is added a little distance below the edge. It is now popular to add a large decorative piece of colorful cloth to the center of the upper triangular area of the apron. Brightly colored commercial cloth is particularly popular for this. A sash is sometimes worn around the waist. This may be made of a plain piece of cloth or may be decorated with strips of cloth and embroidery at the ends. On their heads Phù Lá Hán women wear a headcloth made of a piece of dark blue or black cloth that is often bordered with thin strip of colorful cloth and secured by a string that is decorated with beads and other ornaments.

Xá Phó women wear a short pullover blouse, tubeskirt, sash, and headcloth.[133] The blouse is distinct and Abadie records a Xá Phó legend that accounts for why it is so short: "When the mother made the first clothing for her children, she began with the ancestors of the Thai and Man [i.e. Dao] for which she used large measures. Then the piece of cloth having been more than half used already, she cut a short garment for the ancestors of the Meo [i.e., Hmông]. After this so little remained of the cloth that the ancestors of the Xa Pho could only be given the short jacket worn by the Lolo."[134] The body of Xá Phó blouses is made of two pieces of cloth. The upper piece is folded at the shoulders and then stitched together under the sleeve openings and a square neck opening is cut from the cloth. The area around the neck opening is decorated with embroidery with additional embroidery added elsewhere on the central field of the cloth and often pairs of Job's tears added to form X's as well. The lower part of the body is made from a long piece of cloth that is folded and stitched together on one side and attached to the top piece. This piece is almost completely covered with embroidery. There is also embroidery at the ends of the sleeves.

The tubeshirt is tailored to be narrower at the waist than at the hem and is made of five segments of dark blue or black cotton cloth that are sewn together. Each segment may be made of one or more pieces of cloth to produce the desired skirt width. At the top is a plain waistband. Next is a relatively narrow plain piece that usually has a thin line of embroidery. The next piece is also fairly narrow and it is covered with embroidery and usually features rhomb patterns in different colors, with red being the dominant color. The central segment is usually made from several pieces of cloth. It is relatively wide and the upper part is left plain and the lower part decorated with large discreet embroidered patterns. The hem-segment is also relatively wide and it is covered with two or three rows of embroidered patterns. The traditional sash is made of dark blue cloth with embroidery at the ends. Now it is common to use a piece of commercial cloth, often white, and with no decoration.

There are two types of traditional headcloths worn by Xá Phó women. The traditional everyday headcloth is square and decorated with colored threads and beads. In the past these were made of hand-woven dark blue cloth, but now it is common to make them from four small pieces of black commercial cloth. The other type is made of a long piece of plain dark blue or black cloth and is worn on special occasions. It is wrapped around the head in such a way that there are two points sticking out on the sides like those worn by the Tày Thu Lao. The square style of headcloth is often placed on top of the rectangular ones. Both styles of traditional headcloth have gone out of fashion and it has become common to wear headcloths made of commercial Chinese wool.

Si La. Formerly the Si La in Việt Nam were called Cú Dề Xừ or Khả Pẻ. The latter term refers to Si La women folding and tucking their skirts in the rear rather than in front like Thái.[135] The name Si La was adopted after 1954. There are about 700 Si La living in Mường Tè District, Lai Châu Province. When they first arrived in Mường Tè they settled in the high mountains like the Hmông, but later moved down closer to the Black River (Sông Đà). Si La men wear either Chinese-style highland clothing or generic Western-style clothing. The women wear tubeskirts made of dark blue or black cotton cloth that is undecorated except sometimes with a strip of lighter colored cloth around the hem. At least since the mid–20th century usually they have folded their skirts in the front rather than the back. Their blouse is distinctive. It fastens on the right and the rest of the blouse is made of dark blue or black cloth while the front flap is sometimes made of a lighter color of cloth. The cuffs, collar, and front flap are edged with thin strips of brightly colored cloth (red is popular) and the central area of the front flap in the past was completely covered with silver coins, but now silver colored metal disks are more common. Young women wear a white headcloth and older ones a dark blue or black one. One end is decorated with three rows of silver coins or metal disks like those used on the blouses. The headcloth is folded so that the decorated end hangs down the back of the head.

Cống. There are about 2,000 Cống living in Mường Tè District, Lai Châu Province. The language that they speak is called Phunoi and most Phunoi speakers live in northern Laos. Those that settled in Mường Tè were integrated into the Thái feudal system and in recent years many Cống have inter-married with Tái Dón, Hà Nhì, and Si La. The Cống grow cotton, but do not weave.[136] They trade cotton and baskets with the Tái Dón and also in Laos for cloth and clothing. Cống men dressed like Tái Dón men in the past and these days also sometimes wear generic Western style clothing. Cống women wear tubeskirts like Tái Dón or Thái in Laos. They wear a variety of blouse styles, including front opening blouses like the Tái Dón, blouses that are fastened on the side like the Lự, and front opening blouses that are closed near the bottom to form a wide V-neck opening like the Hmông. The front opening or front flap is usually decorated with cloth of a contrasting color in the fashion of these other groups. The distinguishing feature of Cống blouses is the two or three narrow stripes of cloth in lighter colors than the dark blue or black body of the blouse on the upper part of the sleeves.

5

Ethnic Minorities in Southern Việt Nam

The ethnic minorities discussed in this chapter include the Chăm and Khmer in the lowlands and about twenty-one Mon-Khmer and Malayo-Polynesian speaking groups in the Central Highlands. There are also ethnic Chinese in the lowlands, but they have by and large ceased to weave and to wear distinctive dress. As was discussed previously the Chăm in Việt Nam include two groups. The Eastern Chăm live primarily in Ninh Thuận and Bình Thuận provinces in what was formerly the kingdom of Panduranga. The Western Chăm live near the Cambodian border mainly in An Giang Province. The Central Highlands (*Cao nguyên Trung bộ* or *Cao nguyên Trung phần* in Vietnamese) includes the provinces of Lâm Đồng, Kon Tum, Gia Lai, Đắk Nông, and Đắk Lắk, as well as highland areas of the surrounding provinces from Quảng Bình Province in the north to Đồng Nai and Bình Phước provinces in the south. Malayo-Polynesian speaking groups live roughly in the middle of the Central Highlands with various Mon-Khmer speaking groups living to their north, west, and south.

During the 19th century the Central Highlands was a frontier region that served as a buffer zone between Việt Nam and Siam. Nguyễn influence in the Central Highlands primarily entailed establishing a handful of military outposts and small colonies, collecting tribute and demanding corvée labor from some groups, and promoting a limited amount of trade. Lowland traders travelled through the highlands exchanging lowland products such as bronze gongs and salt for a variety of items found in the highlands including agar wood (aka eaglewood), rhinoceros horns, and honey. In addition, there was periodic slave raiding. Traders from the west were Khmer, Lao, and Chinese, while those coming from the east were Kinh and Chăm. There was some trade in cloth from the lowlands, but it was a minor item. During the latter part of the 19th century Kinh traders often included English cotton cloth in the trade goods that they carried into the highlands.[1]

As was mentioned previously, the French presence in the region began with French Catholic missionaries establishing a base at Kon Tum in the mid–19th century. During the 1880s and 1890s the French sent a series of expeditions into the highlands to secure their claim over the territory, explore, and establish relations with the people in the region. The French presence increased in the early 20th century when the town of Buôn Ma Thuột (aka Ban Mê Thuột) was established in the territory of the Ê Đê Kpă sub-group in 1905 and the resort hill station of Đà Lạt was established in the territory of the Lạt (a Cơ Ho sub-group) in 1907, although significant development of Đà Lạt did not begin until a few years later.

New policies in 1926 led to the development of tea and coffee plantations in the Central Highlands and to the arrival of French settlers and Kinh plantation workers. These were enclaves that employed some local laborers, but a majority of the workers were Kinh. The colonial authorities restricted wider Kinh settlement in the Central Highlands. They also set up a new system of indirect rule for Central Highlanders and gave them inalienable reservation lands. The entire region eventually was made a special Crown Domain directly under the emperor. The French authorities had allowed American and Canadian Protestant missionaries to begin working in Việt Nam in the early 20th century and they were allowed to establish a Central Highlands base at Đà Lạt in the late 1920s.

The anti-colonial war in northern Việt Nam during the 1940s and early 1950s had little impact on the Central Highlands, but outside influence over the region began to change markedly during the latter part of the 1950s. The Land Development Program launched in 1957 the southern government brought Kinh Catholics as well as Thái and Nùng from the north into the highlands. It also initiated a forced assimilation program that deprived the area of its former special status. Opposition to such assimilationist policies by highlanders forced the government to reverse them in 1963, but this and other reforms were overwhelmed by the growing war. Communist infiltration into the highlands starting in the early 1960s brought the war to the Central Highlands. By the time the war had ended in 1975 between 200,000 and 220,000 highlanders out of 1 million had died and 85 percent of their villages had been destroyed or abandoned. The new communist government introduced policies aimed at assimilating people in the Central Highlands and ending what were perceived as "backward customs." It also created New Economic Zones (*Xây dựng các vùng kinh tế mới*) in the Central Highlands and during the latter half of the 1970s and the 1980s over 400,000 Kinh from the north and the Mekong Delta settled in the area (along with a small number of Hmông and Dao). The impact of these changes on textiles and dress in the Central Highlands were similar to those in the north, but somewhat more pronounced. This was especially true with male dress, which traditionally was far more different from the dress of Kinh males than was the dress of males in the northern highlands. An increasing number of males in the Central Highlands began to adopt Western style clothing for everyday wear.

Post-Đổi Mới economic growth in Việt Nam has led to further major changes in the lives of people in the Central Highlands, where the coffee industry in particular has helped to spur economic growth. While some local minority people have benefitted from this growth, poverty persists in the minority population and most of the benefits of economic development in the region have gone to new migrants. Many of these migrants are Kinh from the lowlands, but there have also been a large number of ethnic minority migrants (an estimated 50,000 families) from the northern highlands that have moved to the Central Highlands where they perceive there to be greater economic opportunities.[2] In 1976 the population of the Central Highlands was 1.2 million comprised of 14 official ethnic groups. In 2012 the population had grown to 5.3 million and not only had the percentage of Kinh increased dramatically, but there were people from 47 official ethnic groups represented.[3] These are mostly Hmông, Dao, Tày, and Thái and the majority of them have settled in Kon Tum Province.

We briefly discussed the textiles and dress of many of the southern minority groups in the section on the Kingdom of Chămpa in Chapter 1. There the focus was on the influence of the ancient Chăm on the highland groups and historical influences on one another between highland Malayo-Polynesian Chamic and Mon-Khmer groups. Here we will look at their textile and dress traditions in more detail and at recent developments.

Khmer

At present there are about 1.3 million Khmer or Khmer Krôm (*Khơ Me Crộm* in Vietnamese) scattered throughout the Mekong Delta region of southern Việt Nam, but mainly in Hậu Giang, Trà Vinh, Vĩnh Long, Kiên Giang, An Giang, Bạc Liêu, and Cà Mau provinces. Under Nguyễn and French rule this region received large numbers of Kinh and Chinese migrants and the Khmer became a minority that was subject to considerable cultural influence from the new settlers. While some aspects of Khmer culture survive, such as the widespread adherence to Theravada Buddhism, others have disappeared.

Traditional Khmer clothing includes cotton or silk sarongs for everyday wear and larger wrap-around silk cloths commonly referred to as *sampôt* for special occasions. During the Nguyễn and French periods most Khmer gradually adopted the Kinh style of dress such as the black pants and black blouse (*áo bà ba*) in the case of women. On special occasions older women sometimes wore a style of gown that is stitched down the side and opens near the hip. It is referred to as a *áo tầm vông* or *áo cổ Bà Lai*.[4] One distinctive item of clothing that remained popular is a checked scarf, worn as a headcloth or around the neck. Sericulture and weaving also declined during these periods.

Since the 1970s in particular many Khmer have adopted Western style clothing. During the late 1970s and early 1980s traditional Khmer clothing was worn only in a few communities, such as Bảy Núi in An Giang Province.[5] Khmer weaving had largely disappeared in Việt Nam by the 1970s, but continued in a few communities especially in Tịnh Biên and Tri Tôn districts in An Giang Province.[6] Sericulture was still found in An Giang and Trà Vinh provinces.

Chăm

At present there are a little over 160,000 Chăm in Việt Nam, fewer than the over 200,000 living in Cambodia. In the late 1930s their population had declined to 23,000 in Annam and 8,000 in Cochin China,[7] but recent years in particular have seen the population grow substantially. As was discussed earlier, migration of some Chăm to Cambodia led to the emergence a distinct Eastern Chăm and Western Chăm subgroups. In Việt Nam the Eastern Chăm live mainly in Ninh Thuận and Bình Thuận provinces (constituting the major part of the former Chăm territory of Panduranga), while the Western Chăm live mainly in An Giang Province with some also found in Tây Ninh Province. There are also over 5,000 Chăm living in Hồ Chí Minh City. The majority of Western Chăm follows a local syncretic version of Hinduism, but a significant number are also Muslim. Most Western Chăm Muslims follow a local syncretic version of Islam. All Western Chăm follow variants of Islam like the Malays. The separation of the Chăm into the Eastern Chăm and Western Chăm resulted in the development of a number of differences in the styles of dress of the two groups.[8]

The Eastern Chăm of what formerly was Panduranga who had not been assimilated into local Kinh-Chinese society continued to wear distinctive dress during the Nguyễn Dynasty period. This included both nobles and commoners. Decorative silk and fine cotton cloth for the king and other members of what was left of his court usually was produced by specialist weavers such as those in the village of Mỹ Nghiệp (Ninh Phước District, Ninh Thuận Province), while commoners wove their own cloth. Specialized weaving for nobles largely came to an end in 1832, but some traditions associated with aristocratic dress survived. There was still some demand for the narrow strips of silk cloth with supplementary warp and supplementary weft patterns that were used for special occasion wear and especially on the clothing of priests. Such cloth continued to be woven in Mỹ Nghiệp on the long and narrow *tano pa cako* (*tanung munim jih talah*) loom, although the range of motifs was reduced. Likewise, although most people wore clothing made of plain cotton cloth, some women still wore wrap-around skirts with decorative patterns. In particular, a few people continued to weave some of the motifs previously reserved for skirts worn by nobles. These included the *tu muk* and *tu pik* motifs woven on silk skirt-cloth. The *tu muk* motif consists of a series of zigzag lines and is interpreted as representing either a type of forest vine or a termite (*muk* is usually interpreted as meaning termite). The *tu pik* motif consists of a rhomb with hooks or "wings" (*pik* refers to a wing) and a center that is a different color than the outer part of the motif.

An early 20th century French description of Chăm women's dress mentions that they wore a distinctive headcloth and gown: "The head-dress [of Chăm women] is quite different from that of the Annamese; it is twisted round the hair, and the two ends are allowed to fall on either side of the face to the shoulder. The dress is very much like the *cai ao* [*áo dài*?] of the Annamese, but instead of being a wide flowing garment it fits the figure much more closely."[9] The photograph that accompanies the description show a Chăm woman wearing a plain white headcloth and a plain dark colored gown.[10] As for the color of the gown the author of this account mentions, "Their favorite colour seems to have been green."[11]

Weaving declined considerably in Eastern Chăm communities during the mid- to late 20th century, but began to be revived in the village of Mỹ Nghiệp in particular in the mid–1990s and since then has emerged as an important commercial enterprise supplying textiles not only to the wider Chăm community, but also to the tourist market for domestic and international tourists as well as for export on a small scale. The thread used is entirely commercial, but weavers continue to use the traditional backstrap and the long and narrow *tano pa cako* (*tanung munim jih talah*) looms.[12] Plain white cotton cloth is still widely used by the Chăm for special occasion clothing. Silk cloth with alternating warp float and supplementary warp patterning is woven both for domestic use and for the external commercial market. A few people still weave silk cloth with warp ikat dashes, but such is not popular and is used mainly on skirt worn by elderly women.[13]

At present Eastern Chăm generally wear generic Western style clothing on an everyday basis, but continue to wear distinctive dress for special occasions. On special occasions Eastern Chăm men wear a gown made of plain white cotton cloth. Underneath this they wear a long sarong made of white cotton. The sarongs may be undecorated, but, especially in the case of priests, it is common to add narrow strips of decorative cloth to the side and top of the sarong and wider strips to the hem.[14] The patterns on these strips are woven using a supplementary weft technique. The patterning on the narrow strips is simple, often zigzag lines, while that on the wider pieces includes more complex geometric patterns. Men, priests in particular, also wear headcloths on special occasions with decorative strips of cloth added and fringe at each end.[15]

Eastern Chăm women wear a plain white cotton gown when attending special events.[16] It is common, especially for older women, to wear a wrap-around skirt underneath the blouse.[17] The body of the skirt is often covered with warp directional stripes in a variety of colors (black, red, yellow being most common) with decorative patterning that is woven using warp ikat, alternating warp float, supplementary warp, or supplementary weft techniques. A weft directional band is woven across the ends of the skirt. It is usually plain and woven using thread that contrasts with the colors of the rest of the skirt.

When some of the Western Chăm living in Cambodia migrated to the border region in Việt Nam in the 19th century weaving was still common, but as was discussed earlier Malays in Cambodia as well as Cambodian fashion had influenced their style of dress and weaving techniques. Thus, while some continued to weave on a backstrap loom, most women adopted the Malay style frame loom. The Chăm in Cambodia did not use the long narrow *tano pa cako* loom or produce the array of alternating warp float and supplementary warp patterned textiles woven on this loom as well as silk textiles decorated using the plangi technique. Rather they mainly produced Malay and Cambodian influenced weft ikat and supplementary weft patterns on the frame loom. In addition the Chăm in Cambodia no longer produced silk and cotton thread, but obtained it through trade. By the 19th century such thread was obtained mainly from Chinese traders. The Western Chăm that migrated to Việt Nam in the 19th century brought with them a fairly extensive repertoire of that included a range of weft ikat and supplementary weft patterned textiles, but over time they produced an increasingly narrow range of textiles. The use of natural dyes also declined. The lac used for red dye, for example, was obtained from Cambodia, but this trade had virtually disappeared by the late 20th century. Warfare during the 1960s and early 1907s and subsequent social changes led to a sharp decline in weaving by the Western Chăm in Việt Nam. At present weaving has effectively ceased in Chăm communities in Tây Ninh Province and continues on a regular basis only in a few communities in the Châu Đốc area of An Giang Province. This includes a weaving co-operative in Châu Phong village that is located in Tân Châu district-level town (which is also known for its silk production).

For everyday wear at present the Western Chăm in Việt Nam often wear generic Western style commercial clothing and if they wear Malay-style clothing it is normally made of commercial cloth. Because of religious beliefs men do not wear pure silk cloth, but do wear mixed silk and cotton cloth. Men either wear trousers or Malay-style sarongs, a long-sleeved shirt, and sometimes a headcloth. The sarongs sometimes are made of hand-woven cloth.[18] Dark blue is the most popular color for men's sarongs. It is common for the sarongs to have checks and sometimes they feature warp ikat patterns. There are two main ikat patterns, a relatively small one composed of several dashes that is said they depict a flower and a larger rhomb shaped one. In recent years there has been some innovation in the warp ikat patterns, including large zigzag lines. Men's headcloths usually feature small checks.[19] Western Chăm women in Việt Nam either wear trousers or a skirt (usually a tubeskirt), a long-sleeved blouse, and often a headcloth.[20] Tubeskirts made of silk with Cambodian-style weft ikat or supplementary weft patterning were still woven in the mid–20th century, but are no longer produced. Women's headcloths are generally made of white cloth and it is common to decorate the cloth with a little embroidery near the ends.

Central Highlands Malayo-Polynesian Groups

The Malayo-Polynesian speaking groups in the Central Highlands include the Gia Rai, Ê Đê, Ra Glai, Chu Ru, and Hroi. All of them speak Chamic languages that are closely related to the Cham language and in some respects their cultures reflect an early version of Chăm culture prior to the advent of Hindu and Islamic influence. However, these are also cultures that have evolved in the highlands environment and

5. Ethnic Minorities in Southern Việt Nam

in particular as a result of interaction with neighboring Mon-Khmer speaking peoples. The Chamic groups in the Central Highlands trace descent matrilineally and political organization was village-based.

Gia Rai. The Gia Rai (aka Jarai) live mainly in Gia Lai and Kon Tum provinces. There are over 400,000 Gia Rai in Việt Nam and they speak about ten different dialects. Status differences based on relative wealth were important in traditional Gia Rai society. While traditional political organization was village-based, powerful priests known as the *potao pui* or *sadet* of fire, *potao ia* or *sadet* of water, and *potao angin* or *sadet* of wind exerted considerable influence within Gia Rai society.

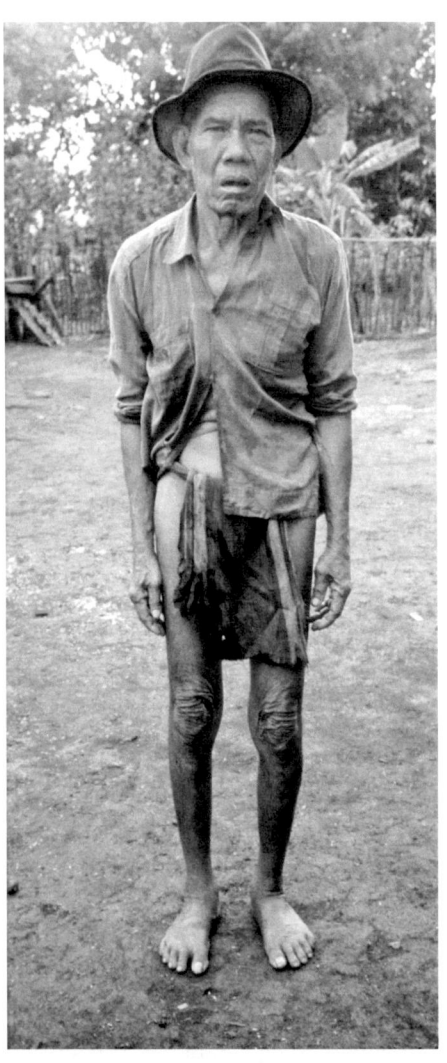

Gia Rai man wearing loincloth and commercial shirt, Gia Lai Province.

Prior to the 1960s the Gia Rai grew cotton, spun cotton thread, dyed thread using a variety of natural dyes, and wove cotton cloth. Dye colors included black, dark blue, two shades of red, and yellow. They also sometimes wove cloth with bast fibers made from wild plants. Aniline dyes were introduced during the French period, but were not widely used (green appears to have been one of the colors produced with aniline dyes). Warfare during the 1960s and first half of the 1970s made growing cotton difficult. After the war it was easier to grow cotton again, but commercial thread also became more readily available. Gia Rai weave cloth on a so-called "Indonesian" type of back-strap loom. Cloth is dyed black or dark blue and is largely undecorated, with narrow colored warp directional stripes being the most common form of decoration. Geometric patterns are produced using the warp float technique and more realistic representations are produced using the discontinuous supplementary weft technique.[21] These discontinuous supplementary weft patterns are made using a needle that traditionally was made from the hair of a hedgehog. Traditional patterns include images of people, animals, plants, and a variety of other objects. During the 1960s and 1970s they added images of objects related to the war such as guns, helicopters, and airplanes.

Traditional clothing worn by Gia Rai men reflects their relative status and includes a loincloth and sometimes a shirt, headcloth, and blanket.[22] There are basically two styles of loincloth. One is relatively plain with decoration consisting of warp directional stripes near each side including plain red stripes and white ones with geometric warp float patterning. This is the type worn by poorer men and by higher status men for everyday wear. In general those worn by poorer men tend to be shorter than those worn by wealthier ones. The second style is wider and a good deal longer (sometimes reaching over 20 feet in length). These loincloths are decorated with a weft directional band near the ends with discontinuous supplementary weft, often a row of Job's tears, and long twined fringe. In the past only by high status men wore such loincloths were. Gia Rai men traditionally often went bare-chested, but sometimes they wore a shirt. Again, there were two styles of shirt. One is a sleeveless pullover that is decorated like the common style of loincloth. The other style is longer in the back, has sleeves, and a number of decorative features. These features include a red rectangle embroidered across the front of the shirt representing bird wings, small lead disks attached across the shoulders and down the sides, and sometimes a weft directional band like the one found on high status loincloths across the lower back of the shirt. In recent decades it has become increasingly common for men to wear generic Western style clothing and

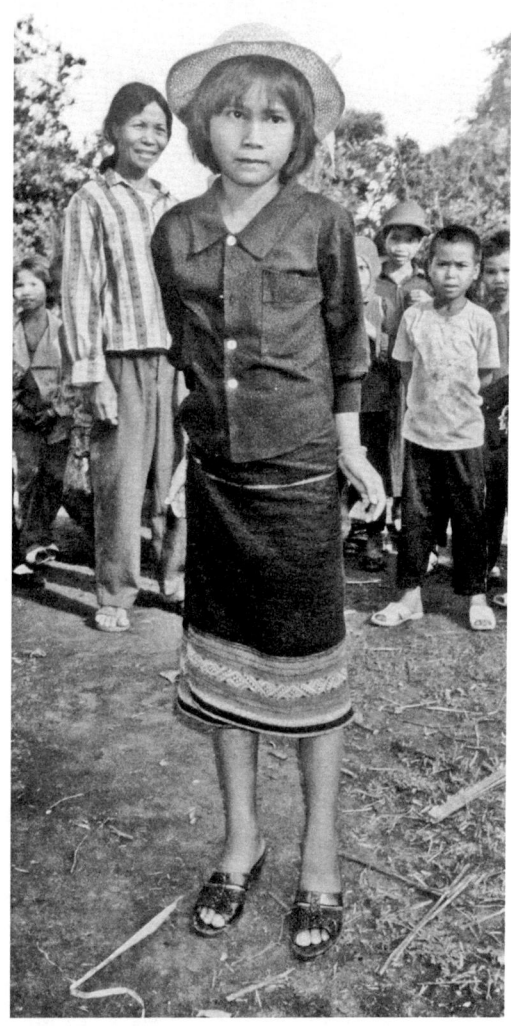

Gia Rai girl wearing traditional handwoven skirt and commercial blouse, Gia Lai Province.

traditional style clothing only on special occasions. In addition if men wear loincloths they usually wear a pair of commercial running shorts underneath. New versions of the high status shirt often open down the front and do not necessarily feature the red embroidered wings on the chest.

Traditional Gia Rai female dress consists of a long wrap-around skirt, pullover blouse, and sometimes a headcloth.[23] Skirts are made of two pieces of cloth that are sewn together. Each piece is largely plain dark blue or black with decoration consisting of thin warp directional stripes near the edges of each piece. These include plain red

5. Ethnic Minorities in Southern Việt Nam

stripes and white ones with geometric warp float patterning similar those on men's clothing but the white stripes on the top and bottom of the skirt are usually a little wider. The blouses are pullovers and usually a little shorter than those worn by men. There are sleeveless blouses and blouses with sleeves. Decoration includes the usual red and white stripes, but it is common for there to be a relatively wide stripe with geometric warp float patterning near the hem. This stripe often includes a series of large distinct patterns like those found on blankets. In recent decades it has also become more common for Gia Rai women to wear generic Western-style clothing and traditional clothing only on special occasions.

Blankets are roughly the same size as skirts. They too are made of two pieces of cloth and are relative plain except for a band of plain red and patterned white warp directional stripes near one edge. There is a relatively wide white stripe at the center of this band that may feature large geometric patterns or discreet representational ones. Blankets are used for sleeping, carrying babies, and may also be folded and worn over men's shoulders.

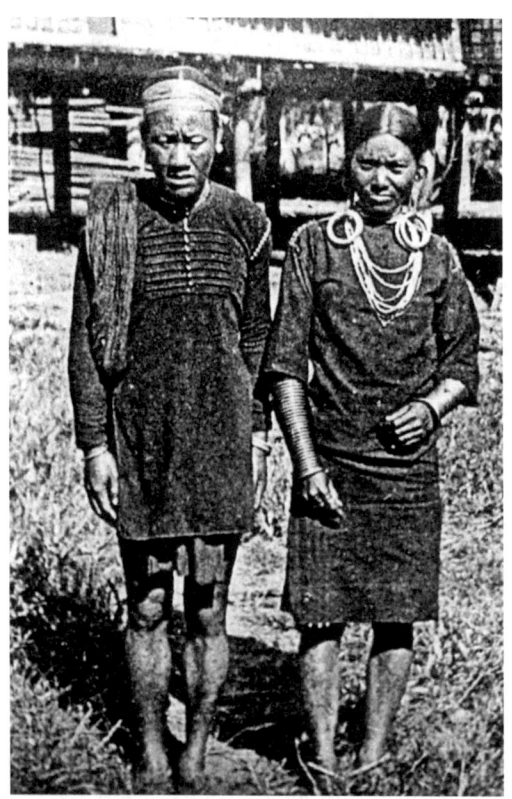

Ê Đê (Bih sub-group) village headman and his wife (from Maître, *Les Jungles Moi*, pl. 47, fig. 85).

As is common throughout the Central Highlands Gia Rai bury the dead with their best clothing.

Ê Đê. There are over 330,000 Ê Đê (aka Rhadé) in Việt Nam. They live to the south of the Gia Rai, mainly in Đắk Lắk Province, and culturally are similar. There are over a dozen Ê Đê sub-groups and six main ones. The dress of all of these is roughly the same, with the exception of the Bih. In addition, Ê Đê dress is similar to that of the Gia Rai and the dress of both is quite distinct from that of other groups in the Central Highlands. Like the Gia Rai the Ê Đê trace descent matrilineally and property is owned by females and passed on from mother to daughter. This relates to clothing, in that even a man's clothing is owned by his mother or wife. Thus, "When a man is to be married his mother will make a loincloth for him; after the marriage this loincloth becomes his wife's property."[24]

Ê Đê cloth is usually made of cotton, although bast fibers were used in the past. Ê Đê of the Kpă sub-group in Krông Bông District, for example, made cloth from

154

ramie.[25] As noted above, both traditional clothing of Ê Đê men and women is roughly similar to that worn by Gia Rai.[26] Among the differences is the manner of decorating blankets. Ê Đê blankets commonly have numerous thin warp directional stripes across the blanket including some relatively wide plain rust red ones along the outer edge.[27] The clothing of the Mdhur sub-group in Phú Yên Province also has some distinctive features.[28] It is common for them to decorate their cloth with yellow, red, and green stripes. Men's shirts commonly open down the front and do not feature the red bird wings in the center. If Ê Đê wear a headcloth it is usually a plain piece of cloth that is wrapped around the head, but Mdhur women sometimes wear a distinctive style of headcloth. It is folded in half and stitched together at one end and worn so the stitched end form a peak over the head with the body of the cloth hanging down the back. Sometimes it is made from a piece of cloth that is decorated like a high status loincloth with a band of discontinuous supplementary weft patterning at the end that hangs down the back.

Both Ê Đê and Gia Rai male priests commonly wear distinctive clothing when carrying out their priestly functions. In the past such attire often included a long-sleeved pullover that is dyed red rather than the usual dark blue or black, a shoulder-bag, and sometimes a shouldercloth. These too are often made of red cloth. It is important to note that in the Central Highlands shoulder-bags were not commonly worn and were only used by priests and other high status men. It is common for these shoulder-bags to feature supplementary warp patterning.[29]

The Bih live adjacent to Lắk Lake in Krông Ana district. They are the southern-most Ê Đê sub-group and are almost completely surrounded by Mnông. Their culture is strongly influenced by the neighboring Mnông. While Bih men dress much the same as their Kpă neighbors, Bih women's dress is distinctive.[30] Their short wrap-around skirts are particularly noteworthy. Neighboring Mnông women also wear short warp-around skirts, but the coloring and decorative patterning of the Bih skirts is different. There are two types of Bih skirt. One is called *yêng sut* and features a rust red lower portion and black upper portion and the other style is called *yêng pal* and is largely black, but with the black area being covered with twill patterning. Both types of skirt also have narrow warp ikat patterned stripes, possibly reflecting Chăm influence. Bih women's blouses are quite plain, except for a narrow strip of red cloth with small lead disks along the top and pairs of distinctive simple red stitched lines coming down from each end of the red strip on the shoulders that are said to represent duck's feat.

Ra Glai. There are over 120,000 Ra Glai in Khánh Hòa and Ninh Thuận provinces. There are four sub-groups and cultural and linguistic differences tend to reflect the influence of each group's particular neighbors (Chăm, Ê Đê, Chu Ru, and Cơ Ho). Three of the king of Chămpa's ten "treasure stores" (monuments where important ceremonial objects were kept) were located in Ra Glai territory. The objects in one of these included the ceremonial dress of the ancestral mother Po inu Nugar. This is still kept by the Ra Glai of Phước Hà in Ninh Thuận Province's Thuận Nam District

5. Ethnic Minorities in Southern Việt Nam

and is brought out once a year for the Kate Festival (the most important annual festival held by the Chăm). The Chăm refer to the Ra Glai as their younger brother and during the Chămpa period they were said to be the youngest child of the king, while the Chăm were the oldest child. By custom among Chamic peoples the youngest child remains with and tales care of the parents and keeps the ceremonial belongings of the family.

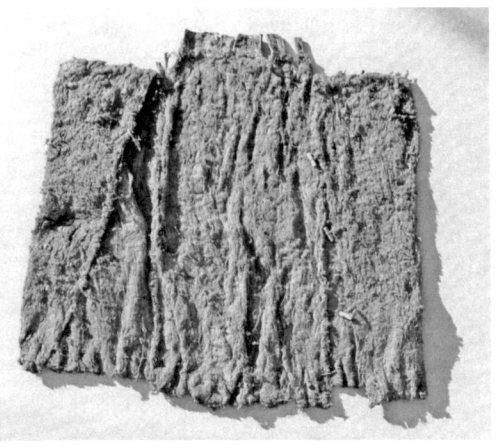

Ra Glai, woman's bark-cloth blouse, Khánh Vĩnh District, Khánh Hòa Province.

The Ra Glai have no tradition of weaving. In the past they made bark-cloth and traded for woven cloth. They planted cotton and traded it as well as various forest products with the Chăm and Cơ Ho for woven cloth.[31] Traditionally men wore loincloths and women short wrap-around skirts made of cloth obtained through trade. They also sometimes wore a blanket and headcloth. During the war Ra Glai males were able to obtain military clothing. After 1975 they were resettled and government stores were set up in larger villages. These provided commercial cloth and clothing. Some older men and women keep loincloths and skirts that they wear on special occasions.

Chu Ru. There are about 20,000 Chu Ru. Most Chu Ru live in Lâm Đồng Province's Đơn Dương District and a few live in Bình Thuận Province. The Chăm influenced their culture.[32] Weaving was not well developed and they traded with the Chăm, Cơ Ho, and Mạ for cloth. In the past Chu Ru men and women dressed like the Chăm. Some of them still do, but wearing generic commercial Western style clothing has become more widespread, especially by men.

Central Highland Mon-Khmer Groups

There are essentially three groups of peoples in the Central Highlands that speak Mon-Khmer languages: Katuic speaking peoples; a northern group of North, Central, and West Bahnaric speaking peoples; and a southern group of South Bahnaric speaking peoples. Katuic speaking groups include the Tà Ôi, Cơ Tu, and Bru (aka Bru-Vân Kiều). The northern groups include the Ba Na, Giẻ Triêng, Xơ Đăng, Hrê, Rơ Măm, and Brâu. The southern groups include the Mnông, Xtiêng, Mạ, Cơ Ho, and Chơ Ro.

Tà Ôi and Cơ Tu. There are about 44,000 Tà Ôi and 62,000 Cơ Tu living in Việt Nam and some living in Laos as well. The Tà Ôi and Cơ Tu lived in the lowlands of Laos until the Lao pushed them into the highlands of Laos and Việt Nam in the 1300s and 1400s. At present in Việt Nam the Tà Ôi and Pa Cô live in an area from A Lưới District in Thừa Thiên–Huế Province in the south to Hướng Hóa District in Quảng Trị Province in the north. The Cơ Tu live to the south of the Tà Ôi in Thừa Thiên–Huế Province's Phú Lộc District and northwestern Quảng Nam provinces. Those categorized as Tà Ôi include people speaking Tà Ôi and Pa Cô, two closely related languages. There are several sub-groups of Cơ Tu. The Cơ Tu had a reputation for being aggressive and frequently raided lowland Kinh communities during the Nguyễn Dynasty period. The French established a single military outpost in Cơ Tu territory in 1904, but generally left them alone until the latter part of the 1930s when additional bases were established and the Cơ Tu gradually brought under French rule.

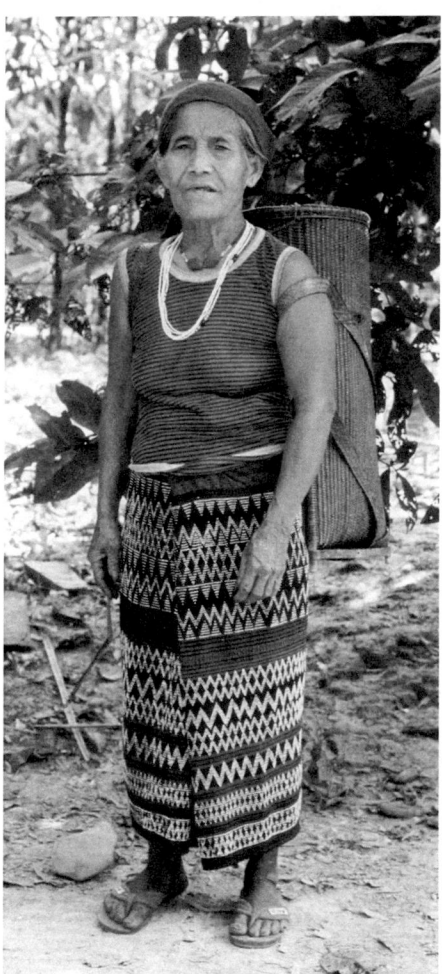 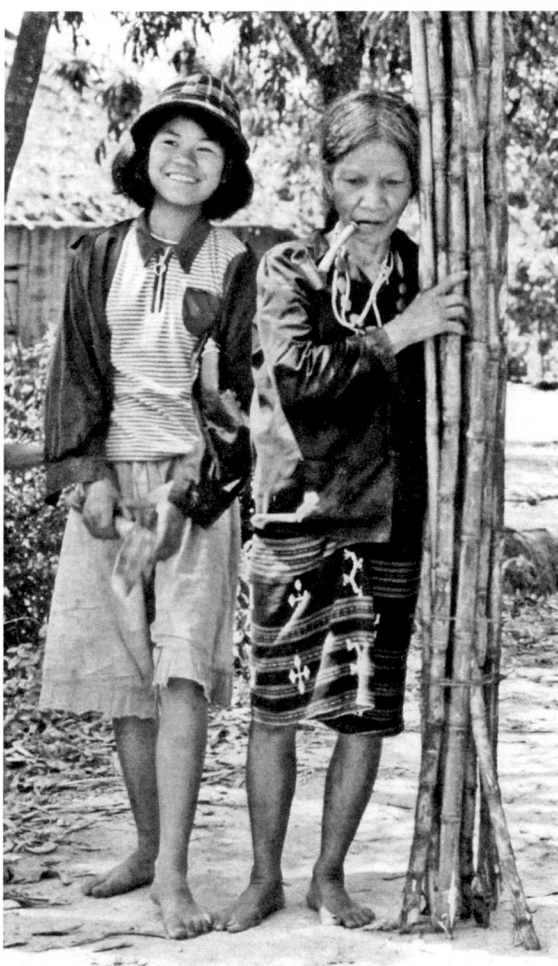

Left: Pa Cô woman, A Lưới District, Thừa Thiên–Huế Province, wearing a tubeskirt with white beads woven by a Tà Ôi woman. *Right:* Young woman in Western attire with Pa Cô woman, A Lưới District, Thừa Thiên–Huế Province, wearing a beaded tubeskirt.

5. Ethnic Minorities in Southern Việt Nam

The Tà Ôi, Pa Cô, Cơ Tu traditionally dressed more or less the same, but most Pa Cô did not weave and obtained cloth from the Tà Ôi.[33] The Tà Ôi and Cơ Tu have traditions of growing cotton and of producing cloth from bast fibers. They also traded forest products with Lao and later with Kinh for cloth. The Tà Ôi and Cơ Tu weave on a foot-braced backstrap loom. At present relatively few Tà Ôi and Cơ Tu still weave. For the past several decades, traditional clothing has been worn mainly on special occasions and most people, men especially, wear generic Western style clothing on an everyday basis.

Large portions of the cloth woven by the Tà Ôi and Cơ Tu are left plain and dyed dark blue or black. At intervals there are plain red and yellow warp directional stripes interspersed with stripes featuring simple alternating warp float patterning.[34] There are three grades of cloth and the lowest grade, which is used to make clothing for poor people is decorated only with these stripes. The two higher grades of cloth have additional decoration in the form of small white glass beads or lead beads that are woven into the weft threads to form discreet patterns. Cloth with white beads constitutes the second grade of cloth and cloth with lead beads the highest grade. Also, while white beads are used in cloth for male and female clothing, lead beads are only used for men's loincloths. The white beads are acquired through trade from the lowlands, while the lead beads are made in the highlands.

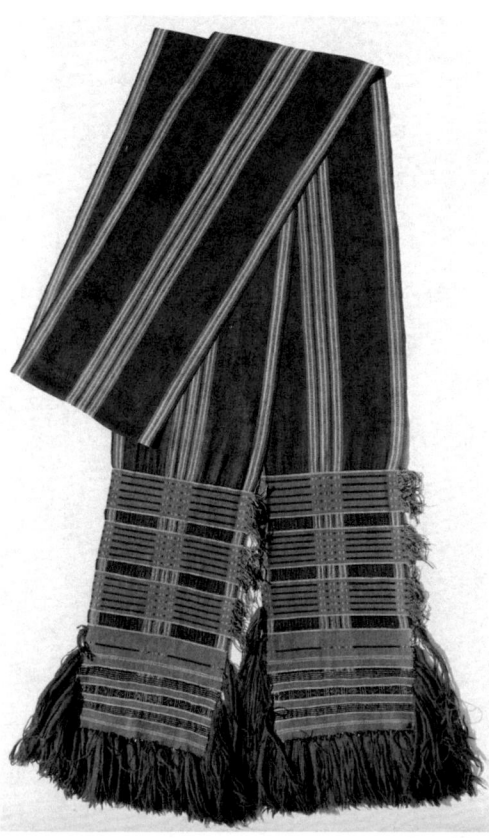

Cơ Tu loincloth decorated with lead beads, Quảng Nam Province.

Men traditionally wore a loincloth and sometimes a blanket folded over the shoulder. Loincloths decorated with beads also feature a large area at each end with numerous weft directional stripes similar to the warp directional ones as well as fringe on all three sides of this area. In between these weft directional stripes there are at least three weft directional bands with patterns made from beads. Lead bead patterns tend to be simple geometric shapes, usually triangles, while white glass bead patterns are more varied and often include at least one band with realistic representations.[35] Loincloths with lead beads were never very common and have now become quite rare. This is because not only are such loincloths no longer made, but the Tà Ôi and Cơ Tu also follow the common Central Highlands practice of burying a person with his or her best clothing.

Traditionally women wore a long tubeskirt and a sash and no blouse.[36] It has become more common for women to wear a shorter tubeskirt and a blouse in recent years. The skirt or skirt and blouse combination is made from a single long piece of cloth that is cut into two pieces and either joined if for a skirt or tailored for a separate skirt and blouse. If the cloth has white bead patterning this is commonly laid out differently along the cloth depending on what part of the clothing a particular piece is intended.[37]

Bru. There are about 75,000 Bru (aka Bru-Vân Kiều) in Việt Nam and about the same number in Laos. The Bru in Laos live in Savannakhét Province where the Phu Tai have influenced them. In Việt Nam most Bru live in Hướng Hoá District, Quảng Trị Province, but they are also found in Quảng Bình and Thừa Thiên–Huế provinces and a group of Bru were resettled in Đắk Lắk Province's Krông Pắk District in 1972.

The Bru were one of the last groups of highland Mon-Khmer peoples commonly to make clothing from bark-cloth. This included loincloths for men and women, with the female loincloths being longer than those worn by men, and shirts and blouses. After the French established an administrative center in Savannakhét town in the 1890s the western Bru came into more contact with the Phu Tai and some began to weave using techniques learned from the Phu Tai and wearing styles of clothing influenced by them, but with distinctive features. This influence slowly spread east to the Bru in Việt Nam during the first half of the 20th century. Bru men gradually started to wear clothing like Lao and Kinh and later adopted generic Western style clothing. Women wear a tubeskirt, blouse, and headcloth.[38] Bru tubeskirts have a waistband that is usually made of two pieces of cloth. There is a plain white one at the top and a narrower striped one below. Skirt bodies are made of a single piece of cloth that is sewn into a tube like those of the Phu Tai. The skirt bodies are decorated with bands of warp float patterning.[39] There are two styles of skirt body. One style features relatively wide bands with thin weft directional yellow stripes and narrower bands with rhomb

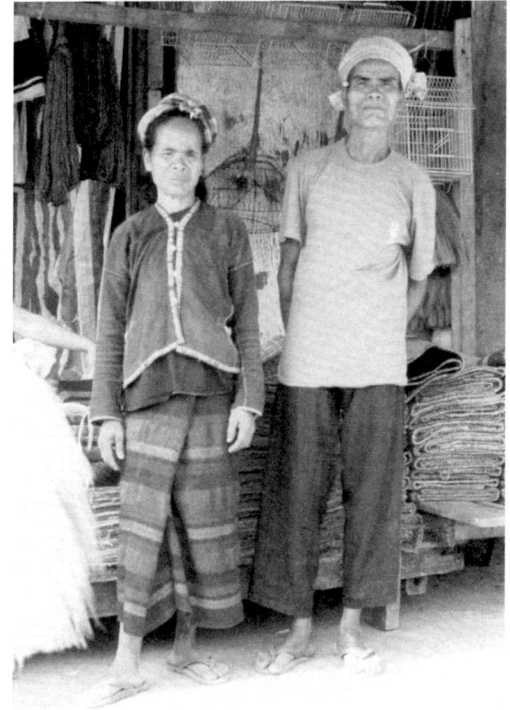

Bru couple at Khe Sanh market, Hương Hóa District, Quảng Trị Province.

patterns woven in a variety of colors. The other style only has the narrow rhomb patterned bands. The blouses are tailored like those of the Phu Tai: cut for a tight fit with a flared bottom, Chinese-style collar, and a front opening fastened with buttons. In the past they were made of dark blue cotton cloth, but now it is more common use black cloth. It is common to add colorful embroidery to the blouse. This includes a fairly wide rectangular area across most of the front and bottom, a narrower strip down the front opening and around the color, narrow bands on each side of the waist, and very narrow stripes where the sleeves are attached to the body. Some older blouses lack this embroidery and instead the front opening was sometimes decorated with one to three rows of French Indochinese coins. Such blouses were not common and are no longer worn. The headcloth is a plain colored long piece of cloth that is wrapped around the head.

Ba Na and Rơngao. The Ba Na number about 230,000 and live mainly in Kon Tum and Gia Lai provinces. There are several Ba Na sub-groups, but cultural differences between them are relatively minor. Ba Na speak a Central Bahnaric language. There are about 18,000 Rơngao (aka Rengao) and they speak a North Bahnaric language that is similar to the language spoken by the Hà Lăng sub-group of Xơ Đăng. They are placed in the Ba Na ethnic category in Việt Nam. The clothing of the Ba Na sub-groups, including the Rơngao, is more or less the same.[40]

Some Ba Na communities have traditions of growing cotton, hemp, and indigo as commercial crops. When Henri Maître visited the Kon Tum area in the early 20th century he found that they were exporting a number of items from the area, including Job's tears (*Coix lacryma-jobi*), and that imports included cloth.[41] The Ba Na weave on an "Indonesian" style of backstrap loom rather than a foot-braced type.

Ba Na male clothing includes a loincloth and sometimes a blanket is draped over one shoulder. Headcloths were worn in the past, but are no longer worn. They were wrapped around the head and tied so as to form a point towards the front. Although similar, there is more variation in the styles of loincloth worn by Ba Na men than Ê Đê and Gia Rai men. The Ba Na also have loincloths with little decoration beyond a few warp directional stripes down each side and others that have more decorative features that are worn by wealthier men of higher status. Some of these loincloths are similar to Ê Đê and Gia Rai and have a weft directional band near the ends with discontinuous supplementary weft patterning, a row of Job's tears, and long twined fringe. However, sometimes the alternating warp float patterning on the warp directional stripes on the sides of such loincloths are more elaborate than is common with Ê Đê and Gia Rai ones.[42] In addition, Ba Na men also sometimes wear loincloths where the warp directional stripes include some with warp ikat dashes along the sides and down the middle.[43]

Ba Na women wear a wrap-around skirt, pullover blouse, and sometimes a blanket draped over one shoulder. In the past the skirts worn by Ba Na women were shorter than those worn by Ê Đê and Gia Rai, but in recent years longer skirts have become popular. The Ba Na skirt has three parts: a waistband, body, and a panel sewn over the body.⁴⁴ Women fold the skirt from the back and secure it in front so that the panel is at the rear. The waistband is longer than the skirt body. Its decorative features can be divided into three parts. One each side there are a series of warp directional stripes. There are plain red stripes, very narrow stripes with white alternating warp float patterning, and wider stripes with dark blue or black and white warp ikat dashes. The central area has a white ground. The middle of this area is left plain and each end is decorated with weft directional bands with supplementary weft patterning. There are a few styles of decorating the skirt body. Most of the body is left plain dark blue or black. One style has a very narrow warp directional band near the top with plain red stripes and stripes with dark blue or black and white warp float patterning and a wider band near the hem with plain red stripes and stripes with dark blue or black and white warp float patterning. Another

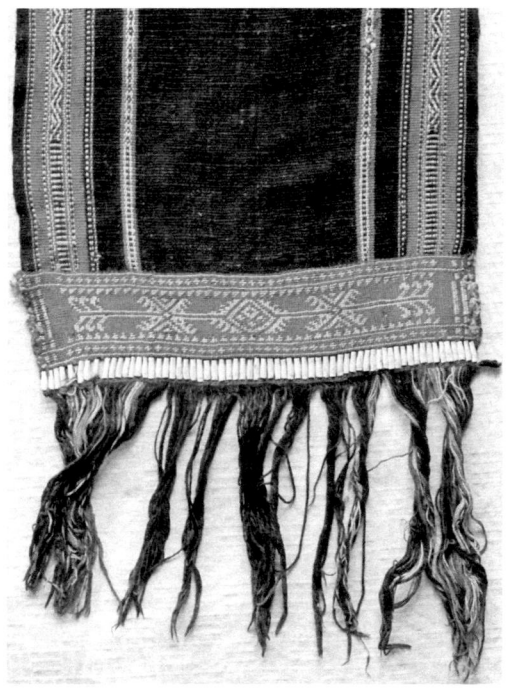

Detail of Rơngao loincloth showing supplementary weft band at end, Đắk Hà District, Kon Tum Province.

style places the narrow band at the hem and has a wide decorative band in the center. This band has a group of stripes on each side similar to those on the sides of the waistband and a stripe in the middle with a white ground and supplementary weft patterns spaced across the length of it. There are pullover blouses that are sleeveless as well as ones with sleeves. The sleeveless version in particular is usually relatively plain except for a narrow decorative band at the top and a wider one near the bottom. The top band has plain red stripes and dark blue or black and white stripes with warp float patterning. The wider one has wider plain red stripes and dark blue or black and white stripes with warp float patterning as well as a stripe in the center with red and white stripe with supplementary weft patterning. A larger portion of the body of fancier blouses is covered with decorative stripes. Usually the entire lower half of the body is covered with stripes and the top and middle of the upper half has stripes. The sleeves are laid out in a similar manner with the end half of the sleeves covered in stripes and the inner half having stripes where it is joined to the body and in the middle. Such stripes often include some with warp ikat patterning. The panel is attached in the center of the body from the waistband down to about the middle of the skirt. The width of these panels varies. Some are fairly narrow while others cover a good deal of the rear of the skirt. They tend to be decorated in a similar way as the skirt body.

Ba Na blankets are made of two long pieces of cloth that are sewn together along the warp.[45] As with Ê Đê and Gia Rai blankets one end of the weft is sometimes sewn together as well. Most of the blanket is plain dark blue or black. The central area is decorated with six or eight narrow warp directional red, white, and sometimes yellow stripes that are evenly placed across the body. Occasionally these stripes include warp ikat dashes. The outer edges of the blanket features two warp directional bands. The one nearest the edge is narrower than the inside one and includes plain red and sometimes yellow stripes and a dark blue or black and white one with warp float patterning. The inner band also includes a combination of plain red and sometimes yellow stripes and dark blue or black and white ones with warp float patterning, but the one of these at the center is fairly wide.

Giẻ Triêng. There are over 50,000 Giẻ Triêng in Việt Nam and a large number of related people in Laos where they are called Talieng. There are four sub-groups: Giẻ, Triêng, Ve, and Bơnoong. They live in the northern part of Kon Tum and Quảng Nam provinces in the vicinity of Ngọc Linh Mountain (the highest mountain in the Central Highlands). They were pushed into this remote area by more warlike peoples engaged in slave raiding, especially the Xơ Đăng (aka Sedang). Despite their remoteness, they developed relations with Lao traders, from whom they learned to pan for gold, which they exchanged for trade goods. The French sent officials into the area in 1927, but did not pacify the Giẻ Triêng until the late 1930s, when many Giẻ Triêng men worked on construction of Colonial Route 14, which passed through their territory.

Although some Giẻ Triêng learned to grow cotton and weave, many communities did not and neither was ever widespread. Some Giẻ Triêng also occasionally wove cloth with bast fibers. Weaving was primarily found in Giẻ and Triêng communities and much less in Ve and Bơnoong communities. In the past they traded for cloth with neighboring groups such as the Cơ Tu as well as with Lao and Kinh. Giẻ Triêng males and females dress much like the Cơ Tu.[46] Thus, Giẻ Triêng men wear loincloths similar to those worn by Cơ Tu and, in fact, often obtain them from the Cơ Tu (including ones with white glass beads).[47] Giẻ Triêng women wear long tubeskirts and no blouse. The skirts are made of two pieces of cloth that are sewn together along the warp and then sewn into a tube along the weft. The skirts are largely plain dark blue or black and each panel has a band at the outer edge and near the center that features plain red and yellow stripes and dark blue or black and white stripes with simple alternating warp float patterning.[48] Men and women sometimes wear a blanket draped over one shoulder. The blankets are made of two pieces of cloth sewn along the warp with decorative bands like those on the skirts, commonly three of these near the outer edges and two on each side of the central area.[49] Bơnoong women sometimes wear leggings made of plain or white cloth.

Unlike most Central Highlands peoples, while a deceased Giẻ Triêng person is dressed in his or her best clothes, family members then inherit the clothing rather than it being buried with the deceased.[50] Less isolated communities, such as those of the Ve sub-group, commonly began wearing generic Western style clothing on an everyday basis and traditional clothing only on special occasions by the mid–20th century, but in some of the more isolated communities traditional clothing continues to be worn on an everyday basis.

Xơ Đăng. There are about 170,000 people in Việt Nam that are categorized as Xơ Đăng. The Xơ Đăng live in remote northern Kon Tum Province and adjacent parts of Quảng Nam Province in the vicinity of Ngọc Linh Mountain. They originally lived further west in the vicinity of the border with Laos, but as slave raiding by the Lao began in the 1600s and later by the Siamese an increasing number of surviving Xơ Đăng fled east towards Ngọc Linh Mountain. Prior to the advent of outsiders carrying out slave raids conflict between Xơ Đăng communities was already common as people sought to capture others for sacrifice. Once slave raiding began Xơ Đăng attacked one another to capture people to be sold as slaves. In addition to subsistence crops, like many other highland groups some Xơ Đăng collected wild cinnamon to trade and in the 1700s began cultivating it. Some Ca Dong, for example, traded cultivated cinnamon for various items including cloth.

Xơ Đăng tend to identify themselves as members of a small local group rather as belonging to a larger ethnic group or even sub-group. The main sub-groups are the Xơ Teng, Mơ Nâm, Tơ Đrá, Ca Dong, and Hà Lăng. There are also some smaller sub-groups like the Châu, which number only about 100. Conflict between villages was common in past. Despite their differences many of the Xơ Đăng sub-groups believe that they are ultimately related and identify with a single culture hero called "Mother Weaver." Mother Weaver lives in a grotto where she sits at her loom weaving an eternal cloth. It is believed: "When she adds a thread, a baby is born. When she breaks a thread, a human being dies and his soul is reincarnated into a new-born baby to return to his former community."[51] When a person dies the soul of the person takes the form of a bird and returns to Mother Weaver's grotto. A legend associated with "Mother Weaver" relates to a great tree named *Luông pling* located near Ngọc Linh Mountain that fell across the landscape.[52] The Tơ Đrá live where the upturned roots are located. Broken pieces of the tree in this area were turned to stone that the Tơ Đrá used to make tools and other objects. This accounts for the Tơ Đrá becoming blacksmiths. Their metal implements have a long history of being traded extensively in the highlands. The Mơ Nâm live where the top of the tree fell and they used its flowers and leaves to make cloth. The Xơ Teng live where the trunk fell and they used the bark of the trunk to make bark-cloth. After death Xơ Đăng believe that their soul turns into a bird and returns to the grotto where Mother Weaver lives.

Not all Xơ Teng have traditions of weaving. Even within a sub-group that weaves, not all communities do so. Bark-cloth was widely worn in the past and people in some remote communities continued to wear it until recently. There are communities of Xơ Teng, Mơ Nâm, and Tơ Đrá known to have produced bark-cloth during the 20th century. Items produced range from simple loincloths to a style of sleeveless front-opening shirt made of a single piece of bark-cloth that is folded over so that it is longer in back than in the front and stitched together below the arm openings. Some Xơ Teng in Đắk Tô District, Kon Tum Province, produce a distinctive type of bast fiber clothing. It is made by plaiting fiber thread using a needle made of hedgehog hair, bone, or bamboo so that it resembles a piece of woven cloth.[53] The bast fiber and bark is mostly a light brown color. Sometimes the clothing is decorated with thin stripes along the edges with bast fiber thread that is a lighter or darker shade of brown. The items made in this manner include wrap-around skirts, pullover sleeveless blouses and shirts, and sleeveless front-opening shirts. Non-weaving communities also obtained woven cloth from neighboring weaving communities of other Xơ Đăng as well as of other ethnic groups and cloth has also been available from traders, mainly from Laos, over the past few centuries.

The Xơ Đăng that weave do so on an "Indonesian" style backstrap loom. Originally cloth was woven from bast fibers made from wild plants collected in the forest. Some Xơ Teng, Ca Dong, and Hà Lăng grew jute and hemp to use as thread and cotton was introduced as a crop more recently, apparently only in the 20th century.[54] Some Tơ Đrá communities were growing cotton by the 20th century and previously did not grow other plants for making thread. The Mơ Nâm have no tradition of growing cotton and only those in Kon Plông District, Kon Tum Province, grew hemp.

Traditional male clothing made of woven cloth includes a loincloth, a headcloth that is wrapped so as to hang down to the neck, and sometimes a blanket that is folded and draped over one shoulder. The particular style of loincloth and blanket worn by Xơ Đăng varies to some extent depending on sub-group and location. Neighboring peoples have influenced weaving styles and men also sometimes wear clothing obtained from these groups rather than woven locally. Thus, in some locales men wear Cơ Tu style loincloths with white glass beads and in others they wear Ba Na style ones featuring a weft directional band near the ends with discontinuous supplementary weft patterning and a row of Job's tears. The Tơ Đrá in Đắk Hà District, Kon Tum Province, often wear a loincloth made of plain white cotton cloth with narrow red lines along the edges. There are also loincloths that exhibit external influence, but that have a distinctive style. An example of this is a loincloth formerly worn by a Mơ Nâm village headman from Kon Plông District that features three sets of plain warp directional stripes down the sides and in the middle with the end areas decorated with three lines of supplementary weft weave triangles at the top of the area, a line of supplementary weft weave rhombs at the end, and fringe at the end and along both side of the area.[55] The blankets worn by men also vary a great deal and many of them are imported from other groups. Some Tơ Đrá and Xơ Teng communities weave a white cotton blanket that is largely plain and undyed with a few narrow warp directional stripes near each edge.[56] Most of the stripes are plain red or yellow (sometimes green as well) and usually there is one on one side that features simple black and white alternating warp float patterning.

Women's traditional dress also varies a great deal depending on sub-group and locale and often other groups have influenced their style of dress. Thus, Hà Lăng women in Sa Thầy District, Kon Tum Province, wear wrap-around skirts and pullover blouses like the Ba Na and the Ba Na also influence the dress of many Xơ Teng women. Some Mơ Nâm in Kon Tum and Quảng Nam provinces wear long Hrê style tubeskirts with a large band with rectangles featuring black and white alternating warp float patterning in the center.[57] Xơ Teng women in Đắk Tô District sometimes wear Ba Na style clothing, but in some communities they also wear a distinctive style of skirt and shouldercloth.[58] The skirt is covered with plain red, yellow, and black warp directional stripes of various widths and a few relative wide stripes with geometric black and white warp float patterning. The shouldercloth is like a large apron and is often worn draped over one shoulder. It consists of a body and another piece of cloth that is sewn across the weft at one end of the body. The body is made of two pieces of cloth that is largely plain white with decorative warp directional bands on each side and in the middle where the two pieces of cloth are joined. The bands feature narrow plain red and yellow stripes and narrow black and white stripes with simple warp float patterning. The piece of cloth at the top of the shawl resembles the waistband of a skirt. The top and bottom parts are covered with stripes like those on the body and in the center there is a band with a series of rectangles with a variety of black and white geometric patterns made using the alternating warp float technique.

The decline of weaving and wearing traditional clothing by the Xơ Đăng was widespread after 1975 and most adopted generic Western style clothing for everyday dress. Increasingly generic Western style clothing was also worn on special occasions or people began to wear a mixture of Western style clothing and one or two traditional items such as a blanket in the case of men or tubeskirt in the case of women, although even the tubeskirts tended to be Lao ones obtained through trade. The cloth that continued to be woven was almost exclusively made of cotton and the use of bast fibers largely ceased after 1975.

Hrê. There are about 130,000 Hrê in Quảng Ngãi and Bình Định provinces. The French commonly referred to the Hrê as Davak (aka Dá Vách). The Hrê originally lived in Laos prior to migrating to their present territory. Chămpa ruled over the Hrê from the 1000s until the defeat of Chămpa by Đại Việt in 1471 and the Chăm exerted considerable influence on Hrê culture. Thus, they are sometimes called Chăm Rê. Đại Việt and the Nguyễn Lords by and large left the Hrê alone. The Nguyễn Dynasty's subsequent effort to assert control over Hrê territory was marked by conflict. The French established outposts in Hrê territory between 1900 and 1902 and the French too met resisted. The Việt Minh seized control over a large part of Quảng Ngãi Province immediately after the Second World War and promoted the settlement of Kinh in Hrê territory. This led to conflict between the Việt Minh and the Hrê culminating in considerable loss of life on both sides in 1949. A great deal of Hrê territory remained under communist control until 1975.

Prior to the Second World War there were significant differences between sub-groups depending on where they lived and the name Hrê itself was commonly used for only one of the sub-groups. Those living in An Lão District, Bình Định Province, near the Định River were called Định people; those living near the Rvá River in Minh Long District, Quảng Ngãi Province, were called Rvá people; those living in Ba Tơ District, Quảng Ngãi Province, near the Liên River were called Liên people; those living near the Hrê River were called Hrê; and those living in Sơn Hà District, Quảng Ngãi Province, near the Krế River, were called Krế people. After the Second World War there was considerable integration of these various sub-groups and gradually they came to view themselves as a single ethnic group.

Depending on the area Hrê communities grew ramie, hemp, and cotton in the past.[59] They also traded hemp and other local products with lowlanders for various goods, including cotton and silk cloth. The Hrê weave on a foot-braced backstrap loom. Alternating warp float weave is the main decorative technique and patterns are geometric and not representational. Black (or sometimes dark blue) is the dominant color of most Hrê clothing, with the alternating warp float patterning being black and white. Plain red warp directional stripes add additional highlights.

Hrê men traditionally wore a loincloth, headcloth, and sometimes a pullover shirt or folded blanket draped over one shoulder.[60] In addition to relatively plain loincloths, fancier versions are relatively long. The central area is usually covered with plain red and black warp directional stripes with a thin stripe with black and white alternating warp float patterning running down the center. There is a rectangular area at each end that has a long warp fringe and shorter weft fringe and weft directional stripes. The latter include narrow plain red, black, and white stripes and two or three wider ones with black and white patterning. The pullover shirt is sleeveless with a rounded neck opening. Common decorative features include bands with several narrow plain black, red, and white stripes alternating with wider bands with black and white alternating warp float patterning (one of these featuring a series of rectangles with patterns). Blankets commonly have a plain black warp directional central area and sets of three warp directional bands with plain red, yellow, and white stripes and one stripe with black and white alternating warp float patterning. By the mid–1970s only old men still wore loincloths and if younger men wore them it was usually with commercial shorts and then only for special occasions. By then if men wore a shirt it was often made of commercial cloth and tailored in Kinh fashion. There are three styles of traditional men's headcloth. One is made from a long piece of plain black cloth that is twisted and then wrapped around the head and knotted in the back so that both ends hang down the back. Another is made from a shorter piece of plain white cloth. It is wrapped around the head and the ends are knotted over the ears. In earlier times when going on a journey or to war men sometimes wore a headcloth made of red material.

Hrê women traditionally wore a relatively long tubeskirt, headcloth, and sometimes a breastcloth or blouse.[61] The skirt is made of two pieces of cloth that are sewn together along the warp. One of these pieces is largely plain. There are bands with plain red warp directional stripes at the top and bottom and two such bands near the center. The other piece of cloth is decorated like the man's pullover shirt with sets of thin plain warp directional stripes and three wider warp directional bands with black and white alternating warp float patterning. Women sometimes would wear on the skirt since it was relatively long. Alternatively they might use a piece of blanket cloth as a bodice or wear a sleeveless five-panel blouse that fastens on the right in Kinh fashion and a Kinh-style breastcloth. It was also common to wear a headcloth. Traditional headcloths have a white ground and decorations in various colors. Since the 1970s it has been common to use a piece of commercial cloth such as a face-towel as a headcloth. At present Hrê women generally wear generic Western style clothing on an everyday basis and traditional clothing only for special occasions.

Rơ Măm. Between 400 and 500 Rơ Măm live in Le village in Sa Thầy District, Kon Tum Province. They speak a dialect of Kaco' (aka Kachok) and there are also Rơ Măm in Cambodia. In the early 20th century the Rơ Măm population was larger and they lived in a dozen Rơ Măm villages. Their population subsequently declined and they were reduced to living in two villages and then as a result of further depopulation as a result of the war in the 1960s and 1970s they came to live only in their present village.

Prior to the 1960s the almost every Rơ Măm family grew cotton and wove cloth.[62] They also traded for cloth with neighboring groups such as the Brâu as well as with Lao traders. By the time the war was over growing cotton and weaving had ceased for the most part. Everyday traditional clothing is largely undecorated and is dyed dark blue. Clothing with decorative patterns generally was reserved for special occasions and the cloth for such clothing was often obtained through trade. Traditional male clothing includes a fairly long loincloth and sometimes a blanket draped over the shoulder. Traditional female clothing includes a tubeskirt that reaches to below the knees, but above the ankles. It is made of a single piece of cloth. If decorated, there is a wide warp directional band in the middle with plain red and yellow stripes and red and white and dark blue and white stripes in the center of the band with simple alternating warp float patterning.[63]

Brâu. There are about 400 Brâu living in Đắc Mế village in Ngọc Hồi district, Kon Tum Province. The Brâu in Việt Nam speak a dialect of Brao and over 50,000 speakers of other Brao dialects live in Ratanakiri and Stung Treng provinces in Cambodia and in Attapeu Province in Laos (where they are known as Lavae). The Brâu lived in fortified villages prior to the advent of French colonial rule because of raids by Siamese.

Traditional male clothing includes a loincloth and sometimes a blanket is draped over one shoulder. Traditional female clothing includes a tubeskirt that reaches to mid-calf and women either went bare-chested or wore a sleeveless pullover blouse. The Brâu in Việt Nam no longer weave and obtain cloth from Brao in Laos (who still weave), from Lao traders, or from Xơ Đăng by trading honey and domestic animals.[64] At present Brâu men generally wear Western style commercial clothing and women either wear commercial clothing or clothing made from cloth obtained through trade.

Mnông. There are over 100,000 Mnông living to the south of the Ê Đê. They are

5. Ethnic Minorities in Southern Việt Nam

commonly divided into three regional groups: the Central and Eastern Mnông in Đắk Lắk and Lâm Đồng provinces, and the Southern Mnông in Bình Phước Province and in Cambodia. Each of these regional groups can be further sub-divided into sub-groups. Central Mnông sub-groups include the Preh, Biêt, and Bu-đâng. Eastern Mnông sub-groups include the Rlâm, Gar, and Chil. Southern sub-groups include the Nông (aka Bu Nông), Prâng, Kuenh, Địp (aka Bu Địp), Poi Loi, as well as a mixed sub-group commonly referred to as the Mnông-Xtiêng. While linguistic differences between sub-groups are relatively minor, there are significant cultural differences depending on where particular communities are located. Thus, Mnông in Đắk Lắk Province often live in close proximity to Ê Đê and share cultural features with them. Mnông in Lâm Đồng Province live close to the Cơ Ho and share cultural aspects with

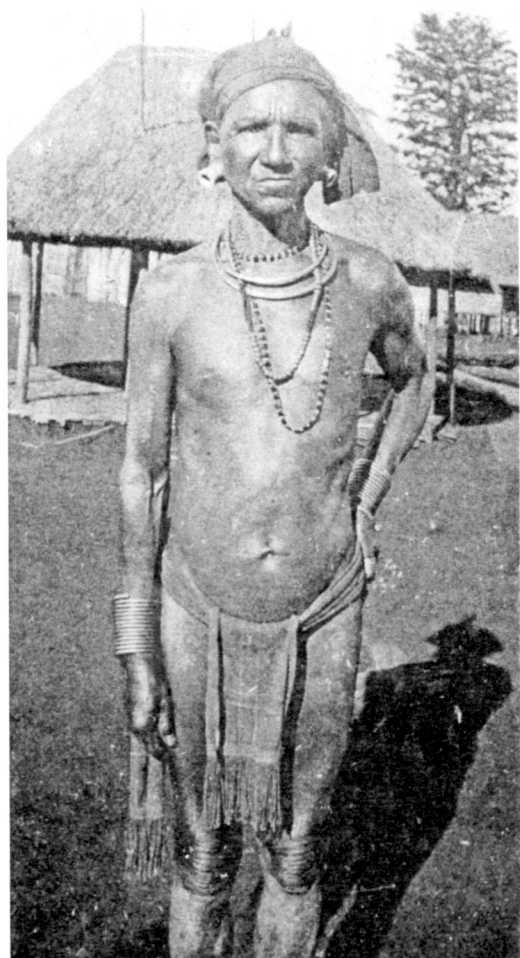 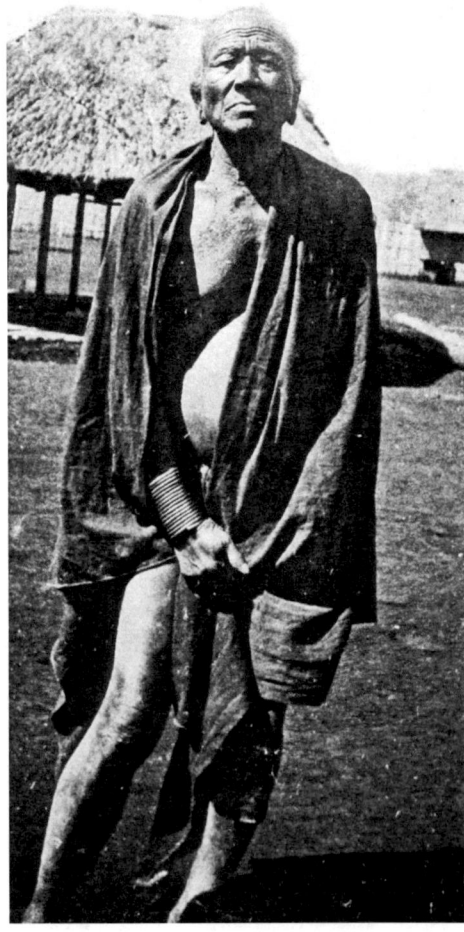

Left: Mnông village headman (from Maître, *Les Jungles Moi*, pl. 11, fig. 19). *Right:* Mnông village headman (from Maître, *Les Jungles Moi*, pl. 11, fig. 20).

them. The Mnông in Bình Phước Province live close to the Xtiêng and share cultural features with them, especially the so-called Mnông-Xtiêng. The Mnông appear to be indigenous to the general area where they live at present.

The Mnông gained a reputation for their resistance to the growing French presence in the early 20th century, especially after one of their chiefs named Pu Trang Lung killed the famous French explorer Henri Maître in 1914.[65] Significant French efforts to pacify the Mnông did not resume until 1930 and the French continued to meet resistance into the late 1930s.[66] Several Biêt villages in particular were involved in the Python God cult that emerged around 1937 and soon spread to several areas of the Central Highlands. Some French believed Kinh that had settled in the vicinity were involved in promoting the cult and pointed to Kinh influence over the cult's leadership, including the wearing of Kinh style of clothing.[67]

French military officers Paul Huard and Albert-Marie Maurice reported that in the 1930s there were Mnông living near Lắk Lake in Đắk Lắk Province and in the upper reaches of the Đồng Nai River in Lâm Đồng Province wearing sleeveless pullover tunics made of bark-cloth.[68] They also note that men were responsible for making bark-cloth. In the late 1990s there were still some elderly Rlâm living in the vicinity of Lắk Lake making sleeveless front-opening shirts and blouses from bark-cloth. These were worn primarily when working in the wet area around the lake.[69]

Mnông women weave on a foot-braced backstrap loom. Weaving has declined considerably in recent years in many Mnông communities and remains common mainly in more isolated areas. Growing cotton was not widespread among the Mnông in the past and it was common to make thread by retting bark and liana fibers. Such bast fibers are no longer widely used and while hand-made cotton thread is occasionally used it is more common to use commercial cotton thread. Traditional colors made from natural dyes include red, yellow, and blue. Textiles are decorated with a variety of geometric and representational patterns woven using supplementary weft and warp float weaves. As in Ê Đê society, status differences are significant in Mnông society and traditionally such differences were reflected in dress with the dress of higher status people tending to have more decorative features.[70] The Mnông traditionally suspended a deceased person's clothing over the gravesite and then abandoned the items. A special large blanket also accompanied the body. The Mnông do not wear traditional clothing on an everyday basis any longer except in remote areas.

Traditional Mnông male clothing includes a loincloth, sometimes a sleeveless pullover shirt or blanket draped over one shoulder, and sometimes a headcloth. Mnông loincloths generally are narrower than those worn by the Ê Đê and their style varies according to region, occasion, and status. There is an undecorated everyday variety, one with only some decoration, and one with numerous decorative features that is worn by high status men on special occasions. In general Eastern Mnông men such as those of the Gar sub-group wear loincloths that are similar to those worn by Ê Đê men, only narrower.[71] Thus, the high status variety features a plain blue center with bands on each wide with plain red warp directional stripes and a blue and white

5. Ethnic Minorities in Southern Việt Nam

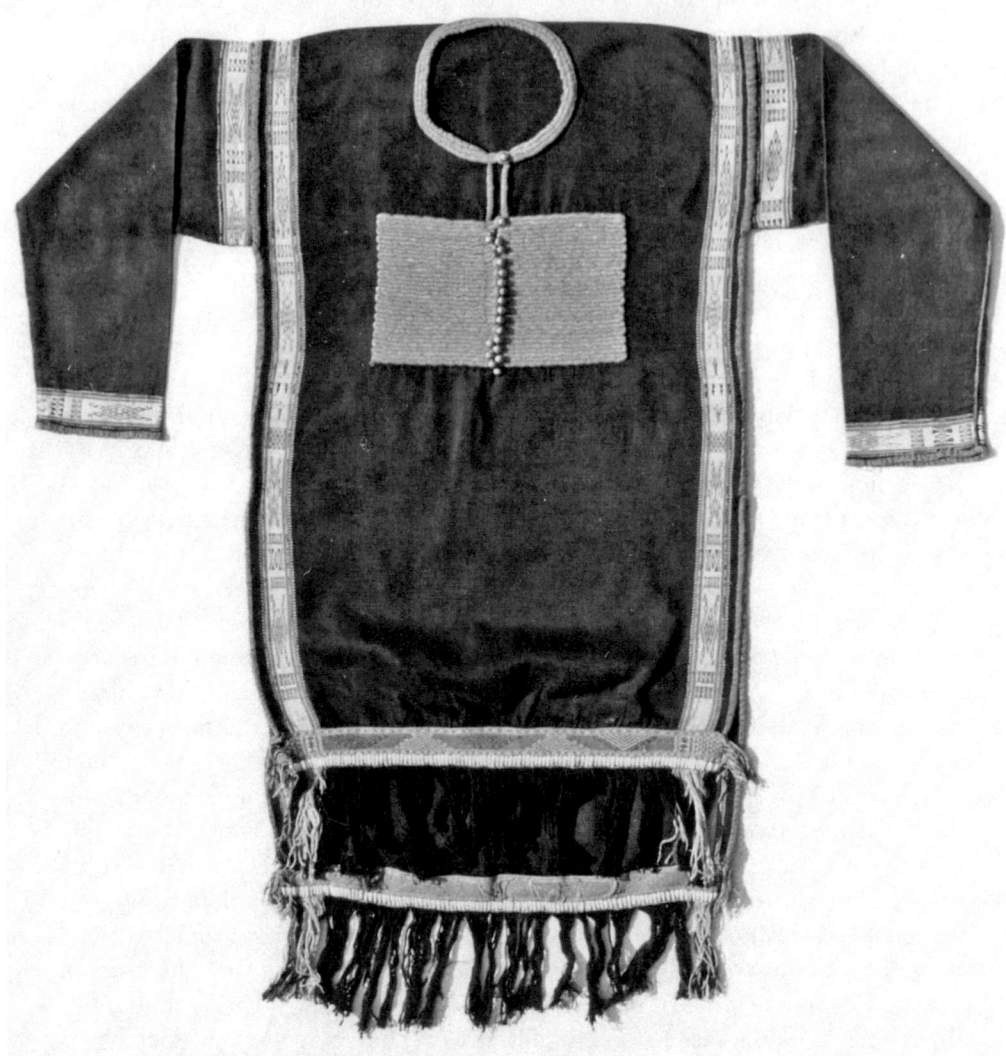

Mnông (Gar sub-group), man's pullover shirt, Lắk District, Đắk Lắk Province.

warp float patterned stripe in the center. The ends have a weft directional band with supplementary weft patterning, a row of Job's tears, and fringe. Elsewhere the high status loincloths worn by Mnông men have warp directional stripes on each side as well as two sets of stripes in the center.[72] Near the ends there is a weft directional band with supplementary weft patterning that is usually a little narrower than on the Ê Đê style loincloths. The supplementary weft patterning is also different. This band is followed by fringe, but there is no row of Job's tears. A short distance above this band is another area with several narrow weft directional stripes with supplementary weft patterning. Another common decorative feature of some of these loincloths is the addition of groups of small metal tubes and red pompoms attached along the sides of the end portion. Brass was a common material for the tubes in the past, but in recent times plastic is often used.

Traditionally Mnông men went bare-chested or draped a folded blanket over one shoulder. Huard and Maurice described sleeveless pullover shirts being worn in the early 20th century, but state that these appear to have been recently adopted and were only worn by men living south of the Đồng Nai River at the time of their research.[73] As with loincloths, shirt styles vary according to area and status. Thus, high status Gar and other Eastern Mnông men wear pullover shirts that are similar to those worn by Ê Đê men with long sleeves, red yarn in the center representing bird wings, warp directional patterned bands down the sides and at each end of the sleeves, and weft directional patterned bands at the front and back hem.[74] Elsewhere the shirt worn is a sleeveless pullover that is sometimes woven from bast fiber.[75] The ground of these shirts is left undyed and they can be relatively plain or on fancier versions most of the central area is covered with supplementary weft patterning. It is common for such shirts to have a large central area with vertical lines of rhombs in red and black and horizontal bands above and below this with distinct patterns. Huard and Maurice also mention that high status Mnông men sometimes wore items of clothing obtained from Kinh, Khmer, or Chinese traders, including red felt shirts, but that such clothing was rare.[76] They describe the headcloths worn by Mnông men at the time of their research as being made of plain black or blue (and rarely red) commercial cotton cloth.[77]

Traditional Mnông female clothing includes a wrap-around skirt and sometimes a blanket. The skirts reach to just below or around the knees and thus are considerably shorter than those worn by Ê Đê women. In the case of older skirts, those made of bast fiber tend to have less decoration than those made of cotton. Skirts are made of a single piece of cloth with either a white or a dark blue or black ground, and decorated with warp directional stripes. Preh skirts tend to be white and those of other subgroups dark blue or black. Eastern Mnông skirts commonly feature two bands near the bottom of the skirt with distinct geometric and representational warp float patterns in the center. The lower band has white patterns over the ground color while the upper band has patterns in various colors surrounded by white thread.[78] There are usually sets of three plain warp directional stripes in between these bands and above the upper band. The top part of the skirt is left plain except for a thin strip near the upper edge. Central Mnông and Southern Mnông skirts are decorated differently. They feature three warp directional bands.[79] There is a relatively wide band in the middle of the skirt with a center featuring black or dark blue and white warp float patterning with narrower plain stripes and stripes with warp float patterning on each side. There are narrower bands near each edge laid out in roughly the same manner but with the central warp float patterned area being much narrower than in the middle band.

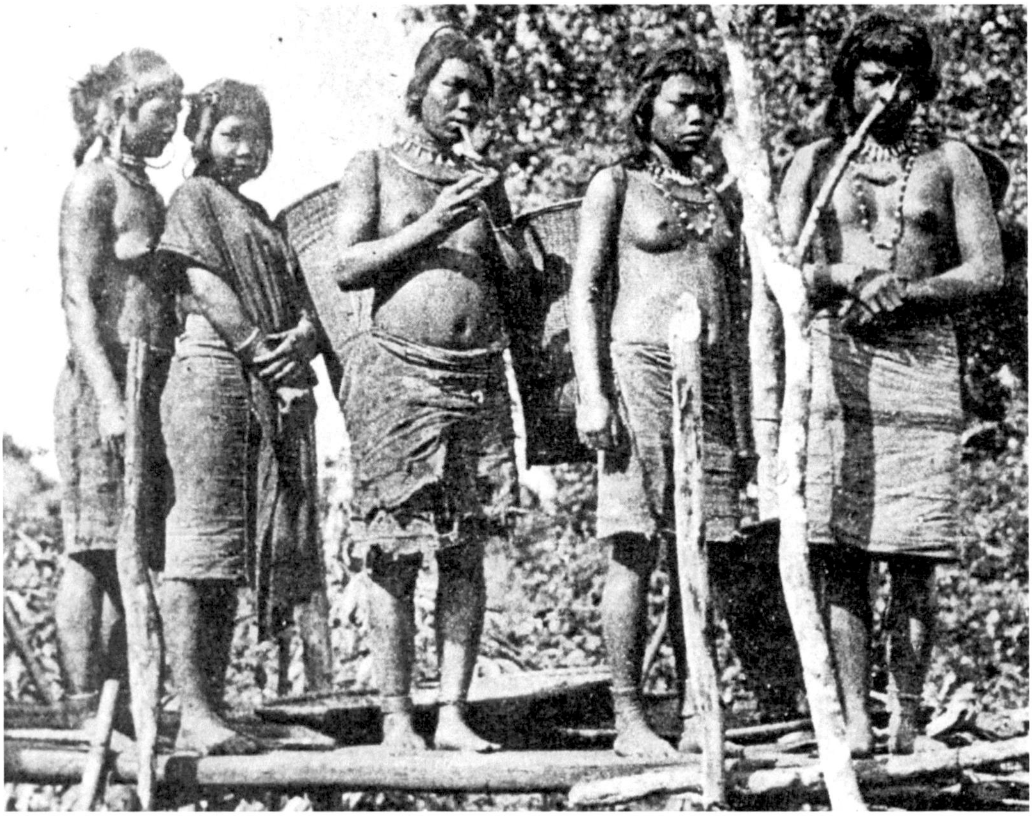

5. Ethnic Minorities in Southern Việt Nam

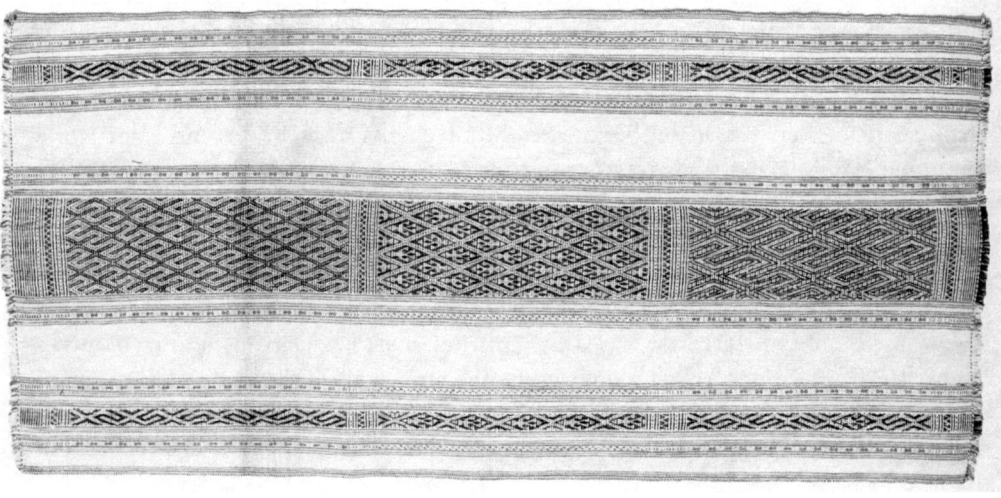

Above: Group of Mnông women (from Maître, *Les Jungles Moï*, pl. 29, fig. 57). *Below:* Mnông (Preh sub-group), woman's wrap-around skirt, Lắk District, Đắk Lắk Province.

Both men and women sometimes wear a blanket when it is cold and women also use them as baby-carriers. The blankets are made of two pieces of cloth joined along the warp and have a dark blue or black ground.[80] The central area of the blanket is largely plain except for a few plain warp directional stripes near the center and sometimes decorative stitching in colored thread where the two pieces of cloth are joined. There are decorative bands near each edge that feature warp float geometric patterning in the center and plain stripes on each side.

Xtiêng. There are over 85,000 Xtiêng (aka Steng) in Việt Nam and over 20,000 in Cambodia. In Việt Nam they live mainly in Bình Phước Province with some also found in Lâm Đồng and Tây Ninh provinces. There are two main sub-groups of Xtiêng: the Bu Đê (aka Đêh), meaning people downstream, and the Bu Lơ, meaning people upstream. Other sub-groups include the Bu Lach and Bu Đíp. Like the Mnông, the Xtiêng appear to be indigenous to the general area where they live at present. Prior to French colonial rule the Xtiêng were relatively isolated from Khmer and Kinh society and outside of Nguyễn rule. French Catholics tried unsuccessfully to establish a mission among the Xtiêng in the 1770s and 1860s.[81] Establishing French control over the Xtiêng was gradual, beginning in 1904, when the first administrative post was established, and often marked by violence. French rule only gained a firm foothold in the late 1930s as Colonial Highway 14 was completed through the region.

The Xtiêng grew cotton in the past, but by the 1960s women were weaving with commercial thread.[82] They weave on a foot-braced backstrap loom, but weaving has been in decline since in the 1970s and people generally wear generic Western style clothing on an everyday basis. Diệp Đình Hoa noted that at the time of his fieldwork men generally wore commercially made shorts and shirts and only a few women still wore traditional skirts. In addition, although many women knew how to weave, they seldom did so any more.[83] Traditional cloth is woven with

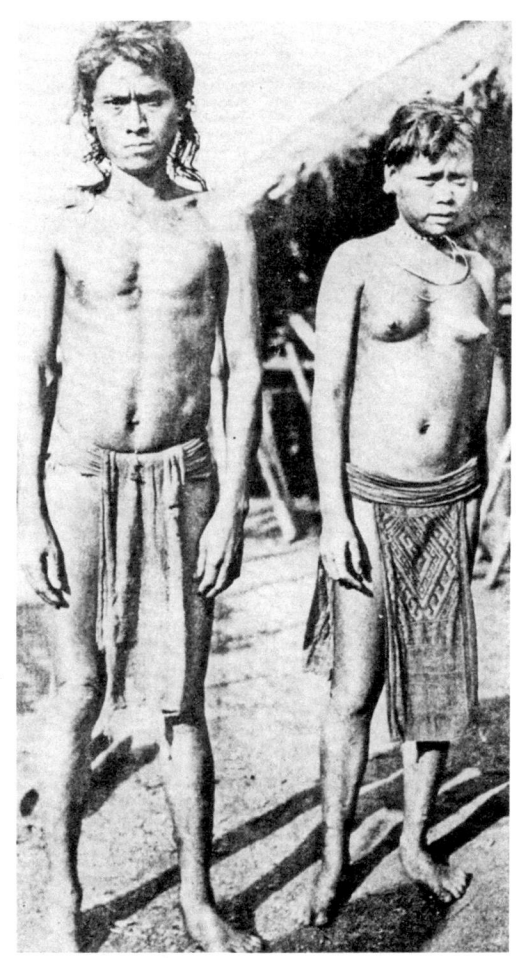

Xtiêng couple (from *Bulletin de la Société des Etudes Indochinoises* 1936).

cotton thread and dominant ground colors are dark blue or black and red. Decorative techniques include supplementary weft and alternating warp float weaves.[84]

Traditional male clothing includes a relatively narrow loincloth and sometimes a sleeveless shirt that opens down the front or blanket wrapped around the shoulders, and headcloth.[85] Everyday loincloths traditionally were plain, fairly narrow, and relatively short. Fancier versions were a little wider and made of three pieces of cloth. The middle piece has a plain dark blue or black center with plain tan or red warp directional stripes along the edges. The end pieces have plain red or tan warp directional stripes along the edges and a central area with a dark blue or black or red ground and several weft directional bands with geometrical supplementary weft patterning (usually one large band in the center with narrower bands on each side). Hickey says that the bands include a "red and white maze design called *mà* ('mother')" and that "the loincloth is woven so that the motifs in front are not aligned with those in the back."[86]

There appear to have been a few different styles of traditional female clothing. Paul Patté, who visited the Xtiêng area in 1904 describes four styles of female dress: (1) a skirt that reaches to about the knees, (2) a loincloth like those worn by men, (3) a loincloth that is slightly shorter and narrower than those worn by men, and (4) a very rudimentary loincloth that is almost a string.[87] Women generally went barebreasted, but sometimes would wear a pullover blouse or wrap a piece of cloth around their shoulders. Xtiêng women wear wrap-around skirts that reach to just below the knees as well as longer one that reach to the ankles (in fact, Patté has a photograph of women wearing such long skirts).[88] In terms of decoration, one style has a plain dark blue or black central area and warp directional bands near the top and bottom. The lower band is wider and includes plain red stripes and a wider stripe in the middle with several rectangular areas with different dark blue or black and white alternating warp float patterns. The upper band is similar, but the stripes are narrower. Another style of skirt is made of three pieces of cloth sewn together along the warp. The pieces on each side are identical and have a red ground with warp several warp directional stripes near each edge. These stripes include a few narrow plain white or yellow stripes, wider stripes with red and white geometric alternating warp float patterning, and near the outer edge an even wider stripe with red and white geometric alternating warp float patterning. The piece of cloth in the center has a dark blue ground with weft directional stripes with continuous dark blue and white supplementary weft patterning. In between many of these stripes are distinct discontinuous supplementary weft patterns in white and red.

Xtiêng blankets are made of three pieces of cloth joined along the warp.[89] The ground is dark blue or black. The outer pieces have a wide band towards the center with plain red stripes, a wide section in the middle with rectangular areas featuring different dark blue or black and white alternating warp float patterns, and narrow stripes in between the plain ones with dark blue or black and white alternating warp float patterns. The outer edge of these pieces has a narrower band that includes plain

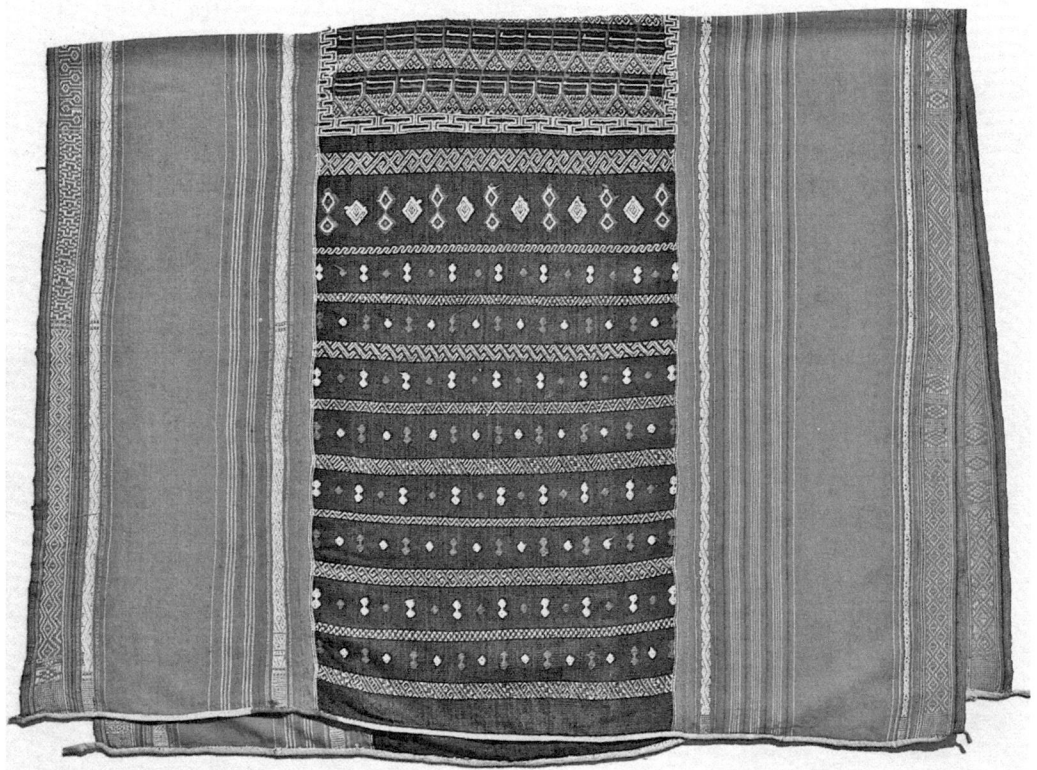

Xtiêng (Bu Lơ sub-group) woman's wrap-around skirt, Bình Long District, Bình Phước Province.

red stripes and a stripe with alternating warp float patterning. The piece of cloth in the middle is largely plain with warp directional bands near each edge with narrow plain red stripes and narrow stripes with dark blue or black and white alternating warp float patterns.

Mạ. About 42,000 Mạ live in the vicinity of the upper Đồng Nai River in western Lâm Đồng Province and eastern Đồng Nai Province. As a result of influence from Fù Nán at one time in the past the Mạ had formed a single political entity and developed a stratified society, but this unity had broken down long before the 19th century when the French visited the area and inter-group warfare and slave raiding was common.[90] Mạ sub-groups include the Xốp, Ngăn, Tô, Krung, and Đạ Đồng.

The Mạ were well known for growing cotton in the past. Cotton cultivation declined during the 1960s and 1970s and then ceased entirely. They weave on a foot-braced backstrap loom. Weaving and wearing traditional clothing also declined during this period. When Phan Xuân Biên and Chu Thái Sơn conducted research a short time later they noted that only older people still wore traditional clothing and that men tended to wear generic Western style clothing and women commercial blouses

5. Ethnic Minorities in Southern Việt Nam

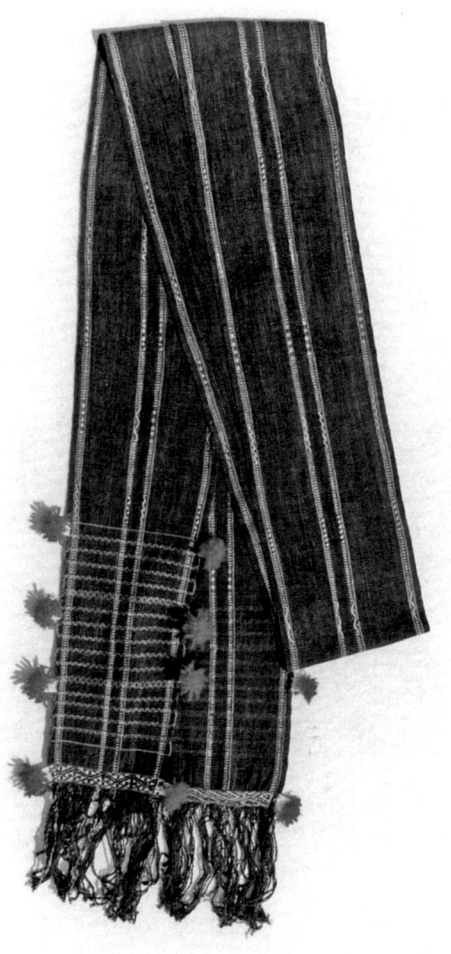

Mạ (Xốp sub-group), man's loincloth, Cát Tiên District, Lâm Đồng Province.

and tubeskirts.[91] At present traditional clothing tends only to be worn on special occasions.

Traditional Mạ male clothing includes a loincloth and sometimes a sleeveless pullover shirt. There are two types of loincloth. The common everyday variety is very narrow and relatively short and plain.[92] It is dark blue and may have pairs of warp directional stripes near each edge and sometimes down the center as well. The fancier versions are wider, but still fairly narrow, and longer than the everyday variety.[93] They are decorated in similar fashion to those worn by Mnông men. Their ground is dark blue or black. They have plain warp directional stripes down the sides and usually in the center as well with alternating warp float patterning in dark blue or black and white. The end areas have ten or more weft directional narrow stripes with supplementary weft patterning and a slightly wider weft directional stripe also with supplementary weft patterning at the end as well as fringe. These loincloths sometimes are decorated with groups of small metal tubes and red pompoms attached along the sides of the end portion like Mnông ones. Likewise, it is now common for plastic to be used for the tubes. Mạ men also sometimes wear sleeveless pullover shirts like those worn by Mnông men.[94]

Mạ women's traditional clothing includes a wrap-around skirt and sometimes a sleeveless pullover blouse. The skirts are similar to those worn by the Mnông, but differ in that they often have a weft directional decorative band near one end (and sometimes a narrower band at the other end).[95] This follows Chăm fashion, but Chăm skirts have similar bands at both ends. The skirt is wrapped around the waist so that this band runs vertically down the right side of the front. The skirts reach to around mid-calf. Older ones are often made of three pieces of cloth and newer ones of a single piece of cloth. The skirts usually have a dark blue or black ground and decorative warp directional stripes in the center and along the edges. The middle area of the skirt may have a wide band in the center with geometric alternating warp float patterning in the middle and narrower plain and alternating warp float patterned stripes on each side or may have three such bands that are narrower with plain spaces in between. Similar warp directional bands are placed along the edges. The weft directional bands at one end of the skirt have similar plain and patterned stripes, but the patterned stripes are woven using a supplementary weft technique. The blouses worn by Mạ women are similar to men's shirts, but tend to be smaller and more tightly tailored than those worn by men.[96]

Cơ Ho. There are about 170,000 people categorized as Cơ Ho living mainly Lâm Đồng Province. Cơ Ho is an ethnic category encompassing several distinct groups. These include the Xrê (aka Sre), Nốp (aka Nộp), Cơ-don (aka Kodu), Chil, Tơ-ring (aka Trinh), Lạt (aka Lạch), Sốp (aka Sộp), and a few other small groups. The Lạt live in the vicinity of Đà Lạt, the Chil to the northeast, the Xrê to the southwest on the Di Linh Plateau, the Nốp to the of the Xrê to the southeast of Bảo Lộc, and the Sốp to the west of Bảo Lộc along the Đạ Tẻh River. The Xrê are the most populous group, followed by the Chil. The Cơ Ho had a long history of contact with the Chăm and Khmer as well as neighboring highland groups and later the Kinh prior to the arrival of the French. The Nguyễn rulers carried out numerous attacks on the Cơ Ho. The French pacified the area in the 1880s and their presence in Cơ Ho territory grew considerably during the early 20th century. Catholic and Protestant missionaries were active in Cơ Ho communities and there were many converts.

Weaving and growing cotton was unevenly developed among the various Cơ Ho groups by the early 20th century. The ground of cloth for textiles usually is either left undyed white or dyed dark blue or black with decorative aspects generally resembling those of the Mạ, Mnông, and Chăm. Many Cơ Ho communities also traded for cloth. Maître mentions Kinh traders purchasing blankets from villages in the west of the Cơ Ho region and then reselling them to other Cơ Ho in the Đà Lạt area that did not weave.[97] Writing a couple of decades later, Queguiner reported that the Xrê were purchasing blankets from the Mạ.[98] Chăm textiles also found their way into Cơ Ho villages. The Xrê in particular were subject to external influence in their style of dress. Quenguiner reported that Xrê men in official positions tended to dress like Kinh.[99] Moreover, as the French presence grew in the Đà Lạt area the Xrê gradually abandoned weaving.[100] It has become increasingly common for Cơ Ho to wear generic Western style clothing on an everyday basis in recent years with traditional clothing worn only in more isolated communities or worn on special occasions.

Traditional Cơ Ho male dress includes a loincloth and sometimes a sleeveless pullover shirt. Cơ Ho loincloths tend to be shorter than those worn by neighboring groups and, while some have a dark blue or black ground, unlike most other highlanders Cơ Ho loincloths often have a white ground.[101] Loincloths are sometimes decorated like those of the Mnông, but less elaborately. A distinctive Sốp loincloth has a white ground that is almost completely covered with red and blue geometric supplementary weft patterning and has weft directional bands at the ends with black and white supplementary weft patterning.[102] The shirts are generally similar to those worn by the Mạ, although sometimes they have different decorative features, such as a Sốp shirt that has warp directional bands with stripes that have black and white alternating warp float patterning and a weft directional band at the bottom with black and white supplementary weft patterning.[103]

Traditional Cơ Ho female dress includes a wrap-around skirt and sometimes a sleeveless pullover blouse or blanket that is wrapped around the shoulders.[104] There is variation in the styles of skirts worn by Cơ Ho women reflecting group differences, location and trade patterns to some extent. Essentially there are two main styles of skirt. The most common type is made of either a single piece of cloth or of two pieces of cloth that are joined along the warp and reaches to the ankles. It usually has a dark blue ground and is decorated with intermittent narrow plain or alternating warp float patterned warp directional stripes and sometimes with thin stripes with warp ikat dashes as well, and has wider warp directional decorative stripes with alternating warp float patterning near each edge. There are also a few thin weft directional stripes at the ends. The Xrê,[105] Nốp,[106] and Lạt[107] commonly wear such in recent years. The Chil also sometimes wear this style of skirt,[108] but some Chil also wear skirts that are similar to those worn by the Mnông.[109] These are made of three pieces of cloth with the outer pieces being identical with a dark blue or black ground and a number of warp directional stripes, some of which are plain and some have alternating warp float patterning. The piece in the center of contemporary skirts often has a red ground with distinct supplementary weft patterns that commonly include representations of animals, humans, and other objects using colorful thread. This style of skirt also has weft directional bands at each end often the alternating red and dark blue or black thread. The decoration of the central piece of cloth has become increasingly colorful in recent years. Sốp women sometimes wore a distinctive style of skirt, but they are rarely seen any more.[110] It is made of a single piece of cloth with a white ground and is decorated with two warp directional bands. One band is near one of the edges and there is another decorative band placed a little further in from the other edge. These bands have stripes with a variety of black and white warp float patterns. There are also weft directional bands at each end with black and white supplementary warp patterning.

Chơ Ro. There are around 27,000 Chơ Ro (aka Chrau). They live mainly in Đồng Nai Province, but are also found in Bình Dương, Bình Phước, Bình Thuận, Lâm Đồng, and Bà Rịa–Vũng Tàu provinces. The name Chơ Ro means "highlander" and refers to a group of people speaking the same language, but that traditionally had no single ethnic identity and identified themselves by local clan names.[111] They are the southernmost Mon-Khmer people in the Central Highlands and have been subject to considerable acculturative influence from lowland peoples for a long time.

In the past Chơ Ro men wore loincloths and sleeveless pullover shirts and women short wrap-around skirts and pullover blouses and sometimes a blanket in the cold season.[112] There are few examples remaining of traditional cloth.[113] It was woven with cotton thread on a foot-braced backstrap loom and has either a dark blue, black, or red ground. Skirts and blouses are made of two pieces of cloth joined along the warp.

There are decorative bands of each side of where the pieces of cloth are joined with plain and warp float patterned warp directional stripes and narrower bands with similar warp directional stripes near each outer edge. Traditional clothing was no longer worn by the 1970s and Chơ Ro men generally wore generic Western style clothing or sometimes Kinh style dress on special occasions and women a mixture of Western style blouses and wrap-around skirts and blankets obtained from neighboring groups such as the Cơ Ho.

Chapter Notes

Introduction

1. John E. Vollmer, "Archaeological Evidence for Looms from Yunnan," in I. Emery and P. Fiske (eds.), *Looms and Their Products* (Washington, D.C.: The Textile Museum, 1979), 78–89; Marie Jeanne Adams, "A 'Forgotten' Bronze Ship and a Recently Discovered Bronze Weaver from Eastern Indonesia," *Asian Perspectives* 22 (1977), 87–109; Michael C. Howard and Kim B. Howard, *Textiles of the Highlands Peoples of Vietnam: Mon-Khmer, Hmong-Mien, and Tibeto-Burman* (Bangkok: White Lotus Press, 2002), 11.

2. See Hans Stübel, *Die Li-Stämme der Insel Hainan: Ein Beitrag zur Volkskunde Südchinas* (Berlin: Klinkhardt & Biermann, 1937).

3. See Michael C. Howard and Kim B. Howard, *Textiles of the Central Highlands of Vietnam* (Bangkok: White Lotus Press, 2002).

4. See Michael C. Howard and Kim B. Howard, *Textiles of the Daic Peoples of Vietnam* (Bangkok: White Lotus Press, 2002), 16.

5. Nguyễn, Thừa Hỷ, *Economic History of Hanoi in the 17th, 18th and 19th Centuries* (Hà Nội: National Political Publishing House, 2002), 155–69.

6. See Naval Intelligence Unit, *Indo-China* (Cambridge, UK: University of Cambridge Press, 1943), 281, 336; L. Delignon, "La production de la Soie en Indochine." *Revue de botanique appliquée et d'agriculture coloniale*, 3rd year, bulletin no. 24 (1923), 530–537.

7. Edward H. Schafer, *The Vermilion Bird: T'ang Images of the South* (Berkeley: University of California Press, 1967), 54.

8. Dieter Kuhn and Joseph Needham, *Science and Civilisation in China: Volume 5, Chemistry and Chemical Technology, Part 9, Textile Technology: Spinning and Reeling* (Cambridge: Cambridge University Press, 1988), 57.

9. Schafer, *The Vermilion Bird*, 180.

10. Kent Gang Deng, *The Premodern Chinese Economy: Structural Equilibrium and Capitalist Sterility* (London: Routledge, 1999), 377.

11. *Hòu Hàn Shū* ("Book of the Later Han"), vol. 26, chapter "Xinanyi Zhuan"; Deng, *The Premodern Chinese Economy*, 377.

12. See Michael C. Howard, *Textiles of the Highland Peoples of Burma, Volume II: The Northern Mon-Khmer, Rawang, Upland Burmish, Lolo, Karen, Tai, and Hmong-Mien-speaking Groups* (Bangkok: White Lotus Press, 2005), 120.

13. James George Scott and J. P. Hardiman, *Gazateer of Upper Burma and the Shan States, Part 1, Volume 2* (Rangoon: Superintendent of Government Printing and Stationary 1900), 363; Howard, *Textiles of the Highland Peoples of Burma, Volume II*, 209.

14. Schafer, *The Vermilion Bird*, 180.

15. Schafer, *The Vermilion Bird*, 72.

16. See Tana Li, *Nguyễn Cochinchina: Southern Vietnam in the Seventeenth and Eighteenth Centuries* (Cornell University, SEAP Publications, 1998), 73.

17. John Crawfurd, *Journal of an Embassy from the Governor-General of India to the Courts of Siam and Cochin China: Exhibiting a View of the Actual State of those Kingdoms*, Volume 2 (Second edition) (London: H. Colburn and R. Bentley, 1830), 278, 279, 318, 319.

18. Crawfurd, *Journal of an Embassy from the Governor-General of India to the Courts of Siam and Cochin China*, Volume 2, 272.

19. Kuhn and Needham, *Science and Civilisation in China*, 57 note d.

20. See Kuhn and Needham, *Science and Civilisation in China*, 30–8.

21. *Yüan-Ho Chun Hsien Thu Chih* ("Topography of the Prefectures and Districts of China in the Reign Period Yuan-ho"), 38, 1075; cited in Schafer, *The Vermilion Bird*, 180.

22. Kuhn and Needham, *Science and Civilisation in China*, 30–1.

23. Howard and Howard, *Textiles of the Highlands Peoples of Vietnam*, 5, 100, 158.

24. See Gina Corrigan, "Hemp and Ramie in Southwest China, *Hali* 113 (2000), 80–83; Howard and Howard, *Textiles of the Highlands Peoples of Vietnam*, 5.

25. Kuhn and Needham, *Science and Civilisation in China*, 50.

26. Kuhn and Needham, *Science and Civilisation in China*, 51.
27. See Schafer, *The Vermilion Bird*, 54.
28. See Howard and Howard, *Textiles of the Highlands Peoples of Vietnam*, 5, 48, 51,115–6, 180–1.
29. Schafer, *The Vermilion Bird*, 158.
30. For a survey of dyes used in Việt Nam see Charles Crevost and A. Pételot, *Catalogue des produits de l'Indochine, Tome VI: Tanins et tinctoriaux* (Hà Nội: Impremerie d'Extrême Orient, 1941).
31. See Dominique Cardon, *Natural Dyes: Sources, Tradition, Technology and Science* (London: Archetype Publications, 2007), 385.
32. Cardon, *Natural Dyes*, 394 fig. 71.
33. See Cardon, *Natural Dyes*, 656–66.
34. Schafer, *The Vermilion Bird*, 180.
35. See Cardon, *Natural Dyes*, 327–8.
36. Cardon, *Natural Dyes*, 475–7.
37. See Howard and Howard, *Textiles of the Highlands Peoples of Vietnam*, 13–4; Howard and Howard, *Textiles of the Daic Peoples of Vietnam*, 139; and Georges Condominas, *From Lawa to Mon, from Saa' to Thai: Historical and Anthropological Aspects of Southeast Asian Social Spaces* (Canberra: Department of Anthropology, Research School of Pacific Studies, Australian National University, 1990).
38. Howard and Howard, *Textiles of the Daic Peoples of Vietnam*, 139–44.

Chapter 1

1. Friedrich Hirth, *The Ancient History of China to the End of the Chóu Dynasty* (Freeport, NY: Books for Libraries, 1969; originally published in 1908), 195.
2. See Nguyễn Khắc Sư, Minh Huyen Pham, and Tong Trung Tin, "Northern Vietnam from the Neolithic to the Han Period," in I. Glover and P. Bellwood (eds.), *Southeast Asia from Prehistory to History* (London: Routledge Curzon, 2004), 177–201.
3. Michael C. Howard, "Introduction," in M.C. Howard (ed.), *Bark-cloth in Southeast Asia* (Bangkok: White Lotus Press, 2006), 3–7.
4. On the oldest beater yet found, dated around 7898 BP, see Dawei Li, Wei Wang, Feng Tian, Wei Liao, and Christopher J. Bae, "The Oldest Bark Cloth Beater in Southern China (Dingmo, Bubing Basin, Guangxi)," *Quaternary International* 30 (2014), 1–6.
5. Judith Cameron, "The Archaeological Evidence for Bark-cloth in Southeast Asia, in M.C. Howard (ed.), *Bark-cloth in Southeast Asia* (Bangkok: White Lotus Press, 2006), 66; See Hà Văn Tấn, "Về những cái gọi là bàn đạp trong các di chỉ văn hóa Phùng Nguyên," in *Những phát hiện mới về Khảo cổ học năm 1979* (Hanoi: Viện Khảo cổ học, 1980), 80–1.

6. See T.V. Holbé, "Quelques mots sur le préhistorique Indochinois à propos des objets receuillis par M. de Pray," *Bulletin des Amis du Vert Hué*, 2ème, Année 43 (1915); Henri Fontaine, "Nouvelles Récoltes d'objets préhistoriques," *Bulletin de la Société des Études indochinoises*, 50, 1 (1975), 75–107.
7. Michael C. Howard, "Introduction," in M.C. Howard (ed.), *Bark-cloth in Southeast Asia* (Bangkok: White Lotus Press, 2006), 2.
8. Howard and Howard, *Textiles of the Central Highlands of Vietnam*, 17–8.
9. Howard, "Introduction," 10.
10. Howard, "Introduction," 2.
11. See Luu Hung, "Bark-cloth of the Ethnic Groups of Highland Vietnam," in M.C. Howard (ed.), *Bark-cloth in Southeast Asia* (Bangkok: White Lotus Press, 2006), 107–114.
12. See Weera Ostapirat, "The Hlai Language," in Anthony Diller, Jerold A. Edmondson, and Yongxian Luo (eds.), *The Tai–Kadai Languages* (New York: Routledge, 2008), 623. On the genetic linkage between the Lí of Hǎinán Island and the Tai (i.e., Zhuang) of Guangxi, see Min-Sheng Peng, Jun-Dong He, Hai-Xin Liu, and Ya-Ping Zhang, "Tracing the Legacy of the Early Hainan Islanders—A Perspective from Mitochondrial DNA," *BMC Evolutionary Biology* 11 (2011), 46, online at biomedicalcentral.com/1471–2148/11/46.
13. See Howard and Howard, *Textiles of the Daic Peoples of Vietnam*, 35–40.
14. *Ying Song ben Taiping huan yu ji bu que* ("Universal geography of the Taiping Era"), (reprinted, Taibei Xian Yonghe Zhen: Wen hai chu ban she, Minguo 52, 1963).
15. Gu Yanwu, *Tian xia jun guo li bing shu* ("On benefits and faults of the empire's local administration") (Shunan: Tong hua shu wu, Guangxu 5, 1879; reprinted, Shanghai: Shanghai gu ji chu ban she, 2002).
16. See Erica Brindley, "Barbarians or Not? Ethnicity and Changing Conceptions of the Ancient Yue (Viet) Peoples, ca. 400–50 BC." *Asia Major* 16, 1 (2003), 1–32; William Meacham, "Defining the Hundred Yue." *Bulletin of the Indo-Pacific Prehistory Association*, 15 (1996), 93–100; Jerry Norman and T.L. Mei, "The Austroasiatics in Ancient South China: Some Lexical Evidence," *Monumenta Serica* 32 (1976), 274–301.
17. See Hui Li, Ying Huang, Laura F. Mustavich, Fan Zhang, Jing-Ze Tan, Ling-E Wang, Ji Qian, Meng-He Gao, and Li Jin, "Y Chromosomes of Prehistoric People along the Yangtze River," *Human Genetics* 122 (2007), 383–388; and Zhou Ying, *The Dawn of the Oriental Civilization: Liangzhu Site and Liangzhu Culture* (Beijing: China Intercontinental Press, 2007).
18. Shelagh J. Vainke, *Chinese Silk: A Cultural History* (New Brunswick, NJ: Rutgers University Press, 2004), 22, 24; Shao Wangping, "The Forma-

tion of Civilization: The Interaction Sphere of the Longshan Period," Allan, Sarah (ed), *The Formation of Chinese Civilization: An Archaeological Perspective* (New Haven: Yale University Press, 2005), 114; "Ancient Tombs Unearthed in East China," *Xinhua News Agency,* 2 July 1999.

19. Constance A. Cook and Barry B. Blakely, "Introduction," in C.A. Cook and B.B. Blakley (eds.), *Defining Chu: Image and Reality in Ancient China* (Honolulu: University of Hawai'i Press, 1999), 2.

20. Leonard Aurousseau, "Le première conquête chinoises pays annamites," *Bulletin de l'École Française d'Etrême Orient* 23 (1924), 255. Lò Yuè/Luò Yuè is sometimes translated as Seabird Yuè, but "seabird" does not seem to be an accurate translation and it more likely refers to the migratory grey heron.

21. See C. Madrolle, "Le Tonkin ancien," *Bulletin de l'École Française d'Etrême Orient* 37, 2 (1937), 319, 325; James R. Chamberlain, "The Black Tai Chronicle of Muang Mouay Part I: Mythology," *Mon-Khmer Studies* 21 (1992), 23.

22. James R. Chamberlain, "The Origins of the Sek: Implications for Tai and Vietnamese History," *Journal of the Siam Society* 86, 1–2 (1998), 38–9.

23. See Amphay Doré, "Le royaume des Ai Lao, une perspective geo-politique," *Inter-Mondes Revue de l'Université Ramkhamhaeng* 1, 2 (1990), 230–236; Howard, *Textiles of the Highland Peoples of Burma, Volume II,* 174.

24. Michael C. Howard, "Searching for the Identity of the Bird on the Dong Son Drums," *Arts of Asia,* 34, 2 (2004), 136–142.

25. Howard, "Searching for the Identity of the Bird on the Dong Son Drums"; Michael C. Howard, "Religious and Status-marking Functions of Textiles among the Tai Peoples of Vietnam," in Jane Puranananda (ed.), *The Secrets of Southeast Asian Textiles: Myth, Status and the Supernatural* (Bangkok: River Books and the James H. W. Thompson Foundation, 2007), 194–215.

26. *Shiji* (aka *Tàishǐgōng shū*) ("Records of the Grand Historian"), chapter 113, 297.

27. Cloth fragments, likely remains of clothing and a shroud, were found in graves dated 530–197 BC at the Châu Can site in Hà Tây Province. Charles Higham, *The Bronze Age of Southeast Asia* (Cambridge: Cambridge University Press, 1996), 114, 116.

28. Lê Ngọc Thắng, *Nghệ thuật trang phục Thái* (Hà Nội: Văn hóa dân tộc, Trung tâm văn hóa Việt Nam, 1990), 170–2.

29. Higham, *The Bronze Age of Southeast Asia,* 119–20.

30. See Wolfram Eberhard, *Kultur und Siedlung der Randvölker Chinas* (Leiden: E.J. Brill, 1942), 178, 364, 365; Wolfram Eberhard, *The Local Cultures of South and East Asia* (Leiden: E.J. Brill, 1968), 273; Herold J. Wiens, *Han Chinese Expansion in South China* (Hamden, CT: The Shoe String Press, 1967), 53; Michael C. Howard, *From Dashes to Dragons: The Ikat-Patterned Textiles of Southeast Asia* (Bangkok: White Lotus Press, 2010), 12.

31. Howard and Howard, *Textiles of the Daic Peoples of Vietnam,* 48, 50, 222.

32. See Howard, "Religious and Status-marking Functions of Textiles among the Tai Peoples of Vietnam."

33. "Spotted Deer Worshipped by Ancient China," *Xinhua News Agency,* 25 Feb. 2001.

34. See Stübel, *Die Li-Stämme der Insel Hainan;* Howard and Howard, *Textiles of the Daic Peoples of Vietnam,* 34–5.

35. Stübel, *Die Li-Stämme der Insel Hainan,* 25, 122, 155, 213.

36. Stübel, *Die Li-Stämme der Insel Hainan,* 122.

37. Stübel, *Die Li-Stämme der Insel Hainan,* 27, 29, 124, 188, 214; Howard and Howard, *Textiles of the Daic Peoples of Vietnam,* 30–2, 34–5, 211–4.

38. See *Huáyáng Guó Zhì* ("Chronicles of Huayang"), volume 4 ("Records of Nanzong").

39. See Robert S. Wicks, *Money, Markets, and Trade in Early Southeast Asia: The Development of Indigenous Monetary Systems to AD 1400.* (Ithaca, NY: Cornell University, Southeast Asia Program, 1992), 33–9.

40. Wang Mingfu and Eric Johnson, *Zhuang Cultural and Linguistic Heritage* (Kumming: The Nationalities Publishing House of Yunnan 2008), 12.

41. Gordon H. Luce (trans.) and G. P. Oey (ed.), *The Man Shu (Book of the Southern Barbarians)* (Ithaca, NY: Southeast Asia Program, Department of Far Eastern Studies, Cornell University, 1961), 23, 33, 36; see Eberhard, *Kultur und Siedlung der Randvölker Chinas,* 312; Howard, *Textiles of the Highland Peoples of Burma, Volume II,* 173.

42. Wang Ningsheng, "Ancient Ethnic Groups as Represented on Bronzes from Yunnan, China," in S.J. Shennan (ed.), *Archaeological Approaches to Cultural Identity* (London: Routledge, 1994), 199–200.

43. Wang, "Ancient Ethnic Groups as Represented on Bronzes from Yunnan, China," 200.

44. Wang, "Ancient Ethnic Groups as Represented on Bronzes from Yunnan, China," 204–5.

45. Wang, "Ancient Ethnic Groups as Represented on Bronzes from Yunnan, China," 200.

46. Wang, "Ancient Ethnic Groups as Represented on Bronzes from Yunnan, China," 202, 205.

47. Wang, "Ancient Ethnic Groups as Represented on Bronzes from Yunnan, China," 204, 205.

48. See Howard, *Textiles of the Highland Peoples of Burma, Volume II,* 115–72.

49. Howard and Howard, *Textiles of the Highland Peoples of Vietnam,* 76, 89–90.

50. Howard and Howard, *Textiles of the Highland Peoples of Vietnam,* 76, 89–90, 91.

51. Howard and Howard, *Textiles of the Highland Peoples of Vietnam*, 76–82.
52. Howard and Howard, *Textiles of the Highland Peoples of Vietnam*, 85–8.
53. Howard and Howard, *Textiles of the Daic Peoples of Vietnam*, 133.
54. *Hòu Hàn Shū* ("Book of the Later Han") volumes 109–113, records 19–23; cited in Wicks, *Money, Markets, and Trade in Early Southeast Asia*, 39. Also see Gordon H. Luce, "The Tan and Ngai-lao," *Journal of the Burma Research Society* 14, 2 (1924): 138–205, reprinted in *Burma Research Society Fiftieth Anniversary Publication No. 2* (Rangoon: Burma Research Society, 1960), 213.
55. From *Shiji*, cited in Yu Ying-shih, *Trade and Expansion in Han China: A Study in the Structure of Sino-Barbarian Economic Relations* (Berkeley: University of California Press, 1967), 113.
56. Berthold Laufer, *Sino-Iranica: Chinese Contributions to the History of Civilization in Ancient Iran, with Special Reference to the History of Cultivated Plants and Products* (Chicago: Field Museum of Natural History, 1919), 491 note 4.
57. Wang and Johnson, *Zhuang Cultural and Linguistic Heritage*, 12.
58. Wang and Johnson, *Zhuang Cultural and Linguistic Heritage*, 25–7, 140.
59. Wang and Johnson, *Zhuang Cultural and Linguistic Heritage*, 23.
60. Wang and Johnson, *Zhuang Cultural and Linguistic Heritage*, 92.
61. See Howard and Howard, *Textiles of the Daic Peoples of Vietnam*, 39.
62. Howard and Howard, *Textiles of the Daic Peoples of Vietnam*, 35, 38.
63. See Geoff Wade, "The Polity of Yelang and the Origin of the Name 'China,'" *Sino-Platonic Papers*, No. 188 (2009); "Chinese Archaeologists Search for Clues on Lost Kingdom," *People's Daily*, 25 October 2002.
64. See Robert D. Jenks, *Insurgency and Social Disorder in Guizhou: The "Miao" Rebellion, 1854–1873* (Honolulu: University of Hawaii Press, 1994).
65. See Jodi L. Weinstein, *Empire and Identity in Guizhou: Local Resistance to Qing Expansion* (Seattle: University of Washington Press, 2014).
66. See Yang Yong, "New Archaeological Discoveries of the Bronze and the Early Iron Age in the Yunnan-Guizhou Plateau and some Related Problems," in Dominik Bonatz, Andreas Reinecke, and Mai Lin Tjoa-Bonatz (eds.), *Crossing Borders: Selected Papers from the 13th International Conference of the European Association of Southeast Asian Archaeologists* (Singapore: NUS Press, 2012), 234–8; Yang Yong, On the Kele Culture," *Chinese Archaeology*, 13, 1 (2013), 186–191; Yang Yong, "Tombs of the Yelang Period at Kele in Hezhang, Guizhou," *Chinese Archaeology* 3, 1 (2003), 14–18.
67. An international seminar on "The Traces of Ye Lang Culture in Vietnam," was held in Hà Nội at the Museum of Vietnamese History on 2 Nov. 2010.
68. *Shiji*, "Account of the Southwestern Barbarians," Burton Watson (trans.), *Records of the Grand Historian by Sima Qian* (Revised edition) (New York: Columbia University Press, 1993), chapter 116.
69. Nationalities Affairs Commission of Guizhou Province, *Ethnic Costume from Guizhou: Clothing Designs and Decorations from Minority Ethnic Groups in Southwest China* (Beijing: Foreign Languages Press, 1987), 84.
70. Nationalities Affairs Commission of Guizhou Province, *Ethnic Costume from Guizhou*, 84; Bian Wei Hui, *Miao Autonomous Prefecture in the Annals of Chi (Guizhou)* (Guizhou: Peoples Publishing House, 1991); and see Howard and Howard, *Textiles of the Daic Peoples of Vietnam*, 25.
71. Li, et al, "Y Chromosomes of Prehistoric People along the Yangtze River."
72. Howard and Howard, *Textiles of the Highland Peoples of Vietnam*, 29–46.
73. Trần Thị Thu Thủy, *Trang phục phụ nữ H'mông Hoa ở Huyện Mù Cang Chải, tinh Yên Bái* (MA thesis, Đại học Quốc gia Hà Nội, Trường Đại học Khoa học Xã hội và Nhân văn, 1998), 62; Howard and Howard, *Textiles of the Highland Peoples of Vietnam*, 38.
74. See Maurice Abadie, *Les Races du Haut-Tonkin de Phong-Tho à Lang Son* (Paris: Société d'éditions géographiques, maritimes et coloniales, 1924), 106; Nguyễn Khắc Tụng, "Dân tộc Dao," in Bùi Văn Cán (ed.), *Các dân tộc ít người ở Việt Nam (Các tỉnh phía bắc)* (Hà Nội: Nhà xuất bản Khoa học xã hội, 1978), 312.
75. Henri Gourdon, *L'Indochine* (Paris: Larousse, 1931), 87.
76. Howard and Howard, *Textiles of the Highland Peoples of Vietnam*, 49.
77. Howard and Howard, *Textiles of the Highland Peoples of Vietnam*, 61–6.
78. See Howard and Howard, *Textiles of the Diac Peoples of Vietnam*, 65–70; J.A. Edmondson and K.J. Gregerson, "Four Languages of the Vietnam-China Borderlands," in K.L. Adams and T.J. Hudak (eds.), *Papers from the Sixth Annual Meeting of the Southeast Asian Linguistics Society* (Tempe, AZ: Arizona State University, Program for Southeast Asian Studies, 2001), 101–33.
79. See Wang Fushi (chief compiler), *Ethnic Costumes and Clothing Decorations from China* (Chengdu: Sichuan People's Publishing House, 1986), 242–7; and for details of textiles see Nationalities Affairs Commission of Guizhou, *Ethnic Costume from Guizhou*, 47 fig. 67, 49 fig. 69, 62 fig. 89, 68 fig. 97, 100 fig. 152, 101 fig. 154.
80. Howard and Howard, *Textiles of the Diac Peoples of Vietnam*, 57.

81. Thaveeporn Vasavakul, "Language Policy and Ethnic Relations in Vietnam," in Michael E. Brown and Sumit Ganguly (eds.), *Fighting Words: Language Policy and Ethnic Relations in Asia* (Cambridge, MA: MIT Press, 2003), 217 note 8.
82. Howard and Howard, *Textiles of the Diac Peoples of Vietnam*, 38.
83. Wang, *Ethnic Costumes and Clothing Decorations from China*, 258.
84. Howard and Howard, *Textiles of the Diac Peoples of Vietnam*, 38.
85. The history of Nan Yue is recorded in the *Shiji*, see "Ordered Annals of Nanyue" (aka "Treatise on the Nanyue"), in Burton Watson (trans.), *Records of the Grand Historian: Han Dynasty*, Chapter 113; also see Michael C. Howard, *Transnationalism in Ancient and Medieval Societies: The Role of Cross-Border Trade and Travel* (Jefferson, NC: McFarland, 2012), 61–2.
86. Wiens, *Han Chinese Expansion in South China*, 134; also see Schafer, *The Vermilion Bird*, 15.
87. Wiens, *Han Chinese Expansion in South China*, 135.
88. See *Hòu Hàn Shū*, chapter 86 ("Treatise on the Nan Man").
89. Wiens, *Han Chinese Expansion in South China*, 140.
90. Wiens, *Han Chinese Expansion in South China*, 136–7.
91. Schafer, *The Vermilion Bird*, 16.
92. Nguyễn Văn Huyên, *The Ancient Civilization of Vietnam* (Hà Nội: Thế Giới Publishers, 1995), 203; the French version: *La civilization Annamite* (Hà Nội: Ecole Française d'Extrême-Orient, 1944).
93. Trinh Hoài Đức, *Gia-dinh-Thung-chi: Histoire et description de la basse Cochinchine (pays de Gia-dinh)*, translated by Louis-Gabriel Aubaret (Paris: Imprimerie Impéril, 1863), 74.
94. Wiens, *Han Chinese Expansion in South China*, 142.
95. Schafer, *The Vermilion Bird*, 45.
96. Wang, Zhongshu, *Han Civilization* (New Haven, CT: Yale University Press, 1982), 53, 59–63, 206; Corrigan, "Hemp and Ramie in Southwest China, 80.
97. Zhou Xun and Gao Chunming (text), The Chinese Costumes Research Group (editing), *5000 Years of Chinese Costume* (Hong Kong: The Commercial Press, 1984), 32.
98. Zhou and Gao, *5000 Years of Chinese Costume*, 32.
99. Zhou and Gao, *5000 Years of Chinese Costume*, 32, and see the drawing on page 38.
100. Zhou and Gao, *5000 Years of Chinese Costume*, 44.
101. Zhou and Gao, *5000 Years of Chinese Costume*, 44.
102. See Zhou and Gao, *5000 Years of Chinese Costume*, 41.
103. Zhou and Gao, *5000 Years of Chinese Costume*, 33.
104. Zhou and Gao, *5000 Years of Chinese Costume*, 73; also see Chang Shana, *Patterns of China Dunhuang Dresses and Adornments in Different Ages* (Beijing: China Light Industry Press, 2000).
105. Qín's rival Zhōu identified with the Fire element, which is associated with the color red.
106. See Sarah Allan, *The Shape of the Turtle: Myth, Earth, and Cosmos in Early China* (Albany, NY: SUNY Press, 1991), 65.
107. Zhou and Gao, *5000 Years of Chinese Costume*, 62.
108. See Thomas John Hudack, *William J. Gidney's Comparative Tai Sourcebook* (Honolulu: University of Hawai'i Press, 2008), 104 number 0337.
109. Zhou and Gao, *5000 Years of Chinese Costume*, 76.
110. See Zhou and Gao, *5000 Years of Chinese Costume*, 88–95 for examples of Sui-Táng styles of female dress.
111. Howard and Howard, *Textiles of the Central Highlands of Vietnam*, 58.
112. On the interaction between Mon-Khmer and Chamic languages see Graham Thurgood, *From Ancient Cham to Modern Dialects: Two Thousand Years of Change* (Honolulu: University of Hawai'i Press, 1999); and Anthony Grant and Paul Sidwell (eds.), *Chamic and Beyond: Studies in Mainland Austronesian Languages* (Canberra: Research School of Pacific and Asian Studies, Australian National University, 2005).
113. Peter Bellwood, *Prehistory of the Indo-Malaysian Archipelago: Revised Edition* (Honolulu: University of Hawai'i Press, 1997), 272.
114. Bellwood, *Prehistory of the Indo-Malaysian Archipelago*, 275.
115. Bellwood, *Prehistory of the Indo-Malaysian Archipelago*, 273.
116. See Higham, *The Bronze Age of Southeast Asia*, 306.
117. See Peter Bellwood, "Southeast Asia Before History," in Nicholas Tarling (ed.), *The Cambridge History of Southeast Asia: Volume One, From Early Times to c. 1800* (Cambridge: Cambridge University Press, 1992), 55–136, 131; Higham, *The Bronze Age of Southeast Asia*, 307.
118. Wilhelm H. Solheim II, "Sa-huỳnh Related Pottery in Southeast Asia," *Asian Perspectives* 3, 2 (1959), 187.
119. Wilhelm H. Solheim II, "Introduction to Sa-Huynh," *Asian Perspectives*, 3, 2 (1959), 102.
120. See Michael C. Howard, *A World Between the Warps: Southeast Asia's Supplementary Warp Textiles* (Bangkok: White Lotus Press, 2008), 16.
121. John N. Miksic, "The Beginning of Trade in Ancient Southeast Asia: The Role of Oc Eo and

the Lower Mekong River," in James C. Khoo (ed.), *Art & Archaeology of Fu Nan: Pre-Khmer Kingdom of the Lower Mekong Valley* (Bangkok: Orchid Press, 2003), 1–33, 22–3.

122. Wang Gungwu, "The Nanhai Trade: A Study of the Early History of Chinese Trade in the South China Sea," *Journal of the Malaysian Branch of the Royal Asiatic Society* 31, 2 (1958), 58.

123. The story also appears in the *Jìn Shū* ("Book of Jin"), written by Fáng Xuánlíng in 648, but the name of the foreigner in given as Hùnhuì and the princess as Yèliǔ.

124. Vo Si Khai, "The Kingdom of Fu Nan and the Culture of Oc Eo," in James C. Khoo (ed.), *Art & Archaeology of Fu Nan: Pre-Khmer Kingdom of the Lower Mekong Valley* (Bangkok: Orchid Press, 2003), 35–85, 69.

125. Vo Si Khai, "The Kingdom of Fu Nan and the Culture of Oc Eo," 70.

126. Georges Maspero, *The Champa Kingdom: The History of an Extinct Vietnamese Culture* (Bangkok: White Lotus Press, 2002), 24.

127. See Emmanuel Guillon, *Cham Art: Treasures from the Dà Nang Museum, Vietnam* (London: Thames & Hudson, 2001), 32–3; Bruce M. Lockhart, "Colonial and Post-Colonial Constructions of 'Champa,'" in Tran Ky Phuong and Bruce Lockhart (eds.), *The Cham of Vietnam: History, Society and Art* (Singapore: NUS Press, 2011), 30.

128. See Lương Thanh Sơn, "Yang Prong—Tháp Chăm ở Đăk Lăk," *Tạp chí Dân tộc học* 3 (1991), 28–32; Adam Dray, "The Cham: Descendants of Ancient Rulers of South China Sea Watch Maritime Dispute from Sidelines," online at news.nationalgeographic.com, 18 June 2014.

129. See Maspero, *The Champa Kingdom*, 6, 15.

130. Maspero, *The Champa Kingdom*, 15.

131. Cited in Graham Thurgood and Ela Thurgood, "The Tones from Proto-Chamic to Tsat [Hainan Cham]: insights from Zheng 1997 and Summer 2004 Fieldwork," in Anthony Grant and Paul Sidwell (eds.), *Chamic and Beyond: Studies in Mainland Austronesian Languages* (Canberra: Pacific Linguistics, Research School of Pacific and Asian Studies, Australian National University, 2005), 247.

132. See Thurgood, *From Ancient Cham to Modern Dialects*, 251; Anthony P. Grant, "The Effects of Intimate Multidirectional Linguistic Contact in Chamic," in Anthony Grant and Paul Sidwell (eds.), *Chamic and Beyond: Studies in Mainland Austronesian Languages* (Canberra: Pacific Linguistics, Research School of Pacific and Asian Studies, Australian National University, 2005), 41; Paul Sidwell, "Acehnese and the Aceh-Chamic Language Family," in Anthony Grant and Paul Sidwell (eds.), *Chamic and Beyond: Studies in Mainland Austronesian Languages* (Canberra: Pacific Linguistics, Research School of Pacific and Asian Studies, Australian National University, 2005), 228–9.

133. See Lockhart, "Colonial and Post-Colonial Constructions of 'Champa,'" 26, 28.

134. Howard, *A World Between the Warps*, 110.

135. Maspero, *The Champa Kingdom*, 2.

136. Howard and Howard, *Textiles of the Central Highlands of Vietnam*, 110.

137. Howard and Howard, *Textiles of the Central Highlands of Vietnam*, 19.

138. Howard, *A World Between the Warps*, 21–4.

139. Howard, *A World Between the Warps*, 20.

140. On Haroi textiles and dress see Michael C. Howard, "The Cham of Vietnam and Their Textiles," *Arts of Asia*, 35, 2 (2005), 123–36; on Bahnar textiles and dress see Howard and Howard, *Textiles of the Central Highlands of Vietnam*, 58–62, 189–93.

141. For a comparison of Haroi and Ba Na textiles see Howard, "The Cham of Vietnam and Their Textiles," 134.

142. Howard and Howard, *Textiles of the Central Highlands of Vietnam*, 56.

143. See Howard and Howard, *Textiles of the Central Highlands of Vietnam*, 84; Bernard Bourette, "Essai d'histoire des populations montagnards du Sud indochinois jusque 1945," *Bulletin de la Société des Etudes Indochinoises* (n.s.) 30, 1 (1955), 40–1.

144. See Howard and Howard, *Textiles of the Central Highlands of Vietnam*, 65–71; Paul Huard and A. Maurice, "Les Mnong du plateau central Indochinois," *Institut Indochinois pour l'Etude de l'Homme, Bulletins et Travaux* 2 (1939), 27–148, 91–113.

145. See Howard and Howard, *Textiles of the Central Highlands of Vietnam*, 209–19.

146. First edition published in 1915 in Leiden by E. J. Brill and the second in Paris and Brussels in 1928 by Les Editions Van Oest.

147. Maspero, *The Champa Kingdom*, 1; *Liáng Shū* ("Book of Liáng"), 54, 53b; *Wénxiàn Tōngkǎo* ("Comprehensive Examination of Literature"), 24, 46a.

148. Maspero, *The Champa Kingdom*, 2–3; *Liáng Shū*, 54, 54a; *Suí Shū* ("Book of Suí"), 82, 37a.

149. Maspero, *The Champa Kingdom*, 18; *Liáng Shū*, 54, 54a.

150. *Xīn Táng Shū* ("New Book of Táng"), 222, 19a; Maspero, *The Champa Kingdom*, 16; Henri Parmentier and Eugène-Marie Durand, "Le trésor des rois Cham," *Bulletin de l'École française d'Extrême-Orient*, 5 (1905), 40.

151. Schafer, *The Vermilion Bird*, 72.

152. Schafer, *The Vermilion Bird*, 72.

153. Maspero, *The Champa Kingdom*, 16; Parmentier and Durand, "Le trésor des rois Cham," 40; *Suí Shū*, 82 ("The Nanman"), 27a; *Xīn Táng Shū* ("New Book of Táng"), 222, 19a.

154. Maspero, *The Champa Kingdom,* 16.
155. Maspero, *The Champa Kingdom,* 136 n. 266; *Liáng Shū* ("Book of Liáng"), 54, 54a.
156. Maspero, *The Champa Kingdom,* 20; and see Parmentier and Durand, "Le trésor des rois Cham," 1–3.
157. Maspero, *The Champa Kingdom,* 137 note 308.
158. Maspero, *The Champa Kingdom,* 137 note 308.

Chapter 2

1. Ngô Đức Thịnh, *Trang phục cổ truyền các dân tộc Việt Nam* (Hà Nội: Nhà xuất bản Văn hoá dân tộc, 1994), 25.
2. Ngô Đức Thịnh, *Trang phục cổ truyền các dân tộc Việt Nam,* 26.
3. Ngô Đức Thịnh, *Trang phục cổ truyền các dân tộc Việt Nam,* 28.
4. Ngô Đức Thịnh, *Trang phục cổ truyền các dân tộc Việt Nam,* 28.
5. Ngô Đức Thịnh, *Trang phục cổ truyền các dân tộc Việt Nam,* 28–9.
6. Zhou and Gao, *5000 Years of Chinese Costume,* 130–1.
7. Zhou and Gao, *5000 Years of Chinese Costume,* 146–7.
8. See photographs of such squares in Zhou and Gao, *5000 Years of Chinese Costume,* 154.
9. Ngô Đức Thịnh, *Trang phục cổ truyền các dân tộc Việt Nam,* 30.
10. Ngô Đức Thịnh, *Trang phục cổ truyền các dân tộc Việt Nam,* 31.
11. Ngô Đức Thịnh, *Trang phục cổ truyền các dân tộc Việt Nam,* 31.
12. Ngô Đức Thịnh, *Trang phục cổ truyền các dân tộc Việt Nam,* 31.
13. Ngô Đức Thịnh, *Trang phục cổ truyền các dân tộc Việt Nam,* 31–2.
14. Ngô Đức Thịnh, *Trang phục cổ truyền các dân tộc Việt Nam,* 32.
15. Ngô Đức Thịnh, *Trang phục cổ truyền các dân tộc Việt Nam,* 32.
16. Hoàng Anh Tuấn, *Silk for Silver: Dutch-Vietnamese Relations, 1637–1700* (Leiden: Brill, 2007), 34.
17. Ngô Đức Thịnh, *Trang phục cổ truyền các dân tộc Việt Nam,* 32.
18. Ngô Đức Thịnh, *Trang phục cổ truyền các dân tộc Việt Nam,* 32.
19. Ngô Đức Thịnh, *Trang phục cổ truyền các dân tộc Việt Nam,* 32.
20. Charles Wheeler, "One Region, Two Histories: Cham Precedents in the History of the Hội An Region," in Nhung Tuyet Tran and Anthony J. S. Reid (eds.), *Viet Nam: Borderless Histories* (Madison: University of Wisconsin Press, 2006), 168, 180.
21. Li, *Nguyễn Cochinchina,* 37–8.
22. Li, *Nguyễn Cochinchina,* 38.
23. Trịnh Hoài Đức, *Gia Định thành thông chí,* 203, cites the date as 1744.
24. Li, *Nguyễn Cochinchina,* 63, 66.
25. Li, *Nguyễn Cochinchina,* 66.
26. Tuan, *Silk for Silver,* 35.
27. Tuan, *Silk for Silver,* 35.
28. Tuan, *Silk for Silver,* 36.
29. Tuan, *Silk for Silver,* 48.
30. Li, *Nguyễn Cochinchina,* 66.
31. Tuan, *Silk for Silver,* 46.
32. Tuan, *Silk for Silver,* 38, 116–7, 163.
33. See Ma Huan (J.V.G.Mills trans.), *Ying-yai Sheng-lan: The Overall Survey of the Ocean's Shores [1433]* (Cambridge: Cambridge University Press, 1970), 79.
34. On the decline of Chămpa's trade in the face of increased competition from neighboring states see Li, *Nguyễn Cochinchina,* 63.
35. Wheeler, "One Region, Two Histories, 168, 180, 183.
36. Ma Huan, *Ying-yai Sheng-lan,* 79–80; also see Ramesh Chandra Majumdar, *Ancient Indian Colonies of the Far East: I: Champa* (Lahore: Punjab Sanskrit Book Depot 1927), 220–2.
37. Ma Huan, *Ying-yai Sheng-lan,* 80 note 1.
38. Ma Huan, *Ying-yai Sheng-lan,* 80.
39. Ma Huan, *Ying-yai Sheng-lan,* 80.
40. Ma Huan, *Ying-yai Sheng-lan,* 80.
41. Ma Huan, *Ying-yai Sheng-lan,* 85.
42. Tomé Pires (Armando Cortesão, trans. and ed.), *The Suma Oriental of Tomé Pires: An Account of the East, From the Red Sea to Japan, Written in Malacca and India in 1512–1515, and The Book of Francisco Rodrigues, Rutter of a Voyage in the Red Sea, Nautical Rules, Almanack and Maps, Written and Drawn in the East Before 1515* (London: Hakluyt Society, 1944), 114.
43. Pires, *The Suma Oriental,* 114.
44. Li, *Nguyễn Cochinchina,* 66.
45. From Shilian Dashan, *Haiwai jishi* ("Record of Travel Overseas") (Taipei: Guangwen shuju, 1969, originally published in 1699); cited in Liam C. Kelly, *Vietnam through the Eyes of a Chinese Abbot: Dashan's Haiwai Jishi (1694–95)* (MA thesis, University of Hawaii at Manoa, 1996), 52–3; and Wheeler, "One Region, Two Histories," 183.
46. Wheeler, "One Region, Two Histories," 183.
47. See Michael Vickery, *Society, Economics, and Politics in Pre-Angkor Cambodia: The 7th-8th Centuries* (Tokyo: The Centre for East Asian Cultural Studies for UNESCO, The Toyo Bunko, 1998), 71–82.
48. Paul Pelliot, "Deux itinéraires de Chine en Inde à la fin du VIIIe siècle," *Bulletin de l'École Française d'Extrême Orient* 4 (1904), 211.
49. See Guillon, *Cham Art,* 15.
50. Tana Li, "The Eighteenth-Century Mekong Delta and Its World of Water Frontier," in Nhung

Tuyet Tran and Anthony J. S. Reid (eds.), *Viet Nam: Borderless Histories* (Madison: University of Wisconsin Press, 2006), 153.
51. Li, "The Eighteenth-Century Mekong Delta and Its World of Water Frontier," 147.
52. On Khmer weaving see Howard, *From Dashes to Dragons*, 128–136.
53. Vickery, *Society, Economics, and Politics in Pre-Angkor Cambodia*, 105, 117, 234–5, 288.
54. Vickery, *Society, Economics, and Politics in Pre-Angkor Cambodia*, 282 note 70, 292.
55. Vickery, *Society, Economics, and Politics in Pre-Angkor Cambodia*, 292.
56. The translation used here is Zhou Daguan, *A Record of Cambodia: The Land and Its People* (Chiang Mai: Silkworm Books, 2007).
57. Zhou, *A Record of Cambodia*, 75–6.
58. Zhou, *A Record of Cambodia*, 76.
59. Zhou, *A Record of Cambodia*, 76.
60. J. Delvert, *Le paysan Cambodgien* (Paris: Mouton, 1961), 145–7; Kikuo Morimoto, *Research Report: Silk Production and Marketing in Cambodia* (Phnom Penh: Institute for Khmer Traditional Textiles and UNESCO, 1995), 28.
61. Forest Inventory and Planning Institute, *Vietnam Forest Trees* (Hanoi: Agricultural Publishing House, 1996), 156.
62. Zhou, *A Record of Cambodia*, 76.
63. Zhou, *A Record of Cambodia*, 76.
64. Zhou, *A Record of Cambodia*, 76.
65. Zhou, *A Record of Cambodia*, 50.
66. Zhou, *A Record of Cambodia*, 50.
67. Zhou, *A Record of Cambodia*, 71; the translator comments (page 119 note 77) that Zhōu uses the phrase "the five colors," which literally refers to "dark green, vermillion, yellow, white, and black," but that it can also refer simply to a variety of colors.
68. Zhou, *A Record of Cambodia*, 50.
69. Ian Mibbett and David Chandler, *The Khmers* (Oxford: Blackwell, 1995), 131.
70. Zhou, *A Record of Cambodia*, 50, 51.
71. Gillian Green, "Textiles at the Khmer Court, Angkor: Origins, Innovations and Continuities," in Jane Purananda (ed.), *Through the Thread of Time: Southeast Asian Textiles* (Bangkok: River Books, 2004), 18.
72. Green, "Textiles at the Khmer Court, 18.
73. Pires, *The Suma Oriental*, 115.
74. Li, *Nguyễn Cochinchina*, 66.
75. See Howard, *From Dashes to Dragons*, 130–1.
76. Howard, "The Cham of Vietnam and Their Textiles," 128.

Chapter 3

1. See Frédéric Mantienne, *Monseigneur Pigneau de Béhaine* (Paris: Editions Eglises d'Asie, 1999).
2. Crawfurd, *Journal of an Embassy from the Governor-General of India to the Courts of Siam and Cochin China*, Volume 2, 311.
3. See Wynn Wilcox "Transnationalism and Multiethnicity in the Early Nguyen Anh Gia Long Period," in Nhung Tuyet Tran and Anthony J. S. Reid (eds.), *Viet Nam: Borderless Histories* (Madison: University of Wisconsin Press, 2006), 194–216, 207; André Salles, *Un Mandarin Breton au service du roi de Cochinchine* (Rennes: Les Portes du Large, 2006); Crawfurd, *Journal of an Embassy from the Governor-General of India to the Courts of Siam and Cochin China*, Volume 1, 391–2.
4. Salles, *Un Mandarin Breton au service du roi de Cochinchine*, 93–5.
5. Crawfurd, *Journal of an Embassy from the Governor-General of India to the Courts of Siam and Cochin China*, Volume 1, 402.
6. Crawfurd, *Journal of an Embassy from the Governor-General of India to the Courts of Siam and Cochin China*, Volume 2, 317.
7. Crawfurd, *Journal of an Embassy from the Governor-General of India to the Courts of Siam and Cochin China*, Volume 1, 440, and see 440–5.
8. Ngô Đức Thịnh, *Trang phục cổ truyền các dân tộc Việt Nam*, 35.
9. Ngô Đức Thịnh, *Trang phục cổ truyền các dân tộc Việt Nam*, 35–6.
10. Oscar Salemink, *The Ethnography of Vietnam's Central Highlanders: A Historical Contextualiztion, 1850–1900* (Honolulu: University of Hawai'i Press, 2003), 43–4.
11. Salemink, *The Ethnography of Vietnam's Central Highlanders*, 36–7.
12. Crawfurd, *Journal of an Embassy from the Governor-General of India to the Courts of Siam and Cochin China*, Volume 2, 277–9.
13. Crawfurd, *Journal of an Embassy from the Governor-General of India to the Courts of Siam and Cochin China*, Volume 1, 404.
14. Crawfurd, *Journal of an Embassy from the Governor-General of India to the Courts of Siam and Cochin China*, Volume 2, 278–9, 281.
15. Crawfurd, *Journal of an Embassy from the Governor-General of India to the Courts of Siam and Cochin China*, Volume 2, 272.
16. Crawfurd, *Journal of an Embassy from the Governor-General of India to the Courts of Siam and Cochin China*, Volume 2, 272–3.
17. Crawfurd, *Journal of an Embassy from the Governor-General of India to the Courts of Siam and Cochin China*, Volume 2, 272, 279.
18. Crawfurd, *Journal of an Embassy from the Governor-General of India to the Courts of Siam and Cochin China*, Volume 2, 280.
19. Crawfurd, *Journal of an Embassy from the Governor-General of India to the Courts of Siam and Cochin China*, Volume 2, 290–1.
20. See Crawfurd, *Journal of an Embassy from*

the Governor-General of India to the Courts of Siam and Cochin China, Volume 2, 317–8, 319, 321.

21. See Crawfurd, *Journal of an Embassy from the Governor-General of India to the Courts of Siam and Cochin China*, Volume 1, 402–3.

22. Ngô Đức Thịnh, *Trang phục cổ truyền các dân tộc Việt Nam*, 38.

23. Naval, *Indo-China*, 201.

24. Naval, *Indo-China*, 203.

25. Naval Intelligence Unit, *Indo-China*, 212.

26. Naval Intelligence Unit, *Indo-China*, 212.

27. Naval Intelligence Unit, *Indo-China*, 254.

28. Naval Intelligence Unit, *Indo-China*, 254.

29. Naval Intelligence Unit, *Indo-China*, 254.

30. Nguyễn Văn Huyên, *Ancient Civilization*, 19.

31. Naval Intelligence Unit, *Indo-China*, 158.

32. Naval Intelligence Unit, *Indo-China*, 470–7.

33. Michael C. Howard, "The Peoples of French Indochina," in *The Art of Jean Despujols and the Peoples of Indo-china*, published online (2014) at http://meadowsfriends.org/about-despujols/.

34. Naval Intelligence Unit, *Indo-China*, 158.

35. See individual entries online at catholic-hierarchy.org/diocese/dbuic.

36. Emperor Bảo Đại was sent to France to study in 1922, first at the *Lycée Condorcet* and then at the *Institut d'études politiques de Paris*. He returned to Huế briefly when his father died in 1926 to be proclaimed emperor and then went back to Paris to resume his studies until 1934.

37. See "The Beauty of Vietnam's Last Queen," *VietNamNet Bridge*, 30 October 2010, online at english.vietnamnet.vn.

38. See "Cát Tường," *Đại học Hoa Sen: Tin tức*, 20 September 2012, online at tintuc.hoasen.edu.vn/vi/1315/tin-chuyen-de/cat-tuong.

39. Justin Corfield, *Historical Dictionary of Ho Chi Minh City* (London: Anthem Press, 2014), 302.

40. Bernard B. Fall, *The Two Viet-Nams: A Political and Military Analysis: Second Revised Edition* (New York: Frederick A. Praeger, 1967), 172.

41. Fall, *The Two Viet-Nams*, 302.

42. Fall, *The Two Viet-Nams*, 178.

43. Fall, *The Two Viet-Nams*, 302; and see Harvey H. Smith, et al, *Area Handbook for South Vietnam* (Washington, DC: U.S. Government Printing Office, 1967), 343.

44. See "Trần Lệ Xuân—Fashionista Việt thập niên 40," *eva.vn: thời trang*, 13 December 2013, online at eva.vn/thoi-trang.

45. Smith, *Area Handbook for South Vietnam*, 102.

46. Nghia M. Vo, *Saigon: A History* (Jefferson, NC: McFarland, 2011), 202.

47. Mick Elmore, "Ao Dai Enjoys A Renaissance Among Women: In Vietnam, A Return to Femininity," *New York Times*, September 17, 1997.

48. See Ann Marie Leshkowich, "The Ao Dai Goes Global: How International Influences and Female Entrepreneurs have Shaped Vietnam's 'National Costume,'" in S.A. Niessen, A.M. Leshkowich, and C. Jones (eds.), *Re-orienting Fashion: The Globalization of Asian Dress* (Oxford: Berg, 2003), 79–116.

Chapter 4

1. See Abadie, *Les Races du Haut-Tonkin*, 63–4; Abadie, *Minorities of the Sino-Vietnamese Borderland*, 92–3; John T. McAlister, Jr., "Mountain Minorities and the Viet Minh: A Key to The Indochina War," in Peter Kunstadter (ed.), *Southeast Asian Tribes, Minorities, and Nations, Volume II* (Princeton, NJ: Princeton University Press, 1967), 780.

2. See the map in Naval Intelligence Division, *Indo-China*, 411 fig. 135.

3. Howard and Howard, *Textiles of the Highland Peoples of Northern Vietnam*, 24–5.

4. See Hy Van Luong, "Wealth, Power, and Inequality: Global Market, the State, and Local Sociocultural Dynamics," in Hy Van Luong (ed.), *Postwar Vietnam: Dynamics of a Transforming Society* (Oxford: Rowman and Littlefield Publishers 2003), 81–106; A. Terry Rambo and Neil L. Jamieson, "Upland Areas, Ethnic Minorities," in Hy Van Luong (ed.), *Postwar Vietnam: Dynamics of a Transforming Society* (Oxford: Rowman and Littlefield Publisher. 2003), 81–106.

5. See Nông Quốc Bình and Michael C. Howard, *Cultural Revival and the Peoples of Ta Van Commune* (Bangkok: White Lotus Press, 2013); Michael C. Howard, "Cultural Revival and Community Development in Ta Van Commune, Sa Pa District, Vietnam," in David B. Wangsgard (ed.), *Culture and Development in Southeast Asia* (Bangkok: White Lotus Press, 2008), 125–35; David B. Wangsgard, "Culture, Civilization and the Preservation of Ethnic Minority Culture in Vietnam," in David B. Wangsgard (ed.), *Culture and Development in Southeast Asia* (Bangkok: White Lotus Press, 2008), 137–58.

6. Jerold A. Edmonson, "Kra or Kadai Languages," in Anthony Diller, Jerold A. Edmondson, and Yongxian Luo (eds.), *The Tai–Kadai Languages* (New York: Routledge, 2008), 653; also see Sebastian Nordhoff, Harald Hammarström, Robert Forkel, and Martin Haspelmath (eds.), "Kadai," in *Glottolog* (Leipzig: Max Planck Institute for Evolutionary Anthropology, 2013), online at glottolog.org/resource/languoid/id/kada1291.

7. Howard and Howard, *Textiles of the Daic Peoples of Vietnam*, 38–9, 216 plate 31.

8. Howard and Howard, *Textiles of the Daic Peoples of Vietnam*, 35, 38, 215–6 plates 25–30.

9. Howard and Howard, *Textiles of the Daic Peoples of Vietnam*, 35.

10. Howard and Howard, *Textiles of the Daic Peoples of Vietnam*, 39–40, 217–8 plates 32–8.

11. See Abadie, *Les Races du Haut-Tonkin de Phong-Tho à Lang-Son,* 35; Abadie, *Minorities of the Sino-Vietnamese Borderland,* 63; Howard and Howard, *Textiles of the Daic Peoples of Vietnam,* 49.
12. Abadie, *Les Races du Haut-Tonkin,* 35; Abadie, *Minorities of the Sino-Vietnamese Borderland,* 63.
13. Abadie, *Les Races du Haut-Tonkin,* 36; Abadie, *Minorities of the Sino-Vietnamese Borderland,* 64; Howard and Howard, *Textiles of the Daic Peoples,* 49–50, 219 plates 39–40.
14. Howard and Howard, *Textiles of the Daic Peoples,* 219 plate 42.
15. Howard and Howard, *Textiles of the Daic Peoples,* 220–1 plates 43–8.
16. Howard and Howard, *Textiles of the Daic Peoples,* 52, 54, 219 plate 41.
17. Howard and Howard, *Textiles of the Daic Peoples,* 59.
18. Howard and Howard, *Textiles of the Daic Peoples,* 59.
19. Howard and Howard, *Textiles of the Daic Peoples,* 61 fig. 3.15, 223 plate 56.
20. Howard and Howard, *Textiles of the Daic Peoples,* 224–5 plates 57–61.
21. Howard and Howard, *Textiles of the Daic Peoples,* 62.
22. Howard and Howard, *Textiles of the Daic Peoples,* 71, 74, 97, 100.
23. Howard and Howard, *Textiles of the Daic Peoples,* 84; Michael C. Howard, "Southeast Asian Textiles as Art," in Michael C. Howard (ed.), *Textile Traditions in Contemporary Southeast Asia* (Bangkok: White Lotus Press, 2012), 17.
24. Howard and Howard, *Textiles of the Daic Peoples,* 86–7.
25. Howard and Howard, *Textiles of the Daic Peoples,* 80.
26. Howard and Howard, *Textiles of the Daic Peoples,* 87.
27. Howard and Howard, *Textiles of the Daic Peoples,* 230 plate 76, 236 plates 97–8.
28. Howard and Howard, *Textiles of the Daic Peoples,* 80–1.
29. Howard and Howard, *Textiles of the Daic Peoples,* 114.
30. Howard and Howard, *Textiles of the Daic Peoples,* 230 plate 76, 236 plates 97–8, 239 plates 107–14, 245 plates 129–32, 247–52 plates 137–58.
31. Howard and Howard, *Textiles of the Daic Peoples,* 234 plates 93–4.
32. Howard and Howard, *Textiles of the Daic Peoples,* 103–5, 241–2 plates 115–9; Howard, *A World Between the Warps,* 7–8, 74–84 plates 28–61.
33. Howard, *A World Between the Warps,* 5–6, 69–71 plates 10–19.
34. Howard, *From Dashes to Dragons,* 29–30.
35. Howard and Howard, *Textiles of the Daic Peoples,* 114; Mattiebelle Gittinger and H. Leedom Lefferts, Jr., *Textiles and the Tai Experience in Southeast Asia* (Washington, DC: The Textile Museum, 1992), 134 fig. 3.47.
36. Howard and Howard, *Textiles of the Daic Peoples,* 261–4 plates 188–91 and 197–9.
37. Howard and Howard, *Textiles of the Daic Peoples,* 114, 260–1 plates 183–7.
38. Howard and Howard, *Textiles of the Daic Peoples,* 259 plates 180–2, 262 plates 192–3, 265–7 plates 202–6 and 211.
39. Howard and Howard, *Textiles of the Daic Peoples,* 235 plate 95.
40. Howard and Howard, *Textiles of the Daic Peoples,* 234 plate 91.
41. Howard and Howard, *Textiles of the Daic Peoples,* 106, 237–8 plates 102–5.
42. Howard and Howard, *Textiles of the Daic Peoples,* 90 fig. 5.8.
43. Howard and Howard, *Textiles of the Daic Peoples,* 82–3, 231 plates 79–82, 233 plate 89,253 plate 163.
44. Howard and Howard, *Textiles of the Daic Peoples,* 108 fig. 6.8, 111 figs 6.9 and 6.10, 116, 117 fig. 6.18, 262–3 plates 193–5, 267–8 plates 212–5, 269 plate 218, 271 plate 226.
45. Howard and Howard, *Textiles of the Daic Peoples,* 235 plate 96.
46. Howard and Howard, *Textiles of the Daic Peoples,* 233 plate 88.
47. Howard and Howard, *Textiles of the Daic Peoples,* 113 fig. 6.13, 255–6 plates 171–3.
48. Howard and Howard, *Textiles of the Daic Peoples,* 232–3 plates 85–7.
49. Howard and Howard, *Textiles of the Daic Peoples,* 256–8 plates 174–9.
50. Howard and Howard, *Textiles of the Daic Peoples,* 242 plate 123.
51. Howard and Howard, *Textiles of the Daic Peoples,* 131, 286 plates 278–9.
52. Howard and Howard, *Textiles of the Daic Peoples,* 272 plates 231–2.
53. Howard and Howard, *Textiles of the Daic Peoples,* 130, 273–7 plates 233–49.
54. Howard and Howard, *Textiles of the Daic Peoples,* 130.
55. Howard and Howard, *Textiles of the Daic Peoples,* 128, 277–9 plates 251–6.
56. Howard and Howard, *Textiles of the Daic Peoples,* 133.
57. Howard and Howard, *Textiles of the Daic Peoples,* 134, 137, 286 plate 280, 287 plate 284.
58. Howard and Howard, *Textiles of the Daic Peoples,* 134–7, 287–9 plates 281–2 and 284–9.
59. Howard and Howard, *Textiles of the Diac Peoples of Vietnam,* 64–6.
60. Howard and Howard, *Textiles of the Diac Peoples of Vietnam,* 66–8, 227 plates 68 and 70.

61. Howard and Howard, *Textiles of the Diac Peoples of Vietnam*, 69–70, 228–9 plates 71–5.
62. Howard and Howard, *Textiles of the Diac Peoples of Vietnam*, 69, 228–9 plates 71–4.
63. Kenneth J. Gregerson and Jerold A. Edmonson, "Some Puzzles in Cao Lan," in S. Burusphat (ed.), *The International Conference on Tai Studies* (Bangkok, Institute of Language and Culture for Rural Development, Mahidol University, 1998), 152.
64. See Gregerson and Edmonson, "Some Puzzles in Ca Lan"; and Sebastian Nordhoff, Harald Hammarström, Robert Forkel, and Martin Haspelmath, "Cao Lan," *Glottolog* (Leipzig: Max Planck Institute for Evolutionary Anthropology, 2013), online at glottolog.org/resource/languoid/id/caol1238.
65. Howard and Howard, *Textiles of the Diac Peoples of Vietnam*, 139.
66. Howard and Howard, *Textiles of the Diac Peoples of Vietnam*, 140; Howard and Howard, *Textiles of the Highland Peoples of Northern Vietnam*, 19–20.
67. See Jeanne Cuisinier, *Les Mường: Géographie humaine et sociologie* (Paris: Institut d'Ethnologie, 1946); Howard and Howard, *Textiles of the Highland Peoples of Northern Vietnam*, 20–5.
68. Howard and Howard, *Textiles of the Highland Peoples of Northern Vietnam*, 154 plate 5.
69. See Vietnam Museum of Ethnology, Vietnam Museum of Ethnology (Hà Nội: Vietnam Museum of Ethnology, 1998), 78.
70. Howard and Howard, *Textiles of the Highland Peoples of Northern Vietnam*, 14–5.
71. Howard and Howard, *Textiles of the Highland Peoples of Northern Vietnam*, 15.
72. Howard and Howard, *Textiles of the Highland Peoples of Northern Vietnam*, 16.
73. Howard and Howard, *Textiles of the Highland Peoples of Northern Vietnam*, 17–8.
74. Howard and Howard, *Textiles of the Highland Peoples of Northern Vietnam*, 18.
75. See Nong and Howard, *Cultural Revival and the People of Ta Van Commune*.
76. Howard and Howard, *Textiles of the Highland Peoples of Northern Vietnam*, 32–5, 157–9 plates 14–20.
77. Howard and Howard, *Textiles of the Highland Peoples of Northern Vietnam*, 157 plate 16.
78. Howard and Howard, *Textiles of the Highland Peoples of Northern Vietnam*, 35–41, 159–63 plates 21–32.
79. E. Diguet, *Les Montagnards du Tonkin* (Paris: Augustin Challamel, 1908), 136; and see Howard and Howard, *Textiles of the Highland Peoples of Northern Vietnam*, 41–4, 164–70 plates 35–58.
80. Howard and Howard, *Textiles of the Highland Peoples of Northern Vietnam*, 170 plate 59.
81. Howard and Howard, *Textiles of the Highland Peoples of Northern Vietnam*, 44–6, 171–3 plates 60–5.
82. Howard and Howard, *Textiles of the Highland Peoples of Northern Vietnam*, 46.
83. Howard and Howard, *Textiles of the Highland Peoples of Northern Vietnam*, 174 plate 68.
84. See Vi Van An, "Les Pa Then," in Nguyễn Văn Huy (ed.), *Mosaïque Culturelle des Ethnies du Vietnam* (Hà Nội: Maison d'édition et d'éducation, 1999), 145–6.
85. Howard and Howard, *Textiles of the Highland Peoples of Northern Vietnam*, 175 plates 71–3.
86. Howard and Howard, *Textiles of the Highland Peoples of Northern Vietnam*, 47–8, 174–5 plates 69–70.
87. Abadie, *Les Races du Haut-Tonkin*, 128–9; Abadie, *Minorities of the Sino-Vietnamese Borderland*, 176–8.
88. Howard and Howard, *Textiles of the Highland Peoples of Northern Vietnam*, 52–9, 176–90 plates 74–126.
89. Howard and Howard, *Textiles of the Highland Peoples of Northern Vietnam*, 57.
90. Abadie, *Minorities of the Sino-Vietnamese Borderland*, 178; Howard and Howard, *Textiles of the Highland Peoples*, 57 fig. 5.6, 185 plates 107 and 108.
91. Howard and Howard, *Textiles of the Highland Peoples*, 179 plates 84 and 85.
92. Howard and Howard, *Textiles of the Highland Peoples*, 183 plates 98 and 99.
93. Howard and Howard, *Textiles of the Highland Peoples*, 176 plate 74.
94. Howard and Howard, *Textiles of the Highland Peoples*, 177 plates 76 and 77.
95. Howard and Howard, *Textiles of the Highland Peoples*, 55–6.
96. Howard and Howard, *Textiles of the Highland Peoples*, 59–61.
97. Howard and Howard, *Textiles of the Highland Peoples*, 62 fig. 5.9, 63–4; Henry Girard, *Les Tribus Sauvages du Haut-Tonkin, Mans et Méos: Notes Anthropometriques et Ethnographiques* (Paris: Imprimerie Nationale, 1904), plate 3; Abadie, *Les Races du Haut-Tonkin*, 134–5; Abadie, *Minorities of the Sino-Vietnamese Borderland*, 182.
98. See N.J. Girardot, *Myth and Meaning in Early Taoism: The Theme of Chaos (hun-tun)* (Berkeley: University of California Press, 1988), 322; David Gordon White, *Myths of the Dog-Man* (Chicago: University of Chicago Press, 1991), 281 note 34.
99. Howard and Howard, *Textiles of the Highland Peoples*, 62–6; Girard, *Les Tribus Sauvages du Haut-Tonkin*, plate 1; Auguste Bonifacy, *Les Groupes Ethniques du Bassin de la Rivière Claire (Haut Tonkin & Chine Méridionale)* (Paris: Extrait

des *Bulletins et Mémoires de la Société d'Anthropologie*, 1906), plate 19 fig. 2; Abadie, *Les Races du Haut-Tonkin*, 134–5; Abadie, *Minorities of the Sino-Vietnamese Borderland*, 182.

100. Diguet, *Les Montagnards du Tonkin*, 121.

101. Howard and Howard, *Textiles of the Highland Peoples*, 72–4, 211 plate 196.

102. Diep Trung Binh, *Patterns on Textiles of the Ethnic Groups in Northeast Vietnam* (Hà Nội: Cultures Nationalities Publishing House, 1997), 103.

103. Diep, *Patterns on Textiles of the Ethnic Groups in Northeast Vietnam*, 104.

104. Diguet, *Les Montagnards du Tonkin*, 122.

105. Howard and Howard, *Textiles of the Highland Peoples*, 67–8.

106. See Bonifacy *Les Groupes Ethniques du Bassin de la Rivière Claire*, plate 17 fig. 1; Howard and Howard, *Textiles of the Highland Peoples*, 68 fig. 5.14, 199–200 plates 155–7.

107. Howard and Howard, *Textiles of the Highland Peoples*, 68 fig. 5.15, 197 plate 148.

108. Howard and Howard, *Textiles of the Highland Peoples*, 199 plates 153–4.

109. Howard and Howard, *Textiles of the Highland Peoples*, 202 plate 167.

110. Howard and Howard, *Textiles of the Highland Peoples*, 200–1 plates 158–62.

111. Howard and Howard, *Textiles of the Highland Peoples*, 201–2 plates 163–65.

112. Howard and Howard, *Textiles of the Highland Peoples*, 70; Abadie, *Les Races du Haut-Tonkin*, 116; Abadie, *Minorities of the Sino-Vietnamese Borderland*, 155.

113. Howard and Howard, *Textiles of the Highland Peoples*, 205 plate 175.

114. Abadie, *Les Races du Haut-Tonkin*, 110; Abadie, *Minorities of the Sino-Vietnamese Borderland*, 148.

115. Howard and Howard, *Textiles of the Highland Peoples*, 208 plate 183.

116. Howard and Howard, *Textiles of the Highland Peoples*, 205 plates 173–4.

117. Howard and Howard, *Textiles of the Highland Peoples*, 69–72, 203–10 plates 169–94.

118. Nguyễn Văn Huy, "Dân tộc Hà Nhì," in Bùi Văn Cán (ed.), *Các dân tộc ít người o Việt Nam (Các Tỉnh Phía Bắc)* (Hà Nội: Nhà Xuất Bản Khoa Học Xã Hội, 1978), 345.

119. Diguet, *Les Montagnards du Tonkin*, 149; Abadie, *Les Races du Haut-Tonkin*, 187; Abadie, *Minorities of the Sino-Vietnamese Borderland*, 250.

120. Diguet, *Les Montagnards du Tonkin*, 149; Abadie, *Les Races du Haut-Tonkin*, 187; *Minorities of the Sino-Vietnamese Borderland*, 250.

121. Howard and Howard, *Textiles of the Highland Peoples*, 90–1, 203–10 plates 169–94.

122. Bonifacy, *Les Groupes Ethniques du Bassin de la Rivière Claire*, plate 20 fig. 1; Howard and Howard, *Textiles of the Highland Peoples*, 77 fig. 6.2; Diguet, *Les Montagnards du Tonkin*, 147; Nguyễn Anh Ngọc, "Dân tộc Lô Lô," in Bùi Văn Cán (ed.), *Các dân tộc ít người ở Việt Nam (Các Tỉnh Phía Bắc)* (Hà Nội: Nhà Xuất Bản Khoa Học Xã Hội, 1978), 377.

123. Abadie, *Les Races du Haut-Tonkin*, 176; Abadie, *Minorities of the Sino-Vietnamese Borderland*, 237.

124. See Thông tấn xã Việt Nam/Vietnam News Agency, *Việt Nam: Hình ảnh cộng đ ng 54 Dân tộc Việt Nam/Vietnam: Image of the Community of 54 Ethnic Groups* (Hà Nội: Nhà Xuất bản Văn hoá dân tộc/Ethnic Cultures Publishing House, 1996), 125.

125. Howard and Howard, *Textiles of the Highland Peoples*, 76–82, 212–8 plates 199–216.

126. See Bonifacy, *Les Groupes Ethniques du Bassin de la Rivière Claire*, plate 20 fig. 1; Howard and Howard, *Textiles of the Highland Peoples*, 77 fig. 6.2.

127. See Bonifacy, *Les Groupes Ethniques du Bassin de la Rivière Claire*, plate 21 figs. 1–2; Howard and Howard, *Textiles of the Highland Peoples*, 76–7, figs. 6.1 and 6.3.

128. See Jamin Pelkey, *A Phula Comparative Lexicon: Phola, Phuza, Muji, Phowa, Azha* (SIL International, 2011).

129. Abadie, *Les Races du Haut-Tonkin*, 185; Abadie, *Minorities of the Sino-Vietnamese Borderland*, 249.

130. Howard and Howard, *Textiles of the Highland Peoples*, 86, 218 plate 27, 219–20 plates 220–1.

131. Abadie, *Les Races du Haut-Tonkin*, 183; Abadie, *Minorities of the Sino-Vietnamese Borderland*, 247.

132. Howard and Howard, *Textiles of the Highland Peoples*, 84 fig. 6.9, 223 plates 231–2; Abadie, *Les Races du Haut-Tonkin*, facing page 176 figs. 337 and 514; Abadie, *Minorities of the Sino-Vietnamese Borderland*, 243 figs. 117–8.

133. Howard and Howard, *Textiles of the Highland Peoples*, 84 fig. 6.8, 86–9, 218–9 plates 218–9, 220–3 plates 223–30.

134. Abadie, *Les Races du Haut-Tonkin*, 186; Abadie, *Minorities of the Sino-Vietnamese Borderland*, 249–50.

135. Nguyễn Văn Huy, "Dân tộc Si La," in Bùi Văn Cán (ed.), *Các dân tộc ít người ở Việt Nam (Các Tỉnh Phía Bắc)* (Hà Nội: Nhà Xuất Bản Khoa Học Xã Hội, 1978), 369; Howard and Howard, *Textiles of the Highland Peoples*, 95.

136. Nguyễn Văn Huy, "Dân tộc Cống," in Bùi Văn Cán (ed.), *Các dân tộc ít người ở Việt Nam (Các Tỉnh Phía Bắc)* (Hà Nội: Nhà Xuất Bản Học Xã Hội, 1978), 363, 365–6; Howard and Howard, *Textiles of the Highland Peoples*, 93–5.

Chapter 5

1. Gerald Cannon Hickey, *Sons of the Moun-*

tains: *Ethnohistory of the Vietnamese Central Highlands to 1954* (New Haven, CT: Yale University Press, 1982), 186.

2. "Ethnic Migrants Seek a Better Life," *Viet Nam News*, 12 November 2012.

3. "Ethnic Migrants Seek a Better Life."

4. Nguyễn Xuân Nghĩa and Phan An, "Dân tộc Khơ me," in Ma Khánh Bằng (ed.), *Các dân tộc ít người ở Việt Nam (Các Tỉnh Phía Nam)* (Hà Nội: Nhà Xuất Bản Khoa Học Xã Hội, 1984), 69.]

5. Nguyễn and Phan, "Dân tộc Khơ me," 69.

6. Nguyễn and Phan, "Dân tộc Khơ me," 67.

7. Naval Intelligence Division, *Indo-China*, 212.

8. Michael C. Howard, "The Cham of Vietnam and Their Textiles," 130; also see Howard, *A World Between the Warps*, 16–20; and Gerard Moussay, "Cham Weaving in Vietnam," in Jane Purananda (ed.), *Through the Thread of Time: Southeast Asian Textiles* (Bangkok: River Books, 2004), 152–61.

9. Gabrielle M. Vassal, *Three Years in Vietnam (1907–1910): Medicine, Chams and Tribesmen in Nhatrang and Surroundings* (Bangkok: White Lotus Press, 1999, originally published in French in 1910), 181–2.

10. Vassal, *Three Years in Vietnam*, 29, plate 33.

11. Vassal, *Three Years in Vietnam*, 182.

12. Howard, *A World Between the Warps*, 102–6 plates 131–43.

13. Howard, *From Dashes to Dragons*, 223 plates 232–3.

14. Howard, "The Cham of Vietnam and Their Textiles," 126 fig. 5.

15. Howard, "The Cham of Vietnam and Their Textiles," 125 fig. 3, 126 fig. 4, 127 fig. 10.

16. Howard, "The Cham of Vietnam and Their Textiles," 127 fig. 6.

17. Howard, "The Cham of Vietnam and Their Textiles," 127 fig. 7, 129 fig. 16.

18. Howard, "The Cham of Vietnam and Their Textiles," 130–1 fig. 21–3; Howard, *From Dashes to Dragons*, 224 plates 235–7.

19. Howard, "The Cham of Vietnam and Their Textiles," 131 fig. 24.

20. Howard, "The Cham of Vietnam and Their Textiles," 130 fig. 18, 132 fig. 25–6; Howard, *From Dashes to Dragons*, 224 plate 235.

21. Howard and Howard, *Textiles of the Central Highlands of Vietnam*, 22.

22. Howard and Howard, *Textiles of the Central Highlands of Vietnam*, 22–3, 153 plates 10–11; Jacques Dournes, "Le vêtement chez le Jorai," *Objets et Mondes*, 3, 2 (1963), 99–114, 16 figs.

23. Howard and Howard, *Textiles of the Central Highlands of Vietnam*, 23, 153–5 plates 12–6; Jacques Dournes, "Le vêtement chez le Jorai."

24. Howard and Howard, *Textiles of the Central Highlands*, 25.

25. Howard and Howard, *Textiles of the Central Highlands*, 158 plates 24–6.

26. Howard and Howard, *Textiles of the Central Highlands*, 24–33, 157–61 plates 21–36; Howard, *A World Between the Warps*, 121–8 plates 203–31; Chu Thái Sơn, et al, *Patterns on Textiles and Other Objects of the Êdê and Mnông in the Central Highlands of Vietnam* (Bangkok: White Lotus Press, 2005).

27. Howard and Howard, *Textiles of the Central Highlands*, 161 plate 36; Howard, *A World Between the Warps*, 126–8 plates 224–31.

28. Howard and Howard, *Textiles of the Central Highlands*, 33, 163–5 plates 41–5.

29. Howard and Howard, *Textiles of the Central Highlands*, 159 plates 27–30, 162 plates 37–8; Howard, *A World Between the Warps*, 124–6 plates 215–22.

30. Howard and Howard, *Textiles of the Central Highlands*, 33, 165–7 plates 46–50; Chu Thái Sơn, et al, *Patterns on Textiles and Other Objects of the Êdê and Mnông in the Central Highlands of Vietnam*, 108–12 plates 60–72; Howard, *A World Between the Warps*, 129 plates 232–3.

31. Howard and Howard, *Textiles of the Central Highlands*, 17–8, 149–50 plates 1–5.

32. See Gerald Hickey, *Sons of the Mountains*, 313–6.

33. Howard and Howard, *Textiles of the Central Highlands*, 39–46.

34. Howard, *A World Between the Warps*, 133–4 plates 248–53.

35. Howard and Howard, *Textiles of the Central Highlands*, 177 plates 77–8.

36. Howard and Howard, *Textiles of the Central Highlands*, 175 plates 71–3, 177–9 plates 79–85.

37. Howard and Howard, *Textiles of the Central Highlands*, 175–6 plates 74–5.

38. Howard and Howard, *Textiles of the Central Highlands*, 35–8, 168–73 plates 51–66; Michael C., Howard and Be Kim Nhung, "Textiles of the Katuic-speaking Peoples of Central Vietnam," *Arts of Asia* 30, 3 (2000), 131–8.

39. Howard, *A World Between the Warps*, 132 plates 244–6.

40. Howard and Howard, *Textiles of the Central Highlands*, 54–5, 58–62, 185–6 plates 100–5, 189–93 plates 114–24.

41. Henri Maître, *Les Jungles Moi: Exploration et histoire des Hinterlands Moi du Cambodge, de la Cochinchine, de l'Annan et du Bas-Lao: Mission Henri Maître (1909–1911) Indochine Sud-Centrale* (Paris: Emile Larose, 1912), 214–5.

42. Howard, *A World Between the Warps*, 144 plates 290–2.

43. Howard and Howard, *Textiles of the Central Highlands*, 190 plate 116.

44. Howard and Howard, *Textiles of the Central Highlands*, 186 plates 103 and 105, 191–2 plates 119–20.

45. Howard and Howard, *Textiles of the Central*

Highlands, 185 plate 102, 192–3 plates 121–4; Howard, *A World Between the Warps,* 144–5 plates 293–4, 147–9 plates 304–10; Howard, *From Dashes to Dragons,* 238 plate 276.
46. Howard and Howard, *Textiles of the Central Highlands,* 47–9.
47. Howard and Howard, *Textiles of the Central Highlands,* 179 plate 86.
48. Howard and Howard, *Textiles of the Central Highlands,* 179 plate 87.
49. See Howard, *A World Between the Warps,* 140–1 plates 277–9, for an example of a Talieng blanket.
50. Gerald Cannon Hickey, *Shattered World: Adaptation and Survival among Vietnam's Highland Peoples during the Vietnam War* (Philadelphia: University of Pennsylvania Press, 1993), 204.
51. Đặng Nghiêm Vạn, *The Sedang of Viet Nam* (Hà Nội: National Centre for Social Sciences and Humanities of Viet Nam, 1998), 145.
52. Đặng, *The Sedang of Viet Nam,* 22–3.
53. Howard and Howard, *Textiles of the Centrtal Highlands of Vietnam,* 51; Howard (ed.), *Bark-cloth in Southeast Asia,* 234–6 plates 3.1–4; Howard and Howard, *Textiles of the Central Highlands,* 180–1 plates 88–90; Đặng, *The Sedang of Viet Nam,* 61 fig. 51–2.
54. Howard and Howard, *Textiles of the Central Highlands of Vietnam,* 51; Đặng Nghiêm Vạn, "Dân tộc Xơ Đăng," in Ma Khánh Bằng (ed.), *Các dân tộc ít người o Việt Nam (Các Tinh Phía Nam)* (Hà Nội: Nha Xuat Ban Khoa Hoc Xa Hoi, 1984), 96.
55. Howard and Howard, *Textiles of the Centrtal Highlands of Vietnam,* 183 plate 97.
56. Howard and Howard, *Textiles of the Centrtal Highlands of Vietnam,* 182 plate 94; Đặng, *The Sedang of Viet Nam,* 59 figure 48.
57. Howard, *A World Between the Warps,* 140 plates 275–6; Howard and Howard, *Textiles of the Centrtal Highlands of Vietnam,* 184 plates 98–9.
58. Đặng, *The Sedang of Viet Nam,* 30 fig. 13, 58 fig. 46–7, 124 fig. 131.
59. Robert L. Mole, *The Montagnards of South Vietnam: A Study of Nine Tribes* (Rutland, VT: Tuttle, 1970), 223–4.
60. Howard and Howard, *Textiles of the Central Highlands,* 57, 187 plates 106–7.
61. Howard and Howard, *Textiles of the Central Highlands,* 57, 187–8 plates 108–12; Howard, *A World Between the Warps,* 31–2, 141.
62. Nguyễn Văn Huy, "Dân tộc Rơ Măm," in Ma Khánh Bằng (ed.), *Các dân tộc ít người o Việt Nam (Các Tinh Phía Nam)* (Hà Nội: Nhà Xuất Bản Khoa Học Xã Hội, 1984), 214; Howard and Howard, *Textiles of the Central Highlands,* 62.
63. Howard and Howard, *Textiles of the Central Highlands,* 189 plate 113; Howard, *A World Between the Warps,* 149 plate 311.
64. Howard and Howard, *Textiles of the Central Highlands,* 63, 194 plates 125–8.
65. Hickey, *Sons of the Mountains,* 289–90.
66. Hickey, *Sons of the Mountains,* 327–9.
67. Hickey, *Sons of the Mountains,* 353.
68. Huard and Maurice, "Les Mnong du plateau central Indochinois," 91–113.
69. Howard and Howard, *Textiles of the Central Highlands,* 200 plate 143; Howard, *Bark-cloth in Southeast Asia,* 237 plate 3.8.
70. Chu Thái Sơn, "Dân tộc Mnông," in Ma Khánh Bằng (ed.), *Các dân tộc ít người ở Việt Nam (Các Tinh Phía Nam)* (Hà Nội: Nhà Xuất Bản Khoa Học Xã Hội, 1984), 134; Ngô Đức Thịnh, "Kiến trúc vật trang trí dân gian." in Ngô Đức Thịnh (ed.), *Văn hóa dân gian M'nông* (Buôn Ma Thuột: Sở Văn hóa-Thông tin Đắk Lắk, 1995), 128–9.
71. Howard and Howard, *Textiles of the Central Highlands,* 201 plate 145.
72. Howard and Howard, *Textiles of the Central Highlands,* 195 plates 129–31, 197 plate 135, 199 plates 138–9.
73. Huard and Maurice, "Les Mnong du plateau central Indochinois," 102.
74. Howard and Howard, *Textiles of the Central Highlands,* 201 plate 144.
75. Howard and Howard, *Textiles of the Central Highlands,* 197 plate 134.
76. Huard and Maurice, "Les Mnong du plateau central Indochinois ," 106–7.
77. Huard and Maurice, "Les Mnong du plateau central Indochinois ," 101.
78. Howard, *A World Between the Warps,* 152 plates 322–4, Howard and Howard, *Textiles of the Central Highlands,* 201 plate 146.
79. Howard, *A World Between the Warps,* 152–3 plates 325–9, Howard and Howard, *Textiles of the Central Highlands,* 196 plates 132–3, 198 plate 136.
80. Howard, *A World Between the Warps,* 154 plates 331–2, Howard and Howard, *Textiles of the Central Highlands,* 196 plates 132–3, 198 plate 137.
81. André Baudrit, "Le fameux Song-Be." *Bulletin de la Société des Etudes Indchinoises* 11 (1936), 10–3; Hickey, *Shattered World,* 76; Paul Patté, *Hinterland Moï* (Paris: Plon-Nourrit, 1906), 3–8.
82. Hickey, *Shattered World,* 90.
83. Diệp Đình Hoa, "Dân tộc Xtiêng," in Ma Khánh Bằng (ed.), *Các dân tộc ít người ở Việt Nam (Các Tinh Phía Nam)* (Hà Nội: Nhà Xuất Bản Khoa Học Xã Hội, 1984), 145.
84. Howard, *A World Between the Warps,* 154–60 plates 333–54; Hickey, *Shattered World,* 90–1.
85. Howard and Howard, *Textiles of the Central Highlands of Vietnam,* 73–7 fig. 5.6 and 5.8–5.12, 202–3 plates 148–50, 205–6 plates 155–8, 208 plate 162.
86. Hickey, *Shattered World,* 90–1.
87. Patté, *Hinterland Moï,* 212–3; Howard and

Howard, *Textiles of the Central Highlands of Vietnam*, 74 fig. 5.9, 76 fig. 5.11, 77 fig. 5.13, 203 plate 151, 207 plate 160, 208 plate 161; Howard, *A World Between the Warps*, 154–5 plates 333–7, 156 plates 338 and 340.

88. Patté, *Hinterland Moï*, facing page 208; Howard and Howard, *Textiles of the Central Highlands of Vietnam*, 74 fig. 5.9.

89. Howard and Howard, *Textiles of the Central Highlands of Vietnam*, 208 plate 163; Howard, *A World Between the Warps*, 159–60 plates 351–4.

90. Jean Boulbert, "Quelques aspects du coutumier (N'dri) des Cau Maa," *Bulletin de la Société des Etudes Indochinoises*, n.s., 32, 2 (1957) 113–78, 140; Bourette, "Essai d'historire des poplations montagnards du Sud Indochinois jusqué a 1945," 31.

91. Phan Xuân Biên and Chu Thái Sơn, "Dân tộc Mạ," in Ma Khánh Bằng (ed.), *Các dân tộc ít người ở Việt Nam (Các Tỉnh Phía Nam)* (Hà Nội: Nhà Xuất Bản Khoa Học Xã Hội, 1984), 134.

92. Howard and Howard, *Textiles of the Central Highlands of Vietnam*, 214 plate 181; Boulbert, "Quelques aspects du coutumier (N'dri) des Cau Maa," fig. 12b.

93. Howard and Howard, *Textiles of the Central Highlands of Vietnam*, 210 plates 167–9, 213 plates 177–8; Howard, *A World Between the Warps*, 164 plates 370–3.

94. Howard and Howard, *Textiles of the Central Highlands of Vietnam*, 210–1 plates 169–71, 213 plates 178–80.

95. Howard and Howard, *Textiles of the Central Highlands of Vietnam*, 209 plate 166, 212 plates 174–6, 214 plates 182–3.

96. Howard and Howard, *Textiles of the Central Highlands of Vietnam*, 211–2 plates 172–4.

97. Maître, *Les Jungles Moi*, 316.

98. Dr. Queguiner, "Notes sur une peuplade Moi de la Chaine Annamitique Sud: Les Cau S're," *Institut Indochinois pour l'Etude de l'Homme: Bulletins et travaux* 6 (1943), 397.

99. Queguiner, "Notes sur une peuplade Moi de la Chaine Annamitique Sud," 397.

100. Phan Ngọc Chiến, "Dân tộc Cơ Ho," in Ma Khánh Bằng (ed.), *Các dân tộc ít người ở Việt Nam (Các Tỉnh Phía Nam)* (Hà Nội: Nhà Xuất Bản Khoa Học Xã Hội, 1984), 110–1.

101. Howard and Howard, *Textiles of the Central Highlands*, 83 fig. 5.19, 219 plate 197; Dam Bo (Jacques Dournes), "Les populations Montagnards de Sud-Indochine," *France-Asia*, Special Issue 5 (1950), plate 3a.

102. Howard and Howard, *Textiles of the Central Highlands*, 219 plate 197.

103. Howard and Howard, *Textiles of the Central Highlands*, 219 plate 198.

104. Howard and Howard, *Textiles of the Central Highlands*, 216 plate 187, 217 plate 191, 218 plate 194; Dam Bo (Jacques Dournes), "Les populations Montagnards de Sud-Indochine," plate 3b.

105. Howard and Howard, *Textiles of the Central Highlands*, 217 plates 191–2.

106. Howard and Howard, *Textiles of the Central Highlands*, 218 plates 194 and 196; Howard, *A World Between the Warps*, 160 plates 355–7.

107. Howard and Howard, *Textiles of the Central Highlands*, 216 plates 187–9.

108. Howard and Howard, *Textiles of the Central Highlands*, 215 plates 184–5.

109. Howard, *A World Between the Warps*, 163 plates 366–9.

110. Howard and Howard, *Textiles of the Central Highlands*, 219 plate 199; Howard, *A World Between the Warps*, 161–2 plates 359–64.

111. Hickey, *Sons of the Mountains*, 18–9.

112. Trần Văn Chi and Chu Thái Sơn, "Dân tộc Chơ Ro," in Ma Khánh Bằng (ed.), *Các dân tộc ít người ở Việt Nam (Các Tỉnh Phía Nam)* (Hà Nội: Nhà Xuất Bản Khoa Học Xã Hội, 1984), 208.

113. See Howard and Howard, *Textiles of the Central Highlands*, 220 plates 200–1.

References

Abadie, Maurice. *Minorities of the Sino-Vietnamese Borderland, with Special Reference to Thai Tribes*. Bangkok: White Lotus Press, 2001. [French edition: *Les Races du Haut-Tonkin de Phong-Tho à Lang Son*. Paris: Société d'éditions géographiques, maritimes et coloniales, 1924.]

Adams, Marie Jeanne. "A 'Forgotten' Bronze Ship and a Recently Discovered Bronze Weaver from Eastern Indonesia." *Asian Perspectives* 22 (1977), 87–109.

Allan, Sarah. *The Shape of the Turtle: Myth, Earth, and Cosmos in Early China*. Albany: SUNY Press, 1991.

Aurousseau, Leonard. "Le première conquête chinoises pays annamites." *Bulletin de l'École Française d'Etrême Orient* 23 (1924).

Baudrit, André. "Le fameux Song-Be." *Bulletin de la Société des Etudes Indchinoises* 11 (1936), 7–42.

Bellwood, Peter. *Prehistory of the Indo-Malaysian Archipelago: Revised Edition*. Honolulu: University of Hawai'i Press, 1997.

_____. "Southeast Asia Before History." In Nicholas Tarling (ed.), *The Cambridge History of Southeast Asia: Volume One, From Early Times to c. 1800*, 51–136. Cambridge: Cambridge University Press, 1992.

Bian Wei Hui. *Miao Autonomous Prefecture in the Annals of Chi (Guizhou)*. Guizhou: Guizhou People's Publishing House, 1991.

Bonifacy, Auguste. *Les Groupes Ethniques du Bassin de la Rivière Claire (Haut Tonkin & Chine Méridional)*. Paris: Extrait des Bulletins et Mémoires de la Société d'Anthropologie, 1906.

Boulbert, Jean. "Quelques aspects du coutumier (N'dri) des Cau Maa." *Bulletin de la Société des Etudes Indochinoises*, n.s., 32, 2 (1957), 113–178.

Bourette, Bernard. "Essai d'histoire des populations montagnards du Sud indochinois jusque 1945." *Bulletin de la Société des Etudes Indochinoises* (n.s.) 30, 1 (1955), 1–133.

Brindley, Erica. "Barbarians of Not? Ethnicity and Changing Conceptions of the Ancient Yue (Viet) Peoples, ca. 400–50 BC" *Asia Major* 16, 1 (2003), 1–32.

Cameron, Judith. "The Archaeological Evidence for Bark-cloth in Southeast Asia." In M.C. Howard (ed.), *Bark-cloth in Southeast Asia*, 65–74. Bangkok: White Lotus Press, 2006.

Cardon, Dominique. *Natural Dyes: Sources, Tradition, Technology and Science*. London: Archetype Publications, 2007.

Chamberlain, James R. "The Black Tai Chronicle of Muang Mouay Part I: Mythology." *Mon-Khmer Studies* 21 (1992), 19–55.

_____. "The Origins of the Sek: Implications for Tai and Vietnamese History." *Journal of the Siam Society* 86, 1–2 (1998), 27–48.

Chang Shana. *Patterns of China Dunhuang Dresses and Adornments in Different Ages*. Beijing: China Light Industry Press, 2000.

Chu Thái Sơn. "Dân tộc Mnông." In Ma Khánh Bằng (ed.), *Các dân tộc ít người ở Việt Nam (Các Tinh Phía Nam)*, 129–41. Hà Nội: Nhà Xuất Bản Khoa Học Xã Hội, 1984.

_____, Nguyễn Đại Lương, Ngô Đức Thịnh, and Michael C. Howard (Kim Be Howard trans). *Patterns on Textiles and Other Objects of the Êđê and Mnông in the Central Highlands of Vietnam*. Bangkok: White Lotus Press, 2005.

Condominas, Georges. *From Lawa to Mon, from Saa' to Thai: Historical and Anthropological Aspects of Southeast Asian Social Spaces*. Canberra: Department of Anthropology, Research School of Pacific Studies, Australian National University, 1990.

Cook, Constance A., and Barry B. Blakely. "Introduction." In C.A. Cook and B.B. Blakley

References

(eds.), *Defining Chu: Image and Reality in Ancient China*, 1–5. Honolulu: University of Hawai'i Press, 1999.

Corfield, Justin. *Historical Dictionary of Ho Chi Minh City*. London: Anthem Press, 2014.

Corrigan, Gina. "Hemp and Ramie in Southwest China." *Hali* 113 (2000), 80–83.

Crawfurd, John. *Journal of an Embassy from the Governor-General of India to the Courts of Siam and Cochin China: Exhibiting a View of the Actual State of those Kingdoms* (Second edition). London: H. Colburn and R. Bentley, 1830.

Crevost, Charles, and A. Pételot. *Catalogue des produits de l'Indochine, Tome VI: Tanins et tinctoriaux*. Hà Nội: Impremerie d'Extrême Orient, 1941.

Cuisinier, Jeanne. *Les Mường: Géographie humaine et sociologie*. Paris: Institut d'Ethnologie, 1946.

Dam Bo (Jacques Dournes). "Les populations Montagnards de Sud-Indochine." *France-Asia*, Special Issue 5 (1950), 931–1208.

Đặng Nghiêm Vạn. "Dân tộc Xơ Đăng." In Ma Khánh Bằng (ed.), *Các dân tộc ít người ở Việt Nam (Các Tỉnh Phía Nam)*, 94–107. Hà Nội: Nhà Xuất Bản Khoa Học Xã Hội, 1984.

_____. *The Sedang of Viet Nam*. Hà Nội: National Centre for Social Sciences and Humanities of Viet Nam, 1998.

Delignon, L. "La production de la Soie en Indochine." *Revue de botanique appliquée et d'agriculture coloniale*, 3rd year, bulletin no. 24 (1923), 530–537.

Delvert, J. *Le paysan Cambodgien*. Paris: Mouton, 1961.

Deng, Kent Gang. *The Premodern Chinese Economy: Structural Equilibrium and Capitalist Sterility*. London: Routledge, 1999.

Diệp Đình Hoa. "Dân tộc Xtiêng" In Ma Khánh Bằng (ed.), *Các dân tộc ít người ở Việt Nam (Các Tỉnh Phía Nam)*, 142–52. Hà Nội: Nhà Xuất Bản Khoa Học Xã Hội, 1984).

Diep Trung Binh. *Patterns on Textiles of the Ethnic Groups in Northeast Vietnam*. Hà Nội: Cultures Nationalities Publishing House, 1997.

Diguet, E. *Les Montagnards du Tonkin*. Paris: Augustin Challamel, 1908.

Doré, Amphay. "Le royaume des Ai Lao, une perspective geo-politique." *Inter-Mondes Revue de l'Université Ramkhamhaeng* 1, 2 (1990), 230–236.

Dournes, Jacques. "Le vêtement chez le Jorai." *Objets et Mondes*, 3, 2 (1963), 99–114.

Dray, Adam. "The Cham: Descendants of Ancient Rulers of South China Sea Watch Maritime Dispute from Sidelines." Online at: news.nationalgeographic.com, 18 June 2014.

Eberhard, Wolfram. *Kultur und Siedlung der Randvölker Chinas*. Leiden: E.J. Brill, 1942.

_____. *The Local Cultures of South and East Asia*. Leiden: E.J. Brill, 1968.

Edmondson, Jerold A. "Kra or Kadai Languages." In Anthony Diller, Jerold A. Edmondson, and Yongxian Luo (eds.), *The Tai-Kadai Languages*, 653–672. New York: Routledge, 2008.

_____, and K.J. Gregerson. "Four Languages of the Vietnam-China Borderlands." In K.L. Adams and T.J. Hudak (eds.), *Papers from the Sixth Annual Meeting of the Southeast Asian Linguistics Society*, 101–133. Tempe: Arizona State University, Program for Southeast Asian Studies, 2001.

Elmore, Mick. "Ao Dai Enjoys A Renaissance Among Women: In Vietnam, A Return to Femininity." *New York Times*, September 17, 1997.

Fall, Bernard B. *The Two Viet-Nams: A Political and Military Analysis: Second Revised Edition*. New York: Frederick A. Praeger, 1967.

Fontaine, Henri. "Nouvelles Récoltes d'objets préhistoriques." *Bulletin de la Société des Études Indochinoises*, 50, 1 (1975), 75–107.

Forest Inventory and Planning Institute. *Vietnam Forest Trees*. Hanoi: Agricultural Publishing House, 1996.

Girard, Henry. *Les Tribus Sauvages du Haut-Tonkin, Mans et Méos: Notes Anthropometriques et Ethnographiques*. Paris: Imprimerie Nationale, 1904.

Girardot, N.J. *Myth and Meaning in Early Taoism: The Theme of Chaos (hun-tun)*. Berkeley: University of California Press, 1988.

Gittinger, Mattiebelle, and H. Leedom Lefferts, Jr. *Textiles and the Tai Experience in Southeast Asia*. Washington, D.C.: The Textile Museum, 1992.

Gourdon, Henri. *L'Indochine*. Paris: Larousse, 1931.

Grant, Anthony P. "The Effects of Intimate Multidirectional Linguistic Contact in Chamic." In Anthony Grant and Paul Sidwell (eds.), *Chamic and Beyond: Studies in Mainland Austronesian Languages*, 37–100. Canberra: Pacific Linguistics, Research School of Pacific and Asian Studies, Australian National University, 2005.

References

_____, and Paul Sidwell (eds.). *Chamic and Beyond: Studies in Mainland Austronesian Languages.* Canberra: Research School of Pacific and Asian Studies, Australian National University, 2005.

Green, Gillian. "Textiles at the Khmer Court, Angkor: Origins, Innovations and Continuities." In Jane Purananda (ed.), *Through the Thread of Time: Southeast Asian Textiles,* 10–25. Bangkok: River Books, 2004.

Gregerson, Kenneth J., and Jerold A. Edmonson. "Some Puzzles in Cao Lan." In S. Burusphat (ed.), *The International Conference on Tai Studies,* 151–164. Bangkok: Institute of Language and Culture for Rural Development, Mahidol University, 1998.

Gu Yanwu. *Tian xia jun guo li bing shu* ("On benefits and faults of the empire's local administration"). Shunan: Tong hua shu wu, Guangxu 5, 1879 (reprinted, Shanghai: Shanghai gu ji chu ban she, 2002).

Guillon, Emmanuel. *Cham Art: Treasures from the Dà Nang Museum, Vietnam.* London: Thames & Hudson, 2001.

Hà Văn Tấn. "Về những cái gọi là bàn đạp trong các di chỉ văn hóa Phùng Nguyên." In *Những phát hiện mới về Khảo cổ học năm 1979,* 80–1. Hà Nội: Viện Khảo cổ học, 1980.

Hickey, Gerald Cannon. *Shattered World: Adaptation and Survival among Vietnam's Highland Peoples during the Vietnam War.* Philadelphia: University of Pennsylvania Press, 1993.

_____. *Sons of the Mountains: Ethnohistory of the Vietnamese Central Highlands to 1954.* New Haven, CT: Yale University Press, 1982.

Higham, Charles. *The Bronze Age of Southeast Asia.* Cambridge: Cambridge University Press, 1996.

Hirth, Friedrich. *The Ancient History of China to the End of the Chóu Dynasty.* Freeport, NY: Books for Libraries, 1969 (originally published in 1908).

Holbé, T.V. "Quelques mots sur le préhistorique Indochinois à propos des objets receuillis par M. de Pray." *Bulletin des Amis du Vert Hué,* 2ème Année 43 (1915).

Howard, Michael C. "The Cham of Vietnam and Their Textiles." *Arts of Asia,* 35, 2 (2005), 123–136.

_____. "Cultural Revival and Community Development in Ta Van Commune, Sa Pa District, Vietnam." In David B. Wangsgard (ed.), *Culture and Development in Southeast Asia,* 125–135. Bangkok: White Lotus Press, 2008.

_____. *From Dashes to Dragons: The Ikat-Patterned Textiles of Southeast Asia.* Bangkok: White Lotus Press, 2010.

_____. "Introduction." In M.C. Howard (ed.), *Bark-cloth in Southeast Asia,* 1–64. Bangkok: White Lotus Press, 2006.

_____. "The Peoples of French Indochina." in *The Art of Jean Despujols and the Peoples of Indo-china.* Published online (2014) at http://meadowsfriends.org/about-despujols/.

_____. "Religious and Status-marking Functions of Textiles among the Tai Peoples of Vietnam." In Jane Purananda (ed.), *The Secrets of Southeast Asian Textiles: Myth, Status and the Supernatural,* 194–215. Bangkok: River Books and the James H.W. Thompson Foundation, 2007.

_____. "Searching for the Identity of the Bird on the Dong Son Drums." *Arts of Asia,* 34, 2 (2004), 136–142.

_____. "Southeast Asian Textiles as Art." In Michael C. Howard (ed.), *Textile Traditions in Contemporary Southeast Asia,* 13–30. Bangkok: White Lotus Press, 2012.

_____. *Textiles of the Highland Peoples of Burma, Volume II: The Northern Mon-Khmer, Rawang, Upland Burmish, Lolo, Karen, Tai, and Hmong-Mien-speaking Groups.* Bangkok: White Lotus Press, 2005.

_____. *Transnationalism in Ancient and Medieval Societies: The Role of Cross-Border Trade and Travel.* Jefferson, NC: McFarland, 2012.

_____. *A World Between the Warps: Southeast Asia's Supplementary Warp Textiles.* Bangkok: White Lotus Press, 2008.

_____ (editor). *Bark-cloth in Southeast Asia.* Bangkok: White Lotus Press, 2006.

_____, and Kim B. Howard. *Textiles of the Central Highlands Vietnam.* Bangkok: White Lots Press, 2002.

_____, and Kim B. Howard. *Textiles of the Daic Peoples of Vietnam.* Bangkok: White Lotus Press, 2002.

_____, and Kim B. Howard *Textiles of the Highlands Peoples of Vietnam: Mon-Khmer, Hmong-Mien, and Tibeto-Burman.* Bangkok: White Lotus Press, 2002.

_____, and Kim B. Howard. "Textiles of the Katuic-speaking Peoples of Central Vietnam." *Arts of Asia* 30, 3 (2000), 131–138.

Huard, Paul, and A. Maurice. "Les Mnong du plateau central Indochinois." *Institut Indochinois pour l'Etude de l'Homme, Bulletins et Travaux* 2 (1939), 27–148.

References

Hudack, Thomas John. *William J. Gidney's Comparative Tai Sourcebook*. Honolulu: University of Hawai'i Press, 2008.

Hy Van Luong. "Wealth, Power, and Inequality: Global Market, the State, and Local Sociocultural Dynamics." In Hy Van Luong (ed.), *Postwar Vietnam: Dynamics of a Transforming Society*, 81–106. Oxford: Rowman and Littlefield, 2003.

Jenks, Robert D. *Insurgency and Social Disorder in Guizhou: The "Miao" Rebellion, 1854–1873*. Honolulu: University of Hawaii Press, 1994.

Kelly, Liam C. *Vietnam through the Eyes of a Chinese Abbot: Dashan's Haiwai Jishi (1694–95)*. MA thesis, University of Hawaii at Manoa, 1996.

Kuhn, Dieter, and Joseph Needham. *Science and Civilisation in China: Volume 5, Chemistry and Chemical Technology, Part 9, Textile Technology: Spinning and Reeling*. Cambridge: Cambridge University Press, 1988.

Laufer, Berthold. *Sino-Iranica: Chinese Contributions to the History of Civilization in Ancient Iran, with Special Reference to the History of Cultivated Plants and Products*. Chicago: Field Museum of Natural History, 1919.

Lê Ngọc Thắng. *Nghệ thuật trang phục Thái*. Hà Nội: Văn hóa dân tộc, Trung tâm văn hóa Việt Nam, 1990.

Leshkowich, Ann Marie. "The Ao Dai Goes Global: How International Influences and Female Entrepreneurs have Shaped Vietnam's 'National Costume.'" In S.A. Niessen, A.M. Leshkowich, and C. Jones (eds.), *Re-orienting Fashion: The Globalization of Asian Dress*, 79–116. Oxford: Berg, 2003.

Li, Dawei, Wei Wang, Feng Tian, Wei Liao, and Christopher J. Bae. "The Oldest Bark Cloth Beater in Southern China (Dingmo, Bubing Basin, Guangxi)." *Quaternary International* 30 (2014), 1–6.

Li, Hui, Ying Huang, Laura F. Mustavich, Fan Zhang, Jing-Ze Tan, Ling-E Wang, Ji Qian, Meng-He Gao, and Li Jin. "Y Chromosomes of Prehistoric People along the Yangtze River." *Human Genetics* 122 (2007), 383–388.

Li, Tana. "The Eighteenth-Century Mekong Delta and Its World of Water Frontier." In Nhung Tuyet Tran and Anthony J.S. Reid (eds.), *Viet Nam: Borderless Histories*, 147–162. Madison: University of Wisconsin Press, 2006.

_____. *Nguyễn Cochinchina: Southern Vietnam in the Seventeenth and Eighteenth Centuries*. Cornell University, SEAP Publications, 1998.

Lockhart, Bruce M. "Colonial and Post-Colonial Constructions of 'Champa.'" In Tran Ky Phuong and Bruce Lockhart (eds.), *The Cham of Vietnam: History, Society and Art*, 1–54. Singapore: NUS Press, 2011.

Luce, Gordon H. "The Tan and Ngai-lao." *Journal of the Burma Research Society* 14, 2 (1924), 138–205 (reprinted in *Burma Research Society Fiftieth Anniversary Publication No. 2*. Rangoon: Burma Research Society, 1960).

_____ (trans.), and G.P. Oey (ed.). *The Man Shu (Book of the Southern Barbarians)*. Ithaca, NY: Southeast Asia Program, Department of Far Eastern Studies, Cornell University, 1961.

Lương Thanh Sơn. "Yang Prong—Tháp Chăm ở Đăk Lăk." *Tạp chí Dân tộc học* 3 (1991), 28–32.

Luu Hung. "Bark-cloth of the Ethnic Groups of Highland Vietnam." In M.C. Howard (ed.), *Bark-cloth in Southeast Asia*, 107–114. Bangkok: White Lotus Press, 2006.

Ma Huan (J.V.G. Mills, trans). *Ying-yai Shenglan: The Overall Survey of the Ocean's Shores [1433]*. Cambridge: Cambridge University Press, 1970.

Maître, Henri. *Les Jungles Moi: Exploration et histoire des Hinterlands Moi du Cambodge, de la Cocninchine, de l'Annan et du Bas-Lao: Mission Henri Maître (1909–1911) Indochine Sud-Centrale*. Paris: Emile Larose, 1912.

Majumdar, Ramesh Chandra. *Ancient Indian Colonies of the Far East: I: Champa*. Lahore: Punjab Sanskrit Book Depot, 1927.

Maspero, Georges. *The Champa Kingdom: The History of an Extinct Vietnamese Culture*. Bangkok: White Lotus Press, 2002. [French editions, *Le Royaume de Champa*. Leiden: E.J. Brill, 1915; Paris and Brussels: Les Editions Van Oest, 1928.]

McAlister, John T., Jr. "Mountain Minorities and the Viet Minh: A Key to The Indochina War." In Peter Kunstadter (ed.), *Southeast Asian Tribes, Minorities, and Nations, Volume II*, 771–844. Princeton, NJ: Princeton University Press, 1967.

Meacham, William. "Defining the Hundred Yue." *Bulletin of the Indo-Pacific Prehistory Association*, 15 (1996), 93–100.

Mibbett, Ian, and David Chandler. *The Khmers*. Oxford: Blackwell, 1995.

References

Miksic, John N. "The Beginning of Trade in Ancient Southeast Asia: The Role of Oc Eo and the Lower Mekong River." In James C. Khoo (ed.), *Art & Archaeology of Fu Nan: Pre-Khmer Kingdom of the Lower Mekong Valley*, 2–33. Bangkok: Orchid Press, 2003.

Mole, Robert L. *The Montagnards of South Vietnam: A Study of Nine Tribes*. Rutland, VT: Tuttle, 1970.

Morimoto, Kikuo. *Research Report: Silk Production and Marketing in Cambodia*. Phnom Penh: Institute for Khmer Traditional Textiles and UNESCO, 1995.

Moussay, Gerard. "Cham Weaving in Vietnam." In Jane Purananda (ed.), *Through the Thread of Time: Southeast Asian Textiles*, 152–161. Bangkok: River Books, 2004.

Nationalities Affairs Commission of Guizhou Province. *Ethnic Costume from Guizhou: Clothing Designs and Decorations from Minority Ethnic Groups in Southwest China*. Beijing: Foreign Languages Press, 1987.

Naval Intelligence Unit. *Indo-China*. Cambridge, UK: University of Cambridge Press, 1943.

Ngô Đức Thịnh. "Kiến trúc vật trang trí dân gian." In Ngô Đức Thịnh (ed.), *Văn hóa dân gian M'nông*, 114–130. Buôn Ma Thuột: Sở Văn hóa-Thông tin Đắk Lắk, 1995.

_____. *Trang phục cổ truyền các dân tộc Việt Nam*. Hà Nội: Nhà xuất bản Văn hoá dân tộc, 1994.

Nguyễn Anh Ngọc. "Dân tộc Lô Lô." In Bùi Văn Cán (ed.), *Các dân tộc ít người ở Việt Nam (Các Tỉnh Phía Bắc)*, 375–82. Hà Nội: Nhà Xuất Bản Khoa Học Xã Hội, 1978.

Nguyễn Khắc Su, Minh Huyen Pham, and Tong Trung Tin. "Northern Vietnam from the Neolithic to the Han Period." In I. Glover and P. Bellwood (eds.), *Southeast Asia from Prehistory to History*, 177–201. London: Routledge Curzon, 2004.

Nguyễn Khắc Tụng. "Dân tộc Dao." In Bùi Văn Cán (ed.), *Các dân tộc ít người ở Việt Nam (Các tỉnh phía bắc)*, 311–336. Hà Nội: Nhà xuất bản Khoa học xã hội, 1978.

Nguyễn, Thừa Hỷ. *Economic History of Hanoi in the 17th, 18th and 19th Centuries*. Hà Nội: National Political Publishing House, 2002.

Nguyễn Văn Huy. "Dân tộc Cống." In Bùi Văn Cán (ed.), *Các dân tộc ít người ở Việt Nam (Các Tỉnh Phía Bắc)*, 363–368 Hà Nội: Nhà Xuất Bản Khoa Học Xã Hội, 1978.

_____. "Dân tộc Hà Nhì." In Bùi Văn Cán (ed.), *Các dân tộc ít người ở Việt Nam (Các Tỉnh Phía Bắc)*, 342–353. Hà Nội: Nhà Xuất Bản Khoa Học Xã Hội, 1978.

_____. "Dân tộc Rơ Măm." In Ma Khánh Bằng (ed.), *Các dân tộc ít người ở Việt Nam (Các Tỉnh Phía Nam)*, 213–216. Hà Nội: Nhà Xuất Bản Khoa Học Xã Hội, 1984.

_____. "Dân tộc Si La." In Bùi Văn Cán (ed.), *Các dân tộc ít người ở Việt Nam (Các Tỉnh Phía Bắc)*, 369–374. Hà Nội: Nhà Xuất Bản Khoa Học Xã Hội, 1978.

Nguyễn Văn Huyên. *The Ancient Civilization of Vietnam*. Hà Nội: Thế Giới Publishers, 1995 (French version: *La civilization Annamite*, Hà Nội: Ecole Française d'Extrême-Orient, 1944).

Nguyễn Xuân Nghĩa and Phan An. "Dân tộc Khơ me." In Ma Khánh Bằng (ed.), *Các dân tộc ít người ở Việt Nam (Các Tỉnh Phía Nam)*, 65–81. Hà Nội: Nhà Xuất Bản Khoa Học Xã Hội, 1984.

Nông Quốc Bình and Michael C. Howard. *Cultural Revival and the Peoples of Ta Van Commune*. Bangkok: White Lotus Press, 2013.

Nordhoff, Sebastian, Harald Hammarström, Robert Forkel, and Martin Haspelmath. "Cao Lan." In *Glottolog*. Leipzig: Max Planck Institute for Evolutionary Anthropology, 2013. Online at: glottolog.org/resource/languoid/id/caol1238.

Nordhoff, Sebastian, Harald Hammarström, Robert Forkel, and Martin Haspelmath. "Kadai." In *Glottolog*. Leipzig: Max Planck Institute for Evolutionary Anthropology, 2013. Online at: glottolog.org/resource/languoid/id/kada1291.

Norman, Jerry, and T.L. Mei. "The Austroasiatics in Ancient South China: Some Lexical Evidence." *Monumenta Serica* 32 (1976), 274–301.

Ostapirat, Weera. "The Hlai Language." In Anthony Diller, Jerold A. Edmondson, and Yongxian Luo (eds.), *The Tai–Kadai Languages*, 623–652. New York: Routledge, 2008.

Parmentier, Henri, and Eugène-Marie Durand. "Le trésor des rois Cham." *Bulletin de l'École française d'Extrême-Orient*, 5 (1905), 1–46.

Patté, Paul. *Hinterland Moï*. Paris: Plon-Nourrit, 1906.

Pelliot, Paul. "Deux itinéraires de Chine en Inde à la fin du VIIIe siècle." *Bulletin de l'École Française d'Extrême Orient* 4 (1904), 131–413.

Peng, Min-Sheng Peng, Jun-Dong He, Hai-Xin Liu, and Ya-Ping Zhang. "Tracing the Legacy of the Early Hainan Islanders—A Perpsective

References

from Mitochondrial DNA." BMC Evolutionary Biology 11 (2011), 46, online at biomedicalcentral.com/1471-2148/11/46.

Phan Ngọc Chiến. "Dân tộc Cơ Ho." In Ma Khánh Bằng (ed.), *Các dân tộc ít người ở Việt Nam (Các Tỉnh Phía Nam)*, 108–109. Hà Nội: Nhà Xuất Bản Khoa Học Xã Hội, 1984.

Phan Xuân Biên and Chu Thái Sơn. "Dân tộc Mạ." In Ma Khánh Bằng (ed.), *Các dân tộc ít người ở Việt Nam (Các Tỉnh Phía Nam)*, 173–287. Hà Nội: Nhà Xuất Bản Khoa Học Xã Hội, 1984.

Pires, Tomé (Armando Cortesão, trans. and ed.). *The Suma Oriental of Tomé Pires: An Account of the East, From the Red Sea to Japan, Written in Malacca and India in 1512–1515, and The Book of Francisco Rodrigues, Rutter of a Voyage in the Red Sea, Nautical Rules, Almanack and Maps, Written and Drawn in the East Before 1515*. London: Hakluyt Society, 1944.

Queguiner, Dr. "Notes sur une peuplade Moi de la Chaine Annamitique Sud: Les Cau S're." *Institut Indochinois pour l'Etude de l'Homme: Bulletins et travaux* 6 (1943), 395–402.

Rambo, A. Terry, and Neil L. Jamieson. "Upland Areas, Ethnic Minorities." In Hy Van Luong (ed.), *Postwar Vietnam: Dynamics of a Transforming Society*, 81–106. Oxford: Rowman and Littlefield, 2003.

Salemink, Oscar. *The Ethnography of Vietnam's Central Highlanders: A Historical Contextualiztion, 1850–1900*. Honolulu: University of Hawai'i Press, 2003.

Salles, André. *Un Mandarin Breton au service du roi de Cochinchine*. Rennes: Les Portes du Large, 2006.

Schafer, Edward H. *The Vermilion Bird: T'ang Images of the South*. Berkeley: University of California Press, 1967.

Scott, James George, and J.P. Hardiman. *Gazateer of Upper Burma and the Shan States, Part 1, Volume 2*. Rangoon: Superintendent of Government Printing and Stationary, 1900.

Shao Wangping. "The Formation of Civilization: The Interaction Sphere of the Longshan Period." In Allan, Sarah (ed.), *The Formation of Chinese Civilization: An Archaeological Perspective*, 85–124. New Haven: Yale University Press, 2005.

Shilian Dashan. *Haiwai jishi* ("Record of Travel Overseas"). Taipei: Guangwen shuju, 1969 (originally published in 1699).

Sidwell, Paul. "Acehnese and the Aceh-Chamic Language Family." In Anthony Grant and Paul Sidwell (eds.), *Chamic and Beyond: Studies in Mainland Austronesian Languages*, 211–231. Canberra: Pacific Linguistics, Research School of Pacific and Asian Studies, Australian National University, 2005.

Smith, Harvey H., et al. *Area Handbook for South Vietnam*. Washington, D.C.: U.S. Government Printing Office, 1967.

Solheim, Wilhelm H., II. "Introduction to Sa-Huynh." *Asian Perspectives*, 3, 2 (1959), 97–108.

_____. "Sa-huỳnh Related Pottery in Southeast Asia." *Asian Perspectives* 3, 2 (1959), 177–188.

Stübel, Hans. *Die Li-Stämme der Insel Hainan: Ein Beitrag zur Volkskunde Südchinas*. Berlin: Klinkhardt & Biermann, 1937.

Thông tấn xã Việt Nam/Vietnam News Agency. *Việt Nam: Hình ảnh cộng đ ng 54 Dân tộc Việt Nam/Vietnam: Image of the Community of 54 Ethnic Groups*. Hà Nội: Nhà Xuất bản Văn hoá dân tộc/Ethnic Cultures Publishing House, 1996.

Thurgood, Graham. *From Ancient Cham to Modern Dialects: Two Thousand Years of Change*. Honolulu: University of Hawai'i Press, 1999.

_____, and Ela Thurgood. "The Tones from Proto-Chamic to Tsat [Hainan Cham]: insights from Zheng 1997 and Summer 2004 Fieldwork." In Anthony Grant and Paul Sidwell (eds.), *Chamic and Beyond: Studies in Mainland Austronesian Languages*, 247–271. Canberra: Pacific Linguistics, Research School of Pacific and Asian Studies, Australian National University, 2005.

Trần Thị Thu Thủy. *Trang phục phụ nữ H'mông Hoa ở Huyện Mù Cang Chải, tỉnh Yên Bái*. MA thesis, Đại học Quốc gia Hà Nội, Trường Đại học Khoa học Xã hội và Nhân văn, 1998.

Trần Văn Chi and Chu Thái Sơn. "Dân tộc Chơ Ro." In Ma Khánh Bằng (ed.), *Các dân tộc ít người ở Việt Nam (Các Tỉnh Phía Nam)*, 205–212. Hà Nội: Nhà Xuất Bản Khoa Học Xã Hội, 1984.

Trịnh Hoài Đức. *Gia Định thành thông chí* (French edition: Louis-Gabriel Aubaret (trans.), *Gia-dinh-Thung-chi: Histoire et description de la basse Cochinchine (pays de Gia-dinh)*. Paris: Imprimerie Impéril, 1863).

Tuấn, Hoàng Anh. *Silk for Silver: Dutch-Vietnamese Relations, 1637–1700*. Leiden: Brill, 2007.

References

Vainke, Shelagh J. *Chinese Silk: A Cultural History*. New Brunswick, NJ: Rutgers University Press, 2004.

Vasavakul, Thaveeporn. "Language Policy and Ethnic Relations in Vietnam." In Michael E. Brown and Sumit Ganguly (eds.), *Fighting Words: Language Policy and Ethnic Relations in Asia*, 211–238. Cambridge, MA: MIT Press, 2003.

Vassal, Gabrielle M. *Three Years in Vietnam (1907–1910): Medicine, Chams and Tribesmen in Nhatrang and Surroundings*. Bangkok: White Lotus Press, 1999 (originally published in French in 1910).

Vi Van An. "Les Pa Then." In Nguyễn Văn Huy (ed.), *Mosaïque Culturelle des Ethnies du Vietnam*, 145–146. Hà Nội: Maison d'édition et d'éducation, 1999.

Vickery, Michael. *Society, Economics, and Politics in Pre-Angkor Cambodia: The 7th-8th Centuries*. Tokyo: The Centre for East Asian Cultural Studies for UNESCO, The Toyo Bunko, 1998.

Vo, Nghia M. *Saigon: A History*. Jefferson, NC: McFarland, 2011.

Vo Si Khai. "The Kingdom of Fu Nan and the Culture of Oc Eo." In James C. Khoo (ed.), *Art & Archaeology of Fu Nan: Pre-Khmer Kingdom of the Lower Mekong Valley*, 35–86. Bangkok: Orchid Press, 2003.

Vollmer, John E. "Archaeological Evidence for Looms from Yunnan." In I. Emery and P. Fiske (eds.), *Looms and Their Products*, 78–89. Washington, D.C.: The Textile Museum, 1979.

Wade, Geoff. "The Polity of Yelang and the Origin of the Name 'China.'" *Sino-Platonic Papers*, No. 188 (2009).

Wang Fushi (chief compiler). *Ethnic Costumes and Clothing Decorations from China*. Chengdu: Sichuan People's Publishing House, 1986.

Wang Gungwu. "The Nanhai Trade: A Study of the Early History of Chinese Trade in the South China Sea." *Journal of the Malayan Branch of the Royal Asiatic Society* 31, 2 (1958), 1–135.

Wang Mingfu and Eric Johnson. *Zhuang Cultural and Linguistic Heritage*. Kunming: The Nationalities Publishing House of Yunnan, 2008.

Wang Ningsheng. "Ancient Ethnic Groups as Represented on Bronzes from Yunnan, China." in S.J. Shennan (ed.), *Archaeological Approaches to Cultural Identity*, 195–206. London: Routledge, 1994.

Wang, Zhongshu. *Han Civilization*. New Haven, CT: Yale University Press, 1982.

Wangsgard, David B. "Culture, Civilization and the Preservation of Ethnic Minority Culture in Vietnam." In David B. Wangsgard (ed.), *Culture and Development in Southeast Asia*, 137–158. Bangkok: White Lotus Press, 2008.

Watson, Burton (trans.). *Records of the Grand Historian by Sima Qian* (Revised edition). New York: Columbia University Press, 1993.

Weinstein, Jodi L. *Empire and Identity in Guizhou: Local Resistance to Qing Expansion*. Seattle: University of Washington Press, 2014.

Wheeler, Charles. "One Region, Two Histories: Cham Precedents in the History of the Hội An Region." In Nhung Tuyet Tran and Anthony J.S. Reid (eds.), *Viet Nam: Borderless Histories*, 163–193. Madison: University of Wisconsin Press, 2006.

White, David Gordon. *Myths of the Dog-Man*. Chicago: University of Chicago Press, 1991.

Wicks, Robert S. *Money, Markets, and Trade in Early Southeast Asia: The Development of Indigenous Monetary Systems to AD 1400*. Ithaca, NY: Cornell University, Southeast Asia Program, 1992.

Wiens, Herold J. *Han Chinese Expansion in South China*. Hamden, CT: The Shoe String Press, 1967.

Wilcox, Wynn. "Transnationalism and Multiethnicity in the Early Nguyen Anh Gia Long Period." In Nhung Tuyet Tran and Anthony J.S. Reid (eds.), *Viet Nam: Borderless Histories*, 194–216. Madison: University of Wisconsin Press, 2006.

Yang Yong. "New Archaeological Discoveries of the Bronze and the Early Iron Age in the Yunnan-Guizhou Plateau and some Related Problems." In Dominik Bonatz, Andreas Reinecke, and Mai Lin Tjoa-Bonatz (eds.), *Crossing Borders: Selected Papers from the 13th International Conference of the European Association of Southeast Asian Archaeologists*, 234–238. Singapore: NUS Press, 2012.

_____. "On the Kele Culture." *Chinese Archaeology* 13, 1 (2013), 186–191.

Yu Ying-shih. *Trade and Expansion in Han China: A Study in the Structure of Sino-Barbarian Economic Relations*. Berkeley: University of California Press, 1967.

Zhou Daguan. *A Record of Cambodia: The Land and Its People*. Chiang Mai: Silkworm Books, 2007.

References

Zhou Xun and Gao Chunming (text), The Chinese Costumes Research Group (editing). *5000 Years of Chinese Costume*. Hong Kong: The Commercial Press, 1984.

Zhou Ying. *The Dawn of the Oriental Civilization: Liangzhu Site and Liangzhu Culture*. Beijing: China Intercontinental Press, 2007.

Chinese Classical Documents

Guang Zhì (aka *Kuang Chih*) ("Extensive Records of Remarkable Things"). Compiled under Guo Yigong (aka Kua I-Kung) about AD 390.

Hòu Hàn Shū ("Book of the Later Han"). Compiled under Fàn Yè, completed around AD 445.

Huáyáng Guó Zhì ("Chronicles of Huayang" or "Records of the Lands South of Mt. Hua"). Compiled under Chang Qu in AD 300s.

Jìn Shū ("Book of Jin"). Compiled under Fáng Xuánlíng, completed in AD 648.

Jiù Táng Shū ("Old Book of Táng"). Compiled under Liu Xu, completed AD 945.

Liáng Shū ("Book of Liáng"). Compiled under Yao Silan, completed in AD 635.

Da Míng hui dian ("The Collected Statutes of the Ming Dynasty"). Compiled by Shen Shixing and Li Dongyang.

Nán Qí Shū (aka *Qí Shū*) ("Book of Southern Qí"). Compiled under Xiāo Zīxiǎn.

Shiji (aka *Tàishǐgōng shū*) ("Records of the Grand Historian"). Compiled under Sīmǎ Qiān, completed around 109 BC. See Watson, *Records of the Grand Historian by Sima Qian*.

Suí Shū ("Book of Suí"). Completed in AD 638.

Tongdian (aka *T'ung-tien, Thung Tien*) ("Comprehensive Institutions" or "Comprehensive Statutes"). Compiled by Dù Yòu between AD 766 and AD 801.

Wénxiàn Tōngkǎo ("Comprehensive Examination of Literature"). Compiled under Mǎ Duānlín, completed in AD 1317.

Xīn Táng Shū ("New Book of Táng"). Compiled under Ōuyáng Xiū, completed in AD 1060.

Ying Song ben Taiping huan yu ji bu que ("Universal Geography of the Taiping Era"). Compiled under Yue Shi in AD 900s (reprinted, Taibei Xian Yonghe Zhen: Wen hai chu ban she, Minguo 52, 1963).

Index

A Lưới 156
Aceh 58
Ái Châu 18, 66; *see also* Thanh Hóa
Ai Lào 13, 14, 27, 32, 37, 38
alternating warp float 59, 60, 150, 152, 153, 154, 158, 159, 160, 161, 162, 164, 165, 166, 167, 169, 170, 171, 173, 174, 176, 178, 179
Amaravati 57
An Giang 13, 78, 80, 146, 148, 149, 151
An Lão 165
Ân Nán 17, 21; *see also* Annam
Angkor 77, 78
Annam 13, 88, 89, 90, 149; *see also* Ân Nán
Antiaris toxicaria 11, 26
áo bà ba 95, 99
áo bào tía 69
áo cánh 95, 97
áo cổ Bà Lai 148
áo dài 2, 5, 9, 22, 52, 73, 94, 95, 97, 98, 99–100
áo dài Bà Nhu 98
áo dài chẽn 96
áo dài chít eo 98
áo dài cổ thuyền 98
áo dài Le Mur 96
áo dài Lê Phổ 96
áo dài mini 98
áo dài Trần Lệ Xuân 98
áo dài với tay raglan 98
áo gấm 86, 93, 94, 100
áo gấm bào 94
áo giao lãnh 72, 73, 87, 90
áo long bào 94
áo long cổn 83
áo ngũ than 87–8, 91, 95
áo tầm vông 148
áo the 87, 94
áo tứ than 87–8, 95, 96, 97
appliqué 36, 39, 43, 44, 104, 114, 118, 126, 132, 133, 140, 141
Arem 25
Artocarpus altilis (breadfruit) 11, 26

asbestos cloth 18
Attapeu 167
Âu Lạc *see* Õu Lò
Âu Việt *see* Õu Yuè
Austro-Asiatic 23, 26
Austro-Tai 9, 13, 23, 26
Austronesian 24
Aya Ru 75; *see also* Phú Yên
Aya Trang 75, 76; *see also* Khanh Hòa

Bã 41
Ba Na 25, 54, 58, 60–1, 84, 160–2, 164, 165
Bà Rịa–Vũng Tàu 57, 178
Ba Tơ 166
Bạ Vì 66
Bắc Giang 121, 131
Bắc Hà 28, 36, 130, 138, 139, 140, 142
Bắc Kạn 45, 105, 107
Bạc Liêu 92, 148
Bắc Ninh 13, 92
Bắc Sơn 133
Bắc Thành 82; *see also* Hà Nội
Bạch Hạc 28
Bahnaric 54, 58, 156
Bai 35, 41
Bai Yuè 26, 27, 41, 48
Baigaur 77
Bali (Balinese) 65
Bàn Vương 132
banana fiber 17, 31
Bảo Đại 91, 93, 94, 96, 98
Bảo Lạc 139, 140
Bảo Lộc 13, 177
Bảo Tró 25
Bảo Yên 119
bark-cloth 2, 11, 23–6, 55, 58, 59, 156, 159, 163, 169
bast fiber 16, 59, 55, 152, 154, 158, 162, 164, 165, 169, 171
Bát Xát 119, 139, 142
Batik 18, 41–3, 44, 45, 46, 125, 126, 127, 128, 134, 135
Bảy Núi 148
beads 134, 157, 158, 162
Bến Nghé 77
Bengal (Bengali) 74, 76

Biêt 168, 169
Bih 60, 154, 155
Bình Định 13, 54, 57, 58, 61, 75, 165
Bình Dương 178
Bình Lư 116, 118, 138, 139
Bình Phước 61, 146, 168, 169, 173, 175, 178
Bình Thuận 54, 58, 75, 146, 149, 156, 178
Black Hà Nhì 139–40
Black Hmông 44, 101, 123, 124, 126
Black La Hủ 142
Black Lô Lô 140, 141–2
Black River 144
Black Tái 37, 53, 104, 109; *see also* Tái Dăm
Blue Hmông 124, 127
Bố Y 17, 41, 44, 119–20; *see also* Bùyī
Bombax ceiba Linn. 11–2, 13; *see also* silk cotton
Bombax malabaricum DC *see* silk cotton
Bơnoong 162
Borneo 24, 25, 54
Bouyi 44, 119
Brao 167; *see also* Brâu
Brâu 167
breadfruit tree *see Artocarpus altilis*
breastcloth 68, 70, 72, 87, 95, 106, 122, 125, 132, 134, 135, 136, 140, 166
broadcloth 86, 87
brocade 13, 47, 51, 54, 56, 69, 94, 98, 100, 122
bronze 2, 9, 23, 28, 29, 30, 31, 33–5, 41, 47, 55, 62, 146
Broussonetia papyrifera (paper mulberry) 11, 26
Bru (Bru-Vân Kiều) 25, 26, 156, 159–60
Bu Đê 173
Bu Đíp (Mnông sub-group) *see* Đíp
Bu Đíp (Xtiêng sub-group) 173
Bu Lach 173

205

Index

Bu Lơ 173, 175
Bu-đang 168
Buddhism 49, 56, 58, 76, 148
Bùlăng 39
Bu Nông see Nông
Buôn Ma Thuột 147
Burma (Burmese) 14, 118; see also Myanmar
Bùyī 41, 42, 44–5, 119; see also Bố Y

Ca Dong 163, 164
Cà Mau 148
Cả River 30
Calico 87
Cambodia 24, 54, 56, 58, 77–8, 80, 90, 146, 149, 150, 151, 167, 168, 173
Cần Thơ 91, 92
Cantonese 89
Cao Bằng 11, 28, 39, 45, 72, 105, 107, 119, 131, 133, 134, 139, 140
CaoLan 121
Catholic 83, 84, 88, 91, 92–3, 94, 101, 146, 147, 173, 177
Cầu Ngang 80
Central Bahnaric 156, 160
Central Highlands 3, 9, 11, 15, 17, 25, 26, 55, 57, 124, 146, 147, 151–79
Central Mnông 168, 171
Central Tai 28, 35, 36, 38, 39, 41, 52, 104, 105, 121
Chaigneau, Jean-Baptiste 83
Chăm 2, 3, 15, 16, 21, 23, 25, 54–65, 73, 75–6, 77, 80–1, 89, 101, 146, 148, 149–51, 155, 156, 176, 177
Chamic 151–2; see also Malayo-Chamic
Chămpa 1, 2, 14, 15, 21, 23, 54–65, 66, 69, 72, 73, 75–6, 77, 80, 148, 155, 156, 165
Champasak 54, 57
Chapa 92, 101; see also Sa Pa
Châu (Xơ Đăng sub-group) 163
Châu Đốc 151
Châu Phong 151
Chè 24
Chéngdū 51, 52
Chéngzōng 78
Chēnlà 14, 56, 77
Chil 61, 168, 177, 178
Chợ Lớn 92, 97
Chơ Ro 178–9
Chrau see Chơ Ro
Christian see Catholic and Protestant
Chủ 27, 46
Chu Ru 55, 58, 59, 151, 155, 156
Chứt 25, 57
Cồ Chồ Hà Nhì 139, 140
Cơ Ho 61, 147, 155, 156, 168, 177–8

Cờ Lao 25, 39, 41, 46, 103; see also Gēlǎo
Cổ Loa 66; see also Phuc An
Cơ Tu 156–9, 162, 164
Cơ-don 177
Cochin China 76, 79, 82, 86, 88, 89, 139
cogon grass (*Imperata cylindrica*) 39, 46
coins 102, 118, 133, 135, 140, 144, 145, 160
Confucianism 50, 69, 84
Cống 139, 145
cotton 1, 13–5, 32, 36, 39, 43, 44, 46, 56, 58, 59, 62, 63, 65, 68, 76, 78, 79, 81, 86, 87, 88, 99, 103, 104, 105, 106, 107, 108, 110, 111, 112, 113, 114, 115, 116, 117, 118, 119, 122, 123, 124, 129, 130, 132, 134, 136, 138, 139–40, 142, 144, 145, 146, 148, 149, 150, 151, 152, 154, 156, 158, 160, 162, 164, 165, 166, 167, 169, 171, 173, 174, 175, 177, 178
Crawfurd, John 85–8
Cù Mông Pass 75
củ nâu see dye yam
Cửa Hàn 85; see also Đà Nẵng
Cuối 121
Cửu Chân 46, 57

Đạ Đồng 175
Đà Lạt 92, 147, 177
Đà Nẵng 57, 85, 92
Đạ Tẻh River 177
Đắc Mế village 167
Dăi 34, 36, 37
Đại Bản 129, 130
Đại Chiêm 58, 62, 75
Đại La 68; see also Thăng Long
Đại Việt 2, 12, 15, 21, 57–8, 66–74, 75, 80, 101, 165
Đắk Hà 161, 164
Đắk Lắk 16, 58, 61, 146, 154, 159, 168, 169, 170, 172
Đắk Nông 146
Đắk Tô 164, 165
Damask 62, 73, 74
Đan Lai 121
Đàng Trong 73
Dao 24, 44, 123, 129–39, 140, 143, 147, 148
Dao Áo Dài 139
Dao Đầu Bằng 138, 139
Dao Đỏ 129, 130, 131–3; see also Red Dao
Dao Lô Gang 130, 131, 133
Dao Quần Chẹt 129, 131, 133–4
Dao Quần Trắng 44, 129, 133, 135, 136–7
Dao Sơn Đầu 133
Dao Thanh Phán 129, 130, 131–3
Dao Thanh Y 129, 135–6

Dao Tiền 42, 129, 134–5
Dao Tuyển 138, 139
Dàxī Culture 42
Dayot, Jean Baptiste Marie 83
Déhóng Dǎi and Jǐngpō Autonomous Prefecture 37
Democratic Republic of Việt Nam (*Việt Nam Dân chủ Cộng hòa*) 96–7, 102
Đèo Văn Trị 111
Di Linh Plateau 177
Diǎn 23, 32, 33–5, 40, 41
Diǎn Yuè 32
Điện Bàn 73
Điện Biên 108, 109, 116, 118, 123, 127, 142
Đinh Bộ Lĩnh 66, 67
Định River 166
Dioscorea cirrhosa Lour. 19, 107; see also dye yam
Diospyros mollis 13, 18, 31, 78
Diospyros mun A. Chev. ex Lecomte 78
Đíp 168
Đổi Mới 99, 102, 147
Doméa 74
Đơn Dương 57, 156
Dòng 41
Đồng Nai (province) 25, 55, 57, 77, 146, 175, 178
Đồng Nai River 57, 169, 171, 175
Đồng Sơn Culture 20, 23, 28, 29, 30, 31, 32, 33, 46, 55, 61
Đồng Văn 104, 140
Dragon 52, 63, 71, 83, 94, 107, 113, 114, 122, 135
Dūnhuáng 42
Dự Tâm 80
Dutch 74
Duy Tân 94
dye (dyes) 2, 18–9, 31, 73, 103, 105, 107, 110, 115, 130, 142, 151, 152, 169
dye yam (*Dioscorea cirrhosa* Lour.) 19, 31, 107, 110

Ê Đê 10, 16, 25, 55, 58, 59–60, 61, 147, 151, 154–5, 160, 162, 168, 169, 170, 171
Ê Đê Kpă see Kpă
Early Lê Dynasty 66
Eastern Chăm 146, 149, 150
Eastern Hàn Dynasty 47, 51, 52
Eastern Jìn Dynasty 49
Eastern Mnông 168, 169, 171
École supérieure des beaux-arts de l'Indochine 95–6
embroidery 36, 39, 40, 43, 44, 46, 70, 83, 86, 104, 113, 114, 115, 118, 120, 123, 126, 127, 130, 132, 133, 134, 135, 136, 137, 138, 141, 142, 143, 144, 153, 159
English 74, 82, 87

Index

Faifo 15, 83; *see also* Hội An
Felt 171
Fibraurea tinctoria Lour. 19
Ficus 11, 26
Filatures 13
Five Dynasties and Ten Kingdoms Period 70
Flowery Hmông 36, 43, 44, 124, 125–6, 139
Flowery Lô Lô 140, 141–2
France (French) 1, 2, 9, 12, 13, 15, 16, 21–2, 66, 82, 83, 88–96, 97, 98, 101–2, 105, 122, 124, 130, 132, 146–7, 148, 152, 156, 159, 162, 165, 167, 169, 173, 175, 177
French Indochina 1, 88, 89, 93
Fù Nán 14, 56, 57, 58, 61, 77, 175
Fújiàn 17, 26, 27, 69, 89

gấm 13, 69
Gâm River 128
Gānsù 51
Gaozu 46, 53, 68
Gar 61, 168, 169, 170, 171
Garuda 65
gauze 76, 83, 84, 86, 115
Gēlǎo 39, 41, 42, 46–7; *see also* Cờ Lao
Gia Lai 58, 146, 152, 153, 160
Gia Long 82–3; *see also* Nguyễn Phúc Ánh
Gia Rai 10, 17, 55, 58, 59–60, 61, 85, 151, 152–4, 160, 162
Giao Chỉ 17, 46, 47, 48
Giáy 44, 119–20, 140, 142
Giẻ 162
Giẻ Triêng 162–3
Gò Công 15
Gold 56, 63, 70, 71, 75, 94, 162
Gossypium arboretum 14, 105, 110
Gossypium barbadense 14
Gossypium herbaceum 105
Gouding 28, 32, 38, 40
grey heron (*Ardea cinera*) 28, 114
Guǎngdōng 14, 16, 17, 24, 26, 28, 44, 49, 121
Guangfulin 31
Guǎngxī 14, 16, 17, 23, 26, 27, 28, 32, 44, 45, 46, 47, 49, 70, 121
Guǎngzhōu 14, 15, 46, 49, 58, 87
Guìzhōu 2, 18, 23, 28, 32, 35, 36, 38, 39, 40–6, 88, 105, 119, 128

Hà Giang 17, 24, 25, 34, 38, 39, 40, 43, 44, 45, 46, 103, 104, 106, 107, 119, 123, 124, 128, 135, 140, 142
Hà Lăng 160, 163, 164, 165
Hạ Long 24, 25

Hà Nì (Hāní) 3 5 139–40, 145
Hà Nội 49, 66, 68, 72, 82, 88, 91, 92, 93, 95
Hà Tây 13
Hà Tĩnh 46, 54
Hải Dương 13, 66
Hải Phòng 74, 91, 92
Hải Vân Pass 57, 73
Hǎinán Island 9, 10, 14, 17, 25, 29, 30, 31, 49, 58
Hǎinánese 89
Hak-kà 89
Hàn (people) 21, 49, 121
Hàn Dynasty 17, 21, 32, 33, 38, 41, 47, 48, 50, 51, 52, 56, 57, 70
Haroi *see* Hroi
Hậu Giang 148
hemp (*Cannabis sativa*) 2, 16–7, 18, 39, 43, 46, 49, 102–3, 121, 124, 125, 127, 135, 160, 164, 166
Hindu (Hinduism, Hindu-ized, Hindus) 56, 58, 62, 65, 149
Hipwrapper (hipcloth, *xiêm, jin xianguan*) 51, 84, 115–6
Hmông 3, 10, 17, 34, 35, 36, 41, 42, 43, 101, 102–3, 123–8, 143, 145, 147, 148
Hmong-Mien 24, 32, 38, 103, 123–39
Họ 121
Hồ Chí Minh 97
Hồ Chí Minh City 77, 149
Hồ Dynasty 121
Hồ Hán Thương 70
Hồ Quý Ly 69, 70
Hoa 119
Hòa An 105
Hòa Bình 102, 108, 109, 115, 121, 134
Hoa Lư 58, 66, 67
Hoabinhian Culture 23
Hoàng Phủ Thiếu Hoa 12
Hội An 15, 58, 73, 74, 76, 83; *see also* Faifo
Hokkien 89
Hónghé Hāní and Yí Autonomous Prefecture 37
Hrê (people) 17, 61, 165–7
Hrê River 166
Hroi 54, 55, 58, 59, 60–1, 76, 151
Huaphanh 116
Húběi 42
Huế 73, 82, 88, 89, 91, 92, 93
Húnán 16, 38, 121, 128
Hundred Yuè *see* Bai Yuè
Hùng Định Vương 12
Hùng kings 12, 27
Hướng Hóa 156, 159

Ikat 30, 31, 32, 59, 60, 81, 110, 113, 114, 117, 118, 150, 151, 155, 160, 161, 162, 178

India 2, 14, 19, 38, 51, 56, 58, 62, 78, 79, 85
Indigo 18, 160
Indigofera tinctoria L. 18
Indrapura 57, 58, 62, 73
Islam 80, 149
Iu Mien 128, 129, 132, 135

jackfruit tree (*Artocarpus heterophyllus* Lam.) 19
jade 47
Japan (Japanese) 13, 16, 54, 72, 73, 74, 122
Jarai *see* Gia Rai
Jiāngchéng Hāní and Yí Autonomous County 37
Jiāozhǐ *see* Giao Chỉ
Jīgōngshān 41
Jìn Dynasty 49, 51, 52, 70
Jīnpíng Miáo Yáo and Dǎi Autonomous County 37
Jiuzhen *see* Cửu Chân
Job's tears (*Coix lacryma-jobi*) 142, 144, 153, 160, 164, 170
jute 164

Kaco' 167
Kadai 20, 23, 24, 25, 26, 31, 39, 41, 46, 103–4
Kam-Sui 26, 41
Kambujadesa *see* Khmer Empire
Kampong Cham 77
kapok 2, 12, 13, 15, 18, 31, 36, 38, 39, 62, 76, 78, 79; *see also* silk cotton
Karen (people) 14, 35
Kate Festival 156
Katu *see* Cơ Tu
Katuic 54, 121, 156
Kauthara 57, 75, 80
Kele 41
Kẹo 121
Khải Định 94
khăn đóng 87, 93, 94, 100
Kháng 20, 121, 123
Khánh Hòa 25, 57, 58
Khmer 54, 73, 76–80, 89, 101, 146, 148, 171, 173, 177
Khmer Empire 21, 77, 78, 79, 80
Khmer Krôm (*Khơ Me Crộm*) 21, 77, 79, 148
Khmu 122; *see also* Khơ Mú
Khổ Bạch 129, 135
Khơ Mú 121, 122
Khu Liên 57
Khúc Thừa Dụ 66
Kiên Giang 148
Kim Mun 129, 135, 137
Kinh 3, 20, 21, 22, 28, 49, 58, 66, 68, 70, 73, 75, 80, 89, 90–6, 97, 99, 100, 101, 109, 121, 122, 147, 148, 149, 156, 158, 159, 162, 165, 166, 167, 169, 171, 173, 177

207

Index

Kompong Krabei 77
Kon Plông 164
Kon Tum 24, 25, 58, 61, 84, 92, 146, 148, 152, 160, 162, 163, 164, 165, 167
Kpă 16, 147, 154, 155
Kra-Dai 103; *see also* Kadai
Krế River 166
Krông Ana 155
Krông Bông 16, 61, 154
Krông Pắk 159
Krung 175
Kuenh 61, 168
Kỳ Sơn 116

La Chí 25, 39, 40, 103–4; *see also* Laji
La Ha 25, 103, 104
La Hủ (Lāhù) 35, 139, 142
La Mi Hà Nhì 139, 140
La Qua *see* Pu Péo
lac (*Kerria chinensis*) 18, 31, 107, 151
Lạc Việt *see* Lò Yuè
Lạch *see* Lạt
Lai Châu 37, 110, 111, 116, 119, 123, 127, 131, 133, 137, 138, 139, 142, 144, 145
Laji 39; *see also* La Chí
Lắk Lake 155, 169
Lâm Đồng 13, 58, 61, 146, 156, 168, 169, 173, 175, 177, 178
Làn Tiên 129, 137–9
Land Chênlà 77
Lạng Sơn 28, 39, 45, 47, 72, 91, 92, 105, 107, 133, 135, 136
Làng Vạc 30
Lào (people) 28, 116–8, 146, 156, 158, 159, 162, 163, 165, 167
Lào Cai 28, 30–1, 35, 36, 39, 43, 101, 104, 105, 106, 119, 120, 123, 124, 125, 126, 127, 139, 130, 138, 140
Lào Khrang 116, 117
Laos 3, 24, 54, 57, 77, 90, 110, 116, 117, 118, 121, 122, 123, 139, 145, 156, 159, 162, 163, 164, 165, 167
Lạt 147, 177, 178
Later Lê Dynasty 71, 72, 74, 101
Lavae 167; *see also* Brâu
Lê Dụ Tông 72
Lê Dynasty *see* Early Lê Dynasty and Later Lê Dynasty
Lê Hiến Tông 71
Lê Hoàn 58, 66, 68
Lê Huyền Tông 72
Lê Lợi *see* Lê Thái Tổ
Le Mur *see* Nguyễn Cát Tường
Lê Phổ 96
Lê Thái Tổ 70, 71
Lê Thái Tông 71
Lê Thần Tông 72
Lê Thánh Tông 71, 75

Le village 167
Lí (people) 9, 10, 25, 26, 29, 30, 32
Liáng Dynasty *see* Southern Liáng Dynasty
Liángzhǔ Culture 26–7
Liáo Dynasty 70
Liên River 166
Lin Yi 57
Lĩng Nán 16, 49
Lò clan 12, 27, 28; *see also* Lò Yuè
Lô Lô 33, 34, 35, 38, 139, 140–1, 143; *see also* Yí
Lô River 14
Lò Yuè 12, 27, 28, 29, 31, 37, 48, 105, 109, 112, 121
loincloth 26, 30, 32, 33, 48, 56, 60, 68, 76, 152, 154, 156, 158, 159, 160, 162, 163, 164, 166, 167, 169, 170–1, 174, 176, 177
Long Biên 49
loofah 135
loom 9–11, 16, 32, 60, 64–5, 78, 81, 105, 107, 110, 122, 123, 124, 129, 149, 150, 151, 152–3, 158, 160, 163, 164, 166, 169, 173, 175, 158
Lự (Lü) 28, 37–8, 116, 117, 118–9, 185
Lung Leng 25
Lương Hòa 80
Lý Dynasty 68–9
Lý Hà 121
Lý Nam Đế 49
Lý Thái Tổ 68–9
Lý Thái Tông 69
Lý Thánh Tông 69

Mạ 61, 156, 175–7
Mã Liêng 25
Mã River 116
Mã Yuán 47, 48
Mạc Đăng Dung 71
Mạc Dynasty 71–2, 74
Madagascar 24
Mai Pha 24, 25
Mak 41
Malay (Malays) 14, 54, 80, 81, 150, 151
Malay Peninsula 24, 58, 80
Malayo-Chamic 54–5, 58, 65, 78, 148
Malayo-Polynesian 9, 10, 23, 24, 25, 54, 55, 57, 146, 148, 151–6
Malaysia 24, 54
Màng 121, 123
Mao suit 97
Máo Zédōng 97
Maonán 41
Marsdenua tinctoria R. Brown 18
Mẫu Sơn Mountain 133
May 25

Mdhur 155
Mekong Delta (*Đồng bằng Sông Cửu Long*) 15, 54, 56, 76–81, 93, 147, 148
Mekong River 15, 32, 54, 57, 77, 121
Mèo Vạc 34, 140
Mĩ clan 27
Miáo Rebellions 41
Mienic 24, 44, 139
Mǐn Yuè 26, 47
Míng (Hàn emperor) 50
Míng Dynasty 41, 70, 71, 73, 74, 75, 139
Minh Long 166
Minh Mạng 84–5, 87
Mnông 61, 155, 167–73, 176, 177, 178
Mnông-Xtiêng 168, 169
Mơ Nâm 163, 164, 165
Mògāo caves 42
Mọn 121
Mon-Khmer 9, 20, 21, 23, 24, 25, 26, 32, 33, 35, 38, 49–50, 54, 55–6, 57, 58, 77, 103, 121–3, 146, 148, 152, 156–79
Mongol 69, 70
Moraceae family (trees) 11, 26
Morinda umbellata L. 18
Mother Weaver 163
Mù Cang Chải 126
Muang Ai 27
Muji 35
Mùlǎo 41
mulberry fruit (*Morus nigra* L.) 18
Mường 20, 70, 102, 121–2
Mường Khương 119, 120, 138, 139, 140, 142
Mường Tè 139, 142, 144, 145
Mường Thanh 37
Mường Vạt 113, 114, 115
Muslims 80, 81, 149
Mỹ Nghiệp 59, 63, 65, 149
Mỹ Tho 91, 92
Myanmar 14, 27, 34, 35, 51, 118, 121; *see also* Burma

Nam Bình 28
Nam Cường 28, 41
Nam Định 13, 15, 69, 91, 92, 97
Nam Phương 94; *see also* Nguyễn Hữu Thị Lan
Nam Việt *see* Nán Yuè
Nán Chào 33, 35, 36, 38, 109, 139
Nán Man 32
Nán Yuè 14, 17, 21, 23, 26, 30, 31, 38, 40, 46–8, 49
Nán Zong 32, 38
Nanlong Rebellion 41, 44, 88
New Economic Zones 147
Ngăn (Mạ sub-group) 175
Ngạn (Tày sub-group) 105
Ngang Pass 54, 57, 72

208

Nghệ An 20, 27, 29, 30, 46, 108, 109, 114, 116, 121, 122, 123, 124, 134
Ngô Đình Diệm 93, 98
Ngô Đình Khả 93
Ngô Đình Nhu 98
Ngô Đình Thục 93
Ngô Quyền 66, 68
Ngọc Hồi 167
Ngọc Linh Mountain 162, 163
Nguyễn Cát Tường 96
Nguyễn Dynasty 82–9, 94, 96, 101, 146, 148, 149, 156, 165, 173
Nguyễn Hoàng 73
Nguyễn Hữu Bài 93
Nguyễn Hữu Thị Lan, Marie-Thérèse 93, 94; *see also* Nam Phương
Nguyễn lords 70, 71, 72, 73–4, 75, 76, 77, 80, 146, 148, 165, 177
Nguyễn Phúc Ánh (Gia Long) 73, 82–3
Nguyễn Phúc Đảm *see* Minh Mạng
Nguyễn Phúc Khoát 73
Nguyệt Hòa 80
Nha Trang 92
Ninh Bình 66, 67, 92
Ninh Phước 59, 63, 65, 149
Ninh Thuận 25, 57, 58, 59, 63, 65, 75, 146, 149, 155
Nòng 38; *see also* Nùng
Nốp (Mnông sub-group) 168
Nốp 177, 178
North Bahnaric 61, 156, 160
Northeastern Mon-Khmer 121
Northern Mon-Khmer 34, 121
Northern Tai 35, 41, 44, 105, 121
Northern Wèi Dynasty 51, 52
Nùng 10, 18, 28, 30, 31, 38, 45, 101, 107–8, 119, 129, 135, 147
Nùng An 11, 107, 108
Nùng Cháo 107
Nùng Dín 45, 46, 107, 108
Nùng Giang 108
Nùng Hua Lài 107, 108
Nùng Inh 107
Nùng Lòi 108
Nùng Phàn Slình 107, 108

Ô Châu 73
Ơ Đu 121, 123
Óc Eo 56
Ōu Lò 28, 29, 41, 46, 105
Ōu Yuè 28, 30, 31, 38, 109; *see also* Tây Âu
Oudon 77

Pa Cô 157, 158
Pa Dí 105, 106, 107
Pà Thẻn 10, 128–9, 133
Pai I 33

Pai Man 33
Palawan 55
Panduranga 57, 75, 146, 149
Panrang *see* Phan Rang
Pānyú 46, 47
Pearl River Delta 24
Persicaria tinctoria (Aiton) Apach 18, 31
Phạm Văn Đồng 97
Phan Hu 135
Phan Rang 75
Phén 105, 107
Philippines 24
Phong Thổ 116, 133, 137, 138, 139
Phôngsali 118
Phù Lá 36, 139, 142–3
Phù Lá Hán 142–3
Phù Lá Lão *see* Xá Phó
Phú Lộc 156
Phú Phong 13
Phu Tai 159, 160
Phú Thọ 27, 131
Phú Xuân 73; *see also* Huế
Phú Yên 54, 57, 58, 59, 75, 76, 155
Phuc An 28
Phunoi 145
Phước Hà 155
Pigneau, Mgr. Pierre Joseph Georges 82
plangi 150
Po inu Nugar 155
Poi Loi 168
Prâng 168
Preh 168, 171, 172
Prey Nokor 77
Protestant 147, 177
Pu Péo 25, 39040, 103, 104; *see also* Qabiao
Puymanel, Olivier de 83

Qabiao 39; *see also* Pu Péo
Qiangshanyang 26
Qín Dynasty 28, 32, 46, 50, 51, 52
Qín Shǐhuáng 50
Qīng Dynasty 41, 47, 51, 52
Quản Bạ 119
Quảng Bình 25, 54, 55, 57, 73, 146, 159
Quảng Nam 13, 57, 73, 75, 76, 156, 162, 163, 165
Quảng Ngãi 54, 55, 57, 61, 165, 166
Quảng Ninh 28, 44, 91, 105, 131, 135, 136, 159
Quảng Trị 57, 156
Quy Nhơn 75, 91, 92
Quỳnh Nhai 142

Ra Glai 25, 55, 58, 151, 155–6
Ramadhipati I (aka Ibrahim) 80
ramie [*Boehmeria Nivea* (L.) Gaudich] 16, 76, 155, 166

Ratanakiri 58, 167
Red Dao 123, 130, 131; *see also* Dao Đỏ
Red Hmông 44, 124, 127
Red River 14, 27, 28, 37, 72, 92, 109, 138, 142
Red River Delta 12, 13, 15, 27, 49–50, 70, 73, 74
Rengao *see* Rơngao
Republic of Việt Nam (*Việt Nam Cộng Hòa*) 97, 102
Rhadé *see* Ê Đê
Rìnán *see* Cửu Chân
Rlâm 61, 168, 169
Rơ Măm 167
Rơngao 160, 161
rose apple (*Syzygium jambos*) 18
Rục 25
Rvá River 166

Sa Huỳnh Culture 55–6
Sa Pa 36, 39, 92, 101, 106, 120, 123, 131, 132, 142
Sa Thầy 165, 167
Sách 25
Sài Gòn 77, 88, 91, 92, 97
Salween River 32
Sán Chay 121
Sán Chỉ 121
sappan tree (*Caesalpinia sappan* L. Leguminosae) 18
Sarawak 55
satin 69, 83, 86, 122, 130
Savannakhét 159
Sedang *see* Xơ Đăng
Self-Strengthening/Self-Help literary group (*Tự Lực văn đoàn*) 96
sericulture 13, 80, 148
Sha 38
Shan 14
Shan State 27
Shǎn Yuè 48
Shì Xiè 48
Shǔ 14, 28, 32, 38, 40, 41, 51–2
Shuǐ 41
Si La 139, 144–5
Siam (Siamese) 76, 77, 78, 80, 85, 88, 101, 146, 163, 167
Sìchuān 14, 32, 41, 42, 46
silk 1, 12–3, 14, 15, 16, 18, 26, 31, 38, 39, 45, 46, 47, 50, 51–2, 54, 56, 62, 63, 65, 68, 69, 70, 71, 72, 73–4, 75, 76, 78, 79, 80, 81, 85, 86, 87, 88, 94, 98, 99, 100, 104, 105, 106, 107, 108, 110, 111, 112, 114, 115, 116, 117, 118, 119, 122, 129, 130, 136, 138, 139, 140, 142, 148, 149, 150, 151, 166
silk cotton 11–2, 13, 25, 31, 62, 78; *see also* kapok
silver 5 6 101, 102, 106, 112, 113, 117, 118, 130, 132, 133,

Index

134, 135, 136, 138, 139, 140, 142, 143, 144, 145
Simhapura 57, 58, 62
Sìn Hồ 142
Sinification 21, 28, 46, 48, 49, 70
Sinitic 103
Sípsong Châu Tái 109
Sipsong Panna 37
Śiva (Shiva) 63, 65
Six Dynasties Period 52, 68
Sơn Hà 166
Sơn La 104, 108, 109, 113, 116, 123, 134, 142
Sòng Dynasty 18, 25, 66, 69
Sòngpíng 49
Sốp 177, 178
Southern and Northern Dynasties 49
Southern Bahnaric 61
Southern Hàn Dynasty 66
Southern Liáng Dynasty 49, 56
Southern Mnông 168, 171
Southwestern Tai 32, 32, 35, 36, 39, 52, 105
spotted deer 31
Spring and Autumn Period 51
Sre see Xrê
Sri Boney 75
State of Việt Nam (*Quốc gia Việt Nam*) 96
Striped Hmông 124, 125
Strobilanthes cusia (Nees) Imlay 18
Stung Treng 77, 167
Sui (people) see Shuǐ
Suí Dynasty 49, 52, 53, 54, 62
Sulawesi 24
Sumatra 54, 58, 80
Sun Yat-sen (Sūn Zhōngshān) 97
supplementary warp 30, 32, 60, 65, 110, 113, 122, 149, 150, 155, 178
supplementary weft 30, 31, 32, 44–5, 47, 60, 63, 65, 107, 110, 113, 114, 115, 116, 117, 118, 119, 129, 149, 150, 151, 152, 153, 155, 160, 161, 164, 169, 170–1, 174, 176, 177, 178

Tà Ôi 156–9
Ta Van 120
Tai 1, 3, 10, 12, 14, 15, 20, 24, 25, 26, 27–8, 31, 32, 33, 35, 36, 37, 38, 44, 46, 47, 48, 49, 52, 53, 55, 56, 57, 78, 104–21
Tái Dăm 12, 27, 109, 110, 111–2, 113, 114, 115, 117, 118, 123; *see also* Black Tai
Tái Dón 109, 110, 111–2, 114, 115, 123, 142, 145; *see also* White Tai
Tài Hú Lake 26
Tái Mai Châu 109

Tái Mười 20, 121
Tái Mường 109, 114, 123
Tái Thanh 109, 123
Tai-Kadai 21, 30, 31–2, 103
Tái-Mèo Autonomous Zone 102
Taiwan 24
Tàizōng 53, 68
Talieng 162
Tân Châu 13, 78, 151
Táng Dynasty 13, 14, 15, 16, 18, 21, 41, 42, 49, 53, 54, 66, 68, 70
tapestry weave 117, 118
Tây 10, 16, 18, 28, 30, 31, 38, 39, 44, 45, 49, 101, 102, 105–7, 109, 121, 129, 135, 140, 148
Tây Âu see Ōu Yuè
Tây Bắc Autonomous Zone 102
Tây Đô 69
Tây Nguyên *see* Central Highlands
Tây Ninh 149, 151, 173
Tày Poọng 121
Temür Khan 78
Teochew 89
Thái 3, 12, 20, 28, 29, 30, 31, 37, 44, 102, 108–16, 117, 119, 121, 122, 123, 142, 143, 144, 145, 147, 148
Thái Nguyên 121, 135
Thailand 3, 24, 34, 55, 80, 113, 116, 118, 121
Thăng Bình 73
Thăng Long 13, 68, 72, 74, 82; *see also* Hà Nội
Thanh Hóa 13, 27, 29, 46, 66, 69, 70, 71, 73, 91, 108, 109, 115, 121
Thành Thái 93, 94
Thổ 121
Thu Bồn River 58, 73, 75
Thu Lao 30–1, 38–9, 105, 106, 140, 144
Thừa Thiên–Huế 57, 73, 156, 159
Thuận Nam 155
Thục Phán 28, 29, 46
Tibeto-Burman 14, 32, 34, 35, 38, 41, 103, 139–45
Tiền Giang 15
Tiểu Bản 129
Tịnh Biên 80, 148
Tĩnh Hải 66
Tô 175
Tơ Đrá 163, 164
Tơ-ring 177
Tonggushān 41
Tonkin 13, 15, 74, 88, 89, 90, 92, 93
Tonlé Sap 80
Tourane 92; *see also* Đà Nẵng
Trà Cú 80
Trà Kiệu valley 57
Trà Vinh 80, 148

Trần Dynasty 69, 73
Trần Lệ Xuân 98
Trần Thái Tông 69
Trần Thuận Tông 69
Trần Văn Hữu 96
Tri Tôn 80, 148
Triêng 162
Triệu Đà *see* Zhào Tuó
Triệu Mạt *see* Zhào Mò
Triệu Xīng *see* Zhào Xīng
Trịnh lords 70, 71, 72, 73, 74
tritik 30, 31, 38–9, 108, 141
Trưng sisters 47
Tu Dí 44, 119, 120
Tu Zhuàng 38–9, 140; *see also* Thu Lao
Tuần Giáo 142
Tǔjiā 41
Tương Dương 123
turmeric (*Curcuma longa* L.) 19
Tuyên Quang 106, 121, 128, 131, 133, 135, 139
twill 144

Văn Lang 12, 27, 28
Vannier, Philippe 83
Vạn Phúc 13
Vạn Xuân 49
Ve 16 2 163
Việt *see* Kinh
Việt Bắc Autonomous Zone 102
Vietic 21, 121
Vijaya 57, 58, 73, 75, 76
Vinh 91, 92
Vĩnh Long 93, 148

Wǎ 34
warp float *see* alternating warp float
warp ikat 30, 32, 59, 60, 81, 110, 150, 151, 155, 160, 161, 162, 178
Warring States Period 50, 51
Water Chēnlà 77
Wénshān Zhuàng and Miao Autonomous Prefecture 28, 38, 39, 46, 140
West Bahnaric 156
Western Chăm 146, 149, 150–1
Western Hàn 47, 51
White Hmông 43, 44, 124, 125
White La Hủ 142
White Tái 37, 109, 111; *see also* Táy Dón
Wrightia laevis J.D.Hooker 18, 31
Wǔ (kingdom) 48, 49, 56
Wǔ of Hàn (emperor, aka Wǔdì) 47, 50
wǔxíng (five elements/phases) 52

Xá Phó 35–6, 142–3
Xiàmén 87

Index

xiêm see hipwrapper
Xieng Khouang 116
Xín Mẫn 142
Xinh Mun 20, 121, 123
Xīshuāngbǎnnà *see* Sipsong Panna
Xơ Đăng 17, 24, 160, 162, 163–5, 167
Xơ Teng 163, 164, 165
Xốp 175
Xrê 177, 178
Xtiêng 169, 174–5

Yang (Yang Guang) 53
Yangtze River 23, 42, 49
Yáo 24, 41, 44, 129; *see also* Dao
Yèláng 23, 30, 31, 32, 40–1
Yellow Dragon 52
Yellow Emperor (Huángdì) 52
Yellow La Hủ 142
yếm see breastcloth
Yên Bái 104, 106, 126, 135, 142
Yên Sơn 133
Yí 34, 35, 41; *see also* Lô Lô
Yizhōu 32
Yongchang 32, 37
Yǒnglè 70
Yuán Dynasty 70
Yuè 27

Yúnguì Plateau 40
Yúnnán 2, 9, 13, 14, 23, 27, 28, 32–40, 41, 44, 46, 51, 104, 116, 118, 123, 139, 142

Zhào Mò 47
Zhào Tuó 28, 46–7, 48, 50
Zhào Xīng 47
Zhào Yīngqí 47
Zhèjiāng 2, 70, 75
Zhongshan suit (*Zhōngshān zhuāng*) 97
Zhuàng 28, 36, 38–9, 41, 44, 45–6, 48, 49, 121
Zongke 32